FREEDOM FROM BONDAGE : SAGA OF FREED BONDED LABOURERS IN BIHAR

FREEDOM FROM BONDAGE : SAGA OF FREED BONDED LABOURERS IN BIHAR

NIL RATAN
Reader in Political Science
A.N. Sinha Institute of Social Studies Patna

SERIALS PUBLICATIONS
NEW DELHI

First Published - 2007

ISBN: 81-8387-069-4

Published by

SERIALS PUBLICATIONS
4830/24, Prahlad Street, Ansari Road
Darya Ganj, New Delhi-110002 (India)
Phone : 23245225. Fax : 91-11-23272135
E-mail: serials@satyam.net.in

Dedicated

to

Freed Bonded Labourers

CONTENTS

PART - IV
An Evaluation of Bonded Labour Rehabilitation Schemes in PATNA District

PART - V
An Evaluation of Bonded Labour Rehabilitation Schemes in WEST CHAMPARAN District

PART - VI
An Evaluation of Bonded Labour Rehabilitation Schemes in MUNGER District

PART - VII
Conclusion

PREFACE

Bonded labour system is evil and wherever it exists, it reminds of the dark ages. Indian society through ages has been developing with the gradual effort to remove slavery and bondage. After independence, the momentum was slow till 1976 when the bonded labour act was enacted into action. The impetus was added by the Honorable Supreme Court with several dynamic judgements, particularly in Bandhua Mukti Morcha v/s Union of India case, which laid the illuminating path for eradicating the bonded labour system.

Bonded labour is an ill product of dreaded poverty and destitution. The liberation and rehabilitation from the adage of debt bonded labour ethos can be meaningful if the freed bonded labourers families can climb the social and economic ladder. They should feel empowered to become independent and free from any socio-economic encumbrances.

The present evaluation in Nawada, Nalanda, Patna, West Champaran & Munger district of rehabilitation schemes for the freed bonded labour has been done with the objective to see the real gains and level of their growth and development from pre-freed status.

ANSISS is grateful to Department of Social Security District Magistrates of respective districts and other district officials for their invaluable support during the study.

The members of the evaluation team Dr. Dinesh Sahay, Dr. Saddruddin, Dr. S.P. Jaiswal and Dipak K. Sinha deserve full appreciation for their co-operation and hard work during the period of survey and preparation of the report. My special thanks to them. This acknowledgement will remain incomplete without putting on record the appreciation for the great amount of pains taken by them in collecting the data.

Last, but not the least we also thank all the respondents spread in the five districts for their valuable time and co-operation.

PART - I

1

INTRODUCTION

A study of society and social life suggests that social stratification is a universal reality and it has existed since the beginning of organized social life. Even the classical literature of ancient days suggests the persistence of inequality and stratification in human society. Plato's 'Republic' throws light on stratification in the analysis of the political state and power distribution. Plato gave the concept of Philosopher state and declared that a state or society consists of three classes of the Philosopher-rulers, the soldiers and the commoners or artisans. He did not include the rural population in it and gave the concept of city-state. In the same way analyzing the concept of State, Aristotle pointed out that society is divided into three classes i.e. upper, middle and lower classes. He advocated for the rule of the middle class and justified his viewpoint. According to his explanation, the upper class is capable of ruling over the state but this class is not in contact with the lower class, hence it cannot understand the problems of the masses or the common people. On the other hand, lower class is not capable of managing the affairs of the state. The middle class is that class which possesses the capability for running the administration of the state and this class is in regular touch with the upper class as well as the common people. Hence this middle class may understand the problems of common people of the society and is also acquainted with the needs and requirements of the upper class people. Hence, this class is the most suitable class for running the affairs of the state.

It appears from the above given views of Plato and Aristotle that they accepted the reality of stratification in human society. In addition to these two classical thinkers of ancient days the social philosophers and thinkers of the 18th and 19th centuries have also analyzed the problem of inequality and stratification and have accepted it as a global phenomenon. Karl Marx gave the concept of the division of society into those who have and have not on the basis of economic factors. According to him, the persons who own and control the means of production constitute the haves. On the other hand, those who neither own the means of production nor have a control over it and simply contribute their labour in the process of production constitute the have nots. According to him, the owner class and working class have existed from the beginning of organized social life and system of production. In the first stage, there were the classes of masters and slaves, and in the following stage the two classes of monarchs and subjects evolved. This stage was followed by the emergence of two classes of feudal and serfs. In the next stage, the classes of capitalists and workers evolved in the society. At every stage, economic inequality was responsible for this stratification. In this way, Marxian analysis also suggests that stratification is a universal reality. The Austrian sociologists Ludwing Gumplowicz also accepted the existence of upper, middle and lower classes in the society and state. In the same way, Pareto gave the concept of heterogeneity of individuals and declared that due to the differences in the degree and type of the domination of residues and due to the variations and differences in family environment, education and intelligence, all the members of the society are not equal in worth and performance. Some are superior and more capable, whereas others are inferior and less capable. In this way, inequality is inevitably found in every society. He himself pointed out, "varying in form, social stratification has existed even in those societies which claimed for equality of men." *[Vilferedo Pareto, Quoted from P.A. Sorokin's Social Mobility and Stratification,* p. 566]. It appears from this remark that social stratification is found in every society whether the society accepts it or claims for social equality.

Presenting social stratification as a universal phenomenon, P.A. Sorokin has pointed out, "any organized social group is always a stratified social body. There has not been and does not exist any permanent social group which is 'flat' and in which all members are equal. Unstratified society with a real equality of its members is a myth, which has never been realized in the history of mankind". [P.A. Sorokin, Social Mobility and Stratification, p. 570]. It appears from this remark that social stratification is the global reality. It is found not only in society, but also in every organized social group.

Analyzing the meaning and concept of stratification Sorokin pointed out, "social stratification means the differentiation of a given population into hierarchically super-posed classed. It is manifested in the existence of upper and lower layers. Its basis and very essence consist in an unequal distribution of rights and privileges, duties and responsibilities, social values and privations, social power and influences among the members of a society. General forms of social stratification are different and numerous". [Ibid, p. 570].

The above given facts suggest that inequality in society has been existing from the very beginning of social life. The stratification and classification of society into different status groups grew more complex with the emergence of different types of occupations. The increasing process of division of labour resulted in the emergence or different occupational groups and with the passing of time in view of the convenience of organized social life; the occupational groups tended to become hereditary. In this way, various occupational groups develop in human society. Analyzing the origin of caste system in India, Nesfield has rightly remarked that the hereditary occupational groups develop into castes or sub-castes with the gradations of different occupations in the society. Some of the occupations were ranked higher and more important and hence the groups associated with these occupations were recorded higher status in the society. On the other hand, the occupations, which were less important were given lower ranking and were graded as inferior. Hence, the groups hereditarily associated with such occupations were given lower status in the society. In this way, social stratification of closed type and rigid in nature developed in the Indian society resulting in the origin of caste system. It appears that the same gradation of occupation developed in different traditional societies and with the division of labour, the gradation of occupation in the light of their importance became the general trend in human societies. In certain societies, in the beginning, the occupations were not hereditary but in many of these societies the occupation became hereditary with the passing of time. Some of the occupations, which were dirty in nature and aroused aversions, were given to the weaker and dominated sections of the society. In most of the cases, the defeated groups or the ruled groups were forced by the ruling group to take these dirty occupations and to serve the society. These weaker, defeated and ruled groups had no alternative and in spite of their unwillingness they had to obey the dictates of the rulers because this was the only way of for their survival. The defeated and ruled groups were also directed and dictated to follow these occupations on the basis of heredity, hence these occupations remained in the same group's generation after generation.

INDIAN SOCIAL STRATIFICATION AND OWNERSHIP

- After the arrival of Aryans in India, Indian society was stratified into three Varnas and then into four Varnas of Brahmin, Khastiya, Vaishya and Sudra. Most of the local and original people who were defeated by the Aryans were given Sudra Varna. Last Varna of Sudra was not given right to property, education, and choice of occupation. [N.D. Kamble, Social Stratification and Regressive Judiciary System in Ancient India, Man in India, Vol. 58, No. 1, Jan-Mar 1978].
- Rigorous Laws were made and were executed for protecting these laws. Laws were regressive and detrimental to the interests of Sudras. Even mere possession of property by the Sudras would injure the Brahmin. Sudra had no right whatsoever to possess property. Brahmins could take this property away with perfect peace as nothing belongs to Sudras but to upper three Varnas. Hierarchical, feudalistic caste system imposed heinous jobs on underprivileged castes. They were deprived of the right to property hence were dependent on others for their survival. The reduction of status and complete dependence laid birth to servitude and slave like practices. Bonded labour in India reflects this continuity from past, since most of them are from the under privileged position in the Varna system.

BONDED LABOUR SCENARIO : CONCEPT, DEFINITION, CONSTITUTIONAL POSITION, AND PERSPECTIVES PREVALENT IN INDIAN SITUATION

- **Bonded Labour debt bondage:** When a family borrows money (for repairs to a house or, more probably, to pay for the wedding or a daughter) from a local landlord, their child or children are put up as surety against the loan. Inevitably, the interest on the loan cannot be paid, let alone the loan itself, so the child is indebted to the landlord for work. However, according to the landlord, the child's upkeep (minimal food and clothing) is more than the pittance the child earns (if the child is paid at all), so the child will forever be bonded to the landlord.

- The system of debt bondage in India is an outcome of certain categories of indebtedness, which have been prevailing for a long time involving certain economically, exploited, helpless and weaker sections of the society. This system originated from the uneven social structure, characterized by feudal and semi-feudal conditions. Bonded Labourers constitute perhaps the weakest section of the rural poor. Bonded Labour as an institution was based on the inter relatedness between ritual compulsions and the pattern of cultivation. The untouchables had been traditionally dispossessed of all social and economic rights, which ensured their total helplessness, and which kept them enslaved through combined operation of ritual and economic domination. In the Hindu moral economy, the two aspects constantly fed on each other. Slavery existed in some form or other till it was abolished legally by the mid- nineteenth century, but forced labour continued to operate. Bonded labour or debt bondage continued after Indian Independence till its legal abolition in 1976.
- Bonded labour is bondage commenced through self sale by adults, or the sale of young family members by guardians in exchange for cash loan or promise of subsistence (national debt) through written agreements, even though here too custom proved to be operative factor. Servitude was supposed to last till the original debt was repaid, and till then the daily expenditure of the total labour power of the debtor constituted on the loan. It was usually stipulated that if the loan remained unpaid in the debtor's lifetime, successive generations would be pledged to bondage until full payment was made. The debtor under bondage, however, had little scope for cash accumulation since the entire labour was pledged to the creditor in exchange for subsistence alone. Hence, the prospect of repayment and release remained notional, and hereditary aspect was more or less assumed right from the beginning.

Operationally, the bonded labour resembled the slave to some extent. The Bonded Labour system means the system of forced, or partly forced labour into which a debtor enters, or has, or is presumed to have entered by an agreement with the creditor. (Dharma Kumar, Bonded Labour, Seminar, February, 1976). The genesis of bonded labour has to be traced to the origins of poverty, which is a result of exploitation. The incidence of debt bondage rose sharply with the monetisation of the rural economy. (MKT., Missing Number, Economic and Political Weekly, Vol. XI, No. 52, December, 1975). In rural India, given the imbalance between the demand and supply of labour in the rural labour market and also the scarcity of the institutional credit, it appears to be almost a consequence of a rural than an exception. (MKT., op. cit.) Bonded labour enter into debt contract for sheer survival which denied them their basic human rights of free movement and offer their labour to the highest bidder. (MKT., op. cit.)

- According to Jan Breman, all forms of agricultural labour in traditional society were characterised by some kind of bondage, which offered wide spectrum. [Patronage and exploitation, London, 1974, p. 7].
- There was an uneven pattern of distribution but this system was profoundly marked in Madras, Bombay, Gujarat, and the Chhota Nagpur region in Bihar. Its incidence was directly correlated to the density of tribal or untouchable communities in these regions, a fact tracked to the subjugation of tribals engaged in shifting cultivation by caste Hindus. [R. Mukherjee, land problems in India, London, 1933, p. 7-8].
- Often bondage was intertwined with several forms of petty tenancies and sharecropping, which were almost equally marked by forced unpaid labour. In the Palamau district of Bihar, bonded labour was known as Kamautti system, under which impure castes of Bhuiyas, Chamars, Kahars, and Dusadhs were bonded to small landlords through debt, which was passed down from generation to generation. The Bihar and Orissa Kamautti Agreement Act of 1920 tried to restrict its scope by making it an annual contract, which had to be registered with copies given to laboures, who were promised fair wages.

- Debt bondage or bonded labour was a form of landless agricultural labour. Debt was almost always the basis of bondage. The striking aspect of this phenomenon was the small amount involved of only a few rupees where a man could sell himself and his descendants to bondage. These loans were taken mainly for urgent domestic expenses, rent payment, ceremonial expenditure (wedding/funeral). The wide spread prevalence of the latter reveals the extraordinary pull of ritual obligations even at the cost of perpetual servitude. Debt bondage was a voluntary submission. The interplay of the dual factors of caste impurity and landlessness led to bonded mode of existence. The prevalence of bonded labour and servitude was always inextricably linked with a particular land ownership pattern.
- Bonded labourers are known by different names in different states and regions of India—Jeeta in Himachal Pradesh, Sevak; Haris in Uttar Pradesh; Kamia, Baramsya and Janasour in Bihar, Hali in Gujarat; Halias and Muliyas or Naga Muliya in Orissa; Padiyal, Charmasand Pannyals in Tamil Nadu; Adimmars, Cherumas, Anchilla Kurichious, Mappila, Paniyans, Kattunaickans, Adyas, Wynad Pulayans in Kerala; Jassigula, Paleras, Gothi and Vethi in Andhra Pradesh; Baramasis, Harwaha and Salkari in Madhya Pradesh; Jeetha in Karnataka: Harwaha and Hariya Sevak in Uttar Pradesh; Chaker and Halia and Nit maoor in West Bengal; Sagari in Rajasthan; Sepi in Punjab; Veta, Segar and Salkari in Maharashtra.
- The genesis of rural poverty in India dates back to the later half of the 18th century, when the erstwhile colonial rulers introduced the Zamindary System. Subsequently, the anti-fanners policies of the colonial government had also contributed towards the indebtedness of a large number of small and medium fanners, and eventually pushing them into the category of landless labourers.
- The problem of bonded labour is closely linked to the broader socio-economic problems of surplus labour, unemployment/under-employment, inequitable distribution of land and assets, low wages, distress migration, social customs etc. With the phenomenon of small, marginal farmers and rural artisan's

steadily becoming landless labourers, it perpetuates the system of bonded labour.

CONCEPTS AND DEFINITIONS

- **Force Labour Convention, 1930 (No. 29) [Article 2 (1)]**—The term forced or compulsory labour shall mean all work or service, which is exacted, from any person under the menace of any penalty and for which the said person has not offered himself voluntarily.
- **Universal Declaration of Human Rights**—On Dec. 10, 1948, the General Assembly of the United Nations adopted and proclaimed the Universal Declaration of Human Rights. Article 4 says: "No one shall beheld in slavery or servitude; slavery and slave trade shall be prohibited in all their forms."
- **UN Supplementary Convention on the Abolition of Slavery (1956)**—Under this convention, debt bondage is defined as "The status and condition arising from a pledge by a debtor of his personal service or those of a person under his control and security for a debt, if the value of those services as reasonably assessed is not applied toward the liquidation of the debt or the length and nature of those services are not respectively limited and defined."
- **As per ILO Report on Stopping Forced Labour (2001)**—The term (Bonded Labour) refers to a worker who rendered service under condition of bondage arising from economic consideration, notably indebtedness through a loan or advance. Where debt is the root cause of bondage, the implication is that the worker (or dependence or heirs) is tied to a particular creditor for a specified or unspecified period until the loan is repaid.
- **As per the Bonded Labour System (Abolition) Act, 1976**
    - 'Bonded labour' means any labour or service rendered under the bonded labour system-Section 2 (e).
    - 'Bonded labourer' means a labourer who incurs, or is presumed to have incurred a bonded debt-Section 2 (f).
    - 'Bonded labour system' means the system of forced, or partly forced, labour under which a debtor enters, or has,

or is presumed to have, entered, into an agreement with the creditor to the effect that would—

(i) render by himself or through any member of his family, or any person dependent on him. Labour or service to the creditor, for a specified period or for any unspecified period, either without wages or for nominal wages;

(ii) for the freedom of employment or other means of livelihood for a specified period or for an unspecified period;

(iii) forfeit the right to move freely throughout the territory of India; or

(iv) forfeit the right to appropriate or sell at market value any of his property or product of his labour or the labour of a member of his family or any person dependent on him.

And includes the system of forced, or partly forced, labour under which a surety for a debtor enters, or has, or is presumed to have, entered, into an agreement with the creditor to the effect that in the event of the failure of the debtor to repay the debt, he would render the bonded labour on behalf of the debtor-Section 2(g).

Through its various judgments, Supreme Court has given a very broad, liberal and expensive interpretation of the definition of the bonded labour. According the interpretation given by the Apex court, where a person provided labour or service to another for remuneration less than the minimum wage, the labour or service falls clearly within the scope and ambit of the words forced labour under the constitution.

CONSTITUTIONAL AND LEGAL PROVISIONS

- The Constitution of India guarantees to all its citizens–justice, social, economic and political, freedom of thought, expression, belief, faith and worship, equity of status and opportunity and fraternity, dignity of individual and unity of the Nation.
- Under Article 23 of the Constitution Traffic in human beings and *beggar* and other similar forms of forced labour are prohibited, any contravention of this provision shall be an offence punishable in accordance with law.

- Bonded Labour System (Abolition) Ordinance was promulgated which was later on replaced by the Bonded Labour System (Abolition) Act, 1976.

SALIENT FEATURES OF THE BONDED LABOUR SYSTEM (ABOLITION) ACT, 1976

- This Act provides for the abolition of the system of bonded labour. It freed unilaterally all the bonded labourers from bondage with simultaneous liquidation of their debts.
- The Act does away with every obligation of a bonded labourer to repay any bonded debt; it also dispenses with the future liability of repaying a bondage debt. The law provides that (a) no suit or other proceedings shall be instituted in any Civil Court for the recovery of any bonded debt, (b) every attachment made before the commencement of the Act for the recovery of any bonded debt shall stand vacated, and (c) such movable property shall be restored to the bonded labourer.
- The district and sub-divisional magistrate have been entrusted with certain duties/responsibilities towards implementation of statutory provisions. Under Section-13 of the Act, Vigilance Committees are required to be constituted at the district and sub-divisional level for implementation of the provisions of the law. They are composite bodies with representatives from different cross sections of the society and have a life of 2 years.
- Registers containing the names and addresses of all freed bonded labourers, their vacation, occupation and income, details of the benefits received are required to be maintained under the Bonded Labour system (Abolition) Rules.
- The Act provides the imprisonment to 3 years and fine up to Rs. 200/- to whoever compels any person to render any bonded labour and whoever advances any bonded debt. An offence under the Act may be tried summarily and any offence under the Act shall be cognizable and bailable.

INTERNATIONAL LABOUR ORGANIZATION AND FORCED/ BONDED LABOUR

- There are two ILO conventions, Convention No. 29 concerning Forced or Compulsory Labour (1930) and Convention No. 105

concerning Abolition of Forced Labour (1957). Government of India has rectified both the conventions.

- Before the 89th Session of the International Labour Conference (June 2001), the Director General of ILO submitted a global report on 'Stopping Forced Labour'. This report contained references regarding incidences of Bonded Labour in India, on the basis of survey conducted by the Gandhi Peace Foundation and National Labour Institute and also estimates of some other NGOs. The Gandhi Peace Foundation and the National Labour Institute conducted a survey in 1978-79, which had estimated the number of bonded labourer as 2.6 million. This survey was based on random sample, drawn from a total of 4,50,199 villages in the 10 selected States. Finally, 1000 villages from out of the 4,50,000 villages were selected. Every 450th villages in the census list of villages of each State starting with a random number was selected for the survey. The findings of the survey in respect of the above 1000 villages were multiplied by 450 to find out the total number of bonded labourers in 10 States. Since the methodology adopted by the Gandhi Peace Foundation was not specific, the Government has not accepted their estimates. The need for having authentic data on number of bonded labourers in India was emphasized. It was urged that comprehensive and authoritative survey might he conducted in this regard.
- From the Government side, it was stated that the Government has strong will and intent to abolish and totally banish the bonded labour system from every nook and corner of the country. It was indicated that Government of India's estimates of bonded labour, as also reported in the following pages, were based on the information submitted by the concerned State Government after conducting detailed survey in the states. The State Governments in the form of affidavits submitted the same information to the Supreme Court in 1977.

One ILO project namely 'Prevention of Family Indebtedness with Micro-Finance Scheme and Related Services' is being implemented in three States, namely Andhra Pradesh, Tamil Nadu and Karnataka. The objective of the project is to introduce existing micro-finance Institutions to develop, test and offer savings and loan products, particularly tailor-made for vulnerable family at the risk of getting into debt traps. The prime focus of the project is on preventing marginal families from falling into debt bondage and also to ensure sustainable rehabilitation of free bonded labourers. Based on its experience on a model could be considered for replication or application in other parts of the country.

The Government of India's statement showing the number of bonded labourers identified released and rehabilitated and those awaiting rehabilitation as on 29.02.1984 as per the reports received from the State Governments.

Figure 1
Breakup of Identified and Freed, Rehabilitated and Remaining for Rehabilitation

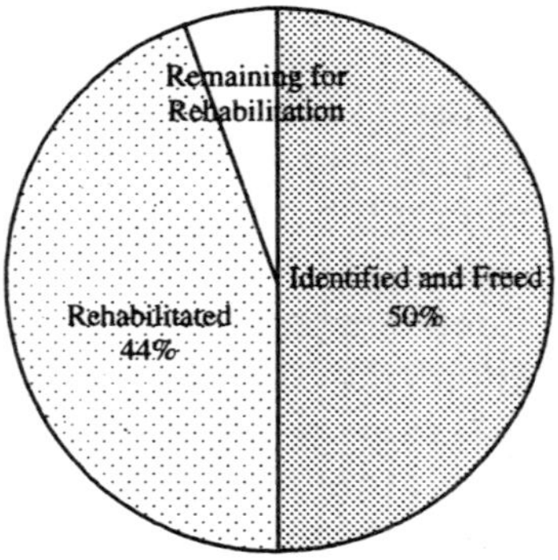

Table 1
State-wise breakup of Bonded Labourers: Identified and Freed, Rehabilitated and Remaining for Rehabilitation

Sl. No.	*States*	*Identified and freed*	*Rehabilitated*	*Remaining for rehabilitation*
1.	Andhra Pradesh	13,491	10,305	3,186
2.	Bihar	8,365	7,431	934
3.	Gujarat	63	63	–
4.	Karnataka	62,699	40,033	22,666
5.	Kerala	829	537	292
6.	Madhya Pradesh	2,020	2,019	1
7.	Maharashtra	540	292	248
8.	Orissa	29,671	17,708	11,665
9.	Rajasthan	6,244	6,190	54
10.	Tamil Nadu	29,934	29,934	–
11.	Uttar Pradesh	8,781	8,682	99
	Total	1,62,637	1,23,194	39,443

Source: Bonded labour in India, V.V. Giri National labour Institute, Noida.

Table 2

Statement Indicating the State-wise breakup: 41 cases Pending for more than per month

S. No.	Name of the States	No. of cases pending
1.	Uttar Pradesh	9
2.	Bihar	7
3.	Madhya Pradesh	6
4.	Andhra Pradesh	2
5.	Jammu & Kashmir	2
6.	Tamil Nadu	1
7.	Gujarat	1
8.	Delhi	1
9.	Karnataka	2
10.	Maharashtra	2
11.	Rajasthan	–
12.	Haryana	2
13.	West Bengal	2
14.	Orissa	2
	Total	41

Source: Bonded labour in India, V.V. Giri National labour Institute, NOIDA, 1979.

PERSPECTIVES

- Bonded labour, which includes beggar and immoral traffic in women [as defined by Art 23 (1) of Indian Constitution], till independence of the country was regarded as vestige of feudal culture. Even after independence, the state machinery and public awareness remained inert to the lot of these depressed people. The singular action taken by the state came in the form of the Bonded Labour Abolition Act of 1976. Yet, six years after that even by the government's own admission, as stated in the Labour Ministry report of 1980-81, 6,21,619 bonded labourers have been identified and only 3,707 of them freed and rehabilitated.
- Bonded labour is not found only in lesser-developed regions alone, but also at those places, which have enjoyed the fruits of green revolution like Punjab and Haryana. [PUCL Bulletin, Dec., 1981,New Delhi, quoting extracts from Seminar on Bonded Labour.]
- Swami Agnivesh refused to accept the Government's claim that the bonded labourers are found only in Karnataka, Tamil Nadu,

Andhra Pradesh, Rajasthan, Bihar, U.P., M.P. and Kerala. He says, "Even a cursory survey will show that bonded labour exists in West Bengal, Maharashtra, Delhi, Chandigarh and Himachal Pradesh also." Referring to the attitude of Haryana Government, Swami Agnivesh has said that the Government refused to accept existence or any such practice in the state initially but confessed only after he had moved the writ petition in the Haryana High Court. [Ibid].

- Starvation in tribal areas because of the takeover of forest by the government and lack of employment opportunities and cultivable land, are the causes of bonded labour, Indebtedness is another cause. Economic stagnation leading to lack of employment prospects has improved the relative strength of the employers.
- The employer knows fully well that his employees have no option other than death and bondage. Usually, the poor men chooses the later, hence the vestige of feudal system is assuming day by day cruel dimensions. [Ibid above]. It is obvious from cases of landlords, who go to the extent of exploiting the halis (as bonded labourers are called in Bihar). In many parts of India, lathaits and gumashtas (local toughs) are patronized by the landlords to intimidate and even kill the labourers who ask for their wages.
- Labourers are compelled to sell themselves to the agents of brick kiln owners or construction companies. In Orissa, a dadan (bonded labour) mortgages his life to the employer and has no right to change the employer. A case from Ratlam states that the employers are well organized with hired hoodlum, to stifle the voice of these bonded labourers. The employers confer with each other and do not allow the employees to change masters. The women of Jansur and Babar willingly go to prostitution centres in Delhi and Meerut in order to free their husbands from debts.
- Even the picture of those rehabilitated is dismaying. Lands given to them in presence of the chief guests have been taken away. Review the rehabilitation schemes of the Government and voluntary agencies. The Government should constitute vigilance committees at district and sub-divisional levels for the identification of the bonded labourers. The forum for

providing relief to the bonded labourers should raise a fund. [PUCL Bulletin, Dec., 1981, New Delhi, quoting extracts from Seminar on Bonded Labour.]

- According to Government of India, the eradication of bonded labour, the identification and rehabilitation of bonded labour is a continuous process. The Labour Secretary has said that it is the responsibility of the State Governments. He said that about 2 lakh 20 thousand bonded labourers have been identified and rehabilitated, since 1975, when the Bonded Labour Act was framed. The Bonded Labour Abolition Act was passed in 1976.
- Article 23 of the Indian Constitution as well as The Bonded Labour (Abolition) Act, 1976 and the SC/ST (POA) Act prohibit bonded labour and mandate stiff punishment for bonded labour employees. The Bonded Labour (Abolition) Act abolishes all agreements and obligations arising out of the bonded labour system. It aims to release all bonded labourers from bondage, cancel any outstanding debts, prohibit the creation of new bonded labour agreements and order the economic rehabilitation of freed bonded labourers by the state. It also punishes offenders with a maximum three years in prison and Rs. 2000 fine. It allotted funds for the identification, release and rehabilitation of bonded labourers.
- *Survey & Identification of Bonded Labourers—a gross underestimate*

• *It is now 46 years since India ratified the ILO Convention No. 29 against Bonded Labour and 24 years since the Indian Government introduced legislation, which prohibits the use of bonded labour. Yet, the GOI has not even taken the first step accessory to implement these proper survey and identification of bonded labourers.*	• *Today when we are talking about whether caste should be put on the agenda of the United Nations, it is clear and obvious that it should be put on the agenda. Any kind of discrimination is relevant to the UN WCAR and caste is the greatest kind of discrimination, which must be totally wiped out from India. Let all Indians, of any caste; go with this agenda to the UN and WCAR, not just Dalits.* *–Dr. Mohini Giri, Former Chairperson, National Commission for Women & Chairperson, Guild of Service, New Delhi.*

- Between 1976, when the Act was passed, and 31 March 1999, the Indian Government has identified a mere 280, 340-bonded labourers.

- However, this figure seems to seriously underestimate the scale of the problem. Commenting on the Indian Government's figure in a letter to Robert Evans MEP (11 April 2000), the Charged Affaires of the EU Delegation of the European Commission in India noted: *"It is obvious that these numbers do not* reflect *the actual situation, although the Government feels that NGO estimates of 5 million adults and 10 million children are exaggerated."*
- Human Rights Watch puts the number of bonded labourers at as high as 40 million.
- A 1978-79 survey, which was carried out jointly by the Gandhi Peace Foundation and the National Labour Institute, estimated that there were 2.6 million bonded labourers in the ten states surveyed. It should be stressed that this survey only looked at bonded labour used in the agricultural sector.
- The more recent report submitted to the Supreme Court by the Commission on Bonded Labour in Tamil Nadu (31 October, 1995) estimated that there were approximately 1.25 million bonded labourers in the state of Tamil Nadu alone.
- Moreover, the evidence shows that the vast majority (80-98%) of bonded labourers in India come from Dalits and Adivasi communities.
- Research carried out in 2000 by the Indian NGO Mine Labour Protection Campaign (MLPC) found that there is a high incidence of bonded labour among the three million mine and quarry workers and that approximately 95% of these workers are Dalits or Adivasis.
- The Gandhi Peace Foundation detailed research indicated a similar pattern in agriculture with 87% of bonded labourers being Dalits or Adivasis.
- A lack of reliable statistics regarding the numbers of bonded labour in India is a serious impediment to eliminating forced labour. An accurate assessment of the number of people, who are bonded, particularly at the local level, is essential if the Government is to develop appropriate action plans to address the problem.
- This glaring, fundamental lacunae in the implementation of the Bonded Labour Act has been recognized by the ILO

Committee of Experts, which recommended in its 2000 report that the [Indian] Government undertake a comprehensive survey using valid statistical methodology to be broken down by gender. The Committee encourages the Government to utilize the services of an independent body to assist in developing the methodology and conducting the survey.

- Action to release bonded labourers and punish employers has not been taken. Even where official survey has identified bonded labourers. NGOs are quick to point out that action to release the bonded labourers in 'the shortest possible period' has not been followed.
- An initial survey in 1997 by the Tamil Nadu State Government identified 25,000 bonded labourers. Of these only 2,444 had been released in the subsequent two and a quarter years, according to a High Court deposition filed by K. Chandra-shekhar on behalf of the Organization of Development and Education for Workers. The deposition also stated that only 50% of those released (1,236) had been given their full rehabilitation assistance of Rs. 9000 (US$197), to which they were entitled under the government regulations.
- Failure to bring prosecutions against those using bonded labour is another blemish, which cripples the efficacy of the Bonded Labour Act.
- Only 32% of identified bonded labour cases lead to arrests and only 0.08% to imprisonment, according to human rights worker Vivek Pandit (Prevention of Atrocities, Vidhayak Sansad, Maharashtra, India, 1995).
- National Human Rights Commission is actively involved in watching Bonded Labour situations in the states.

BIHAR

The State of Bihar was reorganized on 15th November 2000 with 38 districts of erstwhile-undivided Bihar. It is the third largest State in terms of total population size, and occupies the 11th position, in its share of national urban population. Bihar has a rural population of 7,41,99,596 and an urban population of 8,679,200 continues to be predominantly rural even now. It is one of the poorest and the most backward State. However, it is to the credit of the people that they have negotiated and sustained their survival strategies in the most unfavorable structural and functional condition.

The number of community development blocks in the State is 533, contained in 101 sub-divisions of 38 districts. The State consists of two natural divisions North Bihar and Central Bihar. The two regions are largely composed of plains formed by Gangetic alluvial soil divided by the river Ganga. The North Bihar plains, in fact are the most densely populated regions in India. Although the density of population in Central Bihar is equally high, but it is not as crucial as in the North.

The State has an area of 94,163 sq. km. and a population of 82.83 million, according to 2001 census. The population of the State constitutes 8.07 per cent of the country. There is high density of population with 880 per sq. km. The decadal growth rate of population for 1991-2001 has been 28.43 per cent, which is the highest in the country. The literacy rate in the State has been 47.53 per cent according to 2001 census as against 38.50 per cent in 1991 census.

Although, Bihar is predominantly an agricultural State, the State has been changing rapidly. Bihar presents a paradox of poor agricultural performance amidst plenty of rich river streams, high fertility of the soil of the Gangetic plain and land having labour resources.

The poor agricultural performance is also directly related to the slow rate of industrial development because the latter has failed to relieve the pressure of population on neither land nor the agricultural sector is dynamic enough to absorb the surplus.

The survey report of National Council of Applied Economic Research observes "the central weakness of Bihar's economy lies with poor agriculture base which produces neither enough food for its rapidly growing population nor raw materials for its industries seems to be quite appropriate". Bihar is basically a rural and agrarian society as 87.5 per cent people resides in villages.

The economy of the State is predominantly agriculture. Agriculture is the main stay of the State economy and it accounts of people depend on it for their livelihood level is the primary resource in which rural economy is based. Relation with land decides socio-economic relation between groups engaged in agricultural activities directly or indirectly and thus the character of agricultural works, There is strong survival of feudal characteristics. Some of the major areas that require immediate attention are tenancy reforms flood control, assured irrigation etc.

The contribution of agricultural sector to the State domestic product declined from 48 per cent in 1980-81 to 31 per cent in 1996-97. The product increased from around 11 per cent in 1980-81 to 55 per cent in 1996-97 (E.PW Research Foundation 1998). At the time of the 1991 census, the agricultural sector provided livelihood to 81 per cent of the working population in the State (Office of the Registrar General and Census Commissioner, 1991). Paddy, Jowar, Bazra, Tur, Maize, Potato, Onion, Tobacco, Jute, and Sugarcane are extensively cultivated. Kharif and Rabi food grain constitutes 64 and 36 per cent of the total production of food grain in the State, respectively, (Centre for Monitoring Indian Economy, 1991).

The basic cause of Bihar's continuing backwardness is the outdated model of agrarian structure, absentee landownership, large and scattered holdings, insecure tenancies, fragmented holdings and iniquitous agrarian relations. They are constraints to rapid agricultural growth and economic development.

Bihar has been a pioneer in enacting land reforms laws but a laggard in their effective implementation. The first phase of reforms after independence started with the abolition of Zamindari that attempted to bring tenants in direct contact with the Government. Tenancy reforms with a view to providing security to actual cultivators of land against eviction, redistribution of land by imposition of ceiling on agricultural holdings, consolidation of fragmented holdings and updating of land records were other major steps in this direction undertaken in subsequent phases.

However, Bihar's performance in implementing these steps has not only been unsatisfactory but lamentable. Even in the matter of Zamindari abolition, dismal achievement is visible from the fact that besides collecting large amounts of compensation, the big Zamindars extended possession over large areas of land by resorting to large-scale ejection of tenants, under tenants and sharecroppers. Naturally, the bulk of the rural population hardly benefited from the abolition of intermediary interests.

The measures of reforms that could have benefited the disadvantaged groups of marginal peasants, sharecroppers and landless labourers are enforcement of ceiling on agricultural holdings and the redistribution of land, tenancy reform and protection of homestead tenancies. In these areas of land reforms, legislation has fallen short of policy pronouncements and implementation has already been tardily inefficient. Half-hearted and ship-shod efforts spread over three decades to enact, amend and implement ceiling laws have been resulted in the redistribution of only about one per cent of the available land in the State.

Bihar has the dubious distinction of still having a large number of landlords, each owning thousands of acres of land. And the pity of it is that instead of putting their land to proper use, a number of them get it cultivated indifferently through sharecroppers or leaves the land uncultivated. Equally unsatisfactory has been the implementation of tenancy reform; highly exploitative and insecure tenancies in the form of crop sharing arrangements persist in pasts of Bihar [P.S. Appu *"A Modest Programme for the nineties"* in *B.B. Yugandhar and K. Gopal Iyer* (eds.), *Land reforms in India. Bihar Institutional Constraints, Sage Publication,* 1993, *pp.* 51].

Table 3
Land Holding 1990-91, Bihar

Sl. No.	*Type (in Hectare)*	*Total Holding*		*Average*	
		Number 000	*Per cent*	*Area (0.00 Hectare)*	*Percentage*
1.	Below 0.02	1884.869	14.54	31.225	0.29	0.02
2.	0.02–0.5	5719.100	44.11	1650.805	15.37	0.29
3.	0.5–1.0	2589.42	19.97	1908.768	17.77	0.74
Marginal (1+2+3)		10193.392	78.61	3590.798	33.42	0.35
4.	1.0–2.0 (Small)	1437.614	11.09	1954.378	18.19	1.36
5.	2.0–3.0	631.968	4.87	1498.051	13.94	2.37
6.	3.0–4.0	313.152	2.42	1078.171	10.03	3.44
Semi Medium		945.120	7.29	2576.222	23.98	2.73
7.	4.0–5.0	178.215	1.37	786.197	7.32	4.41
8.	5.0–7.5	118.210	0.91	721.464	6.72	6.10
9.	7.5–10.0	55.001	0.42	474.089	4.41	8.62
Medium (7+8+9)		351.426	2.71	1981.750	18.45	5.64
10.	10.0–20.0	32.111	0.24	442.827	4.12	13.79
11.	20.0 & above	6.767	0.05	196.918	1.83	29.01
Large (10+11)		38.898	0.30	639.745	5.96	16.45
	Total	12966.450	100.00	10742:893	100.00	0.83

Source: Agriculture Census 1990-91.

Table 4
Number and Area Operational Holding by Tenure and Status, Area in Hectare

Sl. No.	Size Class (in Hec.)	Total Holding		Wholly owned Self-Occupied Holding		Wholly Leased in Holding		Wholly otherwise operational Holding	
		NO	AREA	NO	AREA	NO	AREA	NO	AREA
1.	Less than 0.02	1884869	31225	1870355	30955	1583	26	4649	81
2.	0.02-0.05	5719100	1650805	5674055	1635196	4804	1408	14108	4287
3.	0.5-1.0	2589423	1908768	2561348	1882795	7137	5405	5988	4520
4.	1.0-2.0	1437614	1954378	1412343	1926881	2758	3386	1296	1905
5.	2.0-3.0	631968	1498051	617957	1468416	1268	3025	675	1708
6.	3.0-4.0	313152	1078171	307153	105950	464	1574	353	1291
7.	4.0-5.0	178215	786197	174593	769814	666	2774	86	370
8.	5.0-7.5	118210	721464	116187	710286	418	2335	26	149
9.	7.5-10.0	55001	474089	54671	471225	169	1391	4	31
10.	10.0-20.0	32111	442827	31978	440961	19	235	2	32
11.	20.0 & above	6787	196918	6746	195655	15	630	-	-
Tolal		12966450	10742893	12827386	10588133	19301	22189	27187	14374

Source: Agricultural census, [(Khajpura, Patna.)]

The growing population and division of the families has brought the size of land holding smaller. Table shows the number of operation holding. One can see that more than 78.61 per cent are such who own less than one-hectare land. The owner of semi-medium land holding of 7.29 per cent and medium class has owned 2.71 per cent. Total area of operational land is 10742.893 hectare. Out of these 33.42 per cent land operated by marginal farmers, 23.98 per cent operated by semi-medium, 18.45 per cent operated by medium class and 5.96 per cent only operated by large farmers.

This table indicates about the operational holding of land. Total operation was holding 10742893 hectare. Out of this, 10588133 hectare land operated by self, 22189 hectare land leased out in fifty per cent share cropping, 14374 hectare land otherwise operational holding.

The poor performance of Bihar in land reforms implementation is rooted primarily in the non-structure of rural power relations and caste alliance at the village levels. Large landowners are not economically affluent but socially and politically powerful. Under the circumstances, it is difficult to enforce a radical transformation of agrarian structure.

The basis goal of fixation of ceiling on agricultural holdings is to ration land in such a way that above a certain level the surplus land is taken away from the present holders and distributed to the landless in accordance with certain principles. It is basically a re distributive measure based on the philosophy of social and economic justice. The disparity in the distribution of land in India with nearly one fourth of the rural households owing no land at all, and another one fifth owning less than one acre provides adequate reason to use ceiling as a means of correcting this imbalance.

The proposal to impose ceiling on surplus land was introduced in the Bihar legislature in 1955 but the Bill could be passed finally in 1959 and the President's assent was received in 1962. Naturally, the landowners got sufficient time-gap to transfer land during the intervening period.

The Bihar land Reforms (Fixation of ceiling Area and acquisition of surplus land) Act, 1961 (Bihar Act XII of 1962) imposed ceiling taking the individual as a unit of for the purpose. It decided to impose a ceiling of 20, 30, 40, 50 and 61 acres of land in each individual. Moreover, it allowed exemptions for educational and health purpose or private plantation etc. Obviously, such a liberal legislation could hardly make any tangible change in the ownership pattern of land. The problem thus acquired a political dimension and the left political parties made it a paint for their gains. Materialization of expected beneficiaries during the later part of seventy lands to land liberation movements to put pressure on the government for taking the Act more effective and useful. Consequently, the Act was amended in 1973 with retrospective effect.

Several important provisions were included in the Act of 1972 (as amended in 1973). Instead of the individual landholders a family consisting of a person, his wife and up to three minor children (below the age of 18 years) was recognized as the unit for ceiling purposes. Secondly, the ceiling areas were reduced to 15, 18, 25, 30, 37.5 and 45 acres of land falling in class I, II, III, IV, V and VI respectively as against 20, 30, 40, 50 and 60 acres of the five categories of land provided in the earlier Act. Thirdly, under the provision of the amended Act, the landowners were not allowed now to retain homestead and orchard lands over and above the ceiling limits. Finally, to provide effective control over Benami and Farzi transfers, the collector is empowered to inquire into cases of transfer of land by a landholder made after 22nd October, 1959.

Table 5
Partly Owned Partly Leased in and Partly Otherwise Operated (Bihar)

Sl. No.	*No*	*Owned Area*	*Area Leased in*	*Area otherwise operated*	*Total Area*
1.	8282	84	61	18	163
2.	26133	5140	3693	1081	9914
3.	14950	11614	1891	2543	16048
4.	21217	13156	5061	3904	22206
5.	12068	15607	4799	4496	24902
6.	5182	12145	4185	3026	19356
7.	2870	8110	2162	2967	13239
8.	1579	5291	1486	1917	8694
9.	157	771	327	345	1443
10.	112	1267	34	298	1599
11.	26	595	-	38	633
Total	92576	73780	23699	20718	118197

Source: Agriculture Census, Khajpura, Patna.

Table 6

Agricultural Census 1995-96 Bihar, Area in Hectare Number of Operational Holdings and Area Operated by Our Size Classes

Nawada	*Marginal Below 1.0*		*Small 1.0-2.0*		*Semi Medium 2.0-4.0*		*Medium 4.0-10.0*		*Large 10.0 & Above*		*All Size*	
	No.	*Area*	*No.*	*Area*	*No.*	*Area*	*No.*	*Area*	*No.*	*Area*	*No.*	*Area*
Male	195086	52529	14062	17587	11869	33515	3684	19066	138	2073	224839	124770
Female	38775	7314	2410	3040	1026	2659	151	724	1	20	42363	13757
Institutional	257	80	63	88	46	130	35	180	13	236	414	714
Total	234118	59923	16535	20715	12941	36304	3870	19970	152	2329	267616	139241
Bihar												
Male	10439329	3583257	1408831	1858439	883196	2410334	196469	1649063	27908	449343	13055933	9950436
Female	892060	280534	113751	154432	54220	144686	15475	88389	694	12278	1076200	680319
Institutional	12584	7189	3907	5024	3670	10503	1877	11233	519	17275	22557	51224
Total	11343973	3870980	1526489	2017895	941086	2565523	213821	1748685	29121	478896	14154690	10681979

Source: Agricultural Census, Khajpura, Patna.

The average annual per capita income of the State increased marginally from 917 in 1980-81 to Rs. 1,010 in 1996-97 at constant (1980-81) prices. At current prices, the average per capita income in the State in 1996-97 is Rs. 3,835 (EPW Research Foundation, 1998).

As per the estimates given by the Planning Commission for 1993-94, 58 per cent of the rural population and 35 per cent of the urban population in Bihar were below the poverty line (Central Statistical Organization, 1999).

A study of poverty numbers of causal factors in Bihar has concluded that between mid-sixties and seventies the proportion of population with incomes below the poverty line showed a fluctuating trend located around a mean of approximately 60 per cent. Now, this percentage stands at 40.8 per cent (1987-88) as compared to India's figure per cent.

Perhaps more alarming is the proportion of population that is very poor with income 25 per cent below the planning commissions poverty line, which remains constant at a little below 40 per cent.

The successive NSS rounds indicate that the absolute numbers of the poor are estimated to have grown by 33 per cent the early seventies and the late eighties. As many as, 77 per cent of farm labourers and 47 per cent of the persons in farm household with land of their own are below the poverty line.

It can easily be suggested that the nature and magnitude of rural poverty in Bihar is primarily attributable to low productivity of agriculture and low wages rather than higher unemployment or under employment.

According to the Rural Labour Enquiry Commission, in the seventies wage paid employment of agricultural labour was around 190 days in the year. The NSS data of 1983-84 further suggested that male rural workers in the State who were not chronically unemployed had 306 days work in the year while it was only 166 days for female workers.

The extent of unemployment in Bihar stands at 2.84 per cent (usual principal status of labour force. The employment and unemployment pattern varies with regard to the rural and urban areas as also between males and females.

The agricultural sector provides the largest percentage of employment and no remarkable change is observed in this regard during the last two decades. While this percentage was 83.2 in 1971

Table 7
District-wise Rural Families Below Poverty Line

Sl. No.	*District*	*No. of Rural Families Below Poverty Line*
1.	Patna	220881
2.	Nalanda	152866
3.	Bhojpur	135088
4.	Buxar	85268
5.	Rohtas	13 5744
6.	Bhabhua	82429
7.	Gaya	294487
8.	Jahanabad	89970
9.	Nawada	162576
10.	Aurangabad	133432
11.	Saran	171431
12.	Siwan	143282
13.	Gopalganj	120822
14.	Muzaffarpur	342388
15.	Sitamardhi	294276
16.	Vaishali	191378
17.	E. Champaran	286090
18.	W. Champaran	254068
19.	Sheohar	53279
20.	Dharbhanga	290889
21.	Samastipur	521785
22.	Madhubani	447695
23.	Saharsa	163507
24.	Supaul	201760
25.	Madhepura	125642
26.	Purnea	272848
27.	Araria	317046
28.	Kishanganj	100038
29.	Katihar	184218
30.	Bhagalpur	218678
31.	Banka	157818
32.	Begusarai	218932
33.	Munger	88062
34.	Jamui	140959
35.	Khagaria	152280
36.	Lakhisarai	87449
37.	Sekhpura	47829
	TOTAL	7077190

Source: District-wise Rural Families Below Poverty Line as per BPL census (1997-2002).

and 79.99 in 1981, it has now increased marginally compared to agriculture, the employment in the industrial and service sectors are at a lower level, but their contribution is increasing.

Industries in Bihar observed 7.2 per cent of labour force in 1972, which increased to 8.81 per cent in 1981, but sharply declined to 4.90 per cent in 1991. In case of service sectors this has increased from 9.6 per cent to 13.00 per cent during this period.

Obviously, no demonstrable diversification of the economy has taken place resulting in slower increase in the percentage share workers in secondary and tertiary sectors. As such, volume of employment generation has to be the largest in the agricultural sector.

The increasing trend in the out-migration of agricultural labourers to Punjab and Haryana particularly from North Bihar has to be seen in the context of dwindling employment opportunities in agriculture and lower level of wages compared to the developed States of North-Western India. Bihar continues to provide extremely low wages despite protections given by the minimum wages acts. The higher wages in these states are directly linked with fairly high productivity of agriculture.

Then there is the issue of under-employment in the agricultural sector as a result of the high man-land ratio in the state. This is essentially a problem of rural employment and under employment that can be only by shifting investment from high capital activities. But for creating infra-structural facilities like power, irrigation and fertilizer etc. some amount of high capital activities have to be adopted.

Bihar has been undergoing a slow process of urbanization. The urban population of India as per the 2001 provisional population totals is 285,354,954 out of which 150,135,894 are males and 135,219,060 are females. The urban population of the country as per 1991 census was 217,611,012 of which 114,908,844 were males and 102,702,168 females. The undivided State of Bihar, in 1991 had an urban population of 11,353,012 out of which 6,156,996 were males and 5,196,016 were females. 2001 census figures reveal that after the separation of Jharkhand, the post divided Bihar has an urban population of 8,679,200 comprising 4,643,27S males and 4,035,922 females.

The growth rate for the total population of the State that during the decade 1991-2001 the total, rural and urban population of the

State have registered decade growth rates of 28.43%, 28.33% and 29.31% respectively. The corresponding growth rates in total, rural and urban population during the decade 1981-91 was 23.28%, 22.61% and 30.45% respectively.

Sex-ratio, which is defined as number of females per thousand males, is one of the important social para males of the society and it indicates balance between males and female in the society.

The Sex-ratio (number of females per one thousand males with State declined from 954 in 1971 to 946 in 1981, 911 in 1991, and 921 in 2001 slightly change. Sex-ratio figures on the basis of the present territorial jurisdiction of the State of Bihar was found sex ratio has generally been adverse to women since 1961. The percentage of population age group 0-14 years declined from 43 per cent to 41 per cent between 1971 and 1991. The absolute population age group 0-14 years 938 to 927 in 2001 census.

According to the Sample Registration system (SRS), fertility in Bihar declined considerately during 1981-91, but it has been

Table 8
Basic Demographic and Health Indicators Bihar and India: A Comparative Statement

Population	*Bihar*	*India*
Total	82878796	1027015247
Male	43153964	531277078
Female	39724832	495738169
Share of India's population	**8.07%**	
Decadal growth rate%		
1981-1991	23.54	23.35
1991-2001	28.43	21.34
Average Annual Exponential Growth rate		
1981-91	2.10	2.14
1991-2001	2.50	1.93
Density of population per sq.km. 2001	880	324
Sex-Ratio		
1991	907	927
2001	921	933
Sex-Ratio (0-6) Years		
1991	953	945
2001	938	927

Source: National Family Health Survey India 1998-99 National Institute for Population

District Educational Set up

Total no. of Panchayat	8471
Total no. of Revenue Villages	45104
Total no. of Schools	51380
Total no. of Primary Schools	41521
Total no. of Upper-primary Schools	9859

stagnating time. The crude birth rate declined from 39.1 per cent 1,000 population in 1981 to 30.7 1991, but has increased slightly to 31.7 in 1997. The total fertility rate also declined substantially from 5.7 children per women in 1981 to 4.4 children per women in 1991, dropping by 1.3 children per women during the 1981-91 decade, but has remained around that level since (4.4 children per women in 1997) mortality decline in Bihar also exhibits a similar pattern, i.e., decline during the 1980s and stagnation during the 1990s. The crude death rate decline from 13.9 per cent 1,000 population in 1981 to 9.8 in 1991. The infant mortality rate declined from 118 per, 1,000 line births in 1981 to 69 in 1991 a decline of 49 per cent. The crude death rate and infant mortality rate in 1997 were 10.0 and 71, respective indicating no improvement since 1991.

The infant mortality rate estimated by the sample Registration system for Bihar 1997 was the same as that for India as a whole (Le.) per 1,000 live births). For 1996-2001, life expectancy is projected to be 65.6 years for males and 62.1 years for females, a substantial increase from the estimates of 55.2 years for male and 53.0 years for females in 1981-86.

Bihar is one of the educationally backward States in India. According to the 2001 census, the literacy rate among the population age seven and above was 47.53 per cent, compared with 65.38 per cent for India as a whole. The literacy rate were 60.38 per cent for males and 33.57 per cent for females in Bihar, compared with 75.76 per cent and 54.28 per cent for males and females respectively, for India. The gap in literacy rates between males and females in Bihar is higher than the gap in India as a whole.

The overall literacy rate for the State of Bihar is 47.53% while the literacy for the country as whole in 2001 census is 65.38%. Out of 37 districts, where literacy rates have been found to be higher than the State average of 47.53% are the district of Patna with a literacy rate high as 63.82% closely followed by Rohtas (62.36%)

and Munger (60.11%) district. The lowest literacy rate of 31.02% has been registered in Kishanganj district during 2001 census.

Table 9
District-wise Literacy Rates

Sl. No.	*District*	*Literacy Rate*
1.	Araria	34.94
2.	Aurangabad	57.50
3.	Banka	43.40
4.	Begusarai	48.55
5.	Bhagalpur	50.28
6.	Bhojpur	57.71
7.	Buxar	57.49
8.	Darbhanga	44.32
9.	Gaya	51.07
10.	Gopalganj	48.19
11.	Jamui	42.74
12.	Jehanabad	56.03
13.	Kaimur (Bhabhua)	55.57
14.	Katihar	35.29
15.	Khagria	41.56
16.	Kishanganj	31.02
17.	Lakhisarai	48.21
18.	Madhepura	36.19
19.	Madhubani	42.35
20.	Munger	60.11
21.	Muzaffarpur	48.15
22.	Nalanda	53.64
23.	Nawada	47.36
24.	West Champaran	39.63
25.	Patna	63.82
26.	East Champaran	38.14
27.	Purnia	35.51
28.	Rohtas	62.36
29.	Saharsa	39.28
30.	Samastipur	45.76
31.	Saran	52.01
32.	Shaikhpura	49.01
33.	Sheohar	37.01
34.	Sitamarhi	39.38
35.	Siwan	52.0]
36.	Supaul	37.80
37.	Vaishali	51.63
	BIHAR	47.53

Source: Census of India, 2001.

Table 10
Educational and Health Indicators : A Comparative Statement

Educational Indicators

Literacy Rate	*Bihar*	*India*
Total	47.53	65.38
Male	60.38	75.76
Female	33.57	54.28
Health Indicators		
Total Fertility Rate (TFR)	4.3	3.2
Contraceptive Prevalence Rate (CPR)	23.4	48.1
Infant Mortality Rate (IMR)	63	68
Crude Birth Rate (CBR)	31.1	26.1
Crude Death Rate (COR)	8.9	8.7
Girls Marrying below 18 years	58.2	36.8

Table 11
District-wise Infant Mortality Rate (IMR) 2001 Census

Sl. No.	*District*	*IMR*	*CBR*	*TFR*
1.	Araria	102	36.76	5.29
2.	Aurangabad	62	35.97	5.24
3.	Banka	00	31.87	4.72
4.	Begusarai	76	35.74	5.38
5.	Bhagalpur	62	31.87	4.72
6.	Bhojpur	55	32.64	4.87
7.	Buxar	00	32.64	4.87
8.	Darbhanga	77	38.30	5.46
9.	Gaya	81	36.83	5.40
10.	Gopalganj	53	37.18	5.54
11.	Jamui	00	40.63	6.16
12.	Jehanabad	81	33.75	4.78
13.	Kaimur (Bhabhua)	00	36.02	5.29
14.	Katihar	77	37.66	5.52
15.	Khagria	85	34.99	5.54
16.	Kishanganj	113	37.97	5.55
17.	Lakhisarai	00	40.63	6.16
18.	Madhepura	82	32.92	4.67
19.	Madhubani	65	34.48	4.75
20.	Munger	70	40.63	6.16
21.	Muzaffarpur	84	34.59	5.08
22.	Nalanda	73	35.09	5.05
23.	Nawada	29	36.22	5.26

Contd....

Sl. No.	District	IMR	CBR	TFR
24.	West Champaran	83	35.76	5.34
25.	Patna	80	35.32	5.13
26.	East Champaran	60	30.80	4.56
27.	Purnia	89	38.06	5.44
28.	Rohtas	67	32.64	4.87
29.	Saharsa	72	32.60	4.51
30.	Samastipur	87	33.08	4.84
31.	Saran	64	33.75	5.07
32.	Shaikhpura	00	35.09	5.05
33.	Sheohar	00	33.66	4.99
34.	Sitamarhi	81	33.66	4.99
35.	Siwan	43	36.25	5.36
36.	Supaul	00	32.60	4.51
37.	Vaishali	46	33.11	5.00

Source: Census of India, 2001.

Table 12
Comparative Statement of Health Indicators

Health Indicator's	*Bihar*	*India*
Infant Mortality Rate (IMR)	63	68
Crude Birth Rate (CBR)	31.1	26.1
Total Fertility Rate (TFR)	4.3	3.2

Source: Family Foundation of India, New Delhi, December 2002, District Profile, and Bihar.

Table 12 indicates the status of TMR, CRR and TFR in the different districts of Bihar.

Table 13
A Comparative Statement of NFHS-I & II in Bihar

Indicators	*NFHS-I (1992-93)*	*NFHS-II (1998-99)*
Infant Mortality Rate (IMR)	89.2	73.0
Neo-natal Mortality Rate	54.8	46.5
Child Mortality Rate (CMR)	42.0	34.6
Total Fertility Rate (TFR)	3.98	3.46
Institutional Delivery (%)	12.1	14.7
Safe Delivery (%)	18.9	23.5
Children Fully Vaccinated	10.7	10.5

Source: Family Foundation of India, New Delhi, and December 2002.

Figure 2
Comparative Statement of NFHS-I & NFHS-II

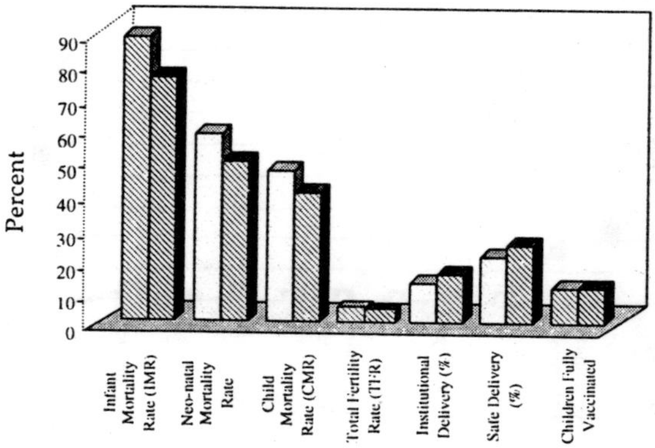

The comparative statement of NFHS-I done in 1992-93 and NFHS-II in the year 1998-99 indicates the clear-cut picture in above stated facts. The infant mortality rate in Bihar is 63 and national rate is 68, which shows improvement in Bihar.

Table 14
Industrial Category of Main Workers (Bihar)

Sl. No.	*Category*	*Persons*	*Male*	*Female*
1.	Total Main Workers	25619038	21513704	4105334
2.	Cultivators	11164519	9867434	1297085
3.	Agricultural Labourers	9512892	7078716	2434176
4.	Livestock, Forestry, Fishing, Hunting and Plantation, Orchards and allied activities	99444	91604	7840
5.	Mining & Quarrying	322741	300485	22256
6.	Planutueturing, Processing, Servicing and Repair in Household Industry V (a)	447008	360300	86708
7.	Manufacturing, Processing, Servicing & Repair in Household Industry V (b)	578537	540347	38190
8.	Constructions	162230	153726	8504
9.	Trade & Commerce	1024837	988900	35937
10.	Transport Storage & Communications	328925	324997	4128
11.	Other Services	1977905	1807395	170510
12.	Marginal Workers	2158033	146393	2011640
13.	Non-workers	38591394	235.11994	35055400

Source: Census of India 1991.

Figure 3
Industrial Category of Main Workers

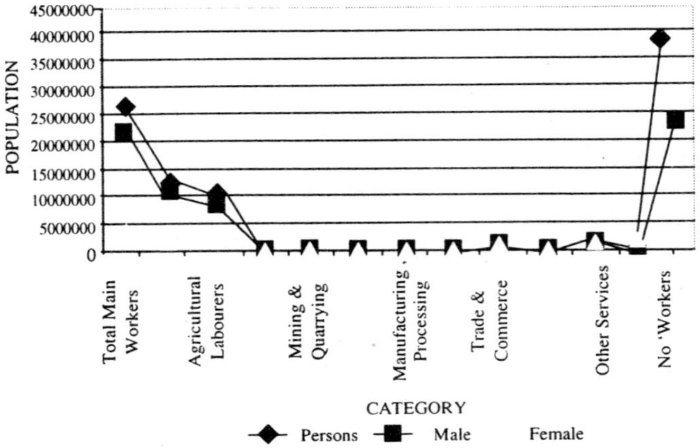

An overall picture of total workers in the State is presented in this table. Total workers include both main and marginal workers. The table shows the clear picture of main workers, cultivators, agriculture labour, livestock, forestry, fishing, hunting and plantation, orchards and allied activities. Persons who work on another person's land for wages in money, kind or share is regarded agricultural labourers. It includes all workers those who have been engaged in some economic activities during the year.

BONDED LABOUR IN BIHAR

- Bonded Labour in Bihar as an institution was based on the inter relatedness between ritual compulsions and the pattern of cultivation. The untouchables had been traditionally dispossessed of all social and economic rights, which ensured their total helplessness, and kept them enslaved through combined operation of ritual and economic domination. In the Hindu moral economy, the two aspects constantly fed on each other. Slavery existed in some form or other till it was abolished legally by the mid-nineteenth century, but forced labour continued to operate. Bonded labour or debt bondage continued after Independence in 1947 till its legal abolition in 1976.
- In the end of nineteenth century, Kamautti system originated in Palamu (now Jharkhand). In Palamau district, bonded labour

was known as Kamautti, under which impure castes of bhuiyas, chamars, kahars, and dusadhs were bonded to small landlords through debt which was passed down from generation to generation. The Kamauti System of bondage rested on the in-debtedness at usurious rates of interest of the labourer on the employer. Palamau was characterized by extremely low productivity and shortage of labour in agriculture. Wages were kept down through the system of bondage and the entire system of labour relations came to rest on the arrangement of debt bondage.

- The Bihar and Orissa Kamauti Agreement Act of 1920 tried to restrict its scope by making it an annual contract, which had to be registered with copies given to laboures who were promised fair wages. Its incidence was directly correlated to the density or tribal or untouchable communities in these regions, a fact tracked to the subjugation or tribals engaged in shifting cultivation by caste Hindus.
- In Bihar, debt bondage or bonded labour was a form of landless agricultural labour. Debt was almost always the oasis of bondage. The striking aspect or this phenomenon was the small amount involved or only a few Rupees where a man could sell himself and his descendants to bondage with a low literacy rate, backwardness and semi-feudal society, it has been a breeding ground for evolution of bonded labour system.
- The first major thrust towards bonded labor identification in the State, since the enactment of the Bonded Labour System (Abolition) Act 1976, came through Supreme Court intervention in the matter of Writ Petition No. 13450 of 1983 in the districts of Dumka and Deoghar, in the then undivided Bihar.

Santhal Pargana Antyodaya Ashram conducted a survey in Saraiyahat Block of Dumka districts and Mohanpur and Deoghar blocks of Deoghar district and identified 3143 bonded labourers. The issue was brought to the notice of concerned Deputy Commissioners. The matter was investigated by B.D.O.s of respective blocks and it was concluded that none of them were bonded labour.

SPAA took the case to the Supreme Court through Writ Petition No. 13450 of 1983. On the prayer to the Court by the SPAA, the

Supreme Court directed Sri K.B. Saxena, I.A.S. to investigate into the matter and report to the Court within six weeks.

Sri Saxena conducted the investigation with the help of six other I.A.S. officers. He concluded that most of them, inclusive of some others who were identified during the investigations, should be recognized as bonded. He suggested that they should be comprehensively rehabilitated after release.

The Supreme Court accepted the report and directed the release of the bonded labours with the payment of an interim relief of Rs. 3,000/- each, Rs. 500/- was to be paid with the release and the remaining amount was to be paid within two weeks. The Court also directed the State Government to prepare a programme for their payment, rehabilitation and also directed to fulfill all obligations under the Act.

The Supreme Court of India in its order dated 11.11.1997, passed in Writ Petition (Civil) No. 3922 of 1985, requested the NHRC to get involved in the monitoring of the implementation of the Bonded Labour System (Ab) Act, 1976.

The NHRC took up the monitoring of the implementation of the Bonded Labour System (Ab) Act, 1976 in early 1998. The present thrust in the implementation of the Act is due to the directions issued by the NHRC for monitoring of the implementation of the Act.

- The Government cf Bihar has identified 8,357 bonded labourers in the state upto March 2003. Among 27 districts of the state, West Champaran tops the list followed by Jamaui and Munger. In West Champaran, a total number of 2,756 bonded labourers were identified; 2,452 were rehabilitated and 294 are yet to be rehabilitated whereas 10 are not available for rehabilitation. Jamaui stands second with 1,938 bonded labourers, and all have been rehabilitated. In Munger, 813 were identified; 765 have been rehabilitated and 48 are yet to be rehabilitated. The rehabilitation process for most of the districts is complete except Darbhanga (3), Madhubani (4), Muzaffarpur (2), Purnea (9), Saharsa (22), and Supaul (2).
- The State Government has identified 8357 bonded labourers. From them, it has rehabilitated 7,906 and 336 are yet to be rehabilitated upto March 2003. 115 could not be rehabilitated, as they were not available due to migration or other reasons.

- Vigilance committees were directed to be constituted at the district and sub divisional level all over the State under the Chairmanship of D.M. and S.D.O. respectively, vide Department of Labour, Employment and Training. Bihar memo No. 301 dated 07.04.98 and memo No. 300 dated 07.04.98. The meeting of Vigilance Committees for identification land rehabilitation of bonded labourers, is required to be held at regular intervals. The above notification was reiterated vide letter No. 1218 dated 21.09.2001 and District Magistrates were directed to reconstitute Vigilance Committees. District authorities were also directed vide letter No. 1472 dated 12.12.2001 to conduct survey of bonded labourers with active participation of Vigilance Committees. Reconstitution of all District Vigilance Committees in the State has been done. A detailed instruction with regard to identification and rehabilitation of bonded labourers was also issued along with extracts of judgments of leading Supreme Court cases.

Table 15
District-wise Figure of Bonded Labour in Bihar
Upto March 2003

Sl. No.	*Name of the District*	*No. of Identified Bonded Labour*	*No. of Rehabilitated Bonded Labour*	*Bonded Labours not available for rehabilitation due to migration or other reasons*	*Bonded Labour to be Rehabilitated*
1.	Araria	1	1		
2.	Aurangabad	56			
3.	Begusarai	504	504		
4.	Bhagalpur	182	182		
5.	Darbhanga	101	98		3
6.	E. Champaran	6	6		
7.	Gaya	146	117	29	
8.	Jahanabad	7	7		
9.	Jamaui	1938	1938		
10.	Katihar	33	33		
11.	Khagaria	626	626		
12.	Kishanganj	4	4		

Contd...

Sl. No.	Name of the District	No. of Identified Bonded Labour	No. of Rehabilitated Bonded Labour	Bonded Labours not available for rehabilitation due to migration or other reasons	Bonded Labour to be Rehabilitated
13.	Madhepura	36	36		
14.	Madhubani	164	145	15	4
15.	Mungher	813	765	48	
16.	Muzaffarpur	29	26	1	2
17.	Nalanda	50	50		
18.	Nawadah	548	548		
19.	Patna	84	84		
20.	Purnea	12	3		9
21.	Rohtas	35	35		
22.	Saharsa	147	113	12	22
23.	Samastipur	13	13		
24.	Sitamarhi	37	37		
25.	Supaul	4	2	2	
26.	Vaishali	25	25		
27.	W. Champaran	2756	2452	10	294
	TOTAL	8357	7906	115	336

Source: Directorate of Social Security, Patna, 2003.

NGO's PERSPECTIVE

- Projected estimate in 1981 by Gandhi Peace Foundation, Delhi of Bonded Labour in Bihar is 1,11,000 (1.7% of agricultural Labour).
- Incidence of bonded labour district-wise (1981).
    1. Very high incidence (20000 and above) Palamau.
    2. High incidence (10000-20000) Saran, Champaran, Mungher, Santhal Pargana (Jharkhand).
    3. Medium incidence (5000-10000) Gaya, Muzaffarpur.
    4. Low incidence (500-5000) Patna, Bhagalpur.
    5. Negligible incidence (0-500) Saharsa, Darbhanga.
    6. No. Bonded Labour Hazaribagh, Ranchi, and Dhanbad, Singhbhum (Jharkhand).

- This data by Gandhi Peace Foundation, Delhi about 1,11,000 (1.7% of agricultural Labour) bonded labour in Bihar was not accepted by Government of India.
- In 1989, National Commission on Rural labour in association with National Academy of Administration, Musoorie commented on the large discrepancies between the high estimates of the Gandhi Peace Foundation's sample survey, and the far lower estimates in the surveys of the State Governments.
- There are no other studies to show the complete data of bonded labour in Bihar except one provided by the Government of Bihar. There are micro-studies of specific areas in Bihar but they do not represent the picture in totality, though they do help in understanding the prevalent social fabric and deplorable conditions of the bonded labour system in parts of Bihar.

REFERENCES & ACKNOWLEDGEMENTS

1. Vilteredo Pareto, Quoted from P.A. Sorokin, Social Mobility and Stratification.
2. N.D. Kamble, Social Stratification and Regencies Judiciary System in Ancient India, Man in India, Vol. 58, No. 1, Jan-March, 1978.
3. Jan Breman, Patronage and Exploitation London, 1974.
4. R. Mukherjee, Land Problems in India, London, 1933.
5. PUCL Bulletin, December, 1981.
6. V.V. Giri National Labour Institute, Noida, Bonded Labour in India, 1979.
7. P.H. Prasad, Pattern of Poverty in Bihar, Geneva, ILO, 1986.
8. M.N. Karna, Bihar: A Profile; ANSISS, 1994.
9. Almas Ali & B.P. Thiagarajan, District Profiles Bihar, PFI, New Delhi, December, 2002.
10. Economic Intelligence Service, Profiles of districts, CMIE, Mumbai.
11. Directorate of Social Security, Patna, 2003.
12. Dharma Kumar, Bonded Labour, Seminar, 198, February, 1976.
13. M.K.T., Missing Number, Economic and Political Weekly, Vol. XI, No. 52, December, 1975.
14. Hussain Dalwai, Bonded Labour Continues, Economic and Political Weekly, Vol. XII, No. 22, May, 1977.
15. Sudipto Mundle, The Bonded of Palamau, Economic and Political Weekly, Vol. XI, No. 18, May, 1976.

16. Sudipto Mundle, Backwardness and Bondage, IIPA, New Delhi, 1979.
17. K. Ilaiah, Bonded Labour in Telengana: A Study, Mainstream, Vol. XVII, No. 30.
18. G.B. Sharma, Abolition of Bonded Labour in India: Some Administrative Dimensions, Administrative Change, Vol. 4, No. 2, Jan-June, 1977.
19. Gandhi Place Foundation and National Labour Institute, New Delhi, National Survey on the Incidence of Bonded Labour, A Preliminary Report, November, 1978.

PART - II

An Evaluation of Bonded Labour Rehabilitation Schemes in NAWADA District

2

NAWADA DISTRICT PROFILE

The district of Nawada, which acquired the status of an independent district on 26th January 1973, has a rich heritage and close linkage with the parent district Gaya. The district consists of 14 Community Development Blocks, viz. Nardiganj, Nawada Sadar, Hisua, Narhat, Sirdala, Rajauli, Akbarpur, Govindpur, Pakari Barwan, Kawakole, Kashichak, Roh, Meskaur and Warsaliganj. The district is bound on the east by Jamui district, on the north by Nalanda and Sheikhpura district and on the west by Gaya district and on the south by Hazaribagh and Giridih district of Jharkhand State.

BRIEF HISTORY

The history of Nawada is a part of the ancient empire of Magadh, which included the undivided districts of Patna and Gaya. This empire gained prominence during the region of king Bimbisar of Haranyakakul dynasty. During this period, both Buddha and Mahavira preached their doctrines. This entire region was full of forests, wild animals and aboriginal tribes. Even today, a considerable part of the district, nearly 20 per cent, is spread over the hills and forests situated towards south and west and mainly contained in the belt of Rajauli, Govindpur, Kawakole, Hisua and Sirdala blocks. The influence of Buddhism and Jainism at that time could extend only to the northern part of district of Nawnda. Lord Buddha stayed in the undivided district of Gaya for a long time and he preached in many parts or the district or Nawada including Kurkihar, Parwati and Tapowan. Lord Mahavira also visited the northern parts of Nawada district.

NATURAL DIVISIONS

The northern and southern part of the district constitutes two distinct natural regions. The northern part, which is plain, formed of alluvial soil, is very fertile. Consequently, it is densely populated and has a rich historical background. The southern part is hilly and undulating with a gentle ascent towards the south merging into hills from the southern fringes of the Chhotanagpur plateau. Fertility of the soil (laterite) is comparatively low. This area remained outside the pale of prosperous Magadh and till 1865 it formed part of the district of Rangarh. The entire southern boundary of the district is a conglomeration of ridges and spurs. Some of these hills attain a height of about 2,250 ft. The area is also inter-spread by base granite rocks of gigantic proportions putting out or the earth. The important hills in the area named after famous Rishis are Durbasa, Shringi, Lomas, Jaghali and Valmiki.

The district of Nawada does not have any important river. Some of these, which are worthily mentioned, are Tailaiya, Ghagra, Khuri, Sakri and Dhanarjya, the last mention having mythological significance. The beds of these rivers are shallow, wide and sandy. They remain dry all through the year except during rainy season when they are virtually in spate. The confluence of all these five rivers takes place at a point near Giriak in Nalanda district from where the river Panchane rises. The district of Nawada also has some important waterfalls such as Kakolat and Had-hadwa. In the southern part of Rajauli block of this district, the famous Safi Mica Mines are situated.

FORESTS

The northern part of the district is devoid of forests as the land is largely under cultivation. However, it is dotted with bamboo groves and mango orchards. Palm, tamarind, papal and banyan trees are found near the village settlements. Bel, Seris, Sisam and Jackfruit trees are also found. In the southern part of the forests of Rajauli, Dilwa and Bhalua have greatly suffered due to unsystematic and large-scale feeling during the Zamindari period. However, some of them are still quite dense and shelter wild animals. Occasionally tigers, panthers, bears, deer, sambhars and wild boars can be seen in these jungles. The Government has banned shooting of wildlife but poaching by the unscrupulous, still poses a great hazard to the dwindling population of wildlife.

CLIMATE CONDITION

The area suffers from extreme of climate. May and June are extremely hot. Although Gaya is said to have the distinction of being the hottest place in India, Nawada may not be far behind. This is mainly due to the barren rocky hills and vast sandy beds of the rivers.

RAINFALL

The major portion of the district falls in the rain shadow zone, The average annual rain fall is 1,047.50 mm and it experiences, on an average, 64 rainy days in a year. The rains generally set in during the middle of June and last till the month of September. The district is always short of adequate rains, and hence declared as a drought prone district.

IRRIGATIONAL FACILITIES

The absence of any major perennial river has deprived the district of any important canal system that could provide water for agricultural operations round the year. The district gets but scanty rainfall. The general slope of the land is also rapid in most of the areas with the results that water runs of quickly.

However, these difficulties have been overcome by the ingenuity and diligence of the people who have devised the system of Ahars and Pynes by which the natural drainage is blocked and the water impounded for use. The river water is also harnessed by diverting it into the pynes. The pynes or diversionary channels are did off from the rivers so as to convey water to the field. Smaller channel or Bhoklas are taken off from the pynes and if necessary, still smaller channels, karhas or field channels are made for conveying water to the fields.

The Ahars on reservoirs of water formed by constructing retaining embankment to act as artificial catchment basin. The embankments are raised on three sides while the fourth side is left open for the drainage water to enter, The Ahars and pynes were constructed by the Zamindars or landlords and used to be maintained by them but after the abolition or intermediary system or Zamindari, the responsibility for their maintenance has developed upon the State Government.

Proper utilization of the Sub-Ferranjan water can be good source of irrigation in such areas of the district where this is feasible. The land being hard and generally rocky, the southern part of the district is unsuitable for sinking deep tube wells. This part comprise Sirdala, Kawakala and parts or Govindpur, Akbarpur and Rajauli and the southern part of Hisua. These areas can have only hand pumps or open wells due to the proximity of the bed rock to the surface and lack of granular material. The areas between the Gaya-Nawada Railway line on the south and the Rajgir hills on the north are suitable for the sinking of small irrigation tube wells with moderate yield. Nawada block is suitable for high yielding tube wells. This narrows towards Rajauli resulting into a marginal zone with moderate yield possibilities. Warsaliganj and Pakri Barawan blocks are considered suitable for sinking large sized tube wells.

A few medium and minor irrigation canals, skricanal scheme being the most important, have been constructed for augmenting the irrigational facilities. But these also are all rain fed and have limited utility.

LAND USE PATTERN

Paddy is the main crop of the district. During recent years, wheat sowing has also been encouraged. Other crops grown are maize, potato, gram, marua, sugarcane and khesari. In the district, 5 types of soil are generally found, these are (i) Loam, (ii) Sandy, (iii) Clay, (iv) Sandly loam and (v) Clay loam. The areas where these kinds of soil are generally found and the crops for which they are indicated below:

MINES AND MINERALS

The district is quite rich in minerals and forests. The district has a number of mica and iron-ore mines, Siger and Dibaur villages near Rajauli have the concentration of mica mines. Ironore is found in Pachamba. Bamboo and canes are found extensively in the forests of the district.

INDUSTRIALIZATION

Nawada is considered to be a backward district mainly on account of lack of industrial development. The development blocks of Rajauli, Govindpur and Kawakole are quite rich so far forest resource in the district are concerned. Catechu sticks are found in abundance in Rajauli block and there is a scope for establishing catechu industry in this belt. Nawada being drought-prone, detores the industrialists from setting up industries in the district since availability of abundant water is an important consideration. Still concerted efforts are being made and many programmes have been launched to improved irrigational facilities as also to develop agriculture production and promote industrialization in the district.

Soil types		*Area*
(i)	Loam	Found in Nawada, Sirdala and Akbarpur blocks.
(ii)	Sandy	Available in some parts of Nawada, Sirdala and Hisua blocks. It is suited for crops like maize, oil seeds and groundnuts.
(iii)	Clay	Available in all parts of Pakri Barawan and Kawakole. It is suited for paddy, gram and wheat.
(iv)	Sandy Loam	Found in the development blocks of Nawada, Warsaliganj, Akbarpur, Narhat and Hisua. It is useful mainly for wheat, maize and paddy.
(v)	Clay Loam	Available in Rajauli and Sirdala blocks. It is useful for paddy, wheat and potato.

In Kadirganj and Gopalganj village of Nawada block, a scheme for production of Tassar silk on loom is underway. Similarly, handloom industry is already in operation in the villages Kadirganj, Gopalganj, Sheikhpura, Masaarla, Nawada, Mirbigha, Pakri Barawan, Jhagibigna in the district. The Government has executed various schemes and programmes in order to popularize household industries such as black smithy, carpentry, pottery, leather industries etc. as well as develop other small-scale industries in the rural areas or the district. A number of gobar gas plants have also recently been established in the district.

COMMUNICATION FACILITIES

The communication facilities are being coming up fast in the entire district. Over and above katcha roads spread over entire district, there are pucca roads including National Highway covering a considerable chunk of the district. There are pucca roads also leading to the main towns of Gaya and Rajgir via Hisua. The Grand Chord line of the Eastern Railway passes through the district headquarters. Nawada is the main station between Keol and Gaya junctions on the route. Further, development of road communication is bound to open up even the remote areas of the district and catalyze the process of development.

ELECTRIFICATION

Electric supply was introduced at Nawada in the year 1953. There are two divisions of the Bihar State Electricity Board for supply of power and the other for construction of electric line. Electric connections have been provided for domestic, commercial, irrigation, State tube wells and industries and transmission of high-tension electrical power.

JURISDICTIONAL CHANGES

As have been mentioned above, Nawada was a sub-division of the old Gaya district until recently. After the reorganization of the districts which look place in the year 1973, Nawada was separated from the old Gaya district to form an independent district consisting of 10 development bocks of the old sub-division and 3 development blocks viz. Atri, Fatahpur and Wazirganj of the Sadar sub-divisions of Gaya district. Later, however, these three development blocks were transferred back to Gaya district thus making Nawada district co-terminus with the old Nawada sub-division.

Table 1
Nawada : Some Important Facts of the District
(Census-2001)

1. Administrative Name : Nawada
2. No. of Sub-division: 02
3. No. of Blocks : 14.
4. No. of Towns : 03
5. No. of Revenue Village : 1094.
6. Area (in sq. kms.) : 2494.
7. No. of Panchayat : 187.
8. No. of Municipal Wards : 2535.
9. Population :

	Rural	*Urban*	*Total*
Male	855675	72963	928638
Female	815084	65703	880787
Total	1670759	138666	1809425

10. Population growth during 1991-2001: 4,49,731 (33.08%)
11. Density of population (per sq. km.): 726
12. Sex ratio (per 1000 male): 948

13. Schools:
    (i) Primary Schools: 995
    (ii) Upper Primary Schools (including High Schools): 246
14. Literacy:

	Male	*Female*	*Total*
Literate	461059	231692	692751
Literacy rate	61.22	32.64	47.36

15. Child population in the age group 0-6

	Rural	*Urban*	*Total*
Male	163747	11802	175549
Female	160025	10990	171015
Total	323772	22792	346564

Source: Provisional Census of India 2001.

Figure 1
Distribution of Population by Sex and Rural and Urban Areas

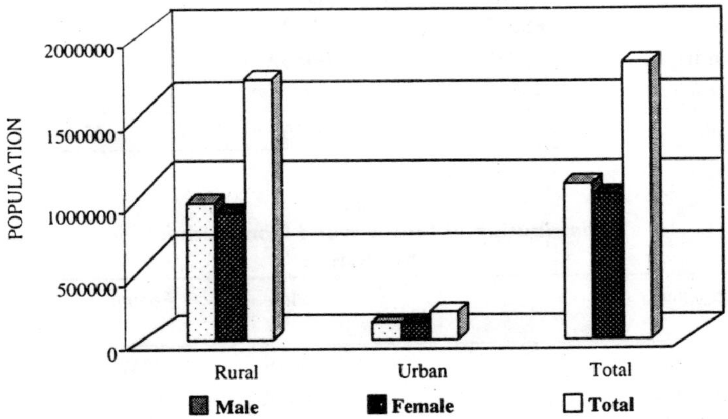

An overall picture of some important facts of Nawada district are presented in this table. Nawada has predominant rural population with strong agrarian base. Literacy rate is 47.36 per cent of total population of the district. The Female literacy is dismal low at 32.64%. The male-female ratio is favouring male. (Sex ratio (per 1000 male): 948 females). Nawada symbolizes an underdeveloped social and economic scenario.

Administratively, the district has two subdivisions and 14 blocks. The table demonstrates a picture of rural and urban population in the different blocks of the district. The district consists of three towns namely—Warsaliganj, Nawada Sadar and Hisua, which represent the urban population.

Table 2
Block-wise Rural and Urban Population of Nawada District (Census 2001)

Sl. No.	*Name of Block*	*Rural*			*Urban*		
		Male	*Female*	*Total*	*Male*	*Female*	*Total*
1.	Kowakole	66512	62656	129168			
2.	Warsaliganj	63804	60033	123837	16324	15006	31330
3.	Nawada Sadar	90654	84494	175148	43737	38552	82291
4.	Rajauli	70264	67424	137688			
5.	Akbarpur	94943	90342	185285			
6.	Hisua	45652	43824	89476	12900	12145	25045
7.	Narhat	43021	42489	85510			
8.	Govindpur	38845	38809	77654			
9.	Pakribarawan	76831	72077	148908			
10.	Sirdala	69433	67143	136576			
11.	Kashichak	34005	31462	65467			
12.	Roh	65093	61929	127022			
13.	Nadriganj	49783	47026	96809			
14.	Meskaur	46835	45376	92211			
	Total	855675	815084	1670759	72963	65703	138666

Table 3
Distribution of Workers and Non-workers in the District

Sl. No.	*Category*	*Male*	*Female*	*Total*
1.	Total workers	448515	227429	675944
2.	Main workers	390652	118301	508953
	(i) Cultivator	190993	80001	270994
	(ii) Agricultural Labour	152571	121702	274273
	(iii) Workers in household Industry	15184	9638	24822
	(iv) Other workers	89767	16088	105855
3.	Marginal workers	57863	109128	166991
4.	Non-workers	480123	653358	1133481

Source: Provisional Census of India 2001.

An overall picture of total workers and non-workers in the Nawada district is presented in this table. The data relating to total workers sub-divided into main and marginal workers and distribution of main workers into the four broad categories of workers viz. Cultivators, Agricultural Labourers, Household

Industry workers and other workers are presented in this table with male and female distribution.

Table 4
Land use (i.e. area under Different Types of Land use in Acres)

Sl. No.	*Types of Land*	*Acres*
1.	Forest	157594.18
2.	Barren and Uncultivated Land	26443.47
3.	Land put to nonagricultural use	58802.67
4.	Water Logging	
	(a) Permanent	7479.77
	(b) Seasonal	17828.81
5.	Miscellaneous Trees, Crops & Groves	875.73
6.	Permanent Pastures and Other Grazing Land	2329.1
7.	Alterable Waste Land	3918.98
8.	Other Fallow Land	19223.21
9.	Current Fallow	66336.61
10.	Net Area Shown	253796.37
11.	Area Shown More Than Once	108407.85
12.	Total Cropped Area Irrigated	362204.22

Source: District Statistical Office, Nawada (Year 2001-02).

The table reveals over all picture of different type of land use (in acres) in the district. Total cropped area irrigated include both net area shown and area shown more than once. Majority of land (15794.28 acres) is covered by the forest and least land (875.73 acres) is used for the purpose of miscellaneous trees, and groves.

The table (given ahead) reveals over all picture of number and area of operation holding by size class (in Hec.) of the district. Majority of operational holdings (163317) are in the group of marginal who use 46897.32 hee. (31.78%) of land for the all-purpose at the average of 0.29 hec. The second highest operational holdings in the group of small category who use 31413 hec. (21.29%) of land at the average of 1.34 hec. The third highest operational holding in the group of semi-medium category who use 38228 hec. (25.91%) of land at the average of 2.67 hec. The fourth highest operational holding in the group of medium category who use 26480 hec. (17.95%) of land at the average of 5.39 hec. The fifth and last category of operational holdings is large in the size class who use 4528 hee. (3.07%) of land at the average of 14.99 hec.

Table 5
Number and Area of Operation Holding by Size Class

Sl. No.	Size Class (in Hec.)	No. of Opera-tional Holding	Inters Percentage of Opera-tional Holding	Area of Opera-tional Holding in use	Inters Percentage of Opera-tional Holding	Average Area per Opera-tional Holding
1.	Below 0.02	21370	10.36	284.32	0.19	0.013
2.	0.02 – 0.5	107841	52.28	22959	15.56	0.21
3.	0.5 – 1.0	34106	16.53	23654	16.03	0.69
Marginal (1+2+3)		163317	79.17	46897.32	31.78	0.29
4.	1.0 – 2.0	23452	11.37	31413	21.29	1.34
Small (4)		23452	11.37	31413	21.29	1.34
5.	2.0 – 3.0	9702	4.71	22608	15.32	2.33
6.	3.0 – 4.0	4594	2.23	15620	10.59	3.4
Semi Medium (5+6)		14296	6.94	38228	25.91	2.67
7.	4.0 – 5.0	2496	1.21	11 022	7.47	4.42
8.	5.0 – 7.5	1784	0.86	10525	7.13	5.90
9.	7.5 – 10.0	636	0.31	4933	3.35	7.76
Medium (7+8+9)		4916	2.38	26480	17.95	5.39
10.	10.0 – 20.0	267	0.13	3437	2.33	12.87
11.	20.0 – 30.0	20	0.01	441	0.30	22.05
12.	30.0 – 40.0	8	–	281	0.19	35.12
13.	40.0 – 50.0	3	–	141	0.10	47.00
14.	50.0 & above	4	–	228	0.15	57.00
Large (10+11+12+13+14)		302	0.14	4528	3.07	14.99
15.	All Sizes	206283	100	147546.32	100	0.72

Source: District Nawada, Agricultural Census 1985 – 86.

The table reveals overall picture of number and area of operational holding by size class (in hec.) of Scheduled caste in the district. Majority of operation holdings (28691) are in the group of marginal who use 5170 hec. (64.16%) of land for the different purposes at the average of 0.18 hec. The second highest operational holdings in the group of small category who use 1752 hec. (21.74%) of land at the average of 1.39 hec. The third highest operational holdings in the group of semi medium category who use 932 hec (11.57%) of land at the average of 2.66 hec. The fourth and last category of operational holding is medium at the average of 5.51 hec. None of the operational holdings of scheduled caste is in the group of large category.

Table 6
Number and Area of Operation Holding by Size Class

Sl. No.	*Size Class (in Hec.)*	*No. of Operational Holding*	*Inters Percentage of Operational Holding*	*Area of Operational Holding*	*Inters Percentage of Operational Holding*	*Average Area per Operational Holding*
1.	Below 0.02	7587	25.01	102	1.27	0.013
2.	0.02 – 0.5	17707	58.36	2704	33.55	0.15
3.	0.5-1.0	3397	11.2	2364	29.34	0.70
Marginal (1+2+3)		28691	94.57	5170	64.16	0.18
4.	1.0 – 2.0	1260	4.15	1752	21.74	1.39
Small (4)		1260	4.15	1752	21.74	1.39
5.	2.0 – 3.0	280	0.92	687	8.53	2.45
6.	3.0 – 4.0	70	0.23	245	3.04	3.50
Semi Medium (5+6)		350	1.15	932	11.57	2.66
7.	4.0 – 5.0	17	0.06	75	0.93	4.41
8.	5.0 – 7.5	17	0.06	103	1.28	6.06
9.	7.5 – 10.0	3	0.01	26	0.32	8.67
Medium (7+8+9)		37	0.13	204	2.53	5.51
10.	10.0 – 20.0	–	–	–	–	–
11.	20.0 – 30.0	–	–	–	–	–
12.	30.0 – 40.0	–	–	–	–	–
13.	40.0 – 50.0	–	–	–	–	–
14.	50.0 & above	–	–	–	–	–
Large (10+11+12+13+14)		0	0	0	0	0
15.	All Sizes	30338	100	8058	100	0.27

Source: District Nawada, Agricultural Census 1985 - 86 (Scheduled Caste).

The table reveals the picture of number of all social groups of operational holdings (Individual, Joint of Institute) by size class. Majority of individual, joint and institutional operational holdings are in the group of marginal category. Further, the table shows that individual, joint and institutional operational holdings are in the 2nd position (small category), semi medium 3rd position, medium 4th position and large category 5th position.

The table reveals the picture of operational holdings (male, Female and Institutional) and area operated by size classes in the Nawada district as well as in Bihar. Majority of operational holdings (Male, Female and Institutional) are in the group of marginal category. Further the table shows that male, female and institutional operational holdings are in the 2nd position (small category), semi medium 3rd position, medium 4th position and large category 5th position.

Table 7
Number and all Social Groups of Operational Holding by Size and Class

Sl. No.	*Size Class (in Hec.)*	*Number*				*All Social Groups*			
		Individual	*Joint*	*Institution*	*Total*	*Individual*	*Joint*	*Institution*	*Total*
1.	Below 0.02	22842	495	21	23358	272	7	-	279
2.	0.02 – 0.5	112722	7069	147	119938	35959	1397	28	37384
3.	0.5 – 1.0	34861	2003	42	36906	26742	1283	27	28052
Marginal (1+2+3)		170425	9567	210	180202	62973	2687	55	65715
4.	1.0 – 2.0	22957	1497	32	24486	25259	2021	51	27331
Small (4)		22957	1497	32	24486	25259	2021	51	27331
5.	2.0 – 3.0	9556	595	35	10186	20354	1375	73	21802
6.	3.0 – 4.0	4369	305	11	4685	13674	1053	39	14766
Semi Medium (5+6)		13925	900	46	14871	34028	2428	112	36568
7.	4.0 – 5.0	2161	225	7	2393	8924	980	30	9934
8.	5.0 – 7.5	1540	175	8	1723	9209	1072	50	10331
9.	7.5 – 10.0	545	65	3	613	4294	578	27	4899
Medium (7+8+9)		4246	465	18	4729	22427	2630	107	25164
10.	10.0 – 20.0	205	32	7	244	2875	428	115	3418
11.	20.0 & above	25	2	5	32	697	57	135	889
Large (10+11+12+13+14)		230	34	12	276	3372	485	250	4307
12.	All Sizes	211783	12463	318	224564	148259	10251	575	159085

Source: District Nawada Agricultural Census 1985-86.

The table shows the overall picture of identified and rehabilitated bonded labour in different blocks of Nawada district. Sirdala block has the highest number of bonded labour identified and rehabilitated (189). Next was Namat block, where 131 were identified and rehabilitated. The third in the list was Akbarpur block with 101. The others were as followings: Pakri Brawan (77), Hisua (27), Govindpur (21), Nawada and Rajauli had the lowest

Table 8
Number of Operational Holdings and Area Operated by Major Size, Classes

Nawada	*Marginal Below 1.0*		*Small 1.0–20*		*Semi Medium 2.0–4.0*		*Medium 4.0–10.0*		*Large 10.0 & above*		*All Size*	
	No	*Area*	*No*	*Area*	*No*	*Area*	*No*	*Area*	*No*	*Area*	*No*	*Area*
Male	195086	52529	14062	17587	11869	33515	3684	19066	138	2073	224839	124770
Female	38775	7314	2410	3040	1026	2659	151	724	1	20	42363	13757
Institutional	257	80	631	88	46	130	35	180	13	236	414	714
Total	234118	59923	16535	20715	12941	36304	3870	19970	152	2329	267616	139241
Bihar												
Male	10439329	3583257	1408831	1858439	883196	2410334	196469	1649063	27908	449343	13055933	9950436
Female	892060	280534	113751	154432	54220	144686	15475	88389	694	12278	1076200	680319
Institutional	12584	7189	3907	5024	3670	10503	1877	11233	519	17275	22557	51224
Total	11343973	3870980	1526489	2017895	941086	2565523	213821	1748685	29121	478896	1415469	10681979

Source: Nawada district, Agricultural Census 1995-96.

Table 9
Bonded Labour in Nawada district

Name of the Block		*Total No. of Bonded Labours*		*Ronking*
		No.	*Percentage*	
1.	Siridala	189	34.49	1
2.	Narhat	131	23.91	2
3.	Akbarpur	101	18.43	3
4.	Pakari Brawan	77	14.05	4
5.	Hisua	27	4.93	5
6.	Govindpur	21	3.83	6
7.	Nawada	01	0.18	7
8.	Rajauli	01	0.18	7
	Total	548	100.00	

Figure 2
Bonded Labour in Nawada District

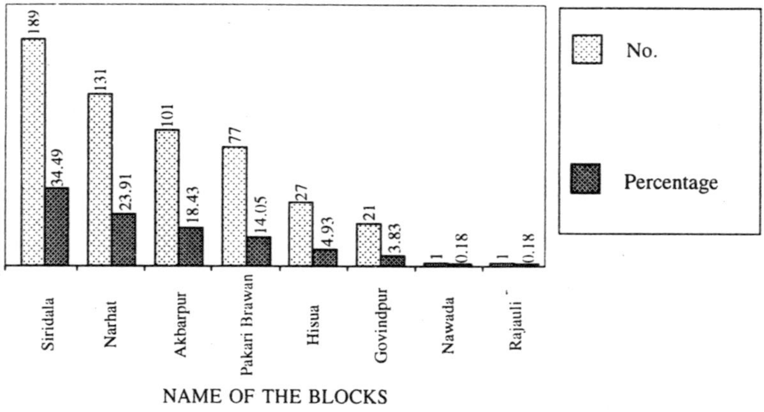

number of identified and freed bonded labourers i.e. One in each block. The total number of freed bonded labourers in the district was 548. No Bonded labourer has been identified in the district from 1987 till date. The district administration holds campaigns about bonded labourers, which is not regular. The campaign includes distribution of leaflets in the blocks and villages (a copy of the leaflet is enclosed in the Annexure), NHRC has been strongly advocating that campaigning for generation of awareness against Bonded Labour System is essential for eradication of this evil system. The thrust of administration should be to keep check on the brick kiln and stone crusher units, where new areas of Bonded Labour System may find new avenues of growth, particularly in the case of migrant workers. The labour department has important role to play in keeping check on these new proliferating units in the district.

REFERENCES & ACKNOWLEDGEMENT

1. Gaya District Gazetteer, P.C. Roy Chaudhry, 1957.
2. Census, 2001.
3. CMIE, Mumbai, Profiles of Districts, EIS.
4. District Magistrate, Nawada Office Documents.
5. Labour & Social Security Department Documents.
6. District Agricultural Census Documents.
7. Agricultural Census Documents.
8. District Census Handbook: Nawada District, 1981, Series –4, Bihar.

3

OBJECTIVE & METHODOLOGY

The evaluation study has been undertaken in Nawada, Nalanda, Patna, West Champaran and Munger districts to assess the impact of different rehabilitation and development plans. It includes focus on who are providing grant/loan for the purpose of effective rehabilitation of bonded labourers, study various programmes undertaken for rehabilitation and impact on bonded labourers.

The general objective of this evaluative study is to appraise the impact on the identified and freed bonded labour of the rehabilitation programmes, which are provided by the Central and State Government in a holistic prospective. The specific objectives of the present evaluation are as follows:

- To identify and ascertain about the freed bonded labour, who have been rehabilitated after been released.
- To find out the background of Freed Bonded Labour.
- To assess the psychological, physical and economic rehabilitation.
- Under the physical and economic rehabilitation, these major components were identified to be evaluated:
    - Allotment of house site and agricultural land.
    - Land development.
    - Provision of low cost dwelling units.
    - Agriculture
    - Provision of credit
    - Animal husbandry

- Training for acquiring new skills and developing existing skills.
- Promoting traditional Arts & Crafts.
- Provision of wage employment and enforcement of minimum wage.
- Health, Medical care and Sanitation.
- Supply of essential commodities.
- Education of children of bonded labourers.
- To find out the infra-structural facilities of FBLs Tolas.
- To assess the various central and centrally sponsored schemes and ongoing schemes of the State Government.
- To evaluate the need or the total requirements of the families of freed bonded labourers to enable them to cross the poverty line on the one hand and to prevent them from sliding back to debt bondage on the other.
- To find out the causes of bonded labour.
- To identify strengths, weakness and their determinants.
- To assess the overall impact of the scheme i.e. ultimate gain through the freed bonded labourers and their families.
- To find out the suggestions from Freed Bonded Labourers to improve their present position.
- To suggest remedial measures so as to enhance their strengths and minimize their weaknesses.

THE STUDY DESIGN: METHODOLOGY

The problem of studying social situation and social phenomena is different from that of analyzing situations and conditions concerning physical and natural environment. The nature of social life is different from the nature of inorganic objects like social, air and water. Hence, the scientific approaches and methods used in physical and natural sciences. The social scientist is required to take into consideration the limitations of the applicability of scientific methods for the study of the social life and social problem. We cannot use the methods of physical and natural science indiscriminately for the study of the social life, social phenomena and social problem. The laboratory studies, conducted in physical and natural science, and the experimental studies, possible in the space of the physical and natural sciences, are not possible in case of social sciences at the same level. They are very few and infrequent studies of this type of the spare of social research. Hence, the social researchers and investigators are required to prepare a plan of systematic and scientific enquiry for studying social problem. This plan is generally known as methodology and study design. This study design is not uniform for all types of social problem. Hence, the social scientists have broadly decided the study design into four types known as "Descriptive study design", "Exploratory study design", "Diagnostic descriptive study design" and "Experimental study design". All these study designs are not informally applicable to all social situations in the study of all types of social problems. A particular study design may be suitable in one situation but inadequate and unsuitable for the study of some other problems or conducting the study of some other in a different situation. The suitability and applicability of the study design depends upon the nature of the problem to be studied and objective of the study design may be adopted by a social scientist for the study of a specific problem.

In the present study also, the present investigating team was required to draw a study design for conducting the psychological and sociological enquiry in a systematic and methodical manner. For this purpose, the present investigating team was required to take into the account the nature of the problem. It is obvious that the socio-economic life of the freed bonded labourers and the impact of liberation on their life are to be studied by the present investigating team in the present study. The objectives of study have been analyzed in details in the chapter. The social situation in which the problem is to be studied is the freed bonded labourers of the districts. The analysis of the objectives of the study reveals that the purpose of present sociological enquiry is neither to explore the underlying cases of specific problem nor to diagnose the evil and cause of evil for suggesting required treatment. Hence, the exploratory study design or diagnostic study design was not required to be prepared in the present case. As regards the experimental study design, it is adopted when there is a possibility of conducting an experiment in a controlled situation. Moreover, the experimental study design cannot be helpful in understudying and analyzing the past conditions rather it may be helpful only in understudying the present condition. At the present, evaluation study and its objectives cover the analysis of the past as well as the present conditions and any experimental study under controlled situation was not possible in the present case. The experimental study design was also not applicable for conducting the proposed sociological enquiry. The objectives of the present study suggest that the present enquiry is concerned with analysis of Psycho, Social and Economic condition of the freed bonded labourers the pre-liberation days and the socio-economic condition and psychological change of this class after liberation or freed life. The differences between the two conditions will help in assessing the impact of rehabilitation programme on the socio-economic and psychological life. Hence, the objectives of the present study demand a descriptive account of the past and present conditions for an analytical discussion. Thus, in the present case, descriptive study design was found to be more suitable and adequately applicable for the study of the problem and for realizing the objectives of the study. It was, therefore, decided to adopt descriptive study design for conducting the present evaluation study and for this purpose the required study design was prepared.

After taking the decision in respect of the type of the study design to be drawn and used in the present study, the task before the team was to decide about the technique or data collection to be used in the present study. It is important to point that in descriptive study design the investigating team may use the technique of observation or questionnaire and interview for conducting the field survey and for collecting the relevant information to prepare a descriptive account if the problem under study. Hence, the present team could also use either of three techniques of data collection for conducting the field survey. But at the same time, it was also needed that an evaluation analysis of these three techniques should be made for finding out the adequacy, suitability and aptness of the technique of data collection in the present case.

The team was to decide what type of interviewing technique should be adopted. Broadly speaking, there are two types of interview known as Structured or Formal interview. The items or questions to be asked from the respondents are already constructed before going to the field.

SAMPLING OF NAWADA

The investigator was to draw a sample from the freed bonded labour belonging to Nawada district in the State of Bihar. It was gathered that the total number of freed bonded labour in the district was 548 and for drawing a sizable sample to represent the whole universe, it was decided to select about 20% of the total number of the freed bonded labour. It is also important to point out that the units considered for drawing a sample was neither village nor the area but the freed bonded labour itself. Hence, the labourers were to be included in the sample.

For drawing a represented part from the universe, the whole district was divided into blocks, which were eight in number. From each block, the number or freed bonded labourers were selected as the units of the sample which was round about 20% with a variation of 5% in each block, but where the number of living freed bonded labourer was only one, it was included in the sample and where the freed bonded labourer was only one but deceased was left out as in case of Rajauli and Nawada blocks respectively.

The number of freed bonded labourer, selected from remaining six blocks, were 38 out of 189 in Sirdala block, 7 out of 21 in Govindpur block, 30 out of 131 in Narhat block, 18 out of 77 in Pakari Barwa block, 32 out of 101 in Akbarpur block and 8 out of 27 in Hisua block. Thus on the whole, 134 persons were included in the sample to constitute a representative part of the whole. It is obvious that for drawing a sample, the district was divided into different blocks and from each block the freed bonded labourers were selected on the basis of random sampling. In this way, the sample was constituted into stages and it may be described as multi-stage sample.

Table 1 shows that the highest numbers of bonded labourers identified are in Sirdala block that is about (189) 34.49 per cent. The next highest (131) 23.91 per cent are in Narhat block and (101) 18.43 per cent are located at Akbarpur block. In Pakari Barwan block there were (77) 14.05 per cent. Only (1) 0.18 per cent bonded labourers were identified at Nawada and Rajauli block. All the identified bonded labourers have been rehabilitated. For the present study, a sample of 24.45 per cent bonded labour (134 FBLs), out of 548 freed bonded labourers in different blocks were undertaken.

Table 1
Percentage Distribution Sample of Bonded Labourer and Total Bonded Labourer

Block		Total No. of Bonded Labourer		No. of Sample bonded labourer	
		No.	Per cent	No.	Per cent
1.	Sirdala	189	34.49	38	20.11
2.	Narhat	131	23.91	30	22.90
3.	Akbarpur	101	18.43	32	31.68
4.	Pakari Barwan	77	14.05	18	23.34
5.	Hisua	27	4.93	08	29.63
6.	Govindpur	21	3.83	07	33.33
7.	Nawada	01	0.18	–	–
8.	Rajauli	01	0.18	01	100.00
	Total	548	100.00	134	24.45

SAMPLING OF NALANDA

The social security department of Nalanda district gave a list of 50 identified and rehabilitated FBLs. After this, the research team decided to include all the FBLs of the district for this evaluation study. It is also important to point out that the units considered for drawing a sample was neither village nor the area but the freed bonded labour itself. Hence, all the FBLs were to be included in the five blocks (i.e. Chandi, Biharsharif, Giriak, Silao and Asthawan) of the district.

SAMPLING OF PATNA

The Patna District Administration gave the list of 86 identified and rehabilitated FBLs. After this, the research team decided to include all the FBLs of the district for this evaluation study. It is also important to point out that the units considered for drawing a sample was neither village nor the area but the freed bonded labour itself. Hence, all the FBLs of respective five blocks (i.e. Barh, Bihata, Fatwah, Naubatpur and Phulwarisharif) of the district were to be included in the present study.

SAMPLING OF WEST CHAMPARAN

The district administration of West Champaran provided a list of 2487 identified and rehabilitated FBLs, who were spread in the different villages of the 16 blocks in the district. During the study, it was found that the provided list was not up-to-date that how many freed bonded laborers had migrated and died. In that unexplained and not clear situation, the ANSISS evaluation team had to draw a sizeable sample to represent the whole universe. So the evaluation team decided to interview about 10% of the freed bonded labourers from all (16) blocks of the district. For this purpose, the evaluation team randomly selected the villages and visited more than 10% of freed bonded labourers individually and contacted 343 FBLs families. It could interview 230 FBLs only from drawn sample because 16 FBLs had migrated and 97 FBLs had died. It is also important to point out here that the units considered for drawings a simple laws neither villages nor the area, but the freed bonded labourers itself.

The total number of 230 freed bonded labourers were interviewed.

SAMPLING OF MUNGER

The district administration of Munger provided a list of 790 identified and freed bonded labourers, who were spread in the different villages of the 6 blocks in the district. But according to provided list, only 745 FBLs were rehabilitated by the district administration. In this situation, the ANSISS research team decided to sample only rehabilitated group of FBLs because the evaluative study was related to impact of rehabilitative package of FBLs. It is also significant here to point out here that during the study, it was found that the provided list was not up-to-date that how many freed bonded labourers had migrated and died. In that unexplained and not clear situation, the ANSISS evaluation team had to draw a sizeable sample to represent the whole universe. So, the evaluation team decided to interview about 20% of the available freed bonded labourers from the 6 blocks of the district. For this purpose, the evaluation team randomly selected the villages and visited more than 20% of freed bonded labourers individually and contacted 332 FBLs household. It could interview 151 FBLs only from the drawn sample because 13 FBLs had migrated and 168 FBLs had died. It is also important to point out here that the units considered for drawing a sample was neither village nor the area, but the freed bonded labourers themselves.

Thus, the total number of 151 freed bonded labourers was interviewed.

PROBLEM IN PERSPECTIVE

The present evaluation study deals at length to the various dimensions of work and domestic, social, economical end political life of freed bonded labourers. The following points have been emphasized in the present condition of freed bondage labourers.

1. Preliminary information has been collected regarding age, caste, literacy, and marital status nature of residence, family income and composition of households.
2. Reasons for the selection of the present occupation and the conditions under which choice was made.
3. Function of the family as well as the nature of relationships that existed within the family.
4. The status of freed bonded labourers as perceived by other residents in the locality, where they reside.
5. Information about the working conditions–nature of work, workload and wages.
6. The protective and welfare measures of the Government and the extent of these benefits for the cause of the labourers.

4

CRITICAL ANALYSIS OF FREED BONDED LABOURERS

In the preceding chapter, the method and technique used for conducting field survey for data collection have been discussed in a systematic and detailed manner. At the outset, it would be prudent to mention here that for methodological purposes the 134 Freed Bonded Labours (FBLs) were sampled out of 548 FBLs of the district and a structural questionnaire was introduced to elicit information from the freed bonded labour. These questions were related with different objectives of the present investigation and also their views and attitude on different dimensions as well as to examine their socio-economic profile. Structural questionnaire provided quantitative data, which was integrated with the qualitative data collected through discussions and was used for analyzing the total picture.

The responses obtained from freed bonded labourers, covers the various aspects of their socio-economic life and about the impact of rehabilitation programmes on them. It has also been mentioned in the objective of the present study in an earlier chapter that the socio-economic life and household conditions of the bonded labourers of Nawada is to be studied not only after they have been liberated rather also in the pre-liberation days. Thus the socio-economic life of the freed bonded labourers of Nawada district is to be studied not only after they have liberated rather also in the pre-liberation days. It will he a comparative analysis of two different conditions, and it will definitely help in understanding the changes taking place after liberation of these freed bonded labourers.

The data about the personal identification of all the respondents have been obtained from the field. These information includes name, age, caste, marital status, age at which bonded labour was taken up, age at which bonded labour was given up, number of children, personal as well as family income, family size, family structure. The personal identification are preliminary in nature and throw light on understanding the variables for the classification of responses regarding various aspects of socio-economic life and freed bonded labour household. The focus on what benefits they have received and impact on them from the rehabilitation programmes of the State Government and Central Government schemes.

The present chapter is concerned with presenting a systematic analysis of collected data. For this purpose, frequency tables have been prepared and the obtained data have been systematically classified on the basis of the different variables for an interpretative analysis of the findings.

Table 1
Age-wise distribution of Freed Bonded Labour

Age Group	*Number*	*Percentage*
41 - 50 years	51	38.06
51 - 60 years	55	41.05
61 - 70 years	15	11.19
71 & above years	13	9.70
Total	134	100.00

Figure 1
Age-wise Distribution of Freed Bonded Labour

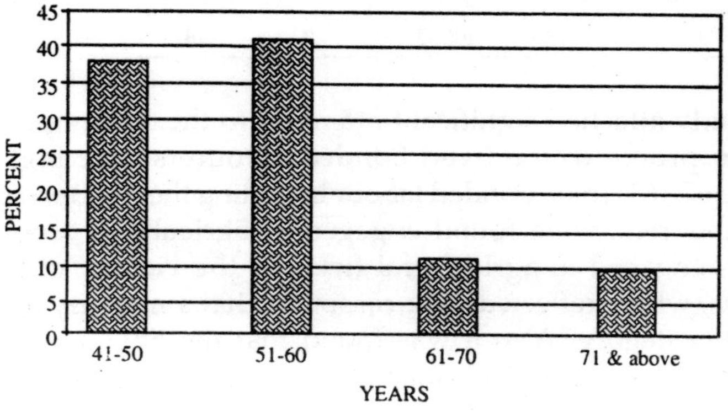

After examining the age pattern of the freed bonded labour, it is evident from the table that the freed bonded labourer belongs to different age groups. They are a composite mix of young, middle age as well as old aged. It is found from the table 1 that the highest percentage of the respondents (41.05%) belongs to the age group of 51-60 years, which suggests that they are old and have been long in the vicious circle of bondage, and were in bulk, till they were freed. The second highest percentage of respondents (38.06%) belongs to the age group of 41-50 years, which implies that they were in the master's clutches also for reasonable period of time. The third highest percentage of the respondents (11.09%) belongs to the age group of 61-70 years. This group was small but provided deep insight into the bondage syndrome. It also suggests that a small percentage survived the hardship of bonded period. They have lived long to tell the tales. This is also true for the following group of 9.70% who are in the age or 71 and above age group. Some from the last two senior groups were bitter for having lived so long, as it emerged during informal discussion. It also emerged that the majority had served their masters for a relatively long time. From age group 50 and above, they are strong 61.94%, which shows the predominance of old freed bonded labourers.

Table 2
Distribution of Occupation of Freed Bonded Labourer

Occupation	*Male*		*Female*		*Total*	
	No.	*%*	*No.*	*%*	*No.*	*%*
Agricultural labour	86	64.18	4	2.98	90	67.16
Non-Agricultural labour	32	23.88	-	-	32	23.88
No Work, Old age	15	8.96	-	-	12	8.96
Total	130	97.02	4	2.98	134	100.00

The study attached significant attention to the contemporary occupation profile of the freed bonded labourers. The highest percentage 67.16% freed bonded labour including the freed women bonded labourers, were found engaged as agricultural labours. They were engaged in agricultural fields in the vicinity of their households, which reflected their reason as that a majority fell in the old age category. Also it was found that the FBLs were not engaged round the year and demand was more seasonal, hence

Figure 2
Distribution of Occupation of Freed Bonded Labourer

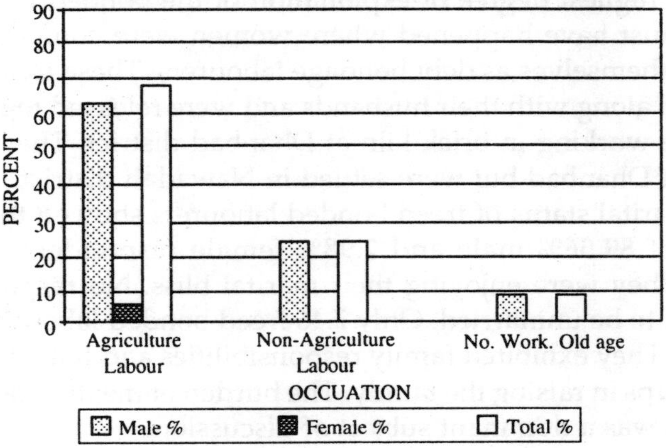

during the lean season they foray into non-agricultural work. The employment was not on long-term basis due to seasonal factor. The 23.88% of freed bonded labour engaged in non-agricultural enterprise like brick kilns, rickshaw pulling, digging, road making work, and house construction works. There were low percentages of freed bonded labourers, who were without work due to old age and sickness.

Thus, the most important and dominant reason appears to be the handling association with the agricultural occupations of freed bonded labour.

Table 3
Distribution of Freed Bonded Labourer by Sex and Marital Status

Marital Status	*Male*		*Female*		*Total*	
	No.	*%*	*No.*	*%*	*No.*	*%*
Married	120	89.56	4	2.98	124	92.54
Unmarried	-	-	-	-	-	-
Widow/Widower	10	7.46	-	-	10	7.46
Total	130	97.02	4	2.98	134	100.00

The pattern of sex distribution among the sampled freed bonded labourers showed 130 males and 4 females, signifying high prevalence of males in bondage but there were female freed bonded labourers too. The presence of females presents a picture where the highest degree of exploitation of the bonded labourer families must have happened where women were compelled to mortgage themselves as debt bondage labourers. These four were mortgaged along with their husbands and were released together. They were working in brick kiln at Dhanbad district. They were released at Dhanbad but were settled in Nawadah district.

The marital status of freed bonded labourers showed that the majority of 89.56% male and 2.98% female respondents were married. They were enjoying their marital bliss. No respondent was found to be unmarried. Only 7.46 freed bonded labours were widowed. They exhibited family responsibilities and talked about the hardships in raising the family. The burden of meeting familial challenges was a dominant subject of discussion.

Table 4
Caste Composition of Freed Bonded Labourer

Caste	*Number*	*Percentage*	*Total*
Schedule Caste	134	100,00	134
Schedule Tribes	-	-	-
Other Backward class	-	-	-
General	-	-	-
Total	134	100.00	134

All freed bonded labourers were from the scheduled caste community. It is significant and true to the history of debt bondage.

Table 5
Classification of Freed Bonded Labourer

Education	*Number*	*Percentage*
Illiterate	131	97.76
Literate	3	2.24
Total	134	100.00

The educational position is appealling. 97.76% of the freed bonded labourers were illiterate and had never received any form of schooling even after been freed under any government non-formal plethora of schemes. No vestige of education had ever touched them, and they were hapless victims of state's gross ignorance and neglect. Only 2.24% were found to be literate or

Figure 3
Educational Status of Freed Bonded Labourer

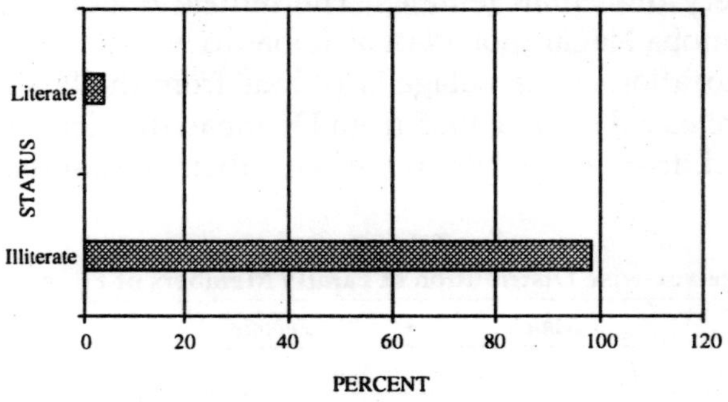

better understood as semi-literate and even they had great difficulty in writing their names. In sum, the freed bonded labourers truly come from the most downtrodden sections of the traditional Indian society or the sociological black hole.

Table 6
Sex wise Distribution of Freed Bonded Labour

Sex	*Number*	*Percentage*
Male	130	97.02
Female	4	2.98
Total	134	100.00

Figure 4
Sex-wise Distribution of FBLs

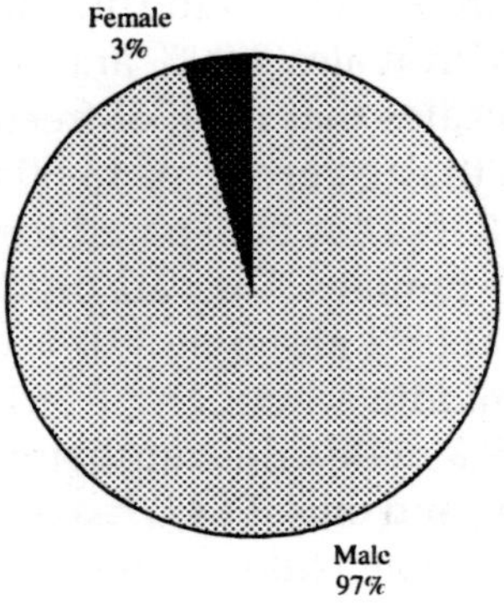

It is evident from the table that the highest 97.02% of freed bonded labourers are males and only 2.98% freed bonded labourers are females, so the representation of male freed bonded labour is very high than females. The female bonded laboures belong to Vinoba Nagar mohallah of Telbadro village in Akbarpur block. The location of the village is 10 kms from the block office. They were released on 3.01.1985 from Dhanbad district, at present in Jharkhand, from brick kiln along with their husbands.

Table 7
Age-sex-wise Distribution of Family Members of FBLs

Sex	*Male*		*Female*		*Total*	
Age group	*No.*	*%*	*No.*	*%*	*No.*	*%*
0 - 5 years	52	5.57	48	5.14	100	10.71
6 - 14 years	154	16.51	108	11.58	262	28.09
15 - 60 years	284	30.44	266	28.51	28.51	58.95
60 & above	14	1.50	7	0.75	0.75	2.25
Total	504	54.02	429	45.98	45.98	100.00

The pattern emerging from the table shows that the freed bonded labourers families belongs to different age groups. They are up to 0 to 5 years, 6-14 years, 15-60 years and 60 and above years. The majority of FBLs (57.45%) were found in the age bracket of 15-60 years, which is evenly between the two-sex i.e.28.94% male and 28.51% female. The next age group of 6-14 years with 28.09% constitutes the second large size with 16.51% males and 11.58% females. The third group size in age group of 0-5 years is 10.71% with males 5.57% and females 5.14%. 3.75% of freed bonded labourers were found in the fourth age group size of 61 and above with males 3.00% and females 0.75%.

Thus, the table indicates that most of freed bonded labourers families were found in the age group of 15-60 years.

The shadow of darkness has not spared the next generation of freed bonded labourer's families. They are predominantly illiterate with figure as high as 92.08% and only 1.02% were literate, 0.60% were educated up to middle school and 0.36% were found to be matriculate. The 14.65% male children between the age group 6-14 years were illiterate and only 3.84% male children were going to school. Among the female children between the age group of 6-14 years, 11.04% were illiterate and were preoccupied in doing their household works only. A small fraction of 1.92% female children go to the middle school but they too drop out and as gathered from discussions girl child education was not so popular and acceptable among the FBLs families.

Table 8
Educational Status of Freed Bonded Labourer's Family Members

Category	*Illiterate*		*Literate*		*Upto Middle*		*Matriculation*		*Total*	
	No.	*%*	*No.*	*%*	*No.*	*%*	*No.*	*%*	*No.*	*%*
Adult Male	280	33.61	10	120	5	0.60	3	0.36	298	35.77
Adult Female	273	32.77	-	-	-	-	-	-	273	32.77
Male Child (6-14)	122	14.65	-	-	32	3.84	-	-	154	18.49
Female Child (6-14)	92	11.04	-	-	16	1.92	-	-	108	12.97
Total	767	92.07	10	10	53	6.36	3	0.36	833	100.00

It is alarming that education is not filtering through next generation, which may keep them tied in disguised servitude to land and propertied masters. There have been no special efforts made by the state education machinery to promote education or raise the educational level of freed bonded labourer's families as a priority and special care sector. Education is empowerment and key to mobility in social and economic sphere but it does not carry any meaning among the FBLs. Self-esteem and confidence was lacking among them. Their main preoccupation is to survive in the existing adversity.

Table 9
Family-size Distribution of Free Bonded Labourers

Sl.No.	*Family Size*	*No. of FBLs*	*%*
1.	Up to 5	34	25.37
2.	6-10	75	55.97
3.	11-15	22	16.42
4.	16-20	03	2.24
	All	134	100.00

The size of the family of FBLs was large. 25.37% of the total FBLS had 5 and less numbers in their families whereas 55.97% FBLs had a family size of 6-10 members. 18.66% of the FBLs had large families. The family size for remaining 2.24% was very large, with maximum family size of 18 members in a family.

Figure 4
Family size of FBLs

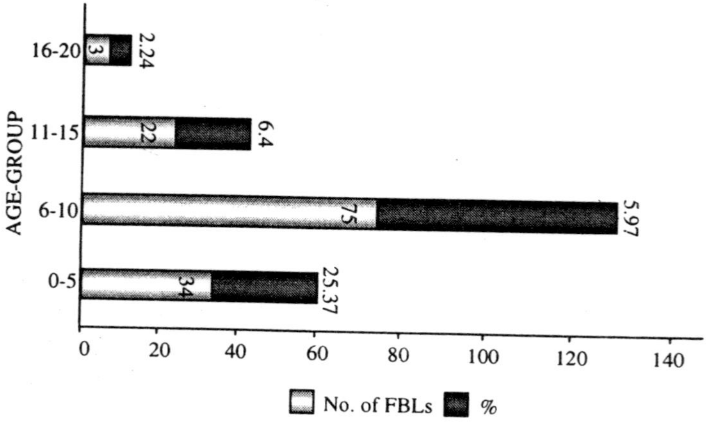

The means of family size comes to 7.75 members. In view of rural family structure, large family is still a prevalent norm and it was true for freed bonded labourer families too. Large families have also been bane for them. It was difficult for them to raise large families or meet any extraordinary situation, where they required money to meet the situation; hence in those situations as well as due to familial pressure many fell into the vicious debt bondage trap. Practically, it was difficult for bonded labourers to escape from bondage since they were unable to repay the loans due to poverty and large family commitments.

The table reveals over all picture of wage-structure of FBLs. The majority of FBLs (80.59%) were working in the agriculture area, and were paid their wages in kind like rice, paddy, wheat etc.10.45% FBLs were working in other than agricultural works like rickshaw pulling, rural road construction work etc., and received their wages in cash ranging from Rs. 35 to 50/- per day. 12 FBLs reported that they don't have any type of work for their livelihood due to their old age and disability, and they are dependent on their family for their day to day requirement.

All FBLs of Narhat block reported that they were receiving very low wages in kind i.e., 2 Kg.-4 Kg. grains like rice paddy, wheat etc. than other block FBLs.

Table 10(a)
Wage-structure of FBLs

Sl.No.	*Wage Structure*	*No. of FBLs*	*Per cent*
	In Kinds (Per day)		
1.	(i) 2 Kg. Grains	08	5.97
	(ii) 3 Kg. Grains	07	5.22
	(iii) 4 Kg. Grains	15	11.19
	(iv) 5 Kg. Grains	78	58.21
	Sub-Total	108	80.59
	In Cash (Per day)		
2.	(i) Rs. 35/-	06	4.48
	(ii) Rs. 40/-	03	2.24
	(iii) Rs. 45/-	03	2.24
	(iv) Rs. 50/-	02	1.49
	Sub Total	14	10.45
3.	No Work	12	8.96
	Grand Total	134	100.00

Table 10(b)
Family Income of FBLs
[The annual family income comprised the combined income of all earning family members]

Sl.No.	*Income categories (Rs.)*	*No. of FBLs*	*%*
1.	Upto 10,000	25	18.65
2.	10,000 - 15.000	28	20.90
3.	15,001 - 20,000	40	29.85
4.	20,001 - 25,000	28	20.90
5.	25,001 & above	13	9.70
	All	134	100.00

The economic status of the FBLs speaks volumes of their economic woes. The poverty syndrome was apparent. The majority of FBL's families have annual family income of Rs. 20 thousand and below. 20.90% FBLs have income of above Rs. 20 thousand to 25 thousand, while another 9.70% FBL have income of more than Rs. 25 thousand. The family income has not grown in a growth mode, as it should have been progressively over the years. Many still receive food grain in kind and cash as part of work rendered in the fields. The majority is not getting the minimum wages as

Figure 5
Family Income of FBLs

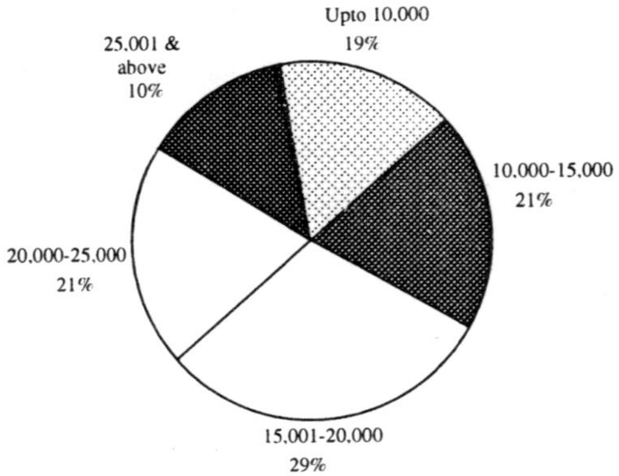

prescribed by the State Government. Even basic awareness about minimum wage was missing.

In view of average FBLs having large family size, the income for sustenance looked low but enough for survival only. It appears uphill task for them to crawl out of poverty manifestation.

DISTRIBUTION OF LIVESTOCK AMONG THE FBLs

Livestock Possession

The FBLs are very poor, even their family members have to work in the land, particularly during busy seasons, and wages are not necessarily higher than elsewhere. Still some have dared to keep livestock in order to supplement their income and other familial diet needs, but it is meager. Those FBLs who work as agricultural labourers had in their possession livestock larger in number than those in non-agricultural occupations.

The distribution of figures in the table demonstrates the complete picture of livestock possession among the FBLs. 44 FBLs out of 134 FBLs have their own livestocks. 9 FBLs had bataidari livestock's which were given by different type of people, likes - farmer, landlords, moneylenders etc. to look after their animals on 50% sharing agreement.

The rest of the FBLs had fewer animals or no animals in their possession. This reflects on their poor supplementary source of income. Many complained that the difficulty of maintaining livestock was mainly of non-availability of grazing lands. Even those who possessed the livestock registered their grievance that there was no help or assistance by Animal and Husbandry official's particularly Veterinary doctors. They had no access or information about artificial insemination centers or mobile clinics. They were maintaining livestock on their traditional knowledge, but had suffered animal casualties due to ignorance or know-how to counter animal diseases. There was no facility available in the neighborhood.

Table 11
Distribution of FBLs by their Livestock Possession

Sl. No.	*Name of Livestock*	*No. of FBLs having*	
		Own Livestock	*Bataidari Livestock*
1.	One buffalo	02	01
2.	Two buffaloes	01	01
3.	Four buffaloes	01	–
4.	One cow	03	
5.	Three cows	02	–
6.	One goat	01	–
7.	Two goats	02	–
8.	Three goats	01	–
9.	One ox	11	01
10.	Two oxen	02	–
11.	One pig	01	–
12.	Two pigs	02	–
13.	Four pigs	01	–
14.	One cow + One goat	04	–
15.	One buffalo + Two goats	–	01
16.	One ox + Two goats	01	–
17.	Two oxen + One goat	01	–
18.	One cow + One ox	02	04
19.	One cow + Two oxen	01	—
20.	One cow + Four oxen	01	–
21.	One Cow + One buffalo	01	–
22.	Two cow + One ox	02	01
23.	One cow + One ox + One goat + One cock	01	–
	TOTAL	44	09

The accessibility of the governmental facilities as basic civic support system for the citizens are an important mark for assessing the reach and welfare measures taken to ameliorate the common man's predicament, particularly in the rural and backward area. In the present table, the availability of governmental infra-structural facilities for the FBLs represents a mixed scenario.

The table reveals that all types of the infra-structural facilities are not available to the FBLs of the district; rather it is insufficient for the FBL families in several areas. Some are fortunate to enjoy the facilities whereas others are deprived of the basic facilities. There is no uniformity in the availability of these government conveniences. The table amply illustrates the tale of missed opportunities by the government agencies in reaching out uniformly to all FBLs families in their neighbourhood.

Table 12
AVailability of Government Infra-structural Facilities in FBLs Villages/Tolas

Sl. No.	*Government Facilities*	*No. of FBLs*	*Percentage*
1.	Post Office	48	35.82
2.	PDS	98	71.13
3.	Health Centre	17	12.67
4.	Electricity	60	44.78
5.	Road facility:		
	(i) Kacha	40	29.85
	(ii) Pucca	50	37.31
	(iii) Mixed	29	21.64
	(iv) No facility	15	11.20
	Sub-Total	134	100.00
6.	Drinking water facility		
	(i) Well	04	2.98
	(ii) Hand pump	86	64.18
	(iii) Well+ Hand pump	44	32.84
	Sub-Total	134	100.00
7.	Educational Facility		
	(i) Primary	98	73.14
	(ii) Upto Middle	05	3.73
	(iii) Upto High School	23	17.16
	(iv) None of these	08	5.97
	Sub-Total	134	100.00
8.	Anganbari Centre	99	73.88
9.	Bank	2	20.90

N = 134.

The picture emerging is like this that 35.82% FBLs can utilise the Post office facilities, whereas 71.13% FBLs can use the Public distribution centre (fair price shop/ration). The health situation is dismal with only 12.67% FBLs having access to the Health centres. Some 44.78% FBLs have the electricity connection, whereas 73.88% use the Anganwari centre. Only 20.90% FBLs have the Bank facilities of any kind.

The positive aspect in this mixed picture is of the drinking water facilities, which are available in any type in all the FBLs village/tola. 64.18% FBL families have hand pump, 32.84% enjoy well and hand pump facilities both.

Figure 6
Government Facilities to FBLs

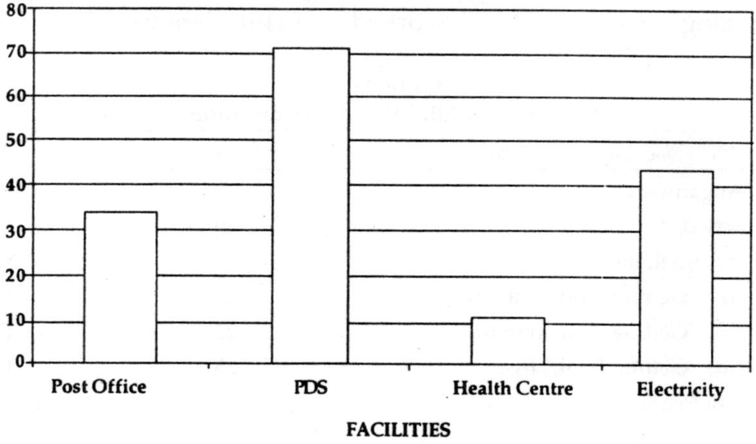

It is only 2.98% of the FBLs dependent on the wells. It is one area where there was little complaint or they talked about. They were satisfied with the availability of drinking water but had complains about the repair of hand pumps. They repair the hand pumps with their meager resources, which they want local officials to do so.

The road facilities were accessible for 50 FBLs families on the pucca road, 40 on the kacha road and 29 FBLs on the mixed road but 15 FBLs did not have any type of road facilities. They use earthen path before reaching any pucca or kachcha road.

Under the educational facilities, 98 FBL's families can benefit from the Primary school in their proximity whereas 5 FBLs up to the Middle school, and 23 FBLs up to High school, but 8 FBLs do not have any educational facility in their neighbourhood.

FBL CHILDREN'S EDUCATION

The distribution of figures in the Table 13 demonstrate about FBLs' children education. Only 21.64% FBLs reported that their children go to school and are getting food materials, cash amount stipend and books free of cost. Only one FBL complained that his children are not getting food materials and books free of cost. 7 FBLs informed that their children don't get cash amount in the school, which is provided by the Government.

Further, the table reveals that majority of 74 (55.22%) FBLs children don't go to school. The majority of FBLs (62.16%) reported that their children were playing here and there. 39 (52.70%) FBLs replied that they are doing work at home. 14.86% were engaged in grazing cattle and 12.16% worked as a child labour.

Table 13
Awareness of FBLs Children Education

Sl.No.	*Where does your child read?*	*No. of FBLs*	*%*
1.	Anganwari	-	0.00
2.	School	29	21.64
	If School, then	Yes	No
	(i) Getting food materials	28	01
	(ii) Getting cash amount	22	07
	(iii) Getting Books free	28	01
3.	Not Reading	74	55.22
	If not reading,		
	(i) Doing work at home	39	52.70
	(ii) Playing here and there	46	62.16
	(iii) Due to long distance of school	08	10.81
	(iv) Working as a child labour	09	12.16
	(v) There is no gain with education	07	9.46
	(vi) No need of education among girls	02	2.70
	(vii) Grazing cattle	11	14.86
	(viii) Dominant caste/people disturb the children inside/outside the school	03	4.05
	(ix) due to low economic condition	01	1.35
4.	Not Applicable	31	23.14

Some did not go to school due to long distance of school (10.81%). There were skeptics who felt that there is no gain in getting educated (9.46%). There were gender-biased families, which felt that there was no need of education among the girls (2.70%). Some children were prevented from going to school by the dominant caste men in their area (4.05%). There were families who wanted to send children to school but could not do so due to poor economic conditions (1.35%).

31 FBLs (23.14%) reported that they have no children or have no school going age children. None of them send their children to the Anganwari Centre due to lack of knowledge and information. There is no approach by the Anganwari Centres or concerned officials to motivate them or extend the Anganwari facilities to them.

Table 14
Distribution of FBLs by Nature and Types of Dwelling Units
Nature and Type of Dwelling of the FBLs

Sl. No.	*No. of rooms*	*Kachcha*		*Pueea*		*Mixed*		*All type*	
		No.	*%*	*No.*	*%*	*No.*	*%*	*No.*	*%*
1.	1	02	1.49	-	0.00	02	1.49	04	2.98
2.	2	15	11.20	05	3.73	29	21.64	49	36.57
3.	3	22	16.42	-	0.00	22	16.42	44	32.84
4.	4+	21	15.67	-	0.00	16	11.94	37	27.61
	All	60	44.78	05	3.73	69	51.49	134	100.00

All FBLs had shelter for themselves, which meant a dwelling unit of some kind. 44.78% FBLs had kachcha (earthen hut) units, 3.73% had pucca units, and rest 51.49% had mixed dwelling units. The mixed dwelling units were a combination of Indira Awas Yojna added to their traditional katcha houses. Such units added more rooms making some livable space for the families, considering many have large family size. But then everyone has not been fortunate to receive the much-needed Indira Awas Yojana units.

The dwelling units had different number of rooms. The distribution was that 27.61% of FBLs had four rooms unit; 32.84% FBLs had three rooms unit, while another 36.57% FBLs had two room set, and 2.98% had one room unit.

The FBLs who had mixed dwelling units had larger number of rooms in comparison to those who were living in kachcha

Figure 7
Dwelling Units of FBLs

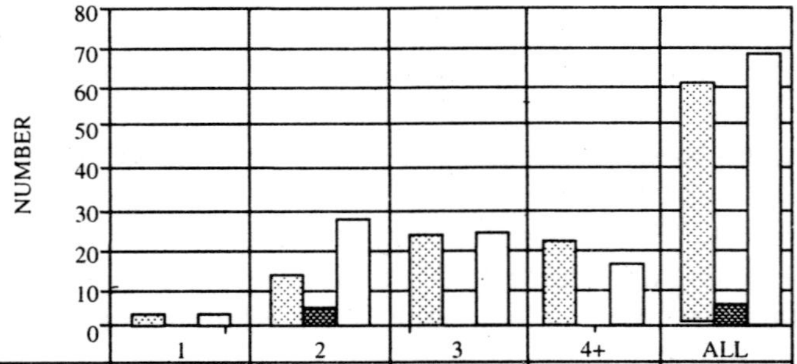

	1	2	3	4+	ALL
Kuchcha	2	15	22	21	60
Pucca	0	5	0	0	5
Mixed	2	29	22	16	69

dwelling units. In the case of pucca and mixed construction, it was seen that these types of constructions were made under the provision of Indira Awas Yojana (IAY).

DRINKING WATER FACILITY

Majority of FBLs use either hand pumps (64.18%) or hand pumps and wells both (32.84%) as the source of potable water supply. Some FBLs (2.98%) use wells only. These drinking water facilities are the community assets, which is provided by the State and Central Govt. resources for use of safe drinking water. Only 2 FBLs of the Tola-Rahulnagar, Village-Bhimbigha, Block-Narhat has installed their own hand pumps.

Table 15
Debt amongst FBLs

Sl. No.	*Sources*	*No. of FBLs under loan*	*%*	*Amount of loan*	*Average amount of Loan.*
1.	Formal Agencies	02	11.11	6000.00	3000.00
2.	Non-formal Agencies	16	88.89	46350.00	2896.88
	ALL	18	100.00	52350.00	2908.33

Debt scenario shows that a majority of 116 FBLs (86.57%) had no debt outstanding and no loan to repay to anyone or agency. The remaining 18 FBLs (13.43%) were in debt and had taken loan. 16 FBLs took loan through non-formal agencies (e.g. landlords, moneylenders etc.) which amounted to a total amount of Rs. 46350.02 FBLs had borrowed loans from the formal agencies (banks) to an amount of Rs. 6000. Thus, a sum of Rs. 525350/- stood as outstanding loan borrowed by 18 FBLs through various agencies. In case of loans from the non-formal agencies, they have to pay a higher rate of interest i.e. 13% per month, which is exploitative in nature.

Table 16
Distribution of FBLs by their Causes for Bonded Labour

Sl. No.	*Statement*	*No. of FBLs*	*%*
1.	Low socio-economic status in the society	21	15.67
2.	Unemployment	61	45.52
3.	Poverty	78	58.21
4.	On the traditional way	08	5.97
5.	Indebtedness	114	85.07
6.	Own choice	02	1.49

Note: Figures are non-additive.

CAUSES OF BONDED LABOUR

The study focussed on finding the causes for becoming bonded labour. The results consolidated on the view that it lies in the deprivation paradigm. They were deprived of a social position in the social order right from the dawn of civilization or creation of Varna order. As all FBLs are in scheduled caste category, they were at the bottom of any social hierarchical order and have paid a heavy price too. They were deprived of position, property, and right to equal opportunities of any fair play in the social order of the day. Consequently, it gave rise to beggary and slavery, indebtedness and subsequently bonded labour system.

The common cord among all were that they never stood at the running line, so they never had an opportunity to compete in an environment of equal social and economic opportunities. The race never began for them. They regretted that they were born losers. The pauperization of the weaker sections is cornerstone of bonded labour ethos and system.

The table reveals that the most significant answers are indebtedness (85.07%) and poverty (58.21%) followed by unemployment (45.52%) and low socio-economic status in the society (15.67%). Some attributed to the traditional family way (5.97%) and own choice (1.49%).

The problem of poverty, hunger, unemployment, no source of income, low socio-economic status in the society, landlessness and the exploitative practices of the dominant landlords sucked them into debt bondage.

PERIOD OF WORKING AS BONDED LABOUR

The table of bondage and servitude unfolds when an in depth analytical findings depict the range of the period of bondage from 3 years to 30 years. Some FBLs related that they never thought that they would be ever free, whereas there were some who worked briefly as bonded labour felt that it was like walking out of a nightmare. The very fact they were free was more important to them.

Table 17
Distribution of FBLs Working Period as Bonded Labour

Sl. No.	*Working Period*	*No. of FBLs*	*%*
1.	Upto 5 years	13	9.70
2.	6 - 10 years	11	8.21
3.	11 - 15 years	34	25.37
4.	16 - 20 years	37	27.61
5.	21 years & above	39	29.11
	Total	134	100.00

The majority of FBLs (56.92%) worked as bonded labour for about 16-30 years. About 33.58% FBLs had worked for more than 6 to 15 years. While 9.70% FBLs reported that they had worked as the Bonded Labour up to 5 years.

The 11 FBLs of Vinobha Nagar tola, village-Telbadaro, block-Akbarpur had the briefest period of 2-3 years in a brick kiln of Dhanbad district, which is situated now in the Jharkhand State.

PERCEPTION OF CHANGE AMONG THE FBLs

This was mother of all the questions that whether they felt any perceptible change after being freed. The response was overwhelming. They cherished the freedom of work, which meant the liberty to choose their workplace. They adored mobility and right to live as they wished. It was a clear departure from bondage to liberty of availing opportunities, as it came through with great hardship in many cases.

Table 18
Perception of Change among Free Bonded Labourers

Sl. No.	*Statement*	*No. of FBLs*	*%*
1.	Freedom of work	116	86.57
2.	Feeling better than earlier	25	18.66
3.	Enhancement in social prestige	03	2.24
4.	No pressure and binding of work	36	26.87
5.	Improvement in food availability	01	0.75
6.	Enhancement of wages	03	2.24
7.	No change	04	2.99

Note: Figures are non-additive.

The table reveals that the most significant answer was freedom of work (86.57%), followed by no pressure and binding of work (26.87%). Those who expressed their feelings of being better than before were 18.66%. Some experienced enhancement in their social prestige (2.24%). A very small section felt improvement in food availability (0.75%) and enhancement in wages (2.24%), but 2.99% felt no change at all.

The revelation of this study was that many FBLs, who were freed, continued to work in their old master's field. They had no complaint against them because the old masters were giving them better wages now than before, and liberty of mobility and choice to work or not with them.

SUGGESTION OF FBLs FOR IMPROVING THEIR PRESENT SITUATION

The expectations of the FBLs were assessed as to what in their opinion the State should take steps to improve their position. The suggestions for improving their present situation gave an inside view to their level of expectations. The table demonstrates that the most significant suggestion was for improving the economic condition of their families (67.91%), in which they demanded loans, vocational training business facilities, land for cultivation and animal husbandry—cattle/piggery rearing skills.

Table 19
Opinion of FBLs on What Steps the Government should take to Improve their Conditions

Sl. No.	Statement	No. of FBLs	%
1.	To improve infra-structural facilities (Electricity, Road, PDS)	42	31.34
2.	Housing, Drinking water, Toilet and Drainage facilities	45	33.58
3.	Medical & Health Care facilities	48	35.82
4.	Educational facilities	06	4.48
5.	For improving economic condition of families (Loan, Vocational training, Business, Land for cultivation, Animal Husbandry—Cattle/Piggery rearing)	91	67.91
6.	Regular work all the year around	24	17.91
7.	Pension facilities and increase in pension amount	23	17.16
8.	More facilities by the Government	59	44.03
9.	Development functionaries should pay visit	03	2.24
10.	HYV/Fertilizer, Agriculture equipments should be provided by the Government	07	5.22
11.	Enhancement of wages	14	10.45
12.	No response	20	14.92

They felt that the Government should provide more Medical and Health Care facilities (35.82%); Housing, drinking water, toilet and drainage facilities (33.58%) and improve the infra-structural facilities (31.34%) like electricity, road and PDS.

17.91% FBLs suggested the need for regular work around the year, while 17.91% FBLs felt that the pension amount should be increased and its delivery made more efficient. There were some suggestions like increase in spread of the educational facilities (4.48%); regular visit of the development functionaries (2.24%); HYV seeds/Fertilizer, agriculture equipment's should be provided by the Government (5.22%) and enhancement of wages (10.45%). 14.92% did not give any suggestion.

During the interview of FBLs, it was found that they depend totally on the Government to improve their economic conditions. They were quiet vocal in telling their plight and expected the government agencies to do more than just one time help. They were anguished on the fact that after their release there has been no substantial attempt to help them except for initial compensation given in kind of livestock or rickshaw. There is need to bring them in mainstream of development a view shared by all freed bonded labourer.

Table 20
Availability of Toilet Facilities in the FBLs-House

Sl. No.	*Response*	*No. of FBLs*	*%*
1.	Yes	11	8.21
2.	No	123	91.79
	All	134	100.00

TOILET FACILITY

Majority of FBL (91.79%) had no toilet facilities in their houses. They use open place out side the village for this purpose. Only 11 (8.21%) FBLs of Vinobanagar tola, Village-Telbadaro, Block-Akbarpur reported to have toilets in their houses. The rural sanitation programme of Government, UNICEF and civil society is non-existence.

DRAINAGE FACILITY

Majority of FBLs (57.46%) reported to have kachcha drains for disposal of wastewater in their tolas. Some of FBLs (15.67%) reported to have Pucca drains. 26.87% FBLs reported that the wastewater spilled here and there in the village lane in the absence of any proper drainage system in the tola.

Table 21
Drainage Facilities in the FBLs-Tola

Sl. No.	*Response*	*No. of FBLs*	*%*
1.	Kachcha	27	57.46
2.	Pucca	21	15.67
3.	Open flow	36	26.87
	All	134	100.00

FBLs ON THEIR UPLIFT AFTER BEING RELEASED

There has been an improvement in financial condition, betterment in food consumption, enhancement in social prestige and increase in voting activities after been released. But none of them have purchased any permanent assets from their income and livelihood.

Table 22
Opinion of FBLs on their uplift after being Released

Sl. No.	Activities	Uplift			
		Gains		No Gains	
		No.of FBLs	%	No. of FBLs	%
1.	Financial condition	93	69.40	41	30.60
2.	Food consumption	96	71.64	38	28.36
3.	Asset acquisition	-	0.00	134	100.00
4.	Social prestige	113	84.33	21	15.67
5.	Voting behaviour	126	94.03	08	5.97

If yes, (i) what type of improvement:

(a) Food according to their will	14	14.58
(b) Takes better food	66	68.75
(c) Improvement in fooding, clothing and Housing	16	16.67
(ii) How many times, do you take food?		
(a) Twice a Day	45	33.58
(b) Thrice a Day	89	66.42

Table 23
Distribution of FBLs by their Possession of Farming Equipments

Sl. No.	Farming Equipment	No. of FBLs	%
1.	Plough	04	2.99
2.	Shovel	56	41.79
3.	Others (Khurpi & Hasia)	134	100.00

The table reveals that about two-third FBLs take their food thrice a day and one-third FBLs take it twice a day. All the FBLs takes rice with potato/salt and chili or rice juice and salt/Chatani and Achar/Chokha etc. They don't consume food rich in protein/carbohydrate/vitamins, particularly non-vegetarian food items, due to low economic condition. Their consumption is still low, but better from past. The intake is more quantitative food compared to qualitative food. Low intake does affect their health standards and longevity of life.

POSSESSION OF FARMING EQUIPMENT

The majority of FBLs are agriculture labourers by occupation. After been released, they acquired some farming equipment, which was tool for their survival and means to earn. Only 4 (2.99%) FBLs reported that they had plough, while 41.79% FBLs reported that they had shovel as the farming equipments. All of them reported that they had Khurpi & Hasia only.

Table 24(a)
Agriculture Facilities provided by Government among FBLs

Sl. No.	Statement	Yes	%	No	%
1.	Farming Equipments provided by the Government	-	0.00	134	100.00
2.	Fertilizer, Seeds and Pesticides at subsidized rate	-	0.00	134	100.00
3.	How you do you irrigate your land?				
	(i) Well	-	0.00		
	(ii) Pond	-	0.00		
	(iii) Canal	22	16.42		
	(iv) N.A.	112	83.58		

None of them got any type of farming equipment or fertilizer, seeds and pesticides at the subsidized rate. There was no irrigation facility like well and tubewell provided by the Government. Those FBLs (16.42%) who had got some agricultural land used canal irrigation. Majority of FBLs (112) was found landless.

Table 24(b)
Distribution of FBLs by providing Land for Cultivation

Sl. No.	Statement	No. of FBLs	Per cent
1.	Land provided for cultivation	22	16.42
	(i) 0.25 - 0.50 acre	18	13.43
	(ii) 0.51 - 0.75 acre	–	–
	(iii) 0.76 - 1.00 acre	04	2.99
2.	Land not in physical possession	07	5.22
3.	No land was given for cultivation	105	78.36

The majority of FBLs (105) reported that they did not receive any agricultural land. 22 FBLs reported that they had received cultivatable land under Bhoodan Andolan, and were cultivating them, but was not enough for their need.

7 FBLs reported that they received land on paper only, under Bhoodan Andolan. They bitterly complained that the lands were not useful for agriculture purposes because it was in the low-lying areas, and there was problem of constant water logging round the year. Many complained that it was far away from their houses also.

Table 25
Working Place of FBLs before Release

Sl. No.	*Statement*	*No. of FBLs*	*%*
1.	Within the same village	91	67.91
2.	Outside the same village but within the block	25	18.66
3.	Outside the block but within the district	07	5.22
4.	Outside the district	11	8.21
	Total	134	100.00

WORKING PLACE OF FBLs BEFORE RELEASE

Majority of FBLs 91 (67.91%) reported that they worked in the same village during the bonded labour period, where they lived. 18.66% FBLs worked outside the village but within their block, while 5.22% FBLs accounted that they worked out side the block but within the district. 8.21% FBLs worked outside the district.

Table 26
Identification Period of FBLs

Sl. No.	*Identification period*	*No. of FBLs*	*%*
1.	1980 – 1981	123	91.79
2.	1985 – 1986	11	8.21

123 FBLs (91.79%) were identified during the year 1980-81, while 11 FBLs (8.21%) were identified during the year 1985-86. The majority have spent 22 years as free persons pursuing their activities on their own terms. Even the other section liberated later, have completed 17 years of freedom from bondage. The Department of Social Security, Government of Bihar and Nawada district officials reported that no bonded labour has been identified after 1986.

Table 27
Knowledge of Minimum wage among FBLs

Sl.No.	*Do you know about the minimum wage ?*	*No. of FBLs*	*%*
1.	Yes	-	0.00
2.	No	134	100.00
	All	134	100.00

Table 27 shows that none of the freed bonded labour knew about the government minimum wage for the agricultural labourers.

Table 28
Distance of Primary Health Centre from FBL's Residence

Sl. No.	*Distance in Km.*	*No. of FBLs*	*%*
1.	1-2	30	22.39
2.	3-4	30	22.39
3.	7-8	20	14.92
4.	9-10	32	23.88
	All	134	100.00

It is evident from the Table 28 that the free bonded labourers face great difficulties to get adequate health care from government health infrastructure due to long distances. 38.80% of the free bonded labour has to cover a long distance of 7 to 10 kms to reach the nearest health center. 54.78% travel 1 to 4 kms to reach a nearest health centre. There is no mobile clinic or any preferential system for Medicare of freed bonded labourers. Non-availability of proper transport makes it more strenuous for sick and old in FBLs to travel. Hence, the free bonded labourers face many difficulties about their family health care.

Table 29
Health & Medicare Facilities among the FBLs

Sl. No.	*Statement*	*No. of FBLs*					
		Yes	*%*	*No*	*%*	*Total*	*%*
1.	Regular check up of Health	-	0.00	134	100.00	134	100.00
2.	Medicare facilities during the illness Period	-	0.00	134	100.00	134	100.00

The Table 29 shows that no Government healthcare of free bonded labour is available at their households. There is no programme, which gives priority to their regular health checkup. There is no fund especially marked to give them medical attention during their severe illness. They are part of Government's general rural medicare approach, but nothing special. The FBLs complained that they do not get medicine at centre. They are given prescription to buy medicine on their own. It was observed that health expenditure on treatment was also draining the FBLs's families to grow, as they should have.

Table 30
Knowledge of Bonded Labour Act among the FBLs

Sl.No.	Statement	No. of FBLs			
		Yes	%	No	%
1.	Do you know about the Bonded Labour Act ?	-	0.00	134	100.00

It is also important to note that 100% freed bonded labour do not know about the Bonded Labour Act, 1976 under which they were freed. They were in consensus grateful to the Government agencies for releasing them from the clutches of bondage.

Table 31
Saving Habit among the FBLs

Sl.No.	Statement	No. of FBLs			
		Yes	%	No	%
1.	Do you have Saving Account in the Bank/Post office ?	14	10.45	120	89.55

It is evident from the Table 31 that saving habit of freed bonded labour is negligible. 89.55% freed bonded labourers do not have any account in Bank or Post office. Only 10.45% freed bonded labourers have their account in Bank or Post office.

The saving attitudes of freed labourers are not satisfactory. The need for more awareness among them about saving habit is needed for their safe and secure future. No effort has been made to educate them or help them in opening account in Post office or bank by Government agencies. Many were not aware about easy access to these facilities but on discussion-expressed desire to open savings account.

Table 32
Availability of Releasing Letters among the FBLs

Sl.No. Statement	No. of FBLs			
	Yes	%	No	%
Have you received any type of Bonded labour release letter issued by D.M./S.D.O.?	134	100	-	-

It is evident from the Table 32 that all freed bonded labourers had received their Release Certificate by the District Administration, but 89.55% of freed bonded labourers have lost their Release Certificate due to carelessness. The Assistant Director, Social Security office, Nawada, gave the name and addresses of released FBLs to ANSISS team.

The distribution of figures in the table 33 demonstrate that majority of FBLs 98 (73.13%) are working wherever they get better opportunity. The interesting revelation was that 25 (18.66%) FBLs were working with their previous landlord where they worked before their release, but on reasonable better wage and working conditions. They were free to move anywhere but were working due to familiarity of work and attractive present working terms and environment. They said that nothing more should be read than what information they gave us. 11 (8.21%) FBLs don't do any type of work due to their old age or disability.

Table 33
Present Working Place of FBLs and his Family Members

Sl. No.	Statements	No. of FBLs							
		Any-where	%	Old emp-loyer	%	Not appli-cable	%	Total	%
1.	Where do you work at present?	98	73.13	25	18.66	11	8.21	134	100.00
2.	Where does other family members work at present?	116	86.57	18	13.43	-	0.00	134	100.00

116 (86.57%) FBL's family members have been working at different places for earning their livelihood, while 18 (13.43%)

FBL's family members have been working with the previous landlord where their father/husband are working.

TRAINING FACILITIES

About 36 (26.87%) FBLs reported that they had received training through labour and employment department at the block level for three days about the animal husbandry. But only 5 FBLs, out of 36, reported that they benefited by this training. Further, the Table 34 reveals that none of them had received any type of loan for starting the business after training.

Majority of FBLs did not receive any training by Government agencies after their release but those who did receive any training did not benefit anything except 5 FBLs to some extent.

NEIGHBOUR OF FBLs

132 families of freed bonded labourers were found living in cluster with the other FBL families only (98.5%). It was easy to reach their cluster in villages, which had a distinct identity. They did not appear segregated but maintained separate physical identity in the villages. It was more due to Government agencies giving them a place as rehabilitation package to stay together. Others informed that they were staying together before entering the bonded labour period. Only 2 FBLs reported that none of his neighbours were bonded Labourers and they live in the village with their own caste people.

Table 34
Training for FBLs

Sl. No.	Statement	No. of FBLs	%
1.	Did you get any type of training at the Govt. level/non-Govt. level after release?		
	Yes	36	26.87
	No	98	73.13
2.	If yes, then what type of training?		
	(i) Animal Husbandry	36	26.87
3.	How many days?		
	(i) 3 days	36	26.87
4.	Are you benefited after training?		
	(i) Benefited	05	13.89
	(ii) Not benefited	31	86.11
5.	Do you get any loan for your business?		
	Yes	-	0.00
	No	134	100.00

Table 35
Neighbours of Freed Bonded Labourer

Sl. No.	*Statement*	*No. of FBLs*	*%*
1.	Was your neighbour bonded labourer ?		
	(i) Yes	132	98.51
	(ii) No	02	1.49
2.	If Yes, how many families?		
	(i) Upto 5	08	6.06
	(ii) 6 - 10	31	23.48
	(iii) 11 - 15	58	43.94
	(iv) 16 - 20	14	10.61
	(v) 21 & above	21	15.91

The distribution of figures in the Table 35 demonstrate that the FBLs live in cluster. 8 members of the total FBLs had 5 and less number of members in their neighbours as FBLs. Another 31 FBLs had a neighbour size of 6-10 freed Bonded Labour members. About 43.94% FBLs had 11-15 members or freed bonded labours in their neighbourhood, while 26.52% FBLs had 16 and above members of freed bonded labours in the neighbourhood.

Table 36
Other Related Programmes for FBL under Poverty Line Scheme

Sl. No.	*Schemes*	*Yes*	*%*	*No*	*%*
1.	IAY	66	49.25	68	50.75
2.	IRDP	14	10.45	120	89.55

REHABILITATION SCHEMES FOR FBLs

The Table 36 reveals that 66 (49.25%) FBLs received Indira Awas Yojana facilities and were using it for residential purposes. 68 (50.75%) FBLs reported that they did not get this type of facility and a long period has passed since they were released. They had no clue as to why they were not provided Indira Awas Yojana house, but they are still hopeful of getting one from the government.

13 FBLs of Budhauli village and 1 FBL of Kachana village reported that about Rupees 1500 to Rs. 1600 were given to them under the IRDP Scheme. But rest got nothing under IRDP assistance.

The Government assistance is evident but in fragmented manner not in totality. There is urgent need to address the issue as to why 68 FBLs (50.75%) were left out.

It can be said that Government programmes, under the below poverty line and bonded labour schemes, are not efficiently provided to the FBLs.

Table 37
Social Security Pension for FBLs

Sl.No.	*Statement*	*Yes*	*%*	*No*	*%*	*Total*	*%*
1.	Do you get said Security Pension?	103	76.87	31	23.13	134	100.00

The distribution of figures in the Table 37 demonstrates the majority of FBLs (103) (76.87%) avails the pension facility of Rs. 100 per month which is provided by the Government under the Bonded Labour Rehabilitaion Scheme.

31 (23.13%) FBLs don't get this type of facility. It was found that the whole sampled village of Narhat Block was deprived of this facility and one case in the village-Kachana of Packaribran Block.

Table 38
Government Compensation Package on been freed

Sl. No.	*Items*	*No. of FBLs*	*Per cent*
A.	**Major things:**		
1.	One Cow + One Buffalo + One Rickshaw	63	47.01
2.	Two Cows + One Rickshaw	38	28.36
3.	Two Buffaloes + One Rickshaw	16	11.94
4.	One Cow + One Rickshaw	05	3.73
5.	Two Cows	04	2.99
6.	Two Buffaloes	08	5.97
	TOTAL	134	100.00
B.	**Except the above major things:**		
1.	Two Goats	35	26.12
2.	Cash	02	1.49

After identification and their release, the bonded labourers were provided compensation by the Government agencies. Under this package, the FBLs were given different type of livestocks, rickshaw and cash money to improve their economic condition and living standard of their family.

The distribution of figures in the table demonstrates that majority of FBLs (63) received one cow, one buffalo and one rickshaw under rehabilitation package through their respective block officials in block offices. 38 FBLs received two cows and one rickshaw, while 16 FBLs received two buffaloes and one rickshaw.

5 FBLs of village Laund, block Sirdala reported that they received one cow and one rickshaw. A woman FBLs out of 134 FBLs, from the tola-Vinoba Nagar, village-Telbadaro, block-Akbarpur reported that they received two cows only. In the same way, 7 FBLs of tola-Vinobanagar, village-Telbadaro, block-Akbarpur and 1 FBL of village-Jamugay, block-Sirdala reported that they received two buffaloes.

Further the Table 38 reveals that 35 FBLs received two goats, and 2 FBLs received cash amount of Rs. 500/- each against the spare amount after purchasing livestock for them.

All compensation was given in lieu of compensatory cash. The respective block officials made the purchases and the distribution.

Table 39
Lal Card and PDS Facilities among FBLs

Sl. No.	*Statement*	*No. of FBLs*			
		Yes	*%*	*No*	*%*
1.	Do you have a Red Card?	128	95.52	06	4.48
2.	If yes, then do you get the related material from PDS at the Govt. rate?	128	95.52	06	4.48
3.	Where are the PDC?				
	(i) Within the village	98	73.13		
	(ii) Outside the village	36	26.87		

It is evident from the above table that 95.52% of the respondents have got the facility of Lal card and a very low percentage (4.48%) did not receive the Lal Card facility which is provided by Government agencies. 95.52% of respondents are getting benefit of kerosene oil only from the PDS network. They complained that the most beneficial would be the availability of foodgrains particularly rice/wheat at subsidized rates in PDS fair price shops (Ration shop).

73.13% FBLs reported that PDS facility was within the village and 26.87% of respondents reported that their PDS was outside their village.

Table 40
Distribution of FBLs Released and Provided Property through the Government

(A) Distribution of FBLs by Seized Property

Sl. No.	*Statement*	*No. of FBLs*			
		Yes	*%*	*No*	*%*
1.	Was your property seized by landlord/money-lender during the Bonded Labour period?	–	–	134	100.00

It is evident from the Table 40 that no property was seized during the bonded labour period by their previous masters/ landlords/money-lenders.

(B) Distribution of FBLs by providing Basgit Paper

Sl. No.	*Have you received Basgit paper?*	*No. of FBLs*	*%*
1.	Yes	100	74.63
	If yes, then:		
	(i) 1-2 decimal	21	15.67
	(ii) 3-4 decimal	38	28.36
	(iii) 5-6 decimal	35	26.12
	(iv) 7-8 decimal	06	4.48
2.	No	34	25.37
	TOTAL	134	100.00

Table 41
Visit of Vigilance Committee Members in the FBL's Village/tola

Sl. No.	*Statement*	*No. of FBLs*			
		Yes	*%*	*No*	*%*
1.	Visit of Vigilance Committee Member	-	0.00	134	100.00

Majority of FBLs (100) reported that they had received basgit papers for their houses, while 34 FBLs reported that they did not receive the basgit papers. Further, the above table reveals that

38 FBLs received 3-4 decimal of land through the basgit paper. 35 FBLs reported that they had received 5-6 decimal of land. 21 FBLs reported that they received 1-2 decimal of land, and only 6 FBLs reported they have received 7-8 decimal of land for their houses.

[Basit Parcha] 74.63% reported that they have Basit Parcha. Only 25.37% respondents do not have Basit Parcha for residence.

VIGILANCE COMMITTEE

For the monitoring the development of socio-economic condition of FBLs, the Vigilance Committee's members have to visit the FBL's village/tola.

The table reveals that the vigilance committee members never visited any FBLs villages/tolas. This indicates that the organizational performance and monitoring system of vigilance committee in the district is non-functional.

5

POLITICAL PARTICIPATION AND HUMAN RIGHTS

Freed bonded labourers are politically aware but not conscious. They do not have direct participation in politics. In recently held elections including the previous panchayat they were not involved.

The visit of political leaders of different parties of National and State level has facilitated in developing a political awareness. All political leaders and parties come to ask them for vote. They do not have much time to spend with them. Their participation in polity is guided by their caste. The leader of the caste decides to a large extent, their voting behaviour. They hardly have made effort to find out to get their names on the voters list.

Their participation of politics in guided by the caste leader who acts as a middleman. Voting behaviour is very much evident, as the freed bonded labour has used their voting right. They were aware of their caste vote. Realisation of right to vote does not bear any meaning for them. They do not take it seriously. What they require is awareness in all walks of life ? As they do not have their own political standing, they fail to associate themselves with existing political system and are deprived of development. The caste factor is dominating feature. The graded social set up does not give scope for others freed bonded labourers are unfamiliar to this system. But all these prevailing political system of any nature really do not suit to the freed bonded labourers. This system can not ensure and does not promote their participation They are mere spectators to the mega game of politics.

FBLs stands for uneducated, very poor, right less and helpless creature and is exploited by the rich and affluent dominant caste in the area. The bonded labourers are still struggling to be recognized with dignity, respect self-respect, rights duties etc.

Being illiterate, they do not know their fundamental rights that a citizen can enjoy. They are not aware of the rights that the Constitution of India provides them. Where right is not known, the question of its violation is missing.

Ask them what they want? The one and simple reply is work-reason it gives them food security. The majority of freed bonded labour do not get sufficient meal in a day. It is a stark reality that a full day hard labour may bring a good fortune to the malik, land owners, proprietor of brick-kiln land others but does not bring much to them.

Right to work round the year is most fundamental need of freed bonded labourers. They do not get proper work. As this study reveals that only for few months they get work in peak season only. They are unemployed for the rest of period.

Non-availability of work, food and right to Education is a sheer violation of natural rights as well as human rights.

The freed bonded labourers seldom realise education as a need. Their children are not attending to school. Their poverty and an alien environment do not inspire them to continue in the school.

A freed bonded labourer child is deprived of food, cloth, love and education. This deprivation can be termed as violation of child rights, an essential part of the human rights.

Freed bonded labourers are not paid their minimum wages. They are not aware about minimum wage as per the norms of the State Government. Facilities of ESI and EPF are non-issues. They have not been visited by any labour enforcement officers nor they do not know about their existence in the block office.

The old members of this community are passing their days in mental and physical agony. Life is unbearable and tough. They pass their days either engaging themselves in minor works, looking after the small children, cleaning utensils, kitchen etc. He cannot enjoy full span of life. What an old aged member requires is proper food, care and medical help to have some basic quality of life and health. Old age increases his vulnerability to fall prey to bad health and mortality eventually.

The blood-sucking moneylenders contribute a lot in the pathetic plight of freed bonded labourers. They collect a regular handsome amount till the death of freed bonded labourers. This becomes an unending vicious circle. If the father dies, son has to pay and it goes on. The principal amount is never realised. This promotes the migration of freed bonded labourers.

The freed bonded labourers are born with the right to earn but for moneylenders only. They need to be freed from the clutches of moneylenders. The labour department can play an important role here. NABARD, Co-operative banks and PACs can help them too. Poor area civil society programme can be extended here to bail them from loans and to provide soft loans.

The block official, also does not show much sympathy for freed bonded labourers. The anti-poverty programmes initiated by central and State Governments for the development of BPL families do not get its due among freed bonded labourer due to lack of interest of officials. The official nexus deprives them of the benefits of development programmes.

Many of them revealed that they are asked to pay bribe for Red Card, PDS and other facilities.

The involvement of the freed bonded labourers in politics is not seen as good sign among the village dominant caste. The existing trend of politics where money, crime, corruption and caste play dominant role, the freed bonded labourers find themselves completely out of place.

The panchayati raj institutions do not support them. Mukhiya does not help them realising their fundamental and constitutional rights. Mukhiya does not play a meaningful role as far as the development of freed bonded labourers is concerned.

VIOLATIONS

- They do not get work and food throughout the year.
- No proper clothing.
- Poor drinking water support.
- Insufficient medical support.
- No employment throughout the year.
- No education intervention.
- Little help from Government and block official.
- No fixed working time.
- No participation and representation in politics.
- Burden of moneylenders.

- Pains of old age.
- Rights of children.
- Role of public distribution system.
- Poor Development programmes for freed bonded labourers.
- Women pre-natal and post-natal care is missing.
- Women and child are not beneficiary of RCH and mother-child safe-hood programme.
- Women and child remain vulnerable to poor health, food and mal-nutrition factors.

6

EVALUATION AND IMPACT ASSESSMENT

The aim of the evaluatory study was:

(a) to scrutinize the impact of existing land-debt related issues;

(b) to study the impact of poverty alleviation programmes and financial assistance provided by various government sources;

(c) to evaluate the on going rehabilitation programmes and their impact on the economic and social conditions of the freed bonded labours in Nawada district.

(d) to assess how the freed bonded labourers had benefited physically, economically and psychologically under the rehabilitation scheme?

1. The present study was concerned with the rehabilitated status of the freed bonded labour in Nawada district. The Department of Social Security, Nawada provided a list of 548 bonded labourers, who were freed in the district. These liberated bonded labourers were scattered in the different villages of Nawada district.

2. The study selected the freed bonded labourers from the villages belonging to eight blocks, namely Akbarpur, Govindpur, Pakriwaran, Narhat, Hisua, Sirdala, Rajouli and Nawada. The number of villages covered in the eight blocks was 25. As per the study sample, 134 FBLs were covered for furnishing information.

3. The Identification of bonded labour and release order certificate given to the bonded labour was done under the

District Magistrate. In 1982-83 release order certificates of 534 bonded laborers and in 1985-86 release order certificates of 14 bonded labourers were issued. A total of 548 bonded labourers were given the release order certificates. All the identified bonded labourers were registered in a register of Social Security Department of Nawada, but the ANSISS team did not find the names of bonded labourers clearly mentioned according to Blocks and Panchayat-wise.

Table 1
Block-wise Distribution of Freed Bonded Labourers

Sl. No.	*Block*	*No. of Bonded labour*
1.	Sirdala	189
2.	Govindpur/Roh	21
3.	Narhat	131
4.	Nawada	01
5.	Pakri Barwan	27
6.	Akbarpur	101
7.	Rajauli	01
8.	Hisua	27
	Total	548

4. After the issue of release order certificates, the rehabilitation programme for bonded labour was launched by the district administration in collaboration with the social security department. The Assistant Director, Social Security, Nawada reported that 534 bonded labourers were rehabilitated in the year 1982-83 and 14 bonded labourers were rehabilitated in the year 1985-86. So, the total rehabilitated bonded labour was 548 in the district.

5. The rehabilitation package was spearheaded by the provisions in the Act of 1976 Bonded Labour (System) abolition, which originally provided for rehabilitation assistance upto a ceiling limit of Rs. 4000/- per bonded labourer. Central and the State Governments concerned on 50:50 basis equally shared the scheme. The rehabilitation assistance was raised to Rs. 6250/- w.e.f. 1.02.1986. It was subsequently increased to Rs. 10000/- per bonded labourer w.e.f. 1.04.1995. Out of this, Rs. 1000/- is to be immediately paid on their his/her release as subsistence allowance.

6. The study shows that, only twice, the bonded labourers were identified and freed in the district, and that was in 1982-83 and in 1985-86. No bonded labourers have been found since 1986 in Nawada district.

Table 2
No. of Freed Labourer, Found by ANSISS, Who had Died after their Rehabilitation?

Sl. No.	*Name of the Block*	*Name of the Village*	*No. of freed labour found by ANSISS, who had died*
1.	Akbarpur	Rajhat	4
		Baksanda	4
		Rajdewar	3
		Farha	2
		Telbadra	3
2.	Govindpur	Sonaro	7
3.	Rajauli	Andharbarin	
4.	Pakri Barawan	Konanandpur	2
		Budhauli	8
		Kachna	
5.	Narhat	Sirsa	3
		Chandail Tala	
		Rahul Nagar Bhim Bigha	8
		Daulatpura	4
6.	Hisua	Bogadar Kaharia	3
7.	Sirdala	Upardih	
		Sahpur	
		Jamugay	4
		Gulabnagar tola	I
		Jharna	
		Hamzabharat	3
		Pipra	
		Kushahan	
		Akauna	5
		Lound	1
8.	Nawada	Samay	1
		Total	66

During the field visit by the ANSISS team, it was discovered that 66 FBLs had died, but there was no information on this account available at the social security office or at the district level. The team updated the current status about FBLs to them.

ABOUT THE BONDED LABOUR REHABILITATION EVALUATION

An attempt was made to examine the nature of the socio-psycho economic existence of the bonded labours in its various aspects. A sample of 134-bonded labourers' households was chosen. For each household only one Questionnaire was used, which included common Questions as well as informal discussions were used as the mode to have the complete picture?

The purpose was to assess the rehabilitation in psychological, physical and economic rehabilitation parameters. This had the following major components:

(1) current social status quo, (2) independence of movement, (3) autonomy in decision-making, (4) freedom of alternatives, (5) feeling no fear from previous employers/landlords, (6) allotment of house-site and agricultural land, (7) land development (including irrigation of lands already in their possession), (8) provision of low cost dwelling units, (9) agriculture, (10) credit (including consumption loan), (11) animal husbandry, dairy, poultry, piggery, fodder cultivation, etc., (12) training for acquiring new skills, (13) developing skills, (14) traditional arts and crafts, (15) Wage employment, (16) enforcement of minimum wages etc., (17) health, medical care and sanitation etc., (18) supply of essential commodities, and (19) education of children of bonded labourers.

PRESENT STATUS OF FREED BONDED LABOURERS

Freed bonded labourers work as agriculture labourer anywhere within the village or outside the village independently. They are free to work with any landlord. Some bonded labourers were working with their same landlord because they reported that the work is available with the landlord and there is no pre-condition laid by the landlords for working. They get the wage, which is prevalent in that area. The relation between landlord and bonded labourers are cordial. Now, the landlords are not abusing the labourers. They enjoy freedom of mobility and have the option to quit anytime. The working conditions are in a different environment and scenario than before.

PERCEPTION OF CHANGE : FBLs ON THEIR UPLIFT AFTER BEING RELEASED

There has been a slight improvement in financial condition, betterment in food consumption, enhancement in social prestige and increase in voting activities after been released. But none of them have purchased any permanent assets from their income and livelihood. The marginal change in economic status of freed bonded labourers was evident in their better food consumption pattern than in the past and in use of clothes. Like the use of rice, Chapati/Roti with vegetable regularly and also the consumption of pulses rarely, was marked progress from the previous bonded life. They were found using neat and clean clothes. Some had accommodation facilities better due to the houses provided under the Indira Awas Yojana.

The status has improved from dark past-but it was not a great leap forward rather a few steps ahead from before. The change is more a positive uplift in psychological level. The liberty matched with freedom of making choices without any compulsion of any kind has created the autonomous identity. It is a definite change in their mental status, despite wretchedness and poverty syndrome.

ABOUT THE PRESENT OCCUPATION

It was noticed that most of the freed bonded labourers were working as agricultural labourers within the village and in the neighbouring villages. Seasonally, they migrated to other places in search for work. Some were found working in non-agricultural sphere like in brick kiln, digging, rickshaw pulling, roadwork, construction work and other works. A small number of freed bonded labourers were without work due to old age and illness. Some FBLs moved for work to nearest towns near their home place. No freed bonded labourers were found in the dairy or poultry or in other business activities.

The family members of the bonded labourers were also working in agriculture, non-agriculture areas like brick-kiln, digging, rickshaw pulling, roadwork and other works. The female members and their children were also working in agriculture sector as agriculture labourers.

About 8 to 10 bonded freed labourers were doing cultivation work on the cultivable land given by the district administration. But they had either no agricultural implements or the appropriate seed, fertilizer, insecticides etc, so their produce of agricultural output was poor.

There was no Government facilitative hand seen in their work sphere. There was no awareness regarding minimum wages, unorganized sector insurance, or primary agricultural cooperative laws among them. There was no NGO activity noticed within the FBLs community for organizing them or in raising their awareness on basic issues. NABARD/similar other institutions which are associated with SELF-HELP GROUPS (SHGs) were completely missing. UNICEF, ILO and other international agencies that work with children, women deprived and old, were conspicuous by their absence.

The FBLs were working with their traditional knowledge and indigenous survival skills with no outside help to their family's occupation. Thus, working in the agriculture field as worker remains the cornerstone of their occupation.

KNOWLEDGE ABOUT THE MINIMUM WAGE

None of the freed bonded labourers knew about the minimum wage, which is prescribed by the government and enforced by the labour department. They were paid according to the existing wage of the area. The working hours of the freed bonded labourers are normally 6 to 8 hours, and they get wage in kind i.e., (Rice or wheat) 5 kg with breakfast of beaten rice (*chura*) or puffed rice (*moori*).

The labour department has to play an important role of teacher, trainer and enforcer of minimum wage.

ABOUT THE DWELLING SITUATION

It was found that the houses of 60 freed bonded labourers had earthen houses (Katcha). The roof of the houses was thatched with straws. The houses of 5 freed bonded labourers had brick/ mortar construction (pucca) and 69 freed bonded labourers had mixed houses. The bonded labourers who had mixed dwelling units had larger numbers of rooms in comparison to those who were living in Kachha dwelling units. In the case of Pucca and mixed construction, it was seen that these types of construction was made under the provision of Indira Awas Yojana (IAY).

The freed bonded labourers live in a habitat and environment, which shows little change for them. His existential condition has not changed for the better even after the rehabilitation housing, schemes. Many still are deprived of IAY houses, which should have been given to them.

The bonded labours are settled in a tola (cluster), which is located in one place, mostly in peripheral areas of the villages. Some FBLs tolas in the villages had the community hall made for their use in social functions. This was a rare sight in the district, and those FBL villages having them were fortunate.

There was an eyesore, that in the Akbarpur block, there were 14 households of freed bonded labourers near village Vinoba Nagar, which were inhabited in such a place, which was 8 to 10 kms far from block headquarters and there was no other household nearby their tola. It showed some sort of their isolation from the rest of the area. They need community sharing and mainstreaming in the nearby local village's environment.

The habitat settlement programme did not appear impressive or satisfactory, since many were still out of the main village community ambit. Even those who had it, were not in the proper physical part of the desired general village settlement zone. It lacked vision, while trying to resettle them with the Government resources. The most important should be the inclusion of the choices of the beneficiary group in any such exercise particularly, in case of the bonded labourer's rehabilitation. After all, they are going to live there permanently.

ABOUT THE DRINKING WATER FACILITIES

It was observed that 86 freed bonded labourers family used hand pump for drinking water, 4 freed bonded labourers family used well and 44 freed bonded labourers family used well and hand pump both for drinking water. The Government had provided them the hand pump and well for drinking water. Only 2 freed bonded labourers had installed their own hand pumps on their premises.

These drinking water facilities are the community assets, which is provided by the State and Central Government resources for use of safe drinking water. It was observed in the case of failure of hand pump, that it is difficult to repair the hand pump because it is public asset then who will repair? This question always arises among the FBLs. At times, they collect donations (*chanda*), then repair the hand pumps. Many times it was found that they quarrel for maintaining the hand pumps. They want the block officials to maintain these pumps. The overall picture was satisfactory in the given rural scenario.

TOILET FACILITY OF BONDED LABOURERS

1. Majority of bonded labourers (123) had no toilet facilities in their houses. They use open place out side the village for defecation purpose. This includes the female population who are forced to in dark only even they get call of nature in day time. This results in stomach diseases. Only 11 bonded labourers of Vinoba Nagar of Akbarpur block reported, that they have toilet facilities in their houses.
2. In every FBLs cluster, provision of low cost sanitation facility such as Sulabh Shauchalaya (toilets), will result in better living conditions and enhancing their quality of living. The female population will feel safe and relieved if this is taken as priority to give toilets in their household vicinity.
3. The performance in the sanitation area was insufficient.

DRAINAGE FACILITIES OF BONDED LABOURER'S HOUSE

Only 21 bonded labourers were fortunate to have (pucca) cemented drains for disposal of wastewater from their houses. The majority of freed bonded labourers [77] reported that they have earth drainage (kachha) for disposal of wastewater from their house. 36 bonded labourers reported that there was no proper wastewater disposal available in their household hence drain water was flowing and collecting near their houses leading to dirty stagnant water around the year.

ABOUT EDUCATION

(a) It was observed that 97.76 per cent of sampled bonded labour are illiterate, and only 2.24 per cent of sampled bonded labour were literate. They have difficulty in even writing their names. The family members of the freed bonded labour are also illiterate. They are not sending their children to school. The school-going children of the freed bonded labour family are doing their domestic work or playing without work. Only five members of the bonded labour family have received education upto middle class and three have matriculated. No female members have received any type of education.

(b) In Narhat block, some FBL family members, who had passed matric, have migrated to Delhi for working in private commercial concerns. Some of the freed bonded labourers' families were not interested in the education of their children, particularly the fathers or the male guardians.

(c) A motivation and hunger for education can keep the school going children of the freed bonded labourers free from being engaged in domestic work or as a child labour. The effort of the District Education Officer and other related Government agencies is to sensitise them towards education. It is the prime duty of the concerned authorities to win all children of FBLs in the nearest Government schools. It is necessary to hold awareness camps and other advocacy methods to raise consciousness of the fact that education enhances status and helps in improving social and economic condition. This area is unsatisfactory and needs total effort from the district officials to mainstream these children in the primary education system of the Nawada district. UNICEF, BEP, DPEP and Sarva Siksha Abhiyaan can facilitate in this effort. The Shiksha mitras (teachers) from local villages and panchayats can help in this process.

PRESENT DEBT AMONG BONDED LABOURERS

(a) Out of 134 freed bonded labourers, 18 freed bonded labourers are in debt. Two bonded labourers have taken loan from bank and 16 have taken loan from the local moneylender (mahajans). They were paying a high rate of interest to the tune of 3 to 10 per cent per month. Most of the loans were taken for meeting their personal consumption, marriage, sickness and other social function expenditures. Many loans were taken as distress loans on high rates to meet immediate crisis. The local moneylenders are part of vicious chain who exploit the situation to their comfort and live well on such a scenario.

(b) The vulnerability existed for all FBLs since they did not have any permanent asset or any worthy savings. The line between them and those who were in debt was very thin. The thrust of the rehabilitation measures can be seen weak here in this context because they were not above below poverty line and were soft preys for mahajans and sahukars. In a way, they were more finacially unstable than being economically stable, so the real threat remained about their exposed position.

(c) The district authorities have to intervene to fortify them economically by their schemes and programmes available within their jurisdiction. The NGOs can play a important role too.

ABOUT THE SAVING ATTITUDE

(a) In the entire 134 freed bonded labourers, only one bonded labourer had a passbook in the bank. They were frank to share that they had two problems. One was that they had little or no idea about savings. Secondly, they had little to save. They were used to local moneylender's loans hence they never thought of post office or the bank. They have no saving attitude or habit. Drinking, eating and wasting money on elaborate social ceremonies were some of the reasons behind no savings. It emerged from them that they thought more of today than tomorrow.

(b) They are perfect illustration for the Government agencies to stimulate them about savings habit. The Department of Savings, Rural Banks, Post Offices and Cooperative Banks can play a significant role. NABARD and other agencies can form Self-Help Groups (SHGs) in order to create an environment for saving and increasing their income potentials.

REHABILITATION PROGRAMME AND SCHEMES AND THEIR IMPACT ON THE FBLs

Government Rehabilitation Assistance on been Freed

(a) After identification and their release, the bonded labourers were provided compensation by the Government agencies. Under this package, the FBLs were given different types of livestocks, rickshaw and cash money to improve their economic condition and living standard of their family.

(b) The majority of FBLs (63) received one cow, one buffalo and one rickshaw under rehabilitation package through their respective block officials in block offices. 38 FBLs received two cows and one rickshaw, while 16 FBLs received two buffaloes and one rickshaw.

(c) 5 FBLs of village Laund, block Sirdala reported that they received one cow and one rickshaw, 4 women FBLs out of 134 FBLs, from the tola-Vinoba Nagar, village-Telbadaro, block-Akbarpur reported that they received two cows only. In the same way, 7 FBLs of tola-Vinoba Nagar, village-Telbadaro, block-Akbarpur and 1 FBL of village Jamugay, block-Sirdala reported that they received two buffaloes.

(d) 35 FBLs received two goats, and 2 FBLs received cash amount of Rs. 500/- each against the spare amount after purchasing livestock for them.

(e) All compensation was given in lieu of compensatory cash. The respective block officials made the purchases and the distribution.

(f) All bonded labourers received the working asset to improve their economic activities. The bonded labourers reported that the quality of assets was very poor. Almost all complained that they sold their cows, buffaloes or they died. They had no proper idea to keep these animals and no training was provided to them for keeping the animals. It appears that without their actual need assessment they were provided the assets, which was not viable and feasible.

(g) This was the major rehabilitation carried by the district authorities as per the provisions of the act, but two basic shortcomings were analyzed during the study. The formulation of schemes was not realistic to the ground reality. The animals were provided to FBLs without basic training regarding its upkeep and how to handle the diseases or whom to contact in the time of crisis. Secondly, it was part of income generating scheme but the implementing agencies did not follow up the marketing of their products. Hence, they were forced to sell because the animals were dying or they did not get enough return. As for the district authorities, they never had a blueprint of follow up. It is the this gap which needs to be filled with constant monitoring of the rehabilitated FBLs. They need direction and guidance to come out of the poverty syndrome with concrete schemes, which matches their skills, or they can be empowered first to handle the schemes or the benefits they receive. A pre-consultation or dialogue between the beneficiaries and the donor can be very fruitful.

Social Security Pension for FBLs

(a) The majority of FBLs (103) (76.87%) receives the pension facility of Rs. 100 per month, which is provided by the Government as Bonded Labour Rehabilitation Scheme. 31 (23.13%) FBLs don't get this type of facility. It was found that the whole sampled village of Narhat block was deprived of this facility and one case in the village-Kachana of Packaribran block.

(b) Why this was been not given to the freed bonded labourers of Narhat block was inquired from the District Social Security Department Officer. It was reported that all allotment funds had been sent to the blocks for distribution without delay. The officials had no explanation to ANSISS team's discovery but assured of prompt action and starting of payment soon.

(c) The administration has done satisfactory work on the pension front. The lapses in Narhat block can be corrected by the corrective action based on ANSISS's team finding.

(d) This pension is lifeline for them and it is recommended that the old family members of the FBL family may be also included in this social security net.

Indira Awas Yojana and IRDP Facilities

(a) 66 (49.25%) FBLs received Indira Awas Yojana facilities and were using it for residential purposes. 68 (50.75%) FBLs reported that they did not get this type of facility and a long period has passed since they were released. The Government assistance is evident, but in fragmented manner not in totality. There is urgent need to address the issue as to why 68 FBLs (50.75%) were left out.

(b) 13 FBLs of Budhauli village and 1 FBL of Kachana village reported that about Rs. 1500 to Rs. 1600 were given to them under the IRDP Scheme. But the rest got nothing under IRDP assistance.

(c) This concerns shelter, which is also one of the foremost and important issues in the case of FBLs. As per the direction of Government of India and the State Government, all DMs have to link the FBLs with IAY scheme as part of convergence and poverty alleviation wholistic strategy, but Nawada has partially failed to meet its mission to provide IAY to all rehabilitated FBLs.

(d) This ANSISS finding can help the DM to take corrective measure and provide IAY to the left ones.

(e) SRY is in practice, since 1999 as an important scheme for poverty alleviation. The FBLs can be brought under the SRY net, which has multiple inputs for the BPL families. It clearly states that within three years with help of all inputs an effort should be made to bring the family above the poverty line.

(f) The convergence with the Department of Rural Development of the State Government is necessary to provide the sustainable cushion to the families of freed bonded labourers. Convergence based on inter-department cooperation should be the key strategy to specifically target them for their upliftment.

Lal Card and PDS Facilities among FBLs

(a) 95.52% of the respondents had the facility of Lal Card and a very low percentage (4.48%) did not receive the Lal Card, which is provided by the district administration agencies.

(b) The Lal cardholders were getting benefit of kerosene oil only from the PDS network. They complained that the most beneficial would be the availability of foodgrains particularly rice and wheat at subsidized rates in PDS fair price shops. (Ration shop).

(c) The majority of the FBLs reported that PDS facility was within their villages but a small number reported that their PDS was outside their village, hence wanted the PDS shop in their villages.

(d) Assistant Director, Social Security, Nawada has promised to provide red card to those who were left out. This has to be followed up.

(e) Red card scheme is useful for the FBLs, but it can become very effective if the Supply department provides them foodgrain at subsidized rate. This was a major question, which is related to hunger and survival, which needs strengthening ?

(f) Convergence in this area requires a top down approach. Hence, it should start from policy level-inter-ministerial, at the level of the highest echelon of bureaucracy, both at the centre and at the state, at the level of field functionaries and going down to the ground level. India today is having surplus food grain stock. It needs vision and commitment from top to down level to reach the needy and deprived population which includes the freed bonded labourers families.

Property Released if they were under Seizure

(a) No property was seized during the bonded labour period by their previous masters/landlords/money-lenders.

Basgit Papers [Basgit Parcha]

(a) Majority of FBLs (100) reported that they had received basgit papers for their houses, while 34 FBLs reported that they did not receive the basgit papers.

(b) 38 FBLs received 3-4 decimal of land through the basgit paper. 35 FBLs had received 5-6 decimal of land. 21 FBLs had received 1-2 decimal of land and only 6 FBLs informed they had received 7-8 decimal of land for their houses.

(c) They were settled in one place. Those had got the basgit parcha have no land for residence. The district authorities had given them the land for home and ownership of land (purcha). This way the majority freed bonded labourers had their home on the homestead land.

(d) There was no uniformity in the size of the homestead given to the FBLs. Some were still deprived of this facility. A corrective action has to be taken to bring all FBLs in the scheme.

(e) There is need to strengthen the mechanism of reporting and feedback. If the State Social Security Department holds quarterly review with the quarterly progress report from the field, then such lapses can be controlled and rectified. ANSISS team on analysis of data found such lapse, which can be plugged by the quarterly progress reports and review at state and district level.

ROLE OF VIGILANCE COMMITTEE IN REHABILITATION SCHEME MONITORING AND KEEPING ATTENTION ON THE PROGRESS OF FBLs SOCIO-ECONOMIC STATUS

Visit of Vigilance Committee Members in the FBL's village/ tola

(a) For monitoring of the rehabilitation programmes of bonded labourers, a vigilance committee has to be constituted at district level and sub-divisional level under the District Magistrate and Sub-divisional Magistrate, as per the provision of the BL (A) Act. The Vigilance Committee members have to visit the FBL's village/tola to monitor the progress. Vigilance Committee works as agent for the district and the Social Security Department to oversee the bonded labour rehabilitation programme. They are legally empowered to follow up the rehabilitation programme of bonded labourers.

(b) Vigilance Committee was constituted at the district level on 1982-83 under the Chairmanship of District Magistrate and the other members were the district level officials, social workers and representatives of the civil society.

(c) It was reconstituted in the year 2002 with District Magistrate as Chairman and the members were Assistant Director, Social Security, three members from Social Welfare, DRDA Director, one member from Lead Bank, Deputy Collector Land Reforms and representatives of civil society.

(d) No Vigilance Committee exits at the sub-divisional level till ANSISS team was in the field. However, in September 2003, a letter has been issued by D.M. to S.D.M., for constituting the Vigilance Committee at Sub-divisional level.

(e) The district vigilance committee members have never visited any FBLs villages or tolas. This indicates about the organizational performance and monitoring system of Vigilance Committee in the district. It is non-functional.

(f) Last meeting of the Vigilance Committee was held on September 1994. After that no meeting has been held by the vigilance committee. According to state circular, the meeting should be held after every two months. According to Assistant Director, Social Security many problem arises because of non-holding of the meeting of Vigilance Committee. At times meetings have been cancelled due to lack of the members present in the meeting.

(g) The follow-up of rehabilitation programme of bonded labour done by the Vigilance Committee was dissatisfactory due to its non-performance.

(h) The BL Act, Government of India and the State Government give a great significance to vigilance committee regarding solving the problem of freed bonded labourers, and for developing future action plans specifically for the rehabilitation of bonded labourers in field.

(i) This was completely missing. The State Government should take corrective action by sensitising the district authorities about the great importance of the role of the Vigilance Committee in order to generate awareness among the officials. Sensitization and capacity building workshops can be organised. The authorities have to be motivated to spread the utility of vigilance committees. It is suggested that FBLs representative can also be made member of the vigilance committees.

Training Facilities

(a) About 36 FBLs of Narhat and Sirdala block recorded to ANSISS team, that they had received training through labour and employment department at the block level for three days, regarding the animal husbandry. It was not useful for all because most of them did not have the animal. Even those who had did not receive any type of loan for starting the dairy business after training. Those who had no animal were not provided loan to buy one. Further, the training, in sum, was futile. It was too little and too late.

(b) The majority of FBLs did not receive any training by Government agencies after their release for self-employment.

(c) Training is an important component of SRY scheme for developing income-generating skills.

(d) The training for acquiring new skills, developing the existing indigenous skills of traditional arts and crafts can be important mode of income. The provision of credit and marketing their products can go a way in economically empowering them.

(e) Vocational training is a means of securing jobs and employment also.

(f) It is suggested that a projection of labour market requirements based on which skill requirements should be assessed.

Distribution of Land for FBLs for Cultivation

(a) The majority of FBLs (105) noted that they did not receive any agricultural land. 22 FBLs reported that they had received cultivatable land under Bhoodan Andolan, and were cultivating them, but there was lack of proper seeds, fertilizer, insecticides or availability of water for proper productivity. They were producing, but it was not enough for their need.

(b) 7 FBLs reported that they received land on paper only, under Bhoodan Andolan. They bitterly complained that the lands were not useful for agriculture purposes because it was in the low-lying areas, and there was problem of constant water logging round the year. Many complained that it was far away from their houses also.

(c) Few bonded labourers had got the agricultural land but this land was outside the village, and quality of land was poor. For cultivation, they were not given any facility by the government. They were unable to cultivate their land. They produced single crop, which is paddy.

(d) The rehabilitation process for the FBLs by giving agricultural land was not satisfactory. It was inadequate and ill-planned.

(e) A comprehensive agricultural strategy should be planned for FBLs by State Government. It should include provision for giving them agricultural land, land development (including irrigation of lands already in their possession), agriculture credit and fodder cultivation. NABARD banks, cooperative, agricultural and other departments can play important role.

(f) The local agricultural research institutes can help in capacity building and transfer of knowledge.

Awareness Programme among the Freed Bonded Labourers

(a) No awareness program was held among the freed bonded labourers. They were not aware about the Government schemes for them except what they had got at time of release.

It is necessary to make them aware about the other assistance schemes and programs.

(b) A regular sensitization and capacity building process was not done in the district for the FBLs. All effort can be done on making them aware about their schemes and how they can benefit from them. It is necessary to inculcate a sense of individual and social identity among them, and also about their basic legitimate rights.

(c) Nukkad *nataks*, plays, street theatres, skits and simulation exercises can be held to drive home about their rights and how to live independently and free from debt bondage.

Difficulties faced in the Fieldwork

(a) The list of freed bonded labourers was not properly maintained in the social security office. There was no mechanism to update the list of bonded labourers. It was not clear that how many bonded labourers were alive or how many had died.

(b) It was not apparent from the social security office that how many bonded labourers had received the pension, and whether they were receiving the correct amount. The Assistant Director, Social Security was not aware that the bonded labourers of Narhat block were not getting the pension.

(c) Mostly bonded labourers were illiterate. So, the responses of many questions were not given like the period in years as debt bonded labour.

(d) Many were not keeping the release order certificate.

(e) Majority of bonded labourers could not reply about their assets and their price.

(f) During the field visit, it was very difficult to talk to some freed bonded labourers because they had local alcoholic drink in early morning and were in drunken stage.

It can be said that government programmes under the below the poverty line and bonded labour schemes were not efficiently provided to the FBLs. No official agency had pursued follow up programme and monitoring to oversee the progress of the freed and rehabilitated bonded labourers. The programmes were implemented mechanically without human touch. Some had benefited while others were left out. There was lack of totality in approach and consistency of purpose. Traditional inspection method for effective implementation of the relevant rehabilitation schemes was missing. There was no communication between the freed bonded labourers and the block, sub-division and district administration officials.

The district administrative has assured that immediate corrective measures would be taken to benefit all freed bonded labourers socio-economic status in the district.

PART - III

An Evaluation of Bonded Labour Rehabilitation Schemes in NALANDA District

7

INTRODUCTION–NALANDA : A PROFILE

BRIEF HISTORY OF THE DISTRICT

The new district of Nalanda was constituted on 9th November, 1972. The sub-division of Biharsharif in-the old Patna district was upgraded as an independent district and named as Nalanda, after a place (about 12 kms. from Biharsharif) internationally renowned for its ancient university. Biharsharif is the chief town, and the headquarter of the district.

The district is bonded on the north by Patna district, on the south by the districts of Gaya and Nawada, on the east by Patna, Lakhisarai and Sheikhpura and on the west by the districts of Patna and Jehanabad. It consists of 20 community development blocks, viz. Karai Parsurai, Nagar Nausa, Harnaut, Chandi, Rahui, Bind, Sarmera, Asthawan, Biharsharif, Noorsarai, Tharthari, Parbalpur, Hilsa, Ekangarsarai, Islampur, Ben, Rajgir, Silao, Giriak and Katrisarai.

According to the Chinese traveller, Hiuen Tsiang, the place assumed the name 'Nalanda' because of the residence of Nagananda here. He has also mentioned that Buddha in his previous birth was the king of this place and on account of his benevolence this place was called Nalanda, which means one capable of giving unlimited gift. However, a more convincing theory has been put forward by Hiranand Shastri, which is that Nalanda is derived from the word Nala because lotus grew profusely in this locality. Thus, Nalanda meant a place, which could give plenty of lotuses Nala.

The name Nalanda has been well-known since very ancient times. The history of this place starts from about 600 B.C. and has been frequently referred to in the Jain and Buddhist scriptures. The Chinese travellers, Itsing and Hiuen Tsiang in the 7th century A.D. and the Tibetan traveller, Dharmaswami in the 13th century have left details, about Nalanda. As the centre of the great Magadh Empire, the district has had a rich and glorious history extending to over 2,500 years.

EARLY HISTORY

Magadh came under the pale of Aryan civilization long after it had been ruled over by the Vratyas, and much later than the other portions of North India. The authentic history of Magadh begins with the 6th century B.C. The Vedic literature mentions Pramaganda as the king of Magadh. The earliest ruling dynasty of Magadh, according to the Mahabharat and the Puranas was that founded by Brihadrath, son of Vasu and father of Jarasandha. The mighty king Jarasandha, who had his capital at Rajgriha (modern Rajgir) succeeded him. The remains of a fortress ascribed to Jarasandha of the pre-historic period are still to be found at Rajgir, as also the ruins the old cyclopean walls built around the city as a part of its fortifications. However, not much is known of the line of the twenty-eight kings believed to have come after Jarasandh.

Magadha reached the Pinnacle of spiritual renaissance in the 6th century B.C. during the reign of king Bimbisar of the Haryanakakula dynasty, when both Gautama Buddha and Mahabir Vardhaman preached their doctrines. The new religions philosophies had profound influence on the history of the country in the next few centuries. Buddha, who lived a life of princely comfort and luxury till age of 29, renounced the world and came to Rajgriha to obtain true knowledge at the feet of two learned Brahmins. Thereafter, he moved on to the place now known as Bodh-Gaya and sat in deep meditation under the now famous peepal tree, where he attained enlightenment. Buddha visited Rajgriha frequently and the sites of Venuvan (bamboo grave) and Gridhra koot (Venture's peak) are often associated with him in the Buddhist literature.

Vardhaman Mahavir was a contemporary of Gautama Buddha. He also forsook the world when he was 32 years old, and preached the Jain doctrines for the rest of his life. He died at Pawapuri, a hallowed place of Jain pilgrimage.

Bimbisar, who was a powerful ruler, annexed the kingdom of Anga with its capital at Champa and entered into matrimonial alliances with Kosala and Vaishali. According to a Chinese pilgrim, he built the city of Rajgriha on an old site. Bimbisar was mudered for the throne by his son Ajatshatru, the founder of Patliputra. Being faced with hospitality of the rulers of Sravasti and also the Vrijjis and Lichchhavis of Vaishali Ajatshatru fortified the village Patligram. His son Udayi who transferred the capital of Magadh from Rajgriha to Patligram, which later came to be known by its more abiding name Patliputra, succeeded Ajatshatru. This place was selected as the capital primarily because or its strategic location and in the expanding empire of Magadh.

Patliputra thereafter remained the capital of Magadh during the reigns of the Sisunag and Nanda dynasties at also under the Maurya dynasty. Ashoka brought about vast improvements in his capital. With the death of Ashoka began the decline of the Mauryan dynasty. Patliputra also fell into comparative insignificance until the rise of the Guptas in the 4th century A.D.

Chandragupta-I extended the kingdom of Magadh upto Allahabad and Patliputra regained its lost glory. His son Samudragupta further extended the empire and transferred the capital to a more central place.

After the death of king Harsa, Magadh entered a period of dark age. Gopal, who founded the pala dynasty, became the king of Bengal in 815 A.D. He was able to consolidate his kingdom and extend his hold over Magadh also. He made the town of Bihar his capital. His descendants were Buddhists and a number of Buddhist Shrines existing at present were erected during their regime (815 to 1200A.D.). Gopal and his successors revived the glory of Magadh. Emissaries were sent to different parts of the country spread the message of lord Buddha. It was during his period that the Lamaisam of Tibet reformed by Atisha who had been educated in Magadh.

THE MUSLIM INVASION

Between 1193 and 1200 A.D. Md. Bin Bakhtiar Khilzi invaded Bihar. He invaded Oddantpuri (Biharsharif) and the monasteries at Nalanda. The Muslim invaders killed a large number of Buddhists. The massacre was so huge that Khilzi did not find even a single monk to explain to him the contents of the Buddhist library. The monks and priests who could do so, escaped and fled, to Tibet, Nepal and South India. Thus, Buddhism was practically effaced from the land of its birth. With the conquest of Muslims over Magadh, the history of this land and other parts of South Bihar got merged with that of Bengal. The district of Nalanda formed part of the territory under the Muslim viceroys of Bengal till 1320 when Emperor Ghiasuddin Tughlak separated Bihar from Bengal. The control of Bihar passed into the hands of the Sherqui dynasty of Jaunpur from 1394 to 1486. After that, it was amalgamated with the Muslim kingdom of Gaur.

The residence of the Muhammedan Governors remained at Biharsharif until 1541, when Sher Shah rebuilt Patna. Patna became a central place and Biharsharif lost its importance. Biharsharif, however, continued to be enriched with buildings by the Muhammedans, and its sacred tombs continued to attract Muhammedan pilgrims for many centuries. The Muhammedan historians rarely mention it, however, until the decline of the Mughals. The Marathas ransacked it in the time of Ali Vardi Khan, and in 1757 Mir Zafar Khan paid it a visit, of which, an account is given in the Sair-ul-Muta Kharin. The Emperor Shah Alam made Biharsharif his headquarters in 1763, and it was near here, at Bara Khurd that he was decisively defeated by carnac. Biharsharif still retains traces of its former importance as a place of Muslim pilgrimage.

The first war of India's Independence, 1857 and also the subsequent Independence Movements inspired the people of Nalanda district to overthrow the foreign yoke. Like other districts of the state Nalanda also has played a prominent role in the country's freedom struggle.

NATURAL DIVISION

The district can be divided into two natural divisions comprising:

(i) An elevated country in the south-east containing the Rajgir hills, and

(ii) Alluvial fertile plains in the remaining portion.

The Rajgir hills are the only natural eminence in an otherwise entirely alluvial and flat region. They form a part of the long range extending from near Bodh Gaya and terminating near Giriak. From Giriak begin two parallel ranges enclosing a narrow revinc. A little south of the present town of Rajgir, the parallel ranges broaden out and enclose a valley which was once upon a time the site of the ancient town of Rajgriha. The two ranges meet again beyond Baibhargiri and Sonagiri.

RIVER SYSTEM

The district does not have any major river of importance. There are, however, some small rivers flowing through it such as Panchane, Sakri etc. Panchane is formed by the confluence of five streams debouching from the neighbouring district, which until near Giriak and then flow northward to Biharsharif. Sakri River, which is even less important, enters the district through the southeast of Biharsharif. Both the rivers fail to attain any great volume, owing the demands made upon them for the purpose of irrigation. These rivers provide water for irrigation and the alluvium brought by them has rendered the district extremely fertile.

CLIMATIC CONDITION

The climate of the district is somewhat extreme. It is very hot in summer and cold in winter. The summer season starts from April. The months of May and first half of June are the hottest. During this period, a hot westerly wind blows. The high temperature and low humidity make the summer oppressive. The easterly wind, which appears in the latter half of June, brings some relief. The rainy season sets in the middle of June and lasts till September. The mercury begins to fall from October end but December and January are the really cold months.

The average rainfall is the heaviest in the month of August in which the number of rainy days varies from 10 to 14 and rainfall from 254 mm to 355 mm. The months of October and November are quite pleasant, as the weather is very bracing. The district receives some winter rains also.

FLORA AND FAUNA

The land in the district is too fertile to be left for wild growth. Except from some jungles in the Rajgir hills the district is devoid of any forest. Forests constitute only 0.36 per cent of the total area of the district. Some afforestation work has been done in the Rajgir hills. The alluvial tract of land yields cereal and non-cereal crops.

Mango orchards and bamboo clumps also can be seen near rural settlements.

Leopard, hyena, jackal, fox and wild cat are some of the carnivore found in the district but their number is very small.

MINES AND MINERALS

The geological formulation of the district is generally alluvial. The Rajgir hills consist of metamorphic schists and slate covered with quartzite. No mineral of any kind is found in the district. The hot water springs of Rajgir are, however, said to contain rich radioactive elements.

LAND USE PATTERN

The land in the district generally consists of Kewal soil. Kewal soil consists of hard clay and is very suitable for growing rice. It has capacity to retain moisture and is suitable for Rabi cultivation also. On uplands near the homestead 'doras' soil is also found which is used for growing potatoes and vegetables. In fields it yields both rice and rabi crops.

The district, which is predominantly agricultural in character, is divided into the hills in the south and low land to the north. The whole district is interested by streams, which in the summer and winter seasons contain little or no water, but at the time of heavy rains are filled from bank to bank.

The main crops of the district are rice, maize, wheat, gram, pulse (masoor) and potato. The district occupies a prominent position in the state in the production of potato. Large-scale trade in potato takes place at the district headquarters, Biharsharif. There are number of cold storages located in and around Biharsharif town.

IRRIGATION FACILITIES

Rains are the main sources of irrigation and the success of crops largely depends on their adequacy and even distribution throughout the agricultural operations. However, rainfall cannot be depended upon as unfailing sources of irrigation. Therefore, artificial irrigation supplements rainfall in varying degree the requirement of water of agriculture. The greater part of the streams in the district is provided with a system of irrigation works intended to store and distribute the water. In the pre-independence period, the main water resources were the artificial reservoirs (ahars), Channels (Pynes), embankments and wells including, tube-wells. In the post-independence period, with the extension of power supply to the rural areas electrically operated tube wells have become major sources of irrigation. Considerable attention has since been paid to the provision of irrigational facilities through execution of various schemes.

LIVESTOCK

Livestock is very important in a district like Nalanda with a predominantly agricultural economy. Cattle of local breed, though hardy and suited to the climate, are generally of a poor variety. Buffaloes are sometimes employed for ploughing the land, especially, when deep mud is prepared for the transplantation of paddy, and are also used for slow draught work. Goats are breeds in almost every village and certain section of people keeps pigs of the usual omnivorous kind.

The quality of the livestock has improved considerably through the effort of the Government and the response of the farmers. In order to protect the livestock from various diseases and epidemics and also to improve the breed, the Animal Husbandry Department of the State Government has adopted some very useful and concrete measures. It has established veterinary hospitals, sub-centres, artificial insemination centres, poultry farms etc., all over the district covering majority of villages. The All India Key Village Scheme sponsored by Government of India also aims at improving the general efficiency of the cattle by adopting scientific methods of breeding, feeding, disease control and marketing. Poultry development has received considerable attention in various community development blocks.

INDUSTRIALIZATION

Potters, carpenters, blacksmiths, coppersmiths and goldsmiths have been carrying on their traditional occupations both in rural as well as in urban areas, although under the impact of modern economy, these classes are fast disintegrating. Rajgir was a centre of paper manufacture. Near Rajgir there were quarries of stone resembling marble from which ornaments used to be made.

There is no large-scale industry or heavy industry worth mentioning in the district. There are, however, few units in the district engaged in small-scale industries such as silk industry, bidi making etc. Cold-storage industry has made rapid strides in this district.

COMMUNICATIONS

The district of Nalanda is well-served by a network of roads. The district headquarter, Biharsharif, is situated on the National Highway provides the road link between North and South Bihar. Roads have been improved considerably in the district after independence. Bridges, culverts and causeways have been constructed on the important roads. Besides the National Highway and the roads maintained by the state P.W.D., there are a few roads managed by the District Board also.

- **Railways** – The Fatwah-Islampur light railway and the Bakhtiarpur Rajgir Branch line pass through the district. The latter has been converted into broad gauge.
- **Riverways** – As there are only small riversand a few streams the district and these too dry up during the summer and winter seasons there is no water communication worth mentioning in the district.
- **Airways** – There is a small landing ground at Biharsharif. It meant for small aircraft only.

TRADE AND COMMERCE

The important trade centres in the district are Islampur, Hilsa and Biharsharif. Trade consists mainly of export of rice, bidi, potatoes and handloom and silk cloth etc., and import of items such as coal, cement, wood, cotton yarn, tobacco leaf, etc. Potato is exported in trucks to the coalfields in Jharia and Dhanbad and on return journey they bring coal both for domestic and industrial purposes.

ELECTRICITY AND POWER

The district receives its entire power supply from the Bihar State Electricity Board. All the towns of the district have electricity. In rural areas also the pace of electrification has been quite fast. Government is paying full attention to rural electrification and a considerable number of villages (approx. 80% of the total villages) have been electrified as a result of this. Domestic and commercial use account for a major portion of the power consumption in the urban areas and for the agricultural use in the rural areas.

SOCIAL AND CULTURAL EVENTS

No major social or cultural event has taken place in the district of Nalanda after its creation as an independent district. However, fairs and festivals are held regularly in the district in complete harmony. Rajgir is famous for the Malmas mela and the one held on the eve of Makar Sankranti.

THE IMPORTANT PLACES OF ATTRACTION FOR VISITORS

(i) **Bihar :** Bihar or Biharsharif, the headquarters of the district lies at a distance of about 30 km South of Bakhtiarpur. It is a railhead also and the Bakhtiarpur-Rajgir line passes through it. It sprang into prominence during the Gupta period and even today, there stands a pillar 14 feet in height, inscribed with the name of Kumar Gupta and Skanda Gupta. It was also the capital of the Pala Kings.

According to the Tibetan Chroniclers, Gopal I, founder of the Pala Empire, had built a vihar or monastery and hence, the name of this town and the state. It contains many graves of pirs, the most famous being that of Makhdumul-Mulkl and, therefore, it has been named as Biharsharif, i.e., Bihar, the place of ascetics.

(ii) **Begampur :** The village is situated 5 km north of Nalanda railway station. It has many unexcavated mounds believed to cover further ruins of the Ancient University of Nalanda. It has two big tanks known as Dighi and Sonaroha.

(iii) **Ghosrawan :** It is a large village lying 3 km east of Pawapuri. The village is noted for its sculptures of stone images. Some ancient stone images have also been found in the village.

(iv) **Giriak Bahbolpur :** The village is situated on the Biharsharif-Ranchi road about 21 km south of Biharsharif. The Giriak Rajgir hill range starts from the western part of this villages. The hilltop in the village contains a round temple, traditionally believed to have been built by Jarasandh, the king of Magadh during the Mahabharat age.

(v) **Islampur :** The village is the headquarters of the block earing the same name. It is noted for its library known as Kutubkhan Quadarea which has many Persian and Arabic manuscripts.

(vi) **Kashmiri Chak :** The village is situated 6 km north of Islampur railway station. It is famous for its tombs of Yusuf Sah and his son Yakub Sah who were believed to have been rebels from Kashmir, hence the name of the village.

(vii) **Nalanda :** The village situated 13 km south of Biharsharif and at the same distance north of Rajgir, is internationally renown as the seat of the Ancient University of Nalanda. The ruins of the buildings of the university attract thousands of visitors every year. There is a museum containing important sculptures and other articles excavated from the ruins. An institute of Pali studies has been set up in Nalanda for the teaching of Pali language.

(viii) **Parnawan :** It is ancient village situated about 5 km west of the block headquarters at Sarmera. It is noted for the old temple called Mahatoji's temple. A one-day fair is held every alternate year on the occasion of Baisakh Purnima.

(ix) **Pawapuri :** It is a large village lying on the Patna-Ranchi road, about 25 km south of Biharsharif. It is a very sacred centre of pilgrimage of the Jains. Lord Mahavira is believed to have attained salvation at this place. It contains a magnificent temple situated in the midst of a large tank. A large fair is held on the occasion of Deepawali every year.

(x) **Rajgir :** It is a small town situated about 25 km south of Biharsharif. It was the first recorded capital of the country. It was a flourishing town in the 6th century B.C. when Lord Buddha was roaring throughout the country to preach Buddhism. It is also a winter health resort. The following are the places of interest in the town :

- **Hot springs :** There are a number of hot springs in the town. The water of the springs is very good health and large number of tourists come to Rajgir in winter for taking bath in the hot springs.
- **Shanti stupa :** The stupa has been constructed on the top of a hill by the Japanese Buddhists.
- **Aerial ropeway chairlift :** It goes up to Shanti Stupa from the foot of the hill and provides a pleasant ride to the tourists who got a panoramic view of the surrounding.

- **Vulture's peak :** It was a favourite abode of Lord Buddha. Here he used to give his sermons. Its rocks are shaped like vultures and hence its name.
- **Cyclopean walls :** Ruins of the ancient walls, which provided protection of the ancient city of Rajgir.
- **Sanda :** It is a large village situated about 5 km south-west of Islampur railway station. It was an ancient centre of Buddhist studies. Remains of stupas, temples, pillars and stone-slabs with inscriptions have been found in the village.

Table 1
Nalanda: Some Important Facts (Census - 2001)

1.	Administrative Name		:	Nalanda	
2.	No. of Sub-Divisions		:	03	
3.	No. of Blocks		:	20	
4.	No. of Towns		:	05	
5.	No. of revenue villages		:	1088	
6.	No. of Panchayats		:	248	
7.	Area (in km)		:	2355	
8.	Total Population:		*Male*	*Female*	*Total*
		Rural	1050249	964635	2014884
		Urban	186218	167225	353443
		Total	1236467	1131860	2368327
9.	Sex Ratio:	Rural	Urban	Total	
	(Per 1,000 male)	918	998	915	
10.	Density of Population (per sq. km.)		:	1006	
11.	Infant Mortality Rate		:	73	
12.	Population growth during 1991-2001		:	370323 (18.54%)	
13.	Literacy		*Male*	*Female*	*Total*
	(i) Literacy		674304	357578	1031882
	(ii) Literacy rate		66.94	39.03	53.64
14.	Child population in the age-group 0-6:				
		Male	*Female*	*Total*	
	Rural	198633	187797	386430	
	Urban	30476	27843	58319	
	Total	229109	215640	444749	
15.	C.D. Block having highest sex rate		:	Giriak (947)	
	C.D. Block having lowest sex rate		:	Karai Parsurai (891)	
16.	C.D. Block having highest literacy rate		:	Biharsharif (62.49)	
	C.D. Block having lowest literacy rate		:	Karai Parsurai (43.65)	
17.	C.D. Block having highest female Literacy rate		:	Biharsharif (50.64)	
	C.D. Block having lowest female Literacy rate		:	Karai Parsurai (29.00)	

An overall picture of some important facts of Nalanda district is presented in the Table 1. The table reveals the distribution of total population in respective of Rural-Urban males, females population, area, density of population, IMR, Literacy rate, child population, highest and lowest sex ratio in the block, highest and lowest literacy rate in the block, highest and lowest female literacy rate in the block etc. Further, the table demonstrates the administrative name of the district is Nalanda. There are 3 sub-divisions, 20 C.D. blocks, 5 towns, 1088 revenue villages and 248 panchayats. The area of the district is 2355.0 kms, density of population is 1006 per sq. km and infant mortality rate is 73. Total population of district is 22368327. Male literacy rate is 66.94%, while female literacy is 39.03%.

Table 2
Distribution of Workers & Non-workers in the District

	Males	*Females*	*Total*
1. Total Population	1236467	1131860	2368327
(i) Total workers	599393	304524	903917
(a) Main workers	494315	641477	700250
(b) Marginal workers	73761	129906	203667
(ii) Non-workers	637074	827336	1464410
2. Total Workers (main + marginal)	599393	304524	903917
(i) Cultivators	224558	98766	323324
(ii) Agricultural labourers	216637	163489	380126
(iii) Household Industry workers	24749	16312	41061
(iv) Other workers	133449	25957	159406

Source: Census of India 2001, Series 11– Bihar.

An overall picture of total workers, main workers, marginal workers and non-workers in respect of male and female workers are presented in this table. The total population is divided into total workers and non-workers. The total workers are divided into main workers, marginal workers. Further, the table reveals that total workers (main + marginal) is sub-divided into cultivators, agricultural labourers, workers in household industry and other workers. Among them, the agricultural labourers (i.e. 380126) are the largest group which defines predominant agrarian base in Nalanda.

Table 3
Block-wise Distribution of Population (Census-2001)

Sl. No.	*C.D. Block*	*Males*	*Females*	*Total*
1.	Karai Parsurai	32228	28722	60950
2.	Nagar Nausa	37031	34682	71713
3.	Harnaut	75595	68208	143803
4.	Chandi	65639	60177	125816
5.	Rahui	66826	61201	128027
6.	Bind	29571	26680	56251
7.	Sarmera	40901	37773	68674
8.	Asthawan	74676	69151	143827
9.	Bihar	206849	187586	394435
10.	Noorsarai	71164	66086	137250
11.	Tharthari	27240	24738	51978
12.	Parbalpur	30335	27998	58333
13.	Hilsa	84979	77450	162429
14.	Ekangarsarai	76364	69715	146079
15.	Islampur	100128	91368	191496
16.	Ben	37687	34402	72089
17.	Rajgir	56856	51998	108854
18.	Silao	64066	58964	123030
19.	Giriak	38836	36775	75611
20.	Katrisarai	19496	18186	37682
	All	1236467	1131860	2368327
	Bihar	43153964	39724832	82878796

An overall picture of block-wise distribution of male and female population is presented in this table. The table reveals, the highest population is in the Bihar block, followed by 2,06,849 males and 1,87,586 females and the lowest population is in the Katrisarai block, followed by 19496 males & 18186 females. Nalanda district contains 2.86% population out of and in the density of population Nalanda district is in 13th position among total population of Bihar.

There are 1,49,668 families below the poverty line in a population of 23,68,327 in Nalanda district. Biharsharif (18,672), Hamaut (13,200), Chandi (12,366) are three blocks having a large number of BPL families. It reveals the socio-economic scenario of Nalanda district.

Table 4
Block-wise List of BPL Families in Nalanda District

Sl. No.	*Block*	*No. of families*
1.	Sarmera	5249
2.	Hilsa	6645
3.	Ben	6010
4.	Katri Sarai	2790
5.	Silao	7827
6.	Harnaut	13200
7.	Bind	4454
8.	Rahui	8576
9.	Nagarnausa	5803
10.	Asthawan	9276
11.	Parwalpur	5063
12.	Islampur	10962
13.	Chandi	12366
14.	Rajgir	7433
15.	Giriyak	5174
16.	Noor Sarai	2166
17.	Karyparsaray	4840
18.	Biharsharif	18672
19.	Tharthari	4840
20.	Ekangarsarai	8322
	Total	149668

REFERENCES & ACKNOWLEDGMENT

1. Patna District Gazetteer, N. Kumar, 1970.
2. Census, 2001.
3. Nalanda DM Office Documents.
4. Nalanda District Social Security Office Documents.
5. CMIF.
6. District Census Handbook : Nalanda District, 1981, Series 4–Bihar.

8

BONDED LABOUR IN NALANDA

The present chapter deals about the present and past status of freed bonded labourers of the district. In respect of this, the district administration and the department of social security provided the list of 50 freed bonded labourers.

Table 1
Freed Bonded Labourers in Nalanda District

Sl. No.	*Name of the Block*	*Freed Bonded Labourers*		*Ranking*
		Number	*Per cent*	
1.	Silao	11	22.00	2
2.	Giriak	7	14.00	4
3.	Biharsharif	9	18.00	3
4.	Chandi	22	44.00	1
5.	Ashthawan	1	2.00	5
	Total	50	100.00	

Table 1 depicts the complete picture of identified and rehabilitated bonded labourers in the different blocks of Nalanda district. Chandi block has the highest number of FBLs (22), rehabilitated by the district administration. Silao block is in the 2nd position, where 11 FBLs were rehabilitated. In the third place, there are 9 Freed Bonded Labourers of Biharsharif block. Another block Giriyak is in the fourth position with 7 FBLs. The Ashathawan block is in the fifth position with one FBL. Thus, the total number of bonded labourers identified and freed in the district was 50. No bonded labourers have been identified in the district from 1995 to 2003.

The district administration holds regular campaigns for identifying bonded labourers. The last survey for the identification of the bonded labourers was done in the year 2002-2003. National Human Rights Commission has been strongly advocating that the campaigning for generation of awareness against bonded labour system is essential for eradication of this evil system. The district administration has shown consistency in holding awareness campaigns.

The thrust of district administration should be to keep check on the brick-kiln and stone crusher units, where new areas of bonded labour system may find new avenues of growth particularly in the case of migrant workers from neighbouring districts and Jharkhand state. The labour department has an important role to play in keeping vigilance on these new proliferating units in the district.

The research team visited all identified freed bonded labourers household on the address provided by the district administration. The Table 2 gives the contemporary position of the actual freed bonded labourers in the district.

Table 2
Block & Village-wise Distribution of FBLs in the Nalanda District

Block	*Village*	*No. of FBLs*			*Total*
		living	*migrated*	*died*	
Silao	Birididih	07	-	03	10
	Mahuri	-	01	-	01
Giriyak	Vijay Nagar (Kandopur)	05	-	02	07
Biharsharif	Pawa	06	-	03	09
Asthawan	Dumrawan	01	-	-	01
Chandi	Sumka	02	04	04	10
	Kharjamma-Gadanpura	05	-	-	05
	Bhalbigha	01	-	-	01
	Noniya Bigha	-	03	-	03
	Jasmat Bigha	01	-	-	01
	Bhathar	-	01	-	01
	Kurthiya	01	-	-	01
	Total	29	09	12	50

Out of 50 FBLs, the team discovered that 12 have died. Many died on account of old age and some due to chronic illness.

The break up is follows:

(a) Silao block = Birididih village = 03

(b) Giriyak block = Kandopur village = 02

(c) Biharsharif block = Pawa village = 03

(d) Chandi block = Sumka village = 04

All died after being freed and rehabilitated.

It was found that 09 have migrated and their neighbours had little or no clue about their present whereabouts. The major reason provided by the neighbours was that they have migrated to look for a better place to earn and live.

The break up for migrant FBLs are as follows:

(a) From Bhathar village in the Chandi block = 01

(b) From Noniya Bigha village in the Chandi block = 03

(c) From Mahuri village in the Silao block = 01

(d) From Sumka village in the Chandi block = 04

This latest information has been passed to the district administration and the local social security office by the ANSISS team. The team met the existing 29 FBLs.

Table 3
Distribution of FBLs by their Causes for Bonded Labour

Sl. No.	*Cause*	*No. of FBLs*	*Per cent*
1.	Low Socio-economic status in the society	14	48.27
2.	Unemployment	09	31.03
3.	Poverty	23	79.31
4.	On the traditional way	11	37.93
5.	Indebtedness	19	65.51
6.	Own choice	02	06.90

Note: The figures are non-additive. It is multiple answer based.

One of the concerns of the study was to find the basis for becoming bonded labourer in Nalanda district. It can be deciphered from the above table that the most significant answer was abject poverty 79.31 per cent, followed by the indebtedness 65.51 per cent. The other major cause was attributed to the low socio-economic status in the- society (48.27 per cent). 37.93 per cent became bonded labour due to following the traditional way 31.03

per cent attributed to the unemployment. Some expressed their own choice (6.90 per cent) in becoming bonded labourer.

There was multiple factors given by all FBLs but the problem of poverty, indebtedness, unemployment, low socio-economic status in the society was dominant cause for falling into vicious bonded labour trap. It is classic example of absolute deprivation praxis in the social and economic structure. The feudal environment and graded caste hierarchy also played a major role in bringing the landless and the helpless in the exploitative practices of the bonded labour system where the dominant landlords lured them into debt bondage.

Table 4
Identification Period of FBLs

Identification Period	*No. of FBLs*	*Per cent*
1980 - 81	18	62.07
1990 - 91	10	34.48
1992 - 93	01	03.45
Total	29	100.00

18 (62.07%) FBLs were identified during the year 1980-81, while 10 (34.48%) FBLs were identified during the year 1990-91. Only one FBL was identified during the year 1992-93. The majority (18 FBLs) have spent 23 years as free persons pursuing their activities on their own terms. The other group (11 FBLs) who was liberated later has completed 13 years of freedom from bondage.

The department of social security, Government of Bihar and Nalanda district officials reported that no bonded labour has been identified after 1992-93 to 2004.

Table 5
Working place of FBLs before release

Statement	*No. of FBLs*	*Per cent*
Within the same village	14	48.28
Outside the village but within the block	-	0.00
Outside the block but within the district	05	17.24
Outside the district but within state	06	20.69
Outside the State	04	13.79
Total	29	1 00.00

It was another significant objective to find out where FBLs were bonded labour before their release. It was important to find that the majority of FBLs (48.28%) reported that they worked in the same village during the bonded labour period, where they lived. This affirms the feudal social environment where these FBLs worked.17.24% FBLs worked out side the block but within their district, while 20.69% FBLs accounted that they worked out side the district but within the state. 13.79% FBLs worked outside the state.

Table 6
Distribution of FBLs Working Period as Bonded Labour

Working Period	*No. of FBLs*	*Per cent*
Upto 5 years	10	34.48
6-10 years	-	-
11-15 years	01	03.45
16-20 years	07	24.14
21 years and above	11	37.93
Total	29	100.00

The Table 6 reveals that out of 29, 11 freed bonded labourers (37.93 per cent) worked as bonded labour for more than 21 years, while 24.14 per cent freed bonded labour reported that they had worked as bonded labour 16 to 20 years. About 34.48 per cent freed bonded labourers worked between 1 to 5 years. 3.45 per cent FBL reported that the period of work was 11 to 15 years. It reveals that the majority was in chains of subjugation and bondage for over a decade and had spent their prime years in servitude.

9

FREED BONDED LABOUR : SOCIAL LIFE

This chapter deals about the social life of Freed Bonded Labourers (FBLs). Under these characteristics of FBLs included age, sex, caste, marital status, family size, family members, neighbours and availability of infrastructure facilities in the village.

The following table gives the details about the social life of freed bonded labourers.

The age composition of the freed bonded labourers is evident from the table shows a range of the freed bonded labourers belong to different age groups ranging from 31 to 71 and above. They are a composite group of young, middle and old age. It is found from the above table that the highest percentage of the respondents (44.82%) belongs to the age group of 61 years and above, which suggests that they are old and have been long in the iniquitous circle of bondage, till they were freed. They have lived long to tell the tales. It also emerged that the majority had served their supreme being for a relatively long time.

Table 1
Age-wise Distribution of Freed Bonded Labourers

Sl. No.	*Age Group (yrs.)*	*Number*	*Per cent*
1.	31 - 40	04	13.80
2.	41 - 50	03	10.34
3.	51 - 60	09	31.04
4.	61 - 70	10	34.48
5.	71 & above	03	10.34
	Total	29	100.00

The second highest percentage of respondents (31.04%) belongs to the age group of 51-60 years, which implies that they were in the master's domain also for reasonable period of time.

The third highest percentage of the respondents (24.14%) belongs to the age group of 31-50 years. This group was small but provided deep insight into the bondage complex. It also suggests that a small percentage survived the hardship during the bondage period.

Table 2
Sex-wise Distribution of Freed Bonded Labourers

Sex	*Number*	*Per cent*
Male	22	75.86
Female	07	24.14
Total	29	100.00

The table demonstrates about the males and females distribution of FBLs in the district. Majority of FBLs (75.86%) are males, where only 24.14% FBLs are females. Thus, the percentage of male FBLs is very high than female FBLs. The females FBLs were found in the Sumka, Gadanpura, Malbigha, Khapraha and Kurthia villages of Chandi block only. The location of these female bonded labourers village was about 2 to 7 kms from the C.D. block office. They were released from the dreaded brick kiln occupation in 1990-91.

Table 3
Family size distribution of Freed Bonded Labourers

Family Size	*No. of FBLs*	*Per cent*
Upto - 5	09	31.03
6 -10	15	51.73
11 - 15	04	13.79
16 & above	01	03.45
Total	29	100.00

The majority of FBLs (51.73%) had family size of 6-10 members, where as 27.24% of FBLs had large family size with 11 and above members. Only 31.03% of FBLs had 5 and less members. Thus, the family size of FBLs was found large in the district because they were related to the village life, where large and joint family is the main characteristic. The families of all rehabilitated FBLs belonged to traditional family system with two or three generations living together and sharing common kitchen worship place and commonly sharing division of family obligations.

Table 4
Age-Sex wise distribution of family members of Freed Bonded Labourers

Age Group	*Male*		*Female*		*Total*	
	No.	*%*	*No.*	*%*	*No.*	*%*
0 - 5	15	6.64	15	6.64	30	13.28
6 - 14	24	10.62	29	12.83	53	23.45
15 - 60	60	26.54	59	26.11	119	52.65
61 & above	17	7.52	07	3.10	24	10.62
Total	116	51.32	110	48.67	226	100.00

The Table 4 shows that the FBLs families belong to different age groups. They are in the age group of upto 5 years, 6-14 years, 15-60 years and 61 and above years.

The majority of FBL's family members (52.65%) were found in the age bracket of 15-60 years, followed by 26.54% males and 26.11% females.

The next age group of 6-14 years with 23.45% constitutes the second largest size with 10.62% males and 12.83% females.

0-5 years (13.28%) age group is in the third position with 6.64% males and females separately.

7.52% males and 3.10% female of FBLs family were found in the fourth age group size of 61 and above.

Table 5
Distribution of Freed Bonded Labourers by Sex and Marital Status

Marital Status	*Male*		*Female*		*Total*	
	No.	*%*	*No.*	*%*	*No.*	*%*
Married	20	68.98	06	20.70	26	86.68
Unmarried	01	03.44	-	-	01	03.44
Widow/Widower	01	3.44	01	3.44	02	6.88
Total	22	75.86	07	24.14	29	100.00

An overall picture of marital status of freed bonded labourers are presented in this Table 5 Majority of FBLs 86.68% were married, followed by 68.98 males and 20.70% females. They were enjoying their marital bliss.

Only one (3.44%) respondent (Suresh Prasad) of village was found unmarried, who is working as a domestic servant with the previous master on his own choice.

Only 3.44% freed bonded labourers were widowed who live in the village and exhibited family responsibilities. They talked about the hardships in raising the family. The burden of meeting domestic challenges was a dominant subject of discussion.

The pattern of sex distribution among the freed bonded labourers showed 22 males and 7 females, signifying high prevalence of males in bondage, but there were female freed bonded labourers too.

The presence of females presents a picture where the highest degree of exploitation of the bonded labourer families must have happened where women were compelled to mortgage themselves as debt bondage labourer. These seven were mortgaged along with their husbands and were released together. They were working in brick kiln at Fathua, Patna and Durgapur (West Bengal). They were released and settled in Nalanda district.

The Table 6 represents the caste situation of FBLs. The majority of FBLs (79.31%) belong to scheduled caste community and another 20.69% FBLs belong to the Other Backward Castes (OBC) group, like-Sonar, Kahar etc. It is significant and true to the history of debt bondage. It fits the absolute deprivation paradigm where ritually low status in graded hierarchical society co-exists with those below the poverty line status. The social and economic level are uniform steeped in the bottom line of a agrarian semi-feudal society.

Table 6
Caste Composition of the Freed Bonded Labourers

Caste	*Number*	*Per cent*
Scheduled Caste	23	79.31
Scheduled Tribe	-	-
Backward	06	20.69
General	-	-
Total	29	100.00

The distribution of figures in the Table 7 demonstrates that the FBLs live in cluster. 2 members of the total FBLs had 2 and less number of members in their neighbours as FBLs.

Table 7
Neighbours of Freed Bonded Labourer

Sl. No.	Statement	No. of FBLs	Per cent
1.	Was your neighbour Freed Bonded Labourer ?		
	(i) Yes	25	86.21
	(ii) No	04	13.79
2.	If Yes, how many families?		
	(i) upto 2	02	6.90
	(ii) 3-4	10	34.48
	(iii) 5-6	13	44.83

Another 10 FBLs had a neighbour size of 3-4 freed bonded labour members, while 44.83% FBLs had 5-6 members of FBLs in the neighbourhood: The social cohesion was among the FBL fraternity and felt psychologically more as an unit due to common background.

The availability of the governmental infrastructure facilities in the society as basic civic support system for the citizens are an important mark for assessing the reach and welfare measures taken to ameliorate the common man's predicament particularly in the rural and backward areas.

Table 8
Availability of Government Infra-structure in FBLs Villages/Tolas

Government Facilities		No. of FBLs	Percentage
1.	Post Office	13	44.83
2.	PDS	22	75.86
3.	Health Centre	11	37.93
4.	Electricity	06	20.69
5.	Bank	07	24.13
6.	Road Facilities		
	(i) Kachcha	14	48.27
	(ii) Pucca	07	24.13
	(iii) Mixed	02	06.96
	(iv) No facility	06	20.69

In the Table 8 the availability of governmental infra-structural facilities for the FBLs represents a mixed scenario.

The table shows that all types of the infra-structural facilities are not available in the FBLs villages/tolas of the district, rather it is insufficient for the FBLs families in several areas. Some are fortunate to enjoy the facilities were as others are deprived of the basic facilities. There is no uniformity in the availability of these Government conveniences. The table amply illustrates the tale of missed opportunities by the Government agencies in reaching out uniformly to all FBLs families in their neighbourhood.

The picture emerging is like this that 44.83% can utilize the post office facilities, whereas 75.86% FBLs can use the public distribution centre (fair price shop/ration). The health situation is dismal with only 37.93% FBLs having access to the health centres. 20.69% FBLs can utilize the electricity connection, whereas 24.13% FBLs have the bank facilities.

The road facilities were accessible for 14 FBLs families Kachcha road, 7 on the Pucca road and 2 FBLs on the mixed road but 6 FBLs did not have any type of road facilities. They use earthen path before reaching any pucca or kachcha road.

The above discussion shows that the Freed Bonded Labourers of Nalanda district reside in an extremely backward area, where there is infra-structural incapacity and limited access to basic amenities.

10

FREED BONDED LABOUR : ECONOMIC LIFE

The present chapter deals about the economic life and conditions of Freed Bonded Labourers. In respect of economic characteristics, the present study includes the occupation, knowledge of minimum wage, wage structure, family income, live stock possession, farming equipments, agriculture lands, dwelling unit, saving habits and debt of the FBLs. Before describing the representative sample, it would be essential to explain the economic conditions of the Freed Bonded Labourers in general.

The kinds of economy, to which the bonded labourers depend, do not fit under the prevalent economic definition. They have transitional and fluid economic status. Their annual income is less. Their economic existence suggests that there is divine power that is keeping the bonded labourers alive. They live a life where the earning depends upon their physical labour, which reflects the primitive economy.

In village level development works, under the Swarn Jyanti Rozgar Yojana and other schemes in which number of works belong, like-digging and carrying of soils, spreading the soil on road, brick work in the village lane etc. are done by the freed bonded labourers. Further, it was also observed that the developmental works were not taken up in their village for last several years.

Men and women, both, work either in the agriculture field or in the brick-kiln work. For other modes of earning, they work as building construction labourers, road construction labourers etc. The older people do minor work such as collection of grass, firewood and play the role of guardian for the small children.

Children also go for rearing of cattle and collection of firewood. They look after small children and minor domestic activities such as cleaning of utensil, storage of water.

It was observed that the bonded labourer works 7 to 10 hours in a day. The work is generally available in the village for five to six months during agricultural seasons only, but there is fear of lean period, which haunts them the most. Work is not available round the year. There is no employment security. At times womenfolk predominantly get employed in agricultural season easily than males.

Freed bonded labourer's work is confined to sowing and harvesting and winnowing. The freed bonded labourers' works in the village from 9 A.M. to 5 P.M. with break at 12 to 1 P.M. with some breakfast. Generally, they get 2.5 kg. of wheat or maize or paddy as wage, which cost approximately Rs. 15 to 20.

The following table give the details about the economic life of freed bonded labourers.

Table 1
Distribution of FBLs in Terms of Land for Cultivation

Sl. No.	*Land provided for Cultivation*	*No. of FBLs*	*Per cent*
1.	Yes	-	-
2.	No	29	100.00
	Total	29	100.00

All FBLs reported that they do not have any type of agricultural land. They work as agricultural labourers with dominant caste people for their livelihood.

The majority of FBLs are agricultural labourers by occupation. After getting freed; they purchased some farming equipment, which were tools for their survival and means to earn. Only 58.62% FBLs reported that they had shovel as the farming equipment. All of them reported that they had Khurpi and Hasua. None of them have plough, which is the most important traditional farming equipment of the village.

All FBLs were found landless. None of them got any type of neither land nor farming equipment. The issue of fertilizer, seeds and pesticides at the subsidized rate and irrigation facility was not relevant in their case due to FBLs landless status.

Table 2
Distribution of FBLs by their Possession of Farming Equipments

Sl. No.	Farming Equipments	No. of FBLs	Per cent
1.	Plough	-	-
2.	Shovel	17	58.62
3.	Others Khurpi & Hasua	29	100.00

Note: The figures are non-additive. It is Multiple response based.

Table 3
Agriculture Facilities provided by Government among FBLs

Sl. No.	Statement	No. of FBLs	Per cent
1.	Farming Equipments provided by the Government	-	0.00
2.	Fertilizer, seeds and pesticides at subsidized rate	-	0.00
3.	How do you irrigate your land ?		
	(i) Well	-	0.00
	(ii) Pond	-	0.00
	(iii) Canal	-	0.00
	(iv) N.A.	29	100.00

The economic condition of FBLs is very poor, even their family members have to work in the agricultural land, particularly during busy seasons. Still, some have kept livestock in order to supplement their income and other familiar diet needs, but it is meagre.

The distribution of figure in the Table 4 shows the complete picture of livestock possession among the FBLs. 10 FBLs out of 29 FBLs have their own livestock. 9 FBLs had bataidari livestock which were given by different types of people likes farmers, landlords, moneylenders etc. to look after their animals on 50% sharing agreement.

The rest of FBLs had no animals in their possession. This reflects on their poor supplementary source of income. Most of them complained that the difficulty in maintaining livestock was mainly due to non-availability of grazing lands. Even those who possessed the livestock registered their grievance that there was no help or assistance by Animal Husbandry official's particularly vetenary doctors. They had no access or information about artificial insemination centres or mobile clinics. They were maintaining livestock on their traditional knowledge, but had suffered animal causalities due to ignorance or know-how to counter animal diseases. There was no facility available in the neighbourhood.

Table 4
Distribution of FBLs by their Livestock Possession

Name of Livestock	*No. of FBLs having*	
	Own Livestock	*Bataidari Livestock*
One buffalo	-	05
Two buffaloes	01	01
One cow	01	01
Two cows	-	-
One goat	01	01
One pig	01	-
Two cocks	01	-
Fourteen cocks	01	-
One cow + One ox	-	01
One goat + Two buffaloes	02	-
One pig + Two buffaloes	01	-
One ox + Two cows + Two buffaloes	01	-
Total	10	09

Table 5 demonstrates the contemporary occupation profile of the FBLs. Majority of FBLs (72.42%), including women bonded labourers, were found engaged as agricultural labourers in the villages or neighbouring villages. They were engaged in the agricultural fields in the vicinity of their households because majority of them, their family members were illiterate and untrained. They don't want to go elsewhere for work due to lack of confidence and boldness. The other reason was their old age and sickness. It was found that FBLs were not engaged round the year and the demand was more seasonal, hence during the dull season they work into the non-agriculture work like brick-kilns, digging, road making work and house construction work in the village or neighbouring area, which is their secondary occupations. The employment was not on long-term basis due to seasonal factor.

Table 5
Distribution of FBLs through their Occupation

Occupation	*Male*		*Female*		*Total*	
	No.	*%*	*No.*	*%*	*No.*	*%*
Agricultural labour	14	48.27	07	24.14	21	72.42
Non-Agricultural labour	01	3.44	-	-	01	3.44
No work/Old age	07	24.14	-	-	07	24.14
Total	22	75.85	07	24.14	29	100.00

Only 3.44% of freed bonded labour was engaged in non-agricultural work round the year because he worked as a domestic servant with their old master.

24.14% FBLs don't do any type of work due to old age and sickness.

Table 6
Wage Structure of FBLs

Wage Structure	*No. of FBLs*	*Per cent*
1. In kinds per day		
(i) 2 Kg. Grains	09	31.04
(ii) 2.5 Kg. Grains	05	17.24
(iii) 3 Kg. Grains	07	24.14
2. No work	07	24.14
3. Not taking wage	01	03.44
Total	29	100.00

The above table shows the overall picture of wage structure of FBLs. The majority of FBLs (72.42%) were working in the agriculture area, and their wages were paid in kind like rice, paddy, wheat etc.

24.14% FBLs were not working due to old age and unable to do anything. 3.44% FBLs is working with their old master without taking any wage and was treated as a family member of their old master.

All FBLs were working in the agriculture field receive very low wages in kind that is between 2 kg to 4 kg grains. Sometimes they and their family members work in non-agricultural area and get very low wage (Rs. 25-35 per day). The wage structure of the FBLs shows their very high level of exploitation in the district.

Table 7
Knowledge of Minimum Wage among FBLs

Sl. No.	*Do you know about the minimum wage ?*	*No. of FBLs*	*Per cent*
1.	Yes	-	-
2.	No	29	100.00
	Total	29	100.00

The above table shows that none of the freed bonded labourers had the knowledge about the government minimum wage for the agricultural and non-agricultural work. Due to lack of knowledge and non-availability of works in the village, they work at low wage. They had no support from Labour Inspectors to enforce minimum wages for them. In fact, they had no idea about minimum wages. No government agency had reached them to raise their information on government prescribed minimum wages. They were still stuck in the old mould of primitive economy where some goods were given in exchange of hard physical labour.

The Table 8 reveals about the economic status of the FBLs family. The poverty syndrome was apparent because all were found below poverty line.

Table 8
Family Income of FBLs

Income categories	*No. of FBLs*	*Per cent*
Upto Rs. 5000/-	02	06.90
Rs. 5001 - 10,000/-	06	20.69
Rs. 10,001 - 15,000/-	11	37.93
Rs 15,001 20,000/-	10	34.48
Total	29	100.00

It can be inferred from the table that their family income is up to Rs. 20,000 per annum and below which is more less below the poverty line amount i.e. Rs. 24,000/- yearly or 2,000/- per month.

Further, the table reveals that majority of FBLs (37.93%) have income of Rs. 10,001 to 15,000, while another 34.48% FBLs have income above Rs. 10 thousands but not more than Rupees 20 thousands. 20.69% of FBLs have income of Rs. 5,001 to 10,000 and only 2 (6.90%) FBLs have income upto Rs. 5,000/-.

The family income has not grown in a growth mode, as it should have been progressively over the years. Many still receive food grains in kind mostly in turn of the services rendered in the fields. The majority was not getting even the minimum wages as prescribed by the State Government. Even the basic awareness about minimum wages was missing.

In view of average FBLs having large family size, the income for sustenance looked low but enough for survival only. It appears uphill task for them to drawl out of poverty manifestation.

Table 9
Saving Attitude among the FBLs

Have you saving account in the Bank/Post office	*No. of FBLs*	*Per cent*
Yes	05	17.24
No	24	82.76
If Yes, then where:		
(i) In the Bank	05	17.24
(ii) In the Post office	-	-

The Table 9 explain about the saving habit of FBLs. 82.76% FBLs do not have any type of account in the bank or Post Office. Only 17.24% FBLs have their account in the Bank. But they did not operate their account for many years.

The saving attitude among of FBLs is not satisfactory. The need for more awareness among them about saving habit is needed for their safe and secure future. No effort has been made to educate them or help them in opening account in the Post office or the Bank by the Government agencies. Many of them were not aware about easy access to these facilities but on discussion - expressed desire to open saving account. The other reason is lack of literacy education among them. The national savings department has not held any awareness camps for inculcating saving habits.

The Table 10 shows that out of 29 FBLs, 21 FBLs (72.41%) had no debt outstanding and no loan to repay to anyone or any agency. The remaining 8 FBLs 27.59% were in debt and had taken loan from non-formal agency (i.e. landlords, moneylenders, etc.) which amounted to a total amount of Rs. 37,700/-. For getting loans from, the non-formal agency, they had to pay a higher rate of interest (i.e. 6-10 per cent per months) which is exploitative in nature.

Table 10
Debt among FBLs

Source	*No. of FBLs under loan*	*Per cent*	*Amount of Loan*	*Average Amount of Loan*
Formal agency	-	-	-	-
Non-formal agency	08	27.59	37700	471.25
Total	08	27.59	37700	471.25

Table 11
Present Working Place of FBLs and their Family Members

Statement	*Anywhere*		*Old employer*		*Not applicable*		*Total*	
	No.	*%*	*No.*	*%*	*No.*	*%*	*No.*	*%*
Where do you work at present ?	17	58.62	05	17.24	07	24.14	29	100.00
Where does other family members work at present ?	21	72.41	07	24.14	01	3.45	29	100.00

The distribution of figures in the Table 11 demonstrate that majority of FBLs 17 (58.62%) are working wherever they get better opportunity. 5 (17.24%) FBLs revealed that they were working with their previous landlord, where they worked before their release but today they are working there on slightly better wage and working condition 7 (24.14%) FBLs don't do any type of work due to their old age and physical disability.

21 (72.41%) FBLs family members have been working at different places for earning their livelihood, while 7 (24.14%) family members were working with the previous landlord where their father/husband were working.

Above table shows that all FBLs had their own shelter, which meant a dwelling unit of some kind. Majority of FBLs had katcha (earthen hut) units, 17.24% had pacca units and rest 34.48% had mixed dwelling units. The mixed dwelling units were a combination of Indira Awas Yojana added to their traditional katcha houses. But everyone had not received the Indira Awas Yojana units. Such units added more rooms making liveable space for the families, considering many have large family size. But then everyone has not been fortunate to receive the much-needed Indira Awas Yojana units.

Table 12
Distribution of FBLs by Nature and Types of Dwelling Units

Sl. No.	No. of rooms	Kachcha		Pucca		Mixed		All Type	
		No.	%	No.	%	No.	%	No.	%
1.	1	07	24.14	05	17.24	-	-	12	41.38
2.	2	05	17.24	-	-	04	13.79	09	31.03
3.	3	02	6.90	-	-	04	13.79	06	20.69
4.	4+	-	-	-	-	02	6.90	02	06.90
Total		14	48.28	05	17.24	10	34.48	29	100.00

The dwelling units had different number of rooms. The distribution of dwelling units in the above table shows that majority of FBLs (41.38%) had one room unit, 31.03% FBLs had two rooms unit, another 20.69% had three rooms unit and only 6.90% FBLs had four rooms set.

The FBLs who had mixed dwelling units had larger number of rooms in comparison to those who were living in kachcha dwelling units. In the case of pucca and mixed construction, it was seen that these types of constructions were made under the provision of Indira Awas Yojana (IAY).

11

EDUCATION SCENARIO : FREED BONDED LABOURERS AND THEIR FAMILIES

Education is empowerment. It can be used as an instrument to bring qualitative change in the life of freed bonded labourer. 53.64 per cent is the literacy rate of Nalanda district. {66.94 (male), 39.03 (female)}. The rate of illiteracy suggests that the government sponsored illiteracy programmes have to make inroads to cover the vulnerable areas of deprived and under privileged. The present literacy and education district administration's initiative has not percolated to the freed bonded labour and their families. FBLs remain under the dark zone of ignorance.

Table 1
Classification of Freed Bonded Labourer on the basis of Education

Education	*Number*	*Per cent*
Illiterate	26	89.66
Literate	-	-
Middle	01	3.48
Upto Matriculation	02	6.96
Total	29	100.00

The educational position of freed bonded labourers is dismal because majority of them (89.66%) is illiterate and has never received any form of schooling, before and even after been freed under any government's non-formal plethora of schemes. No ray of light of any form of education had ever touched them, and they were hapless victims of states gross ignorance and neglect. Only 3.48% were found to be received middle class education. But it is also important to know that 6.96% respondents received education upto Matriculation. In sum, the freed bonded labourers truly come from the most oppressed, deprived and downtrodden sections of the traditional Indian Society or the sociological black hole.

Table 2
Educational status of Freed Bonded Labourers' Family Members

Category	*Illiterate*		*Literate*		*Upto Middle*		*Matri-culation*		*Total*	
	No.	*%*	*No.*	*%*	*No.*	*%*	*No.*	*%*	*No.*	*%*
Adult Male	63	32.14	08	4.08	04	2.04	02	1.02	77	39.28
Adult Female	63	32.14	02	1.02	01	0.51	-	-	66	33.67
Male (6-14 yrs)	23	11.74	-	-	01	0.51	-	-	24	12.5
Female (6-14 yrs)	28	14.29	-	-	01	0.51	-	-	29	14.80
Total	177	90.31	10	5.10	07	3.57	02	1.02	196	100.00

As regards literacy and educational status of FBLs, the table shows, the shadow of darkness has not spared the next generation of FBL's families. The 29 FBLs had in all 196 family members. Thus, there were 77 adult males, 66 adult females, 24 male child and 29 female child labourers' families. They are predominantly illiterate with figures high as 91.30% and only 5.10% literate. 3.57% were educated upto middle school and 1.02% were found to be matriculate. 11.74% male children between the age group 6-14 years were illiterate and only 0.51% male children were going to school. Among the female children between the age group of 6-14 years, 14.29% illiterate and were preoccupied in doing their household works only. A small fraction of 0.51% female children go to the middle school but they too drop out. As gathered from discussion female and male child education was not so popular and acceptable among the FBLs families.

It is alarming that education is not filtering through next generation, which may keep them tied in disguised servitude to land and propertied masters. There have been no special efforts made by the state education machinery to promote education or raise the educational level of freed bonded labourer's families as a priority and special care sector.

Education is empowerment and key to mobility in social and economic sphere but it does not carry any meaning among the

FBLs. Self-esteem and confidence was lacking among them. Their main pre-occupation is to survive in the existing adversity.

The distribution of figures in the table 3 demonstrates about the FBLs children education. Only one female of village-Sunka, Block-Chandi FBL reported that her children go to school and are getting food materials and books free of cost, but she complained that her children are not getting cash amount stipend. One female FBL of village Sunka, Block-Chandi reported that her children go to the Anganwari center and are getting mid-day food.

Further, the Table 3 reveals that majority of 19 (65.52%) FBLs children don't go to school. The majority of FBLs (44.83%) reported that their children were playing here & there. 12 (41.38%) FBLs replied that they are doing work at home. 10.34% worked as a child labour while 6.90% were engaged in grazing cattle.

Table 3
Awareness of FBLs Children Education

Sl. No.	*Where does your child read?*	*No. of FBLs*	*%*
1.	Anganwari	01	3.45
	If Anganwari, then		
	(i) Getting food :	01	3.45
2.	School	01	3.45
	If school, then :		
	(i) Getting food materials	01	3.45
	(ii) Getting cash amount	-	0.00
	(iii) Getting books free	01	3.45
3.	Not reading	19	65.52
	If not reading :		
	(i) Doing work at home	12	41.38
	(ii) Playing here & there	13	44.83
	(iii) Due to long distance of school	04	13.79
	(iv) Working as a children	03	10.34
	(v) There is no gain with education	05	17.24
	(vi) No need of education among girls	07	24.14
	(vii) Grazing cattle	02	6.90
	(viii) Dominant caste people disturb the children inside/outside the school	02	6.90
	(ix) Due to low economic condition	04	13.79
4.	Not Applicable	09	31.03

Note: Figures are non-additive.

Some didn't go to school due to long distance of school (13.79%). There were sceptics who felt that there is no gain in getting educated (17.24%). There were gender-biased families, which felt that there was no need of education among the girls (24.14%). Some children were prevented from going to school by the dominant caste men in their area (6.90%). There were families who wanted to send children to school but could not do so due to poor economics conditions (13.79%).

9 (31.03%) FBLs reported that they have no children. Table 3 showing political similarities and differences of different groups or have no school-going age children. Many of them don't send their children to the Anganwari centre due to lack of knowledge and information. There is no approach by the Anganwari centres or concerned officials to motivate them or extend the Anganwari facilities to them.

Table 4
Availability of Educational Facilities in the FBL's Village/tola

Sl. No.	*Facilities*	*No. of FBLs*	*Per cent*
1.	Anganwari	17	58.62
2.	School		
	(i) Primary School	04	13.79
	(ii) Middle School	07	21.14
	(iii) High School	18	62.07
	(iv) None of these	-	0.00

Note: Figures are non-additive.

Availability of educational facilities in the society is basic need and civic support system for the citizen, today. It brings important and dimensional change in the life of the people. The present table represents the availability of governmental educational facilities for the FBLs in the village/tola.

The table shows that all type of educational facilities is not available in the FBLs villages/tolas of the district, rather it is insufficient for the FBLs families in several areas. The picture emerging is like this that 58.62% FBLs can utilize the Anganwari facilities, where the FBLs can utilize schooling facilities for their children. Further, the table reveals that majority of FBLs (62.07%) can use schooling facilities upto high school, whereas 21.14% FBLs can utilize these facilities up to middle school. Only 13.79% FBLs have to get primary education for their children.

In spite of these facilities, the light of education is not spread among the FBLs families. This shows lack of thinking about education among FBLs families and has not taken proper attention.

From above discussion and on the basis of the field experience, it is recommended that freed bonded labour need some special literacy and education package. A focused approach is needed to bring them in education cover totally. The school presently running in the village has failed to cater the needs of freed bonded labour children.

There are some suggestions given by freed bonded labourers themselves regarding the promoting of education and literacy among them:

- Set up fully assisted residential government school, especially for free bonded labour.
- Teacher/instructor should come from their society because they can have better interpersonal communication with the student.
- Female teachers to educate the girl and women of the society.
- Education should be job oriented.
- Educational avenues and opportunities of job and employment after education.

There are many factors behind the low percentage of literacy and education rate among the freed bonded labour. Important among these are poverty, hard work, unlimited working time, lack of awareness, lack of motivation, dearth of avenues and opportunities of work and employment, collapse of government sponsored programmes etc.

12

FREED BONDED LABOUR : HEALTH

Freed Bonded labourers do not have knowledge of good health. The idea of good health among Freed Bonded labourers is little known due to their poor economic condition. Although they survive by doing physical work, they have little time or resources to take their care when their health goes down. They consider themselves healthy and fit as long as they can earn by hard toil, but once they are down then they realise the significance of good health and concept of health care but do they have resources for bailing out. Minor ailments like cold and cough, abdominal disease, fever etc. are ignored among freed bonded labourers. They pay attention to major ailments, but at times it is too late to do anything to salvage their health situation. Majority of them are suffering from some ailment around the year. There is no proper diagnosis and medical check up programmes undertaken among freed bonded labourers through the district administration.

The availability of safe drinking water is the major problem for the poor people and key to good health. Thus, the present table tries to examine the drinking water facilities for the FBLs.

Table 1
Drinking Water Facilities of FBL's

Source	*No. of FBLs*	*Per cent*
Well	06	20.69
Hand Pump	23	79.31
Total	29	100.00

The positive aspect in this mixed picture is that some type of drinking water facilities is available in all the FBLs village/tola.

79.31% families have hand pump facilities and 20.69% enjoy well facilities of drinking water. They were satisfied with the availability of drinking water facilities but had complains about the repair of hand pumps and wells. They repair the hand pumps and wells with their meagre resources, which they want local officials to do so.

They do not know whether the water available is safe for drinking. They simply know food and water is important for survival. Sometimes, joint water sharing by man and animal from the same pot can be seen in the houses of freed bonded labourers. Water is kept in open and this is due to lack of awareness and mainly because of the want of proper storage system and required utensils.

Table 2
Availability of Toilet Facilities in the Homes of FBLs

Response	*No. of FBLs*	*Per cent*
Yes	-	0.00
No	29	100.00
Total	29	100.00

It is evident from the Table 2 that there isn't any type of toilet facilities available in the FBLs houses. They use open defecation in places outside the village for this purpose. There is no provision of toilets and bathrooms. They do it in open. Even the female satisfies herself from the long call of nature in open. They are bound to bear this humiliation.

Table 3
Availability of Drainage Facilities in the Villages/Tolas of FBLs

Response	*No. of FBLs*	*Per cent*
Kachcha	-	0.00
Pucca	07	14.14
Open flow	22	75.86
All	29	1 00.00

It is so harmful for their health and the environment. The rural sanitation programme of Government, UNICEF and Civil Society is non-existence in the whole district. The rural sanitation programme is completely silent on this segment of freed bonded labourers and their families. Health and sanitation are closely related which needs strengthening on priority for this critical group.

Majority of FBLs (75.86%) reported that the wastewater spilled here and there in the village land in the absence of any proper drainage system in the village/tola. Some of FBLs (24.14%) reported to have pucca drains for disposal of wastewater in their tolas.

Table 4
Distance of Primary Health Centre from FBL's Residence

Distance in Km.	*No. of FBLs*	*Per cent*
1-2	11	37.93
3-4	08	29.59
5-6	03	10.34
7-8	07	24.14
Total	29	100.00

The above table shows that the FBLs face great difficulties to get adequate care from Government health infrastructure due to long distances.

34.48% of the FBLs have to cover a long distance of 5 to 8 kms to reach the nearest health centre.

29.59% travel 3-4 kms to reach the nearest health centre, while 37.93% travel 1-2 kms to reach the nearest health centre.

There is no mobile clinic or any preferential system for medicare of FBLs. Non-availability of proper transport makes it more strenuous for sick and old FBLs to travel. Hence, the FBLs face many difficulties about their family health care.

Table 5
Medicare Facilities for FBLs

Statement	*No. of FBLs*					
	Yes	*%*	*No*	*%*	*Total*	*%*
Regular check up of Health	05	17.24	24	82.76	29	100.00
Medicare facilities during the illness period	05	17.24	24	82.76	29	100.00

The table demonstrates the present status of Government health care system for the freed bonded labourers and their households. No government health care for freed bonded labour is available at their doorstep. There is no programme, which gives priority to their regular health check up or medical team visits for annual check up since they belong to the critical sector of society. The FBLs complained that they do not get medicine at health centre. They are given prescription to buy medicine on their own cost. Only 17.24% freed bonded labourers reported to get medical facilities during their illness in government's primary health centre outdoor service.

Though health centres at block level existly, but it is not accessible for them. Doctors do not visit them. ANM are available, but are of little use. They are aware of quacks. They confide more in the quacks. The vicious nexus of touts and FBLs exists in their area. There is need for proper planning by district civil surgeon and others to include FBLs in their health planning programme. They are vulnerable to diseases more due to their poor conditions. PHC and APHC should be provided FBL list with proper direction to give them medicare regularly.

13

EVALUATION OF REHABILITATION SCHEMES AND THEIR IMPACT

The present study was concerned with the rehabilitation status of the freed bonded labourers in Nalanda district. The department of social security, Nalanda provided a list of 50 bonded labourers, who were freed in the district. These liberated bonded labourers were scattered in the different blocks in the different villages of Nalanda district.

The study team visited all freed bonded labourers present (29) in the villages spread to five blocks namely Silao, Giriyak, Biharsharif, Chandi and Asthawan. All (29) the identified and rehabilitated freed bonded labourers were in depth covered for furnishing information. Out of 50 FBLs, only 29 FBLs were available, the rest have died or migrated. (See Chapter - II).

Table 1

Sl. No.	*C.D. Blocks*	*No. of FBLs*
1.	Silao	11
2.	Giriyak	07
3.	Biharsarif	09
4.	Chandi	22
5.	Ashthawan	01
	Total	50

The identification of bonded labourers and release order certificate given to the bonded labourers was done under the District Magistrate.

In the year 1980-81, release order certificate of 18 bonded labourers.

In 1990-91, release order certificate of 10 bonded labourers.

In 1992-93, release order certificate of 1 bonded labourer was issued.

A total of 50 bonded labourers were given the release order certificate. All the identified bonded labourers are registered in a file of social security department of Nalanda.

Table 2
Identification Period of 29 Available Freed Bonded Labourers in Nalanda

Sl. No.	*Identification Period*	*No. of FBLs*	*Per cent*
1.	1980-81	18	62.07
2.	1990-91	10	34.48
3.	1992-93	01	03.45
	Total	29	100.00

After the issue of release order certificate, the rehabilitation programme for bonded labourers was launched by the district administration in collaboration with the social security department. The Assistant Director, Social Security Department Nalanda reported that 18 bonded labourers were rehabilitated in the year 1980-81, 10 bonded labourers were rehabilitated in the year 1990-91 and one bonded labourer were rehabilitated in the year 1992-93. Thus, 29 identified bonded labourers were rehabilitated in the district.

The study shows that, only thrice, the bonded labourers were identified and freed in the district and that was in 1980-81, 1990-91 and 1992-93. No bonded labourers have been found since 1992-93 in Nalanda district.

During the field visit, it was discovered that 12 FBLs had died and 9 FBLs had migrated, but there was no information on this account available at the social security office or at the district level. The team updated the current status about the freed bonded labourers to them.

An attempt was made to examine the nature of the socio-psycho-economic existence of the bonded labourers in its various aspects. For each household only one questionnaire was used, which included common questions as well as discussion were used as the mode to have complete picture.

Table 3
Block and Village wise Distribution of FBLs in the Nalanda District

Sl. No.	Block	Village	No. of FBLs			
			Living	Migrated	Died	Total
1.	Silao	Bindidih	7	-	3	10
		Mahuri	-	1	-	01
2.	Giriyak	Kandopur	5	-	2	07
3.	Biharsarif	Paws	6	-	3	09
4.	Asthawan	Dumrawan	1	-	-	01
5.	Chandi	Sumks	2	4	4	10
		Gadanpura	5	-	-	05
		Malbighs	1	-	-	01
		Noniysbighs	-	3	-	03
		Jasmatbighs	1	-	-	01
		Bhathar	-	1	-	01
		Kurthiys	1	-	-	01
		Total	29	09	12	50

PRESENT STATUS OF FREED BONDED LABOURERS

Freed bonded labourers work as agriculture labourer anywhere within the village or outside the village independently. They are free to work with any landlord. One bonded labour was working with the same landlord. He is alone and there is no body to take his care except his previous landlord. FBL reported that landlord treated him as a family member.

PERCEPTION OF CHANGE: FBLs ON THEIR UPLIFT AFTER BEING RELEASED

There has been a slight improvement in financial, betterment in food consumption, enhancement in social prestige and increase in voting activities after been released. But none of them have purchased any permanent assets from their income and livelihood. The marginal change in their better food consumption pattern than in past and in use of clothes. Like the use of rice, bread with vegetable regularly and also the consumption of pulses after a day or two, was marked progress from the previous bonded life. They were using neat and clean clothes. Some had better accommodation facilities due to houses provided under the Indira Awas Yojana.

ABOUT THE PRESENT OCCUPATION

It was observed that most of the freed bonded labourers were working as agricultural labourers within the village and in the neighbouring. Seasonally, they migrated to other place in search for work. Some were found working in non-agricultural like in brick-klin, digging, roadwork, construction work and other works. A small number of freed bonded labourers were without work due to old age and illness. Some FBLs moved for work to nearest towns near their home place.

The family members of FBLs were also working in agriculture, non-agriculture areas like brick-klin, digging, roadwork and other works.

There was no government facilitative hand seen in their work sphere. There was no awareness regarding wages in unorganized sector, insurance cover or primary agricultural co-operative laws among them. There was no NGO activity noticed within the FBLs community for organizing them or in raising their awareness on basic issues. NABARD/similar other institutions, which are associated with Self-Help Group, were completely missing. ILO and other international agencies that work with children, women deprived and old were conspicuous by their presence.

The FBLs were working with their traditional knowledge and indigenous survival skills with no outside help to their family's occupation. Thus, working in agriculture field as workers remains the corner stone of their occupation.

KNOWLEDGE ABOUT THE MINIMUM WAGE

None of the freed bonded labourers knew about the minimum wage, which is prescribed by the government and enforced by the labour department. They were paid according to the existing wage of the area. The working hours of the freed bonded labourers are normally 6 to 8 hours and they get wage only in kind that is 2 to 3 kg rice with breakfast.

The labour department has to play an important role to implement minimum wages for them from their employers.

GOVERNMENT REHABILITATION ASSISTANCE OF FREED BONDED LABOURERS

(a) After identification and their release, the bonded labourers were provided compensation by the Government agencies.

Under this package, the FBLs were given different types of livestock, horse cart and cash money to improve their economic condition and living standard of their family.

Table 4
Government Compensation Package for the FBLs

Sl. No.	Major things	No. of FBLs	Per cent
1.	One buffalo	05	17.23
2.	Five pigs	03	10.34
3.	One cow + Five pigs	04	13.79
4.	One cow + One buffalo	01	03.45
5.	One buffalo + Cash Rs. 5000/-	04	13.79
6.	One buffalo + Cash Rs. 3000/-	02	06.90
7.	One buffalo + Cash Rs. 2500/-	01	03.45
8.	Five pigs + Cash Rs. 5000/-	02	06.90
9.	Horse cart + Cash Rs. 3000/-	02	06.90
10.	Horse cart + Cash Rs. 2500/-	01	03.45
11.	Cash Rs. 6000/- for shop	01	03.45
12.	Cash Rs. 6000/-	02	06.90
13.	Not received any type of assistance	01	03.45
	All	29	100.00

(b) The majority of FBLs (5) received one buffalo.

(c) 4 FBLs received one cow and 5 pigs.

(d) 4 FBLs received one buffalo and cash Rs. 5000/-.

(e) 2 FBLs received one buffalo and cash Rs. 3000/-, 1 FBLs received one buffalo and cash Rs. 2500/-.

(f) 3 FBLs received five pigs.

(g) 2 FBLs receive a five pig and cash Rs. 5000/-.

(h) 2 FBLs received one horse cart and cash Rs. 3000/-.

(i) 1 FBL received one horse cart and cash Rs. 2500/-.

(j) 3 FBLs received only cash Rs. 6000/- for shop, and

(k) 1 FBL did not receive any type of assistance because he refused and lives with his master.

28 bonded labourers received working assets to improve their economic activities. The bonded labourers reported that the quality

of assets was very poor. Almost all sold their cow, buffalo, pig and horse or they died. Cash amount received by the FBLs for business was consumed and they did not start their business.

This was the major rehabilitation carried by the district authorities as per the provisions of the act, but two basic shortcomings were analyzed during the study. The formulation of schemes was not realistic to the ground. The animals were provided to FBLs without basic training regarding its upkeeps and how to handle the diseases or whom to contact in the time of crisis. There was no linkage to Department of Animal Husbandry and Vetenary for training on animal maintenance and upkeep.

Secondly, it was part of income generating scheme but the implementing agency did not follow up the marketing of their product or training on animal care. They were forced to sell because the animals were dying or they did not get enough return.

As for the district authorities, they never had a blueprint of follow up. The FBLs need direction and guidance to come out of the poverty syndrome with concrete scheme, which matches their skills. They can be empowered first to handle the schemes and its benefits.

Pre-consultation between the beneficiaries and the donor can be very fruitful in planning such a big exercise.

Table 5
Social Security Pension for FBLs

Sl. No.	*Statement*	*No. of FBLs*					
		Yes	*%*	*No*	*%*	*Total*	*%*
1.	Do you get Social Security Pension ?	24	82.76	05	17.24	29	100.00

(a) The distribution of figures in the Table 5 demonstrates that the majority of FBLs (82.76%) avail the social security pension facility of Rs. 100/- per month which is provided by the Government under the Bonded Labour Rehabilitation Scheme.

(b) 5 (17.24%) FBLs don't get this type of facility. It was found that four cases (each cases of Sumka, Malbigha, Khaprachan and Kurathiya village) of Chandi block and one case was in the village-Dumrawan of Asthawan block.

(c) Why this had been not given to the freed bonded labour, was inquired from the district social security department officer. He reported that I have no knowledge about this, why they have not been paid by the social security pension giving section. He has promised to implement it soon.

(d) The administration has done satisfactory work on the pension front. The lapse regarding 5 FBLs can be corrected by corrective action.

(e) This pension is lifeline for them and it is recommended that the old age family members of the FBLs may be also included in these social securities.

Table 6
Indira Awas Yojana and IRDP Facilities

Sl. No.	*Scheme*	*No. of FBLs*					
		Yes	*%*	*No*	*%*	*Total*	*%*
1.	IAY	09	31.03	20	68.97	29	100.00
2.	IRDP	03	10.34	26	89.66	29	100.00

- The table reveals that 9 (31.03%) FBLs received Indira Awas Yojana (IAY) facilities and were using it for residential purposes.
- More than two-third (68.97%) FBLs reported that they didn't get this type of facility and a long period has passed since they were released. They had no clue as to why they were not provided IAY house, but they are still hopeful of getting one from the Government.
- 3 FBLs reported that they received one buffalo under IRDP scheme. But the rest got nothing under IRDP assistance.
- The Government assistance is evident but in fragmented manner not in totality. There is urgent need to address the issue as to why 20 (68.97%) FBLs were left out from the IAY scheme.
- It can be said that the Government programmes, under the below poverty line and bonded labour schemes, are not efficiently provided to the FBLs.
- This scheme is about shelter, which is also one of the foremost and important issues in the case of FBLs. As per the direction

of the Government of India and the State Government, all DMs have to link the FBLs with IAY schemes as a part of Government and poverty alleviation holistic strategy.

- Nalanda district has failed to meet its mission to provide IAY and other development scheme to all rehabilitated FBLs.
- SJGSY is in practice since April 1999 as an important scheme for poverty alleviation. The FBLs can be brought under SJGSY, which has multiple input for BPL families. It clearly states that within three years with help of all inputs an effort should be made to bring the family above the poverty line.

Table 7
Lal Card and PDS Facilities among FBLs

Sl. No.	*Statement*	*No. of FBLs*	*Per cent*
1.	Do you have a red Card?		
	(i) Yes	17	58.62
	(ii) No	12	41.38
2.	If yes, then what type of materials received by you at the Govt. rate ?		
	(i) Kerosene Oil	14	48.28
	(ii) Kerosene Oil & grains	03	10.34
3.	Where are the PDS?		
	(i) Within the Village	22	75.86
	(ii) Outside the Village	07	24.14

- It is evident from the above table that 58.62% of FBLs have got the facility of Lal Card.
- 41.38% of FBLs didn't receive the Lal Card facility which is provided by the Government agencies.
- 48.28 of FBLs are getting benefit of kerosene oil only from the PDS net work.
- While 10.34% of FBLs (two FBLs of tola-Vidaynagar, vill-Kandopur, Block-Giriyak and one FBL of village-Pawa, Block-Biharsharif) reported that they are getting benefit of kerosene oil and food grains particularly 15 kg. Rice and 20 kg. Wheat in a month.
- They complained that the most beneficial would be the availability of food grains particularly rice/wheat at subsidized rates in PDS fair price shop (Ration shop).

- 75.86 FBLs reported that PDS facility was within the village and 24.14% of FBLs reported that their PDS was outside their village.

It is evident from the Table 8 that their previous employer seized no property during the bonded labour period.

Table 8
Property Released and Provided Property through the Government

(a) Distribution of FBLs by Seized Property

Sl. No.	Statement	No. of FBLs			
		Yes	%	No	%
1.	Did employer seize your property during the Bonded Labour Period?	-	0.00	29	100.00

(b) Distribution of FBLs by providing Basgit paper

Sl. No.	Have you received Basgit Paper?	No. of FBLs	%
1.	Yes	12	41.38
	If Yes, then:		
	(i) 2 decimal	01	3.45
	(ii) 3.5 decimal	06	20.69
	(iii) 10.5 decimal	05	17.24
2.	No	17	58.62
	Total	29	100.00

- Majority of FBLs (17) reported that they did not receive the basgit papers for their houses.
- While 12 FBLs reported that they had received basgit papers, Moreover, 6 FBLs of village Pawa Block-Biharsharif reported that they had received 3.5 decimal of land through the basgit paper.
- While 5 FBLs of tola-Vijaynagar, village-Kandopur, block-Giriyak reported they had received 10.5 decimal of land.
- And only one FBL of village-Kurthiya, block-Chandi reported that they had received 2 decimal of land for their houses.
- Thus 41.38% FBLs reported that they have Basgit paper for their houses.

Table 9
Visit of Vigilance Committee Members in the Villages/tolas of FBLs

Sl. No.	*Statement*	*No. of FBLs*			
		Yes	*%*	*No*	*%*
1.	Visit of Vigilance Committee Members	-	0.00	29	100.00

- For the monitoring the development of socio-economic condition of FBLs, the vigilance committee's members have to visit the FBLs Village/tola to monitor the progress.
- The table reveals that the vigilance committee members never visited any FBLs villages/tolas.
- This indicates that the organizational performance and monitoring system of vigilance committee in the district is non-functional.

TRAINING FACILITIES

(a) None of the FBLs had received any training by any Government agency after their release for self-employment.

(b) Training is an important component for learning skills for self employment to generate regular income.

(c) The training for acquiring new skills, developing the existing indigenous skills, traditional arts and crafts can be important mode of income.

(d) Vocational training is a means of securing jobs and employment also.

AWARENESS PROGRAMME AMONG THE FREED BONDED LABOURERS

(a) No awareness programme was held among the freed bonded labourers. They were not aware about the government scheme for them except what they had got at the time of release. It is necessary to make them aware about the other assistance, schemes and programmes.

(b) A regular sensitization and capacity building process was not done in the district for the FBLs. All efforts can be done on making them aware about their schemes and how they can benefit from them.

(c) Exercises can be held to drive home about their right and how to live independently and free from debt bondage.

It is evident from the table 10 that all FBLs had not received their Release Certificate by the District Administration.

The Social Security Office, Nalanda gave the name and addresses of released FBLs to ANSISS team.

Table 10
Availability of Releasing Letters among the FBLs

Have you received any type of Bonded Labour release letter issued by DM/SDO ?	*No. of FBLs*	*Per cent*
Yes	-	-
No	29	100.00
Total	29	100.00

Table 11
Opinion of FBLs on what Steps the Government should take to Improve their Conditions

Statement		*No. of FBLs*	*Per cent*
1.	To improve infra-structural facilities–Electricity, Road, PDS	21	72.42
2.	Housing, Drinking water, Toilet and Drainage Facilities	18	62.07
3.	Medical & Health care facilities	15	51.73
4.	Educational facilities	12	41.38
5.	For improving economic condition of families loan, vocational training, Business, Land for cultivation, Animal Husbandry–Cattle, Piggery	27	93.11
6.	Pension facilities and increase in Pension Amount	04	13.80
7.	Regular work all the year around	14	48.28
8.	More facilities by the Government	07	24.14
9.	Development functionaries as should pay visit	05	17.255
10.	Enhancement of wage	11	37.941
11.	No response	02	6.90

- The expectations of the FBLs were assessed as to what in their opinion the state should take steps to improve their position.

The suggestions for improving their present situation gave an inside view of their level of expectations.

- The table demonstrates that most significant suggestion was for improving the economic condition of their families (93.11%) in which they demand loans, business facilities, land for cultivation and animal husbandry, cattle/pig-rearing skills.
- They felt that the Government should provide more medical and health care facilities (51.73%).
- Housing, drinking water, toilet and drainage facilities (62.07%).
- And (72.42%) want improvement in the infra-structural facilities like electricity, road and public distribution system.
- (13.80%) FBLs suggested that the pension amount should be increased and payment regularly.
- (41.38%) FBLs have demanded educational facilities for their children.
- (17.25%) of FBLs felt that the development functionaries should pay visit in the FBLs village/tolas.
- (37.94%) of FBLs wants the increase of their wages for the betterment of their living condition.
- 48.28% of FBLs have demanded regular work all the year around.
- Very low (6.90%) of FBLs did not given any suggestions.
- During the interview of FBLs it was found that they totally depend on the Government to improve their economic conditions.

Table 12
Knowledge of Bonded Labour Act among the FBLs

Do you know about the Bonded Labour Act ?	*No. of FBLs*	*%*
Yes	-	-
No	29	100.00
Total	29	100.00

All FBLs of the district don't know about the Bonded Labour Act, 1976 under which they freed.

They were in consensus grateful to the Government agencies for releasing from the clutches of bondage.

The most important questions is that whether they felt any perceptible change after being freed. The response was overwhelming. They cherished the freedom of work, which meant liberty to choose their workplace. They adored mobility and right to live as they wished. It was a clear departure from bondage to liberty of availing opportunities, as it came through with great hardship in many cases.

Table 13
Perception of Change among FBLs

Sl. No.	*Statement*	*No. of FBLs*	*Per cent*
1.	Freedom of work	24	82.76
2.	Feeling better than earlier	15	51.72
3.	Enhancement in social prestige	04	13.79
4.	No pressure/binding of work	18	62.07
5.	Improvement in food availability	01	3.45
6.	Enhancement of wages	01	3.45
7.	No Change	02	6.90

Note: Figures are non-additive.

- The above table reveals that the most significant answers were freedom of work (82.76%), followed by no pressure and binding cf work (62.07%).
- Those who expressed feelings of being better than before were 51.72%.
- Some experienced enhancement in their social prestige (13.79%).
- A very small section felt improvement in food availability (3.45%) and enhancement in wages (3.45%).
- But 6.90% felt no change at all.

The revelation of this study was that many FBLs. who were freed, continued to work in their old master's field. They had no complaint against them because the old master were giving them better wages now than before and liberty and mobility and choice to work or not with them.

There has been an improvement in financial condition, betterment in food consumption enhancement in social prestige and increase in voting activities after their released.

Table 14
Opinion of FBLs on their uplift after being Released

Activities	*Uplift*			
	Gain		*No Gain*	
	No. of FBLs	*%*	*No. of FBLs*	*%*
Financial condition	22	75.86	06	20.69
Food consumption	24	82.76	04	13.79
Asset acquisition	01	3.45	27	93.10
Social prestige	27	93.10	01	3.45
Voting behaviour	27	93.10	01	3.45
No response	01	3.45		

Table 15

Sl. No.	*Statement*	*No. of FBLs*	*%*
(A)	(1) Gain in food consumption		
	(i) What type of improvement ?		
	(a) Food according to their will	5	20.83
	(b) Take better food	12	50.00
	(c) Improvement in fooding, Clothing & housing	7	29.17
	(ii) How many times, do you take food ?		
	(a) Twice a day	10	41.67
	(b) Thrice a day	14	58.33
	(2) No gain	04	13.79
	(3) No response	01	3.45
(B)	Gain in asset acquisition, then what type of asset ?		
	(a) Purchasinq of land	01	3.45

The above table demonstrates that the majority of FBLs (50.00%) take better food at present. 29.17% of FBLs reported that they have experienced improvement in fooding, clothing and housing, while 20.83% FBLs reported that they take food according to their will, which is just enough for subsistence.

The table 15 further reveals that 58.33% take their food thrice a day and 41.67% of FBLs take it twice a day. All the FBLs take rice with potato/salt and chili or rice juice (Maar) and salt/chatani and achar/chokha etc. They don't consume food rich in protein and vitamins, particularly non-vegetarian food items, but to their low economic condition. Their consumption in quality food is still low but improved from past. The thrust of intake is more on the quantitative food compared to qualitative food. Low intake does affect their health standard and longevity of life.

But except one FBL of village Khhapracha (Yashmatbigha), block-Chandi who purchased 3 decimal land after the release, none of them have purchased any permanent assets for their income and livelihood.

DIFFICULTIES FACED IN THE FIELDWORK AND FEEDBACK

(a) The list of freed bonded labourers was not properly maintained in the social security office. No register is maintained. The list of bonded labourer is in file, which is not properly recorded, and file is not in the proper place.

(b) The list of bonded labourers was not up-to-date. It was not clear that how many bonded labourers were alive or how many had died or migrated.

(c) It was very surprising that the Assistant Director, Social Security was not aware about the rehabilitated freed bonded labourers in the district. He was not aware about the social security pension and how many bonded labourer had received it.

(d) Mostly bonded labourer was illiterate so the response of many questions was not given properly.

(e) Many FBLs are not keeping the release order certificate.

- It can be said that Government programmes under below the poverty line and bonded labour schemes were not efficiently provided to the FBLs.
- No official agency had pursued follow up programme and monitoring to oversee the progress of the freed and rehabilitated bonded labourers.
- The programmes were implemented mechanically without human touch. Some had benefited while others were left out. There was lack of totality in approach.

- There was no set up between the freed bonded labourers and the block, subdivision and district administration officials to interact on periodic basis in order to ascertain their economic as well as social upliftment. The vigilence committee could have filled up this gap, but it was not functional.
- The district administrative has given assurance to use corrective measures on priority for all FBLs and their upliftment.

PART - IV

An Evaluation of Bonded Labour Rehabilitation Schemes in PATNA District

14

INTRODUCTION–PATNA : A PROFILE

The district of Patna was constituted in the year 1865 out of portions of the then existing districts of Bihar and Tirhut. There were some minor changes of jurisdiction between 1861 and 1931, but its boundaries remained virtually intact therefore until 1972 when the subdivision of Biharsharif was separated and upgraded as the independent districts of Nalanda. The district is now with six subdivisions viz. Patna city, Patna Sadar, Danapur, Barh, Masauri and Paliganj consisting of 24 community development Blocks cum Anchals.

The district of Patna lies virtually in the heart of the South Bihar Plain. It is a constituent district of Patna division. The city of Patna besides being the headquarters and the state capital since 1911. The district is bounded on the north by the Ganges and to the east lies the district of Begusarai and Lakhisarai and in the south district of Jehanabad and Nalanda. Patna is separated from Bhojpur district on its West by the river Sone.

According to the district Gazetteer of Patna (1970), the district is named after its principal city, Patna. Various legends exist regarding its origin. The most popular legend ascribes it to a prince named Putraka, who created it with a stroke of his magic staff and named it in honour of his wife, the princes of Patali. It is also said that originally appears to have been princes of Patali. It is also said that originally appears to have been derived from 'Patali' or trumpet flower. Megasthenes called it Palibhotra. It is, however, generally accepted that Patna stands on the site of the ancient metropolies of Patna or Patliputra.

As the centre of the great Malady Empire, the district has rich and glorious history.

EARLY HISTORY

The varatyas referred to in the Atharvaveda constituted pre-vedic civilization in the origin of Magadh. The autochthonose tribes gave way to the incoming Aryans and migrated south to hilly regions of the Chhotanagpur Plateau which is now the stronghold of the tribes of Bihar. Thus, Bandhayana (6th century B.C.) spoke of Magadh as a tract containing a people of mixed origin outside the pale of Arya civilization.

Epic literature describes valiant feats of the mighty king Jarsandha who had its capital Rajgriha (now in Nalanda district). However, not much is known of line of the twenty-eight kings believed to have came after Jarasandha. Magadh reached the heights of spirituals renaissance in the sixth century B.C. during the reign of king Bimbisar of the Haryana Kakula dynasty when both Gautam Buddha and Mahavir Vardhaman preached their doctrines.

Bimbisar was a powerful ruler. He annexed the kingdom of Anga with its capital at champa and entered into matrimonial alliances with Kosala and Vaishali. According to a Chinese pilgrim, the city of Rajgriha was built by him at an old site-Bimbisar was murdered for the throne by his son Ajatshatru, the founder of Patliputra. Being faced with hostility of the rulers of Sravasti and also the Vrijis and Lichchvis of Vaishali,. Ajatshatru fortified the village of pataligram which lay just south of the confluence of the Ganges and the Sone. This little village soon become the metropolis of the country and remained so fan over four hundred years. Lord Buddha had prophesied that of all famous places, busy centres of commerce, Patliputra would be greatest, but three dangers, viz. fire, water and internal strife will threaten it. Ajatshatru was succeeded by his son Udayi who transferred the capital of Magadh from Rajgriha to Patligram which subsequently came to know by its more abiding name Patliputra. This place was selected as the capital primarily because of its strategic locations facile river communication and more central position in the expanding empire of Magadh.

After Udayi, the history of Magadh became rather obscure. His successors Aniruddha, Munda and Hagddasaka were all incapable. The citizen of Patliputra became indignant and banished the last ruler and an amatya (minister), Sishunag by name, was raised to the throne. After the full of the Sishunag dynasty (circa 400 B.C.), the Nandas came to power. They, in their turn, were replaced by the Mauryas Chandragupta, the founder of Maurya dynasty was a native of Magadh. He was a great Conqueror and brought the whole of Northern India and large parts of peninsular India under his scepter. With the help of Kautilya or Chanakya, Chandragupta built up an efficient system of administration and wielded considerable power. He successfully defeated the invading army of Seleukas Hikator, the Greek of Alexander and king of Syria and married his daughter. He extended his empire over a vast territory stretching from the Bay of Bengal to the Arabian Sea. Megasthenes was sent by Seleukas as an ambassador to his court.

Chandragupta reigned for about 24 years. The extent of the Mauryan empire sums to have remained undiminished during the region of his successor. Ashoka ascended the throne of Magadh in 272 B.C. During the first thirteen years of his reign, he continued the traditional Mauryan Policy of expansion within India and or friendly relations with the foreign powers. Ashoka conquered and annexed Kalinga and placed it under a Kumar with capital at Tosali. Subsequently, he recorded in one of the rock edicts his feelings of profound sorrow and remorse caused by the misereies of the people daring his Kalinga Campaign. This proved to be a turning point in the career of Ashoka. It introduced a momentous change in the Mauryan policy by substituting Dharmavijaya for Digvijaya. Ashoka adopted Buddhism as his religion and Magadh became the centre of Buddhist missionary activities. It was during his regime that the third Buddhist synod was held at Patliputra. Ashoka brought about vast improvement in his capital. A masonry well was build around the city. Numerous stone building were erected replete with rich decorations. A hospital was constructed for the animals. Fa-hien visited the city in the fifth century A.D. when some of the buildings of the Ashoka period were still standing.

With the death of Ashoka began the decline of the Mauryan dynasty. Patliputra also fell into comparative oblivion until the rise of the Guptas in the fourth century A.D. The Sunga period in between was rather uneventful.

Chandragupta I extended the kingdom of Magadh up to Allahabad and Patliputra regained its lost glory. His son Samudragupta further extended the empire and transferred the capital to a more central place, though Patliputra continued to be an important and a great city. Fa-hien, a Chinese pilgrim who toured India in Circa 424 A.D. during the regime of Chandragupta II, the son of Samudragupta found the city of Pataliputra in a prosperous condition. It was a centre of learning and was visited by scholar from different parts of the world.

Hiuen Tsang, another Chinese traveller who visited Patliputra between 630 and 645 A.D. during the reign of Harsha. However, found the city deserted though the remained of splendid palaces were reminiscent of their glorious past. Devastation was probably due to the invasion of the barbarous Hun in the latter dealt of the sixth century A.D. and of Sasanka was an enemy of Buddhism and he tried to uproot the religion. The persecution of the Buddhists did not last long for the got a patron in king Harshavardhan (600-618 A.D.) Although Patliputra was in ruins when Hiuen visited it, Magadh continued to be the peaceful abode of Buddhists. After the death of king Harsha, Magadh entered a period of dark age.

THE MUSLIM INVASION

Sometime after 1193 but before 1200 A.D. Md. Bin Bakhtiar Khilji invaded Bihar. The Muslim invaders killed a large number of Buddhist. Buddhist was practically effaced from the land of its birth with the conquest of the Muslims over Magadh, the history of this land and other parts of South Bihar got merged with that of Bengal. The district Patna formed part of the territory under the Bengal viceroys till 1320 when Emperor Ghiyasuddin Tughlak separated it.

MUGHAL PERIOD

Bihar, the first Mughal Emperor, came to manner in 1529 to curb the rebellious Afghan chiefs. After Babar's death, Sher Shah defeated Humayun and sized power. On his way back from Bengal in 1541, Sher Shah passed through a small town on the solution bank of the Ganges. He was greatly impressed by the place and got a Fort constructed there little town was none other than Patna. After the building of the Fort Patna again became a central place. It was soon a centre of trade and commerce. The Portuguese merchants visited the place in circa 1520. Patna was described by Tavernier as a large town in Bengal most famous for its trade.

Daud Khan, an Afghan chief who became the Governor of Bengal in 1573, established his headquarters at Patna and Hajipur in view of the strategic importance of these two places. He was attacked in 1574 at Patna by the Mughal army commanded by Munim Khan but without any success. Emperor Akbar then moved to supervise the military operations and eventually Patna was conquered by the Mughals. Therefore, Patna became the headquarters of the Mughal Governors and a centre of political activity. The town was raided in 1612 by Khusru, the pretender to the Mughal throne, who proclaimed himself palace at Patna. His forces plundered the city. Patna was recaptured by Shah Jehan in 1622 during his rebellion against his father. Another Magdha prince Prawez Shah, son of Jahangir, ruled over the city for some time. The still existing stone mosque known as Father-ki-Masjid was built by him in 1626.

The city of Patna progressed considerably during the Governorship of Azim-us-Shah, the grandson of Aurangzeb. In 1704, he named the city after himself as Azimabad. He endeavored to make Patna a great city, second only on the imperial capital of Delhi. With this end in view he induced many nobles to come down to Patna and settle here. Azim-us-Shah's efforts, however, did not entirely succeed on account of the war that broke out after Aurangzeb's death of Azim-us-Shah who was swallowed alive in quicksand in the year 1712, the Siyed brothers of Burah played the role of king-makers in the 18th century on the fall of the Saiyed brothers, the province of Bihar (including Patna) was once again merged with the Subah of Bengal.

ADVENT OF THE BRITISH

The first English trade mission to visit Patna consisted of Hughes and Parker who came in 1620 to purchase cloth and to establish a business house. However, it was only after the East India Company had firmly established itself in Bengal that the English again thought of setting up a factory at Patna. A batch of pioneers came in 1650 and succeeded in founding a small settlement. By 1658 they had a factory on the northern bank of the Ganges opposite Patna for refining sculpture since the saltpeter fields were situated there. The English began as humble traders. The chief article of commerce was sculpture, which was in great demand all over Europe for the manufacture of gunpowder. The flourishing trade of the English soon came to the notice of the Mughal Governor, Shaista Khan on finding that by paying a very small price for sculpture they were exploiting the people, he imposed certain duty on the company's goods on their refusal to play, he imprisoned peacock, the chief of the English factory at Patna. This was the beginning of a difficult time for the company which lasted for over 30 years.

During this period very often they had to suspend their business and close their factories.

THE MARATHA AND AFGHAN RAIDS

The imperial throne of Delhi had become weak and several aspirants for power has begun to assert themselves. In 1740, Ali Vardi Khan defeated Nawab Sarfaraz Khan and became the master of Bihar and Bengal. Soon after, Patna was threatened by a Maratha invasion. In 1741, the fortification of the city was improved, the city wall was repaired and the most outside was desilted to ensure protection to city dwellers. Mustafa Khan, the Afghan General of Ali Vardi Khan, laid siege to Patna in 1745 but was eventually defeated. The Marathas attacked in 1746 and the Afghans aided them, but Ali Vardi Khan managed to repulse both of them. In 1748 the Governor of Patna was assassinated and the Afghans of Darbhanga plundered the city. For a few days until the arrival of Ali Vardi Khan there was a reign of terror in Patna created by the Afghans. The Afghans eventually suffered a crushing defeat at Rabi Sarai near the present Railway station of Fatwah.

In 1757, the English made Mir Jafar Khan, the Nabab of Bengal. He was escorted to Patna by an English force commanded by Robert Clive. Mir Zafar made Ram Narain, the Deputy Governor of Bihar. Emperor Shah Alam came to Patna in 1759 to enforce his claim over the province. In the battle that followed between the English forces and Shah Alam, thereafter, the English forces ultimately succeeded in driving out Shah Alam to Burdwan. Shah Alam returned again with forces reinforcement and Jean Law, the French adventurer, to aid him. Shah Alam's attempt to ransack Patna again net with failure. Later in 1761 Shah Alam and Jean Law were defeated at Manpur near Gaya. In spite of their victory, the English came to terms with Shah Alam who was proclaimed the Emperor of India at Patna. Mir Kasim was then made the Nawab of Bihar, Bengal and Orissa.

Mir Kasim and the English could not remain on good terms for long and soon quarrels started. The English attempted to seize Patna, but were forced by Mir Kasim to remained inside their factories. Mir Kasim and the English were constantly at war. Mir Kasim came to Patna in October 1763 when he was shocked to learn that his fort at Munger had been surrendered to the English and he ordered complete annihilation of English at Patna. As a result 198 Englishmen's women and children were butchered in what came to be known as the great massacre of Patna. The cemetery near Patna city still contains a cenotaph commemorating these persons. Hearing of this massacre, the English forces under major Adams hurriedly moved to Patna and laid seize to the city. After a great deal of fighting Mir Kasim lost on the 6th November, 1763 and escaped to the territory of the Vazir of Oudh. On the 23rd October 1764 the English won a decisive victory at Buxar which made them the masters of the lower provinces of Bengal.

1857 MOVEMENT

The next event of importance in the district was the war of Indian Independence or the Great Mutiny of 1857 as it is sometimes called. The events in the up-country had inspired the people of Bihar also and they prepared to over throw the foreign yoke. The latters found in the house of Pir Ali, a bookseller at Patna, in the course of search of his house on the 4h July, 1857 confirmed that the rising was not a sepoy muting but a planned effort to free the country from foreign rule.

Tayler was then the Commissioner of Patna. He wanted General Lloyd, who was in command of the military divisions at a Danapur, to disarm them the General viz. hesitant, and at long last he reluctantly agreed to take away the percussion-caps of the sepoys. The Indian soldiers could not tolerate the insult inflicted upon them. In the war that followed, the Indian soldiers took their arms, left their lines and marched towards Arrah to join the Valiant Babu Kuer Singh.

On the 4th August, Taylor was replaced by Samuels. 200 British soldiers and two guns protected the city of Patna. The success of the freedom fighters in Gorakhpur and other places inspired the people. The Indian soldiers who had broken away from the British, moved about in the country-side. Several Governments then were stormed and destroyed. The English were not able to stop the activities of the rebels in mufassil areas, though Patna remained quiet. The struggle of 1857, however, ultimately failed and the English rule over the country continued for another ninety years. The district of Patna played a very vital role in the struggle for country's freedom.

NATURAL DIVISIONS

The district can be divided into two natural divisions comprising : (i) a narrow strip of somewhat high land about 8 km in width along the southern bank of the Ganges having vary fertile soil, and (ii) alluvial fertile plains in the remaining portions.

After creation of the new district of Nalanda (which contains the Rajgir hills) the territory of the present district of Patna does not contain any hilly region. It has an entirely alluvial and flat region.

The Ganges and the Sone are the two major rivers of the district. The next important river of the district is the Punpun. The greater part of the district is watered by streams which decend from the Chhotanagpur plateau to join the Ganges.

The Ganges, which runs all among the northern boundary of the district, separates it from Saran, Tirhut and Darbhangha divisions. It is the largest river of the district. It enters the district at its confluence with the Sone and flows for 148 kms, it in the eastern direction up to Dumara. The Gandak joins the Ganges just opposite Patna. The river is so wide in this region that Patna has sometimes been likened to a part of the Ganges which is, of course, navigable throughout the year.

The Sone, rising in the Maikal range near Amar Kantak in the Deccan plateau (which incidentally is also the source of another greats river in India, the Narmada) and after traversing some 624 kms touches the district of Patna at Mahabalipur from where it flows in northerly direction for 65 km until it joins the Ganges. The river constitutes a natural boundary between the district of Patna and Bhojpur. It has along rail-cum-road bridge at Koilwar. The river receives no tributaries in the district and is normally constituted of a narrow stream of water. In the dry season, the river is a wide stretch of drifting sand with landlocked pools and narrow serpentines streams of water. During the rains, however, the river receives washings from the uplands in its earlier stages and generally overflows its banks, including the surrounding area. The lead of the Sone, constitutes an important source of sand for house building.

The Punpun enters the district from the south and flows the north-easterly direction. It crosses the Patna-Gaya railways line near Punpun railway station and joins the Ganges near Fatwah after flowing for 85 km, through the district. It is joined by the Morhar and the Dardha before it meets the Ganges.

CLIMATIC CONDITIONS

The district of Patna has an extreme type of climate. It is very hot in summer and cold in winter. The summer commences in April. The month of May and the first half of June are the hottest. During this period, a hot westerly wind which develops into a heat wave (100) blows. High temperature and low humidity make the summer really oppressive. The easterly wind appears in the latter half of June bringing rains and a slight relief from summer. The rainy season lasts upto September. The mercury begins to fall from October and, but December and January are the really cold months.

During the last decade 1991-2000, the highest temperature of 46°C was recorded in 1998 in the month of June. Generally, the maximum temperature in the district varies between 45–46°C. The average rainfall is the heaviest generally in the month of August in which the number of rainy days varies from 12 to 16 and the actual rainfall from 266 mm to 368 mm. The month of October and November are quite pleasant, as there is neither too much heat nor too much cold.

FLORA AND FAUNA

The land in the district is too fertile to be left for wild growth. The district is devoid of any forest wealth of consequence. The alluvial tract of land yield rice, sugar-cane and other food grains. The area under cultivation is studded with mango orchards and bamboo clumps. In the fields adjoining the Ganges weeds such as ammannia, utricularia, hygrophyte and sesbania grow. But Palmyra and date palm and mango orchards are found near habilitations. Dry shrub jungles are sometimes seen in the villages away from the rivers. Trees commonly met with arbel, neem, siris, jack fruit and the red cotton tree.

Leopard, hyena, jackal, fox and wild cat are some of the carnivore found in the district, but their number is very small.

LAND USE PATTERN

The district may be divided into three broadly marked tracts comprised within the Patna Sadar, Patna City, Barh, Danapur, Masaurhi and Paliganj subdivisions. These areas are: (i) the diara lands along the river Ganges, (ii) a long narrow strip of high land along the banks of the Ganges, and (iii) a broad belt of low-lying country south of the above upland strip.

The district of Patna is an extensively cultivated district in the state of Bihar. The diara lands are most fertile in the district. They grow bhadai (early kharif) crops before the river rise and rabi crop in the cold weather, both yielding excellent harvests.

Rice is the main crop of the district. It accounts for more than one-third of the gross area sown. Other important food-grains grown are maize, pulse and wheat. Non-food crops consist mostly of oil-seeds. Cash crop such as vegetables, water-melons etc. are also grown in diara belt.

The soil found in the district are mainly of four kinds, viz. (i) kewal, (ii) doras, (iii) balsundari, and (iv) rehra. The kewal soil consists of hard clay and is suitable for rabi cultivation also. The Mokamah tal consists mainly of this soil. As the tal is under water most of the time, only rabi crops are grown in it. The doras soil is formed of clay and sand mixed in almost equal proportions on uplands near the home steed it is used for growing potatoes and vegetables. In fields, it yields both rice and rabi crops. Balsundari soil has a greater proportion of sand than clay in it. It produces rabi crops and spices. Rehra soil contain carbonate of sands in it and is not suitable for cultivation except where the soda contents is very low.

IRRIGATIONAL FACILITIES

Patna is one of the few districts of state which have a network of irrigation canals since the British days. Even so, after independence in 1947, considerable attention has been paid to the provision of irrigational facilities. Besides the various irrigational projects executed in the district, tube-wells under the Patna-Barh-Ekangarsarai-Bihta emergency river pump and technical co-operation administration schemes were installed in the district and some pynes were also renovated.

MINES AND MINERALS

The geological formation of the entire district is alluvial built-up with the alluvium brought down by the Ganges and deposited by it and its tributaries. No mineral of any kind is found in the district.

FISHERY

The extensive bed of the river Ganges in Patna and other places in the district offers one of the best fishing grounds. The spawn of rehu, kaws and hilsa is also collected from the river Ganges. It is in great demand in other parts of Bihar and West Bengal. It is stocked in specially prepared nursery tanks. It develops to fry and fingerling stages within a fortnight, and then it is ready for stocking in tanks.

Fishing practically begin in October and the peak season is December, January and February, when a variety of fish can be seen in the fish market. The Fisheries Development Schemes of the district are managed by the District Fisheries Office located in Patna under the administrative control of the Director of Fisheries, Government of Bihar.

INDUSTRIALIZATION

Patna had been famous in the part for the excellence of its handicrafts which have commended respect of foreign markets on account of their finish, generally attributable to master craftsman who have existed their skill from, generation to generation besides potters, carpenters, blacksmiths, coppersmiths and goldsmiths have been carrying on their traditional occupation both in rural as well as urban areas, to earn their living. However, under the impact of modern economy, these classes are fast disintegrating.

Among the large industrial establishments of the district are Shri Lakshmi Cold Storage Ltd., Patna city; Pradip Lamp Works, Patna city; South Bihar Sugar Mill Ltd., Bihta; Bata Shoe Co. Ltd., Digha Ghat and Mokamah. The Bihar Cotton Mills, Phulwarisharif; Shri Baidyanath Ayurvedic Bhawan Ltd., Patna, Hidustan Manufacturing and Industrial Corporation Ltd., Phulwarisharif; Britannia Engineering Co. Ltd., Mokamah and Medòned and Co. (Distillery) Hathidah.

LIVESTOCK

Livestock plays an important role in the predominantly agricultural economy of the district. Though the cattle of the local breed has generally been of medicore quality, in the last two decades the quality has improved considerably due to the efforts of Government and the response of the farmers. The Bankipur breed of cattle, more commonly known as 'Taylor breed' is still found in the district. The Brahmani bulls have been replaced by the Tharparkar bulls. For the improvement of breed, key village schemes and artificial insemination centre have been started in the district. The cows and bullocks of Shahabad breed are also found in the district and are very suitable. These cows are good milch-cattle and the bullocks are used draught animals and for ploughing. This breed is usually found in villages on the bank of river Ganges. Buffaloes are also utilized for plough, but main value is for milk which they yield in large quantity.

The number of veterinary hospitals, dispensaries and artificial insemination centres has increased considerably over the decades. This has resulted in decline in the incidence of cattle mortality. The district has got a veterinary college located at Phulwarisharif in Patna.

The Government Poultry Farm at Patna has become very popular and its eggs are in greats demand in the city. The city is also served by a dairy plant known as the Patna Dairy Project, which is being managed by the National Dairy Development Board at present.

COMMUNICATIONS

The district of Patna is well-served by a network of roads. National Highway No. 31 passes through Danapur, Patna and Patna City. While one branch goes to Barauni via Barh, another proceeds to Nawada via Bihar. All the sub-divisional headquarters of the district (except the newly created sub-division of Masaurhi) are situated on this National Highway which provides the road link between North and South Bihar. The number of metalled and black-topped roads has considerably increased over the decades. Bridges, culverts and causeways have been constructed on the important roads.

The main line of the Eastern Railway passes through the entire length of the district running parallel to the Ganges. There are three railway lines running across the district from north to south, viz., the Patna-Gaya Branch link, the Fatwah-Islampur Light Railway and the Bakhtiarpur-Rajgir Branch line. Except the Light Railway, the other two are branches of the Eastern Railway. With the opening of the famous Patna-Hazipur Bridge (Mahatma Gandhi Setu), the ferry service connecting the capital with the North-Eastern Railway system has ceased to function.

The Ganges is navigable throughout the year and there is considerable boat traffic for transporting cargo. The smaller river, e.g., Punpun and Dardha become navigable only during the rains when they are use for transporting agricultural produce to the grain market at Fatwah.

Patna is connected by air to Kolkata and New Delhi and a few other places by daily flights. There is an aerodrome near Phulwarisharif and another at Bihta.

TRADE AND COMMERCE

Patna town in the district of Patna occupies a place of considerable importance as a commercial centre. Its central position at the junction of three great rivers, viz., the Sone, the Gaṇdak and the Ganges gives it an additional advantage for the purpose of transport by river. The city proper comprises the large business quarters such as Marufganj, Mansurganj, the Chauk with Mirchaiganj, Maharajganj and other petty bazars. Marufganj is by far the most important of any of the marts in the city. Besides the city of Patna, other important trade centres in the district are Danapur, Barh, Mokama, Fatwah and Masaurhi.

In Patna district, trade consists mainly of export pulses, dry chillies, castor seed, milk products and vegetables and import of cotton textile, iron and steel products, cement, coal and consumer goods.

ELECTRICITY AND POWER

The district receives its entire power supply from the Barauni Thermal Power Station, the Patratu Thermal Power Station and Patna electricity supply undertaking.

All the 12 towns of Patna district have electricity. In rural areas also, the pace of electrification has been comparatively fast and in terms of proportion Patna is, better provided than many other districts of the state. Out of 1,294 inhabited villages in the district 986 villages accounting for 76.20 per cent have been electrified so far. The Government is paying full attention to provide electricity to villages under the Rural Electrification Scheme. The main consumption of electricity in the rural areas is for agricultural purposes.

SOCIAL AND CULTURAL EVENTS AND NATURAL AND ADMINISTRATIVE DEVELOPMENT

Except the flood caused by the river Sone in the year 1975, which had inundated the entire town of Patna, no other natural calamity has occurred in the district during the last decade.

After creation of Nalanda district, Patna district was left with only 16 development blocks-cum-anchals viz., Patna rural, Fatwah, Phulwarisharif, Punpun, Dhanaura, Masaurhi, Danapur-cum-Khagaul, Naubatpur, Paliganj, Bikram, Bihta, Maner, Barh, Bakhtiarpur, Pandarak and Mokameh. At present, district of Patna has 24 community development blocks-cum anchals viz., Maner, Danapur-cum-Khagaul, Patna Rural (a), Patna Rural (b), Sampatchak, Phulwarisharif, Bihta, Naubatpur, Bikram, Dulhin Bazar, Paliganj, Masaurhi, Dhanarua, Punpun, Fatwah, Daniawan, Khusrupur, Bakhtiyarpur, Athmalgola, Belchi, Barh, Pandarak, Ghoswari, Makanph. Fairs and festivals are held regularly in the district. Sombari mela is held in the immediate vicinity of the Patna civil court building on each Monday in the month of Shravana (July-August). The main articles put up for sale during this fair are furniture, utensils and plants of fruits and flowers.

PLACES OF RELIGIONS, HISTORICAL AND ARCHAEOLOGICAL IMPORTANT IN VILLAGE AND PLACES OF TOURIST INTEREST IN THE TOWNS OF THE DISTRICT

1. **Baikatpur :** It is a village in Fatwah block situated on the southern bank of the Ganga. It is noted for its Shiva temple said to have been built by Raja Man Singh the famous General of Akbar's army. Weekly fairs are held on every Monday in the month of Shravana (July-August) and an annual fair on the occasion of Shivaratri.
2. **Varanasi :** The village lies on the southern bank of the Ganga about 3 km north of Barh railway station. It is noted for its old temple of Umanath. A large annual fair is held on the occasion of Shivaratri.

3. **Bharatpura :** The village is situated 14 km south of Bikram on the Bihta-Pali road. It is noted for its old library which has about 2500 rare and old books, manuscripts and tamrapatras (copper plates).
4. **Bihta :** The village lies on the main line of the Eastern Railway about 25 km west of Patna. It is the headquarters of the block bearing the same name and has a sugar mill and a large rice market. A large annual fairs is held on the occasion of Shivaratri.
5. **Bijapur :** It is a village situated about 14 km east of Taregna railway station. It is famous for its Kanhaiya-astern built in the beginning of the 19th century.
6. **Bir-Oiara :** The village is situated about 10 km east of Nadwan railway station. It is noted for its Shiva temple containing four feet high image. Large fairs are held here on the occasion of Shivaratri and Basant Panchmi.
7. **Goraila :** The village is situated 5 km south of the block headquarter at Naubatpur. It is famous for the tomb of the father of Makhdum Saheb of Biharsharif. It is a place of pilgrimage for Muhammadans.
8. **Naubatpur :** The village is the headquarters of the block bearing the same name. It has an Arya Samaj Temple built in the beginning of this century.
9. **Nawada :** A village situated about 6 km north-east Barh railway station. It contains an old tomb of Muslim saint which is held in reverence not only by the Muslims but also the Hindus.
10. **Nisarpura :** It is a village situated on the bank of river Punpun about 1.5 km south of the block headquarter at Naubatpur. It is noted for its large fairs held on the occasion of Makar Sankranti and Bisua.
11. **Pakri :** The village situated on the river Punpun, is the headquarter of Punpun block. A large number of Hindu Pilgrims congregate here during pitripaksh, the second fortnight of Bhadrapad (September-October) to offer oblation to their deceased ancestors.
12. **Seonar :** The village is situated about 1.5 km west Mokameh. It is famous for its temple of Nilkant-Mahadeo. An annual fair is held on the occasion of Shivaratri.

13. The village lies about 13 km south of Bikram on the Bihta-Pali road. It is famous for its temple of Sun-God. An annual fair is held on the occasion of chhat in Kartik every year.

14. Patna : Patna is the largest town and headquarters of Patna district, Patna division and Bihar state. It lies on the main line of the Eastern Railway and is well connected by road. It is mainly an administrative and educational centre. It has, however, a few ancient sacred places as also places of tourist interest, the details of which are indicated below:

(i) The temple of Bari and Chhoti Patan Devi for the Hindus.

(ii) The mausoleum and Patsher-ki-Masjid at Sultanganj for Muslims.

(iii) Harmandir and Gurudwara in Patna City for Sikhs.

(iv) Padri-ki-Haveli (a Roman Catholic Church built in the 18th century) for the Christians.

(v) *Martyr's Memorial :* It is a cart in bronze and mounted on a pedestal and is installed on the eastern gate of the old Secretariat as a solemn tribute to the seven students who became martyrs in police firing on 9th August 1942 in their attempt to hoist the national flag on the Secretariat building.

(vi) *Sadaquat Ashram :* It is situated in Digha, on Patna-Danapur road and in the pre-in-dependence days guided the freedom movement in Bihar. It is associated with the memories of Mahatma Gandhi, Dr. Rajendra Prasad, Maulana Mazharul Haque and other leaders.

(vii) *Patna Museum :* It is public museum, situated on Buddha Marg and possesses some of other rare exhibits.

(viii) *Golghar :* This historic monument is a unique piece of architecture. It was originally built as a granary and is now used as a Government grain godown.

(ix) *Gandhi Museum :* It is located on Ashok Rajpath at the north-western corner Gandhi Maidan and contains pictorial and other records showing the association of Mahatma Gandhi with Bihar.

(x) *Kumhrar :* The excavation sites of Kumhrar are situated on Patna by pass road, off Gulzarbagh Railway Station.

Among the exhibits, the Mauryan monolithic stone pillar is note worthy.

15. **Phulwarisharif :** Phulwarisharif town is situated on Patna-Khagaul road and is the headquarters of the block bearing the same name. It is an important place for the Muslims as it contains an old Khankah where the hair of Prophet Mohammad as preserved. Every year on the occasion of Fateh-Duaz-Dahum (the birthday of prophet) a large fair is held. It attracts an all Indian gathering. Phulwarisharif also has an old mosque built of red stone and known as Sangi-Masjid, believed to have been built by Emperor Humayun in 1533 A.D.

16. **Maner :** The town is situated about 27 km west of Patna on Patna-Arrah road and is the headquarters of the block bearing the same name. The village derives its name from King Maniar, the remains of whose fortress still exist. It is traditionally believed that the marriage party of Lord Rama halted at Maner both on the outward and inward journeys from Ayodhya to Janakpur. The village has a magnificent tomb of the Muslim saint Makhdum Saheb, said to have been constructed by Emperor Jehangir in 1660 A.D.

The Table 1 shows an overall picture of some important facts of Patna district. The table reveals, the distribution of total population in respect of Rural-urban males and females population, area, density of population, IMR, literacy rate, child population, highest and lowest sex ratio in the block, highest and lowest female literacy rate in the block etc. Further, the table demonstrates the administrative name of the district is Patna. There are six sub-divisions, 24 C.D. blocks, 12 towns, 1419 revenue villages and 340 panchayats. The area of the district is 3202.0 sq. km., density of population is 1471 per sq. km. and infant mortality rate is 80. The total population of the district is 4709851 followed by 2514949 males and 2194902 females. Male literacy rate of district Patna is 73.81% while female literacy rate is 52.17%.

The Table 2 demonstrates over all picture of block-wise population (male, female and total) of Patna district. The district belongs to 4709851 persons followed by 2514949 males and 2194902 females. Patna Rural (a) block has the highest population (i.e. 1076128 persons) followed 590047 males and 486081 females, while Belchhi block has the lowest population (i.e. 48467 persons) followed by 25406 males and 23061 females.

Table 1
Patna: Some Important Facts (Census - 2001)

1.	Administrative Name		:	Patna	
2.	No. of Sub-divisions		:	06	
3.	No. of C.D. Blocks		:	24	
4.	No. of Towns		:	12	
5.	No. of Revenue villages		:	1419	
6.	No. of Panchayats		:	340	
7.	Area in (km./sq.)		:	3202.0	
8.	Total Population :				
		Male		*Female*	Total
	Rural	1449850		1291077	2740927
	Urban	1065099		903825	1968924
	Total	2514949		2194902	4709851
9.	Sex ratio :	*Rural*		*Urban*	*Total*
	(Per 1000 male)	890		849	873
10.	Density of population (per sq. Km.): 1471				
11.	Infant Mortality Rate : 80				
12.	Population growth during 1991-2001 : 1086626 (30.17%)				
13.		*Male*		*Female*	*Total*
	(i) Literacy :	1554868		943056	2497924
	(ii) Literacy rate :	73.81		52.17	63.82
14.	Child population in the age-group 0-6 :				
		Male		*Female*	*Total*
	Rural	268820		260681	529501
	Urban	139633		126708	266341
	Total	408453		387389	795842
15.	CD Block having highest sex ratio : Bikram – 924				
	CD Block having lowest sex ratio : Patna Rural (a) – 824				
16.	CD Block having highest literacy rate : Patna Rural (a) - 84.76				
	CD Block having lowest literacy rate : Ghoswari - 37.81				
17.	CD Block having highest female literacy rate : Patna Rural (a) - 78.54				
	CD Block having lowest female literacy rate : Ghoswari - 21.71				

The Table 3 shows an overall picture of total workers, main workers and non-workers in respect of male and female workers. The total population is divided into total workers and non-workers. The total workers are divided into main workers & marginal workers. Further, the table reveals that the total workers (main + marginal) is sub-divided into cultivators, agricultural labourers, workers in household industry and other workers. Among them, the agricultural labourers (i.e., 473292) are the largest group, which defines predominant agrarian base in Patna.

Table 2
Block wise Distribution of Population (Census - 2001)

Sl. No.	*Name of the C.D. Block*	*Population*		
		Male	*Female*	*Total*
1.	Maner	113374	94640	208014
2.	Danapur-cum-Khagaul	171414	148739	320153
3.	Patna Rural (a)	590047	486081	1076128
4.	Patna Rural (b)	230859	202345	433204
5.	Sampatchak	35851	32801	68652
6.	Phulwarisharif	100341	89919	190260
7.	Bihta	109242	98100	207342
8.	Naubatpur	89601	80861	170462
9.	Bikram	72273	66758	139031
10.	Dulhin Bazar	53843	49554	103397
11.	Paliganj	107744	98433	206177
12.	Masaurhi	106863	98047	204910
13.	Dhanarua	91252	883390	174642
14.	Punpun	61598	55540	1117138
15.	Fatwah	82072	71987	154059
16.	Daniawan	31768	28128	59896
17.	Khusrupur	42612	37824	80436
18.	Bakhtiarpur	92399	79806	172205
19.	Athmalgola	35249	30665	65914
20.	Belchhi	25406	23061	48467
21.	Barh	86707	75671	162378
22.	Pandarak	64870	58580	123450
23.	Ghoswari	30286	26026	56312
24.	Mokameh	89278	77946	167224
	Total	2514949	2194902	4709851

Table 3
Distribution of Workers and Non-workers of Patna district
(Census- 2001)

			Males	*Females*	*Total*
1.	Total Population :		2514949	2194902	4709851
	(i)	Total workers	1138866	289831	1428697
		(a) Main workers	1004183	162554	1166737
		(b) Marginal workers	134683	127277	261960
	(ii)	Non-workers	1376083	1905071	3281154
2.	Total workers :				
	(i)	Cultivators	265983	48986	314969
	(ii)	Agricultural labourers	305235	168057	473292
	(iii)	Workers in household industry	38143	15696	53839
	(iv)	Other workers	529505	57092	586597

REFERENCES & ACKNOWLEDGMENT

1. Economic Intelligence Service, Profile of districts, CMIE, Mumbai.
2. District Census Handbook, Patna district, 1981, Series–4, Bihar.
3. Patna District Gazetteer, N. Kumar, Gazetteer Branch, Revenue Department, 1970.
4. Census 2001.

15

BONDED LABOUR IN PATNA

This chapter reflects about the overall status of freed bonded labourers of Patna district. In view of this, the district administration provided the list of 86 freed bonded labourers.

Table 1
Freed Bonded Labourers in Patna district

Sl. No.	*Name of the Block*	*Freed Bonded Labourers*		*Ranking*
		Number	*Per cent*	
1.	Barh	06	6.98	3
2.	Bihta	01	1.16	5
3.	Fatwah	36	41.86	2
4.	Naubatpur	02	2.33	
5.	Phulwarisharif	41	47.67	1
	Total	86	100.00	

The above table demonstrates the complete picture of identified and rehabilitated bonded labourers in the different blocks of district. The district contains 24 C.D. blocks. The administration over with regular campaigns of identification of bonded labourers, it has identified only 86 bonded labourers FBLs in the respective 5 C.D. blocks. Phulwarisharif block has the highest number of FBLs (41), rehabilitated by the district administration.

The research team visited all identified freed bonded labourers household on the address provided by the district administration. The above table shows the present position of the freed bonded labourers in the district.

Table 2
Block and Village-wise Distribution of FBLs in the Patna district

Sl. No.	Block	Village	No. of FBLs			Total
			Living	Migrated	Died	
1.	Barh	Malahi	02	-	-	02
		Husainganj	-	-	01	01
		Salarpur	03	-	-	03
2.	Bihta	Painal	01	-	-	01
3.	Fatwah	Baruna	17	01	06	24
		Bhuski	07	-	03	10
		Deolalpur	01	-	-	01
		Adalpur	01	-	-	01
4.	Naubatpur	Khajoori	02	-	-	02
5.	Phulwarisharif	Babhanpura	07	-	03	10
		Mahangupur	08	01	07	16
		Chakbairiya	01	-	-	01
		Manoharpur	03	01	-	04
		Udaini	04	-	01	05
		Hasanpur	05	-	-	05
		Total	62	03	21	86

The Fatwah block is in the 2nd position with 36 FBLs. Barh block is in the 3rd position, where 6 FBLs were rehabilitated. Another block Naubatpur is in the 4th position with 2 FBLs. The Bhita block is in the 5th position with one FBL. Thus, the total number of bonded labourers identified and freed, in the district was 86. No bonded labourers have been identified in the district, from 1994 till date.

The district administration holds regular campaigns for identifying bonded labourers. The last survey for the identification of the bonded labourers was done in the year 2002-03. National Human Rights Commission has been strongly advocating that the campaigning for generation of awareness against bonded labour system is essential for eradication of this evil system. The district administration has shown consistency in holding awareness campaigns.

Out of 86 FBLs, the team discovered that 21 FBLs have died. Many died on account of old age and some due to chronic illness.

The break up for died FBLs are 33 follows:

(a) Barh block	(i) Husainganj village	- 01
(b) Fatwah block	(ii) Baruna village	- 06
	(iii) Bhuski village	- 03
(c) Phulwarisharif block	(i) Babhanpura village	- 03
	(ii) Mahangupur village	- 07
	(iii) Udaini village	- 01

All died after being freed and rehabilitated.

It was found that 03 have migrated and their neighbours had little or no clue about there present whereabouts. The major reason given by the neighbours was that they have migrated to look for a better place to earn and live.

The break up for migrant FBLs are as follows:

(a) Fatwah block	(i) Baruna village	- 01
(b) Phulwarisharif block	(i) Mahangupur village	- 01
	(ii) Manoharpur village	- 01

This latest information has been passed to the district administration and the social security department office by the ANSISS research team. The team met the existing 62 FBLs.

Table 3
Distribution of FBLs by their Causes for Bonded Labour

Cause	*No. of FBLs*	*Per cent*
Low socio-economic status in the society	15	24.19
Unemployment	11	17.74
Poverty	26	41.94
On the traditional way	05	8.06
Indebtedness	58	93.55

Note: The figures are non-additive. It is multiple answer based.

One of the main objectives of the study was to find out the reason for becoming bonded labour in Patna district. It can be observed from the above table that the most significant answer was indebtedness 93.55 per cent, followed by the poverty 41.94 per cent. The other major cause was attributed to the low socio-economic status in the society 24.19 per cent, followed by the unemployment 17.74 per cent and on the traditional way 8.06 per cent.

In respect of causes of bonded labour, there was multiple answers given by the FBLs but the problem indebtedness, poverty, low socio-economic status in the society and unemployment was most dominant causes for falling into vicious bonded labour trap. It is classic example of absolute deprivation praxis in the social and economic structure. The feudal environment and graded caste hierarchy also played an important role in bringing the landless and the helpless in the exploitative practices of the bonded labour system where the dominant landlords lured them bondage.

Table 4
Identification Period of FBLs

Identification Period	*No. of FBLs*	*Per cent*
1981-82	35	40.70
1984-85	10	11.63
1986-87	22	25.58
1991-92	19	22.09

The above table shows about the identification period of freed bonded labourers. 35 (40.70%) FBLs were identified during the year 1981-82, while 10 (11.63%) FBLs were identified during the year 1984-85. 22 (25.58%) FBLs were identified during the year 1986-87 and 19 (22.09%) of FBLs were identified during the year 1991-92.

Table 5
Working Place of FBLs before Release

Statement	*No. of FBLs*	*Per cent*
Within the same village	45	72.58
Outside the village but within the block	17	27.42
Outside the block but within the district	-	0.0
Outside the district but within state	-	0.0
Outside the State	-	0.0
Total	62	100. 00

The office of Patna Social Security, Government of Bihar and Patna district officials reported that no bonded labour has been identified after 1992-93 till date (June, 2004), though surveys are held regularly.

Another major objective of the study was to find out where the FBLs were bonded labour before their release and rehabilitation. It was important to find that the majority of FBLs (72.58%) reported that they worked in the same village during the bonded labour period, where they lived. This affirms the feudal social environment where these FBLs worked. The rest 27.42% FBLs reported that they worked outside the village but within the block. All FBLs identified and released were agricultural labourers.

It is suggested that the area of brick-kilns may be subjected to intense verification, because it is a potential area for indebted bondage cases. It is important to point out here that there are many brick-kilns near the bank of the river Ganges in the district. The district administration must cover this area for identification.

Table 6
Distribution of FBLs Working Period as Bonded Labour

Working Period	*No. of FBLs*	*Per cent*
Up to 5 years	11	17.74
6 -10 years	19	30.65
11- 15 years	18	29.03
16 - 20 years	08	12.90
21 years and above	06	09.68
Total	62	100.00

The above table reveals that out of 62, 32 (51.61%) FBLs worked as bonded labour for 11 years and above, while 30.65% FBLs reported that they had worked as bonded labour for 6 to 10 years. About 17.74% FBLs worked between 1 to 5 years. It reveals that the majority was in chain of subjugation and bondage for over a decade and spent their prime years in servitude.

16

FREED BONDED LABOUR : SOCIAL LIFE

The social status of an individual has been affected and even determined by the nature of the occupation from which he derives his livelihood. Certain occupations are linked to the rank of graded social hierarchical life in which he is born. He follows traditional occupation to make a livelihood. The social situation in the village remains embedded with traditional pattern of hierarchical occupation. It has exercised, and still exercises a marked influence on the Hindu social system in the villages. The whole social life spectrum is build around his caste status. The majority of the FBLs in Patna belonged to Scheduled Caste Category (93.55%) and the rest belonged to OBC category (6.45%).

Before describing the data, it would be essential to note these freed bonded labourers are from ritually deprived strata of society and isolated in graded social hierarchy of unequal and extremely backward community of peasant village society. The continuity of sociologically disadvantaged position combines with economic deprivation. Their backwardness reflected not only their ascribed position but also from their achieved position. The general living condition of FBLs and quality of life was found at the lowest ebb of any social-economic scale. It was also found during evaluation study that as a whole, this community (FBLs) still suffers from social disabilities and economic feebleness. The mainstreaming in the local social situation was not visible and they were apparently peripheral and insignificant. The freedom from yoke of bondage had made them free, but liberty was socially limited.

The following table gives details about the social life of freed bonded labourers.

Table 1
Age-wise Distribution of Freed Bonded Labourers

Sl. No.	*Age Group (yrs.)*	*Number*	*Per cent*
1.	31-40	03	4.84
2.	41-50	19	30.65
3.	51-60	28	45.16
4.	61-70	08	12.90
5.	71 and above	04	6.45
	Total	62	100.00

The pattern of age distribution among freed bonded labourers is presented in this table. It is evident from the Table 1 that the freed bonded labourers belong to different age groups ranging from 31 to 71 and above. They are composite mix of young, middle age as well as old age group.

It is found from the above table that the highest percentage of the respondents (45.16%) belongs to age group of 51-60 years.

The second highest percentage of respondents (30.65%) belongs to the age group of 41-50 years.

The third highest percentage of the respondents (12.90%) belongs to the age group of 61-70 years. This group was small but provided deep insight into the bondage syndrome.

The fourth highest percentage of respondents (6.45%) belongs to 71 and above age groups. They are old and not in a position to work hard.

And the last percentage of freed bonded labourer belongs to 31-40 years having (4.84%). These age groups are young and hard working.

Table 2
Sex-wise Distribution of Freed Bonded Labourers

Sex	*Number*	*Per cent*
Male	62	100.00
Female	-	0.00
Total	62	100.00

The table shows the distribution of male and female freed bonded labourers in the district. It is evident from the table that there are no female freed bonded labour in the district because the only female freed bonded labour, Smt. Durgabati Devi, w/o Late Ram Chandra Ram of village-Mahangupur, block Phulwarisharif, who was identified during 1984-85, had died. Thus, all the respondent of district are male freed bonded labourer.

Table 3
Family size-wise Distribution of Freed Bonded Labourers

Family Size	*No. of FBLs*	*Per cent*
Upto - 5	14	22.58
6 - 10	33	53.23
11 - 15	14	22.58
16 & above	01	01.61
Total	62	100.00

The above table shows that the majority of FBLs (53.23%) had family size of 6-10 members, whereas the category of 11-15 members and upto 5 members family size belongs to same percentage (22.58%). Only one FBL's family belongs to 16 and above members. Thus, the family size of FBLs were found large in the district because they are related to the village life, where large and joint family are common due to myth of more hands.

Table 4
Age and Sex wise Distribution of Family Members of Freed Bonded Labourers

Age Group	*Male*		*Female*		*Total*	
	No.	*%*	*No.*	*%*	*No.*	*%*
0-5	22	4.36	19	3.77	41	8.13
6-14	109	21.63	89	17.66	198	39.29
15-60	134	26.59	120	23.81	254	50.40
61 +	07	1.39	04	0.79	11	2.18
Total	272	53.97	232	46.03	504	100.00

The age pattern emerging from the table shows that the freed bonded labourers families belongs to different age groups. They are up to 0 to 5 years, 6-14 years, 15-60 years and 61 and above. The majority of FBLs (50.40%) were found in the age group of 15-60 years, which had 26.59% males and 23.81% females.

The next age group of 6-14 years with 39.29% constitutes the second largest group having 21.63% males and 17.66 females.

Another age group of 0-5 years with 8.3% constitutes the third largest group with 4.36% males and 3.77% females.

1.39% males and 0.79% females were found in 11 FBLs families (2.18%) in the fourth age group size of 61 and above.

Thus, the table indicates that majority of FBLs families were found in the age group of 15-60 years and this age group is more hard working and more earning group.

Table 5
Distribution of Freed Bonded Labourers by Marital Status

Marital Status	*No. of FBLs*	*Per cent*
Married	58	93.55
Unmarried	-	0.00
Widower	04	06.45
Total	62	100.00

In the above table, it is observed that a high (93.55) percentage were married and only (6.45%) of respondents were found widower. No FBLs were found unmarried. It appears that majority are strong believers of family life. The role of the state is to give them secure work, food and health environment to protect their families.

Table 6
Caste Composition of the Freed Bonded Labourers

Caste	*Number*	*Per cent*
Scheduled caste	58	93.55
Schedule tribe	-	0.0
Backward	04	06.45
General	-	0.00
Total	62	100.00

The Table 6 indicates the caste structure of freed bonded labourers in Patna district. The majority of FBLs (93.55%) belongs to scheduled caste (Chamar, Mushar and Dusadh) community while 6.45% of FBLs belongs to backward caste (Koiri, Mallah and Kahar) category. None of the FBLs were found in the category of general and scheduled tribe. It is significant and true to the history of debt bondage. It fits the absolute deprivation paradigm where ritually low status in graded hierarchical society co-exists with those below the poverty line status. The social and economic levels are uniformly steeped in the bottom line of an agrarian semi-feudal society.

Table 7
Neighbours of Freed Bonded Labourer

Sl. No.	*Statement*	*No. of FBLs*	*Per cent*
1.	Was your neighbour Freed Bonded Labour?		
	(i) Yes	58	93.55
	(ii) No	04	6.45
2.	If Yes, how many ?		
	(i) upto 5	19	30.65
	(ii) 6-10	22	35.48
	(iii) 11 and above	17	27.42

Above given table shows that majority of FBLs (93.55) were found in cluster, while 6.45% of FBLs were not found in cluster It indicates that the district administration identified & rehabilitated bonded labourer in cluster.

Further, the table demonstrate that 35.48% FBLs had a neighbour size of 6-10 FBLs members while 30.65% FBLs had upto 5 members of FBLs in the neighbourhood. 27.42% of FBLs had 11 and above members of FBLs in the neighbourhood. The social cohesion was among the FBLs fraternity and felt psychologically more as an unit due to their common background.

The response obtained in the above table from freed bonded labourers, reflects the availability of governmental infrastructure in FBLs village and their tolas.

The accessibility of the governmental facilities as basic civic support system for the citizens are an important work for assessing the reach and welfare measures taken to ameliorate the common mens predicament, particularly in the rural and backward areas. In the present table, the availability of governmental infra-structure facilities for FBLs represents a mixed scenario.

The table reveals that all types of the infra-structural facilities are not available in the FBLs village/tolas of the district, rather. It is insufficient for the FBLs families in several areas. Some are fortunate to enjoy the facilities were as others are deprived of the basic facilities. There is no uniformity in the availability of these government conveniences. The table also demonstrate that missed opportunity by the government agencies in reaching out uniformly to all FBLs families in their neighbourhood. The table also indicate that (37.10%) can utilize the post office facilities, whereas (79.03%) can use the public distribution centre (fair price shop/ration). The health situation is dismal with only (38.71%) FBLs having access to the health centres. 70.97% of FBLs can utilize the electricity connection. Bank facility is not found in the FBLs village.

Table 8
Availability of Government Infra-structure Facilities in FBLs Villages/Tolas

Sl. No.	*Government Facilities*	*No. of FBLs*	*Per cent*
1.	Post Office	23	37.10
2.	PDS	49	79.03
3.	Health Centre	-	38.71
4.	Electricity	44	70.97
5.	Bank	-	0.00
6.	Road Facilities		
	(i) Kachcha	24	38.71
	(ii) Pucca	30	48.39
	(iii) Mixed	08	12.90
	(iv) No facility	-	0.00

The next important issue is transportation by road facilities. The road facilities were accessible for 3871% in connecting by kachcha road, (4839%) connecting pucca road and only (12.90%) use the mixed road facilities. The FBLs also reported that the difficulties in rainy seasons. The administration can increase the rural connectivity by implementing Pradhan Mantri Gramin Sadak Yojana on priority for FBL clusters and tolas. The FBL families can also be employed during the road construction work which can provide them limited livelihood.

The infra-structure support to FBL clusters requires a holistic approach where all aspects can be provided to lessen their problem. It needs humanistic outreaching and administrative will to uplift their social life.

17

FREED BONDED LABOUR : ECONOMIC LIFE

In the village level development, the Central Government and State Government schemes are rays of hope for employment like Swarn Jayanti Rojgar Yojana and other schemes where there are number of work like digging and carrying of soils, spreading the soil on road, brick work in the village lane etc. The work is given to the weaker section of the society but it was observed that little or no development have been taken up in FBL villages. Further, it was observed that the development works were not taken up in their village for last several years.

The FBL and their families work either in the agriculture field or in the non agriculture works like brick-kiln, building construction, road construction, Rickshaw/Thela pulling, digging and carrying of soils etc. The older people helps in the collection of grass, rearing the cattle, collection of firewood and looking after the children. They also help in domestic activities.

It was seen that the bonded labourers works 8 to 10 hours in a day. The work is generally available in the village for five to six months during agriculture season only. Work is not available round the year in agriculture sector. There is no employment guarantee for work in all seasons.

Freed bonded labourers work is confined to sowing, harvesting and winnowing. The freed bonded labourers work in the villages from 8 A.M. to 6 P.M. with some food at 1 P.M. to 3 P.M. with some breakfast. Generally, they get Rs. 35 to Rs. 70 as daily wage in the agriculture and non-agriculture work. They get highest wage in the busy season, particularly in the rainy season, in the agricultural area. In the non-agricultural area, they get maximum wage, when they go to work in neighbouring town area.

The following table gives the details description about the economic condition of freed bonded labourers.

Table 1(a)
Distribution of FBLs in terms of land provided for Cultivation through the District Administration

Sl. No.	*Land Provided for Cultivation*	*No. of FBLs*	*Per cent*
1.	Yes	-	0.00
2.	No	62	100.00
	Total	62	1 00.00

All freed bonded labourers reported that they have not received agriculture land through the district administration. They work as agricultural labourers with the landlord for their livelihood.

60 FBLs are landless 2 FBLs of village Khajuri, block Naubatpur have 50 decimal land each which was purchased from rehabilitation package.

Table 1(b)
Distribution of FBLs in terms of own Land for Cultivation

Sl. No.	*Have you own land for Cultivation ?*	*No. of FBLs*	*Per cent*
1.	Yes	02	3.23
2.	No	60	96.77
	Total	62	100.00

The majority of freed bonded labourers are agricultural and non-agricultural labourers by occupation. After getting freed, they purchased some farming equipments, which were tools for their work to agriculture and non-agricultural sector. Only 75.81 per cent of freed bonded labourers reported that they had shovel as the farming equipment. All of them reported that they had Khurpi and Hasua. None of them have plough, which is the most traditional farming equipment of the village.

Table 2
Distribution of FBLs by their Possession of Farming Equipments

Sl. No.	Farming Equipments	No. of FBLs	Per cent
1.	Plough	-	0.00
2.	Shovel	47	75.81
3.	Others Khurpi & Hasua	62	100.00

Note: The figures are non-additive. It is multiple answer based.

Table 3
Agriculture Facilities provided by Government among FBLs

Sl. No.	Statement	No. of FBLs	Per cent
1.	Farming Equipments provided by the Government	-	0.00
2.	Fertilizer, seeds and pesticides at subsidized rate	-	0.00
3.	How do you irrigate your land ?		
	(i) Well	-	0.00
	(ii) Pond	-	0.00
	(iii) Canal	02	3.23
	(iv) N.A.	60	96.77

Majority of FBLs 60 (96.77%) were found landless except 2 (3.23%) of FBLs of Khajoori village, block-Naubatpur. None of them got any type of farming equipments by the district administration. Due to landless of freed bonded labourers the issue of fertilizer, seeds, pesticides and irrigation facility is baseless. Only 2 FBLs of village Khajoori use canal to irrigate their land.

Freed bonded labourers are economically very poor even their family members have to work in the agricultural and non-agricultural sector. Besides these some bonded labourers kept livestock to supplement their income and other familiar diet needs, but it is meager.

The distribution of figure in the Table 4 shows the complete picture of livestock possession among the freed bonded labourers. 22 freed bonded labourers out of 62 freed bonded labourers have their own livestock. Only 5 freed bonded labourers had bataidari livestock, which were given by different types of people to look after their animal on 50 per cent sharing basis.

Table 4
Distribution of FBLs by their Livestock Possession

Sl. No.	Name of Livestock	No. of FBLs having	
		Own Livestock	*Bataidari Livestock*
1.	One buffalo	03	01
2.	Two buffaloes	02	02
3.	One cow	02	-
4.	Two cows	-	01
5.	One ox	01	-
6.	One goat	06	-
7.	Two goats	03	-
8.	Six pig	01	-
9.	One cock	01	-
10.	One pig + one buffalo	-	01
11.	One Goat + one buffalo	02	-
12..	One Goat + two buffaloes	01	-
13.	One Ox + three buffaloes	01	-
	Total	22	05

The rest of freed bonded labourers had no livestock in their possession because they have no means to keep it. This reflects on their poor supplementary source of income.

Table 5
Distribution of FBLs through their Occupation

Sl. No.	Occupation	No. of FBLs	Per cent
1.	Agricultural labour	57	91.94
2.	Non-Agricultural labour	01	1.61
3.	No work/Old age	04	6.45
	Total	62	100.00

The above Table 5 demonstrates the contemporary occupation profile of the freed bonded labourers. Majority of freed bonded labourers (91.94%) were found as agricultural labourers in the village or neighbouring village. They were engaged in agriculture fields in the vicinity of their households because majority of them and their family members were illiterate and untrained. They do not want to go elsewhere for work due to lack of confidence. The other reason was their old age and sickness. It was found that freed bonded labourers were not engaged round the year and the demand was more seasonal, hence during the dull season they work in to the non-agriculture work, which is their secondary occupations.

Only 1.61 per cent of freed bonded labourers were engaged in non-agricultural work round the year. 6.45 per cent freed bonded labourers do not do any type of work due to old age and sickness.

Table 6
Wage Structure of FBLs

Wage Structure	*No. of FBLs*	*Per cent*
1. In cash per day		
Rs. 31-40	34	54.84
Rs. 41-50	16	25.81
Rs. 51-60	03	4.84
Rs. 61-70	05	8.06
No work	04	6.45
Total	62	100.00

The table shows that the overall picture of wage structure of freed bonded labourers. Majority of bonded labourers 91.94 per cent were working in the agriculture area and their wage were paid in cash between Rs. 31/- to Rs. 70/- per day. The difference of wage in agriculture sector depends on pick and dull seasonal work.

Table 7
Knowledge of Minimum wage among FBLs

Sl. No.	*Do you know about the minimum wage ?*	*No. of FBLs*	*Per cent*
1.	Yes	-	0.00
2.	No	62	100.00
	Total	62	100.00

The above table shows that none of the freed bonded labourers had the knowledge about the Government's minimum wage for the agriculture and non-agriculture sector. Due to lack of knowledge and non-availability of work in the village, they work at low wage. They had no support from labour inspector to enforce minimum wage for them.

Table 8
Annual Family Income of FBLs

Income categories	*No. of FBLs*	*Per cent*
Upto Rs. 5000/-	03	4.84
Rs. 5001 - 10,000/-	19	30.64
Rs. 10,001 - 15,000/-	21	33.87
Rs. 15,001 - 20,000/-	13	20.97
Rs. 20,000 - 25,000/-	06	9.68
Total	62	100.00

The Table 8 stated about the economic status of freed bonded labourers family. The poverty line syndrome was apparent because 91.22% were found below poverty line.

It can be inferred from the table that their family income is up to Rs. 20,000/- per annum and below which is more or less below the poverty line amount that is Rs. 24,000/- yearly Rs. 2000/- per month.

Only 9.68 per cent of freed bonded labourers family earned Rs. 20,000/- to Rs. 25,000/- in the year which shows that they were above the poverty line.

Further the table reveals that the majority of freed bonded labourers (33.87 per cent) have income of Rs. 10,001/- to Rs. 15000/- while another 30.64 per cent FBLs have income of Rs. 5001/- to Rs. 10,000/- and 20.97 per cent FBLs have income of Rs. 15001/- to Rs. 20,000/-. Only 4.84 per cent of FBLs have earned to Rs. 5000/-.

The Table 9 explains about the saving habit of the freed bonded labourers. 74.19 per cent FBLs do not have any type of account in the bank or Post office. Only 25.81 per cent FBLs have their account in the Bank, but they did not operate their account for many years. The saving attitude among FBLs is not satisfactory. The need for more awareness among them about saving habit for their safe and secure future.

Out of 62 freed bonded labourers, 52 freed bonded labourers had no debt outstanding and no loan to repay to any commercial agency. The remaining 10 freed bonded labourers in Table 10 were in debt and had taken loan from, formal and non-formal agency, which amounted to a total amount of Rs. 29200/-. Only one FBL of village Mahangupur, block -Phulwarisharif had taken loan from a non-formal agency and he had to pay a higher rate of interest, which was exploitative in nature.

Table 9
Saving Attitude among the FBLs

Have you saving account in the Bank/Post office ?	*No. of FBLs*	*Per cent*
Yes	16	25.81
No	46	74.19
If yes then where:		
(i) In the Bank	16	25.81
(ii) In the Post office	-	0.00

Table 10
Debt among Freed Bonded Labourers

Source	*No. of FBLs under loan*	*Per cent*	*Amount of Loan*	*Average Amount of Loan*
Formal Agency	09	90.00	27000.00	3000.00
Non-formal Agency	01	10.00	2200.00	2200.00
Total	10	100.00	29200.00	2920.00

Table 11
Present Working place of FBLs and their Family Members

Statement	*Anywhere*		*Old employer*		*Not applicable*		*Total*	
	No.	%	No.	%	No.	%	No.	%
Where do you work at present ?	58	93.55	-	0.00	04	6.45	62	100.00
Where does other family members work at present ?	61	98.39	-	0.00	01	1.61	62	100.00

The above table explains about the working place of the freed bonded labourers and their families. The distribution of figure in the table shows that the majority of freed bonded labourers 58 (93.55 per cent) are working wherever they get better opportunity. They were free to work. None of them were found working with their old employer 4 (6.45 per cent) freed bonded labourers do not do any type of work due to their old age and physical disability.

98.39 per cent of freed bonded labourer family members have been working at different places for earning their livelihood.

Table 12

Distribution of FBLs by Nature and Types of Dwelling Units

Sl. No.	*No. of rooms*	*Kachcha*		*Pucca*		*Mixed*		*All Type*	
		No.	*%*	*No.*	*0,10*	*No.*	*%*	*No.*	*%*
1.	1	02	3.23	07	11.29	-		09	14.52
2.	2	13	20.97	34	54.84	01	1.61	48	77.42
3.	3+	03	4.84	01	1.61.	01	1.61	05	8.06
Total		18	29.04	42	67.74	02	3.22	62	100.00

The above table show that all freed bonded labourers had their own shelter, which meant a dwelling unit of some kind. The majority of freed bonded labourers 42 (67.74%) had pucca houses, which has been made by help of the district administration under Indira Awas Yojana scheme. 18 (29.04%) of freed bonded labourer had kachcha houses, and the rest 3.22 per cent had mixed dwelling units. The mixed dwelling units were a combination of Indira Awas Yojana added to their traditional kachcha houses. But 18 (29.04 per cent) FBLs had not received the Indira Awas Yojana. This was a serious matter.

The dwelling units had different numbers of rooms. The distribution of number of rooms in the above table shows that majority of FBLs 48 (77.42 per cent) had two rooms unit, 14.52 per cent had one room unit and 8.06 per cent FBLs had three rooms unit.

18

EDUCATION SCENARIO : FREED BONDED LABOURERS AND THEIR FAMILIES

Education is most significant instrument for changing the society. Education is the most crucial investment in human development. Education strongly influences health, hygiene, demographic profile, productivity and practically all that is connected with the quality of life. Education is empowerment. It can be used as basic process to bring positive change in the life of free bonded labourers. The literacy rate of Patna district is 63.82 per cent followed by male 73.81 per cent and female 52.17 per cent. The rate of illiteracy suggests that the Government sponsored illiteracy programmes have still to make inroads to cover the poor and under privileged. The present literacy and education initiative has not benefited the freed bonded labourers.

Table 1
Classification of Freed Bonded Labourers on the basis of Education

Sl. No.	*Education*	*No. of FBLs*	*Per cent*
1.	Illiterate	48	77.42
2.	Literate	06	9.68
3.	Middle	06	9.68
4.	Up to matriculation	02	3.22
	Total	62	100.00

The educational position of freed bonded labourers are poor because majority (72.42%) are illiterate, and have never received any form of schooling. Even after freedom they have received education under any Government's non-formal educational schemes. Only 9.68% of FBLs were found literate in the sense of that they take social security cheque with signature, and another 9.68% were found to have received middle class education. But it is also important to know that 3.22% of FBLs received education upto matriculation. In sum, the freed bonded labourers truly come from the most downtrodden sections.

Table 2
Educational Status of Freed Bonded Labourers' Family Members

Category	*Illiterate*		*Literate*		*PTO Middle*		*Matriculation*		*Total*	
	No.	*%*	*No.*	*%*	*No.*	*%*	*No*	*%*	*No.*	*%*
Adult Male	105	22.68	10	2.16	19	4.10	07	1.51	141	30.45
Adult Female	121	26.13	01	0.22	01	0.22	01	0.22	124	26.79
Male (6-14 yrs)	86	18.57	-	0.00	23	4.97	-	0.00	109	23.54
Female (6-14 yrs)	71	15.34	-	0.00	18	3.88	-	0.00	89	19.22
Total	383	82.72	11	2.38	61	13.17	08	1.73	463	100.00

As regards literacy and educational status of freed bonded labourers family, the table shows that the shadow of gloom has not spared the next generation. The 62 FBLs had total 463 family members followed by 141 adult males and 124 adult females. There were 109 male child and 89 female child in the freed bonded labourers families. They are predominantly illiterate with highest figure 383 (82.72 per cent) and only 2.38 per cent literate. 13.17 per cent were educated up to middle school and 1.73 per cent was found to be matriculate. 18.57 per cent male children and 15.34 per cent of female children between the age group of 6-14 years were not going to school. Only 4.97 per cent male children and 3.88 per cent female children were going to school. It is alarming that education is not reaching the next generation. There have been no major imitative made by the district education agency to facilitate education among the freed bonded labourers families as key intervention to uplift their status.

Education is significant medium for mobility in social and economic sphere, but it means little to the freed bonded labourers. They were low and depressed. Their main battle is to beat the massive odds in order to have some livelihood.

The distribution of figures in the Table 3 shows about the freed bonded labourers children education. Out of 62 FBLs, only 15 FBLs reported that their children go to school and they reported that they are getting food reading materials and books free of cost but they are not getting any cash stipend. Two FBLs reported that their children go to the Anganwari centre and they are getting mid day meal.

Table 3
Awareness of FBLs Children Education

Where does your child read?	No. of FBLs	Per cent
Anganwari	02	3.23
If Anganwari, then :		
(i) Getting food	02	3.23
(ii)		
School	15	24.19
If School, then :		
(i) Getting food materials	15	24.19
(ii) Getting cash amount	-	-
(iii) Getting books free	15	24.19
Not reading	35	56.45
If not reading :		
(i) Doing work at home	25	40.32
(ii) Playing here & there	23	37.10
(iii) Due to long distance of school	06	09.68
(iv) Working as a children	11	17.74
(v) There is no gain with education	05	08.06
(vi) No need of education among girls	02	03.23
(vii) Grazing cattle	14	22.58
(viii) Dominant caste people disturb the children inside/outside the school	03	04.84
(ix) Due to low economic condition	07	11.29
Not Applicable	11	17.74

Note: Figures are non-additive.

Further, the table reveals that majority of 35 (56.45 per cent) FBLs children do not go to school. The majority of FBLs 40.32 per cent reported that their children were doing work at home; 37.10 per cent FBLs children were playing here and there. 17.74 per cent FBLs children worked as a child labour, while 22.58 per cent FBLs children were occupied in grazing cattle.

9.68 per cent FBLs children did not go to school due to long distance. 8.06 per cent FBLs felt that there is no gain in getting education. There were gender-biased families (3.23 per cent), which felt that there was no need of education among the girls. Some FBLs children were prevented from going to school by the dominant caste men in the area (4.84%). There were 11.29 per cent families, who wanted to send children to school but could not do so; because of their bad economic conditions.

Majority of freed bonded labourers family do not send their children to the Anganwari center due to lack of knowledge and information. There is no approach by the Anganwari centres or the concerned officials to meat them or extend the Anganwari appear to them.

Table 4
Availability of Educational Facilities in the FBLs Village/tola

Sl. No.	*Facilities*	*No. of FBLs*	*Per cent*
1.	Anganwari School	42	67.74
	(i) Primary School	34	54.84
	(ii) Middle School	23	37.10
	(iii) High School	05	08.06
	(iv) None of these	-	00.00

Note: Figures are non-additive.

Availability of educational facilities is basic need for society. It brings significant change in the life of commoners. The present table represents the availability of governmental educational facilities for the freed bonded labourers in the village/tola.

The Table 4 indicates that all type of educational facilities are not available in the FBLs village/tola of the district, rather it is insufficient for the FBLs families in several areas. The picture emerging is like that 67.74 per cent freed bonded labour can utilize the Anganwari facilities whereas all the FBLs can utilize schooling facilities for their children. Further, the table reveals that majority of FBLs (54.84 per cent) can use schooling facilities up to primary school, whereas 37.10 per cent FBLs can utilize these facilities up to middle school. Only 8.06 per cent of FBLs can utilize these facilities up to high school for their children.

In spite of these facilities, education has not been priority among the FBLs families. This shows that FBLs families have low interest in education. There is no hunger for education. The hunger for food over takes the craving for education.

The pedagogy of the economical oppressed and deprived need special pedagogical intervention for educational upliftment and climbing the stair of socio-economic mobility. Education should be the cornerstone of all major government initiative to bring around a substantive and fundamental change in freed bonded labour's status.

19

FREED BONDED LABOUR : HEALTH

To be healthy is one of the basic need of the people as well as the society. A healthy person can survive better than an unhealthy person. But the light of health does'nt spread for all the sections of society equally. The weaker and economically backward section of the society is totally backward in the health awareness.

They fall victim to diseases which requires intensive medical care and money to save them from mortality or incapacitation.

Health cannot be placed on priority basis among the FBLs where two squares meal in a day is a more important priority. They do not know and understand malnutrition and its consequences, which is essential part of life. The food taken by FBLs is not nutritious. FBLs are engaged in hard physical work, the food they take is not enough to keep them fit for long and disease makes early entry, which debilitates them, and most grow old in their prime youth. The lack of rural medicare particularly for FBLs hits them early and hard. The issue of mortality looms large. Longevity is intertwined with sound health policy for the FBLs.

One of the prime necessities for the better upkeep of man is the provision of safe drinking water. Most of the diseases can be attributed to contaminated water. Water facilities available to the FBLs are by no means adequate.

They are not aware that the water available is not hygienic for drinking. These drinking water facilities are the community assets, which is provided by the State and Central Government resource for use of safe drinking water.

The availability of safe drinking water is the major problem. Thus, the present table tries to examine the drinking water facilities for the FBLs.

Table 1(a)
Availability of Drinking Water Facilities in the FBLs Villages/Tolas

Source	*No. of FBLs*	*Per cent*
Well	25	40.32
Hand Pump	21	33.87
Well + Hand Pump	12	19.36
No facility	04	6.45
Total	62	100.00

The positive aspect in this mixed picture is that some type of drinking water facilities is available in the villages/tolas of FBLs. The majority of FBLs use the facility of well for drinking water purposes which is available in their villages/tolas, while 33.87% FBLs can use the facility of hand pump and 19.36% FBLs can use well & hand pump both. 4 (6.45%) of FBLs vill-Udaini, block-Phulwarisharif reported that there is not any type of drinking water-facility in their tolas. They bring water for drinking from neighbouring village/tola.

Table 1(b)
Drinking Water Facilities used by the FBLs

Source	*No. of FBLs*	*Per cent*
Well	27	43.55
Hand Pump	31	50.00
Well + hand pump	04	06.45
Total	62	100.00

It is evident from the above table that majority or FBLs (50.00%) use hand-pump for drinking water while 43.55% of FBLs use well and only 6.45% of FBLs use well and hand pump both.

Drinking water facilities are the community assets, which is provided by the State and Central Government reserves for use of safe drinking water. Safe drinking water is the basic need of weaker section people.

Above table shows that there is not any type of toilet facilities available in the FBLs houses. They use open defecation in places out side the village for their nature's call. There is no facility of toilet and bathrooms. They go in open fields. Even the female satisfies herself from the long call of nature in open away. It leads to severe diseases among female because they can go to open for defecation during night only, thus forcing them to keep stool for a longer periods. They are the worst sufferers on both account-health and dignity.

Table 2
Availability of Toilet Facilities in the Homes of FBLs

Response	*No. of FBLs*	*Per cent*
Yes	-	0.00
No	62	100.00
Total	62	100.00

Open defecation harmful for their health and village environment. The rural sanitation programme of government, UNICEF and civil society is non-existence in the district. The rural sanitation programme has not touched this segment of freed bonded labourers and their families. Health and sanitation are closely related, which needs strengthening on priority. It is evident from the above table that the majority of FBLs (74.19%) reported that the waste water spilled here and there in the village land in absence of any proper drainage system in the village/tola. (14.52%) FBLs reported that they have katcha drains for disposal of waste water in their tola. Only (11.29%) have the facility of pucca drains for their waste water disposal.

Table 3
Availability of Drainage Facilities in the Villages/Tolas of FBLs

Response	*No. of FBLs*	*Per cent*
Kachcha	09	14.52
Pucca	07	11.29
Open flow	46	74.19
All	62	100.00

Above table reveals the situation of Government Primary health centres and its distance from FBLs residence. The freed bonded labourers face great difficulties to get adequate health care from Government health infrastructure due to long distances. 48.39% of FBLs have to cover a long distance of 5 to 8 Kms. to reach the nearest health centre while 51.61% FBLs have to travel 1 to 4 Kms. to reach health centre for treatment. There is no mobile clinic or any preferential system for medicare of freed bonded labourers. The non-availability of proper transport makes it more strenuous for sick and old FBLs to travel. Hence, the freed bonded labourers encounter many problems in treatment of their family.

Table 4
Distance of Primary Health Centre from FBL's Residence

Distance in Km.	*No. of FBLs*	*Per cent*
1 - 2	30	48.38
3 - 4	02	03.23
5 - 6	19	30.65
7 - 8	11	17.74
Total	62	100.00

Table 5
Medicare Facilities for FBLs

	Yes	*%*	*No*	*%*	*Total*	*%*
Regular check up of Health	-	0.00	62	100.00	62	100.00
Medicare facilities during the illness period	-	0.00	62	100.00	62	100.00

It is evident from the table about the present status of Government health care system for the freed bonded labourers and their family members. There is no programme, which gives priority to their regular health check-up. There is no fund especially marked to give them medical attention during their severe illness. The FBLs complained that they do not get medicine at Government health centre. They are given prescription to buy medicine on their own cost. All FBLs reported that no regular check up of health and medicine is given during the illness period. They are dependent on the village quack doctors and untrained health workers. During maternity, many female members have suffered due to the unavailability of trained female dais/health workers.

It was observed during field work that almost all freed bonded labourers were not having proper meal. They are suffering from malnutrition. They are only concerned with quantity of the food (*roti, chawal, subzi*), not its quality. The food intake lacks nutritional value. Personal cleanliness and daily health do not get place in the daily life. The Government doctors should hold regular camps to sensitize them about health, hygiene and nutritious food for good living. In absence of a proper medicare they are dependent for medical help by village quacks. They confide more in the quacks and their touts who visits them regularly, than the nearest primary heath center or the additional primary health center. There is a strong need to build bridge of communication and inter personal relationship by the Government PHC and Addl. PHC staff with the freed bonded labourer's family. They need special medical attention after been liberated from years of bondage and medical neglect.

20

EVALUATION OF REHABILITATION SCHEMES AND THEIR IMPACT

The present evaluative study was concerned with the rehabilitation status of the freed bonded labourers in Patna district. The district administration, Patna provided the list of 86 freed bonded labourers, who were freed between 1981-82 to 1992-93. These liberated bonded labourers were scattered in different blocks in the different villages of Patna district.

Table 1
Block-wise Distribution of Freed Bonded Labourers

Sl. No.	*Block*	*No. of freed bonded labour*	*Per cent*
1.	Barh	06	6.98
2.	Bihta	01	1.16
3.	Fatwah	36	41.86
4.	Naubatpur	02	2.33
5.	Phulwarisharif	41	47.67
	Total	86	100.00

The research team visited all freed bonded labourers present (62) in the villages spread to five C.D. blocks namely, Barh, Bihta, Fatwah, Naubatpur and Phulwarisharif. All (62) identified and rehabilitated freed bonded labourers were in depth covered for furnishing information. Out of 86 FBls, only 62 FBls were available for giving the respective information. The rest have died or migrated.

Table 2
Block and Village-wise Distribution of FBLs in the Patna District

Sl. No.	Block	Village	No. of FBLs			
			Living	Migrated	Died	Total
1.	Barh	Malahi	02	-	-	02
		Husainganj	-	-	01	01
		Salarpur	03	-	-	03
2.	Bihta	Painal	01	-	-	01
3.	Fatwah	Baruna	17	01	06	24
		Bhuski	07	-	03	10
		Deolalpur	01	-	-	01
		Adalpur	01	-	-	01
4.	Naubatpur	Khajoori	02	-	-	02
5.	Phulwarisharif	Babhanpura	07	-	03	10
		Mahangupur	08	01	07	16
		Chakbairiya	01	-	-	01
		Manoharpur	03	01	-	04
		Udaini	04	-	01	05
		Hasanpur	05	-	-	05
		Total	62	03	21	86

Table 3
Identification Period of Freed Bonded Labourers in Patna

Sl. No.	Identification Period	No. of FBLs	Per cent
1.	1981-82	35	40.70
2.	1984-85	10	11.63
3.	1986-87	22	25.58
4.	1991-92	19	22.09
	Total	86	100.00

The identification of bonded labour and release order certificate given the bonded labour was done under the district Magistrate.

In the year 1981-82 release order certificate was given to 35 bonded labourers.

In 1984-85 release order certificate was given to 10 bonded labourers.

In 1986-87 release order certificate was given to 22 bonded labourers.

In 1991-92 release order certificate was given to 19 bonded labourers.

A total of 86 bonded labourers were given the release order certificates. All the identified bonded labourers are registered in a file of revenue department of Patna district.

After the issue of release order certificates, the rehabilitation programme for bonded labourer was launched by the district administration in collaboration with social security department. The Assistant Director, Social Security Patna reported that all FBLs were rehabilitated through the district administration, except one FBL of village Painal, block-Bihata, who was not given the rehabilitation package due to non-availability of fund.

The study shows that, only four times the bonded labourers were identified and freed in the district, and that was in 1981-82, 1984-85, 1986-87 and 1991-92. No bonded labourers have been found in Patna district by district administration since 1992-93.

During field visit, it was discovered that 21 FBLs had died and 3 FBLs had migrated, but there was no information on this account available at the social security office or at the district level. The team updated the current status about the freed bonded labourers to social security office.

An attempt was made to examine the nature of the social-psycho- economic existence of the bonded labourers in its various aspects. For each household, only one questionnaire was used, which included common questions as well as interactive discussions were used as the made to have the complete picture.

PRESENT OCCUPATION OF FBLs & THEIR FAMILIES

The freed bonded labourers work as agricultural labourers within the village or outside the village independently. They are free to work with any landlord. Seasonally, they migrate to other places in search of work. Some were found working in non-agricultural work like digging, roadwork, construction work and other works. A small number of freed bonded labourers were without work due to old age and illness. Some FBLs go for work to nearest towns adjacent to home place.

The study shows that, only four times the bonded labourers were dentified and freed in the district, and that was in 1981-82, 1984-85, 1986-87 and 1991-92. No bonded labourers have been found in Patna, district by district administration since 1992-93.

During field visit, it was discovered that 21 FBLs had died and 3 FBLs had migrated but there was no information on this account available at the social security office or at the district level. The team updated the current status about the freed bonded labourers to social security office.

An attempt was made to examine the nature of the social-psycho- economic existence of the bonded labourers in its various aspects. For each household, only one questionnaire was used, which included common-questions as well as interactive discussions were used as the made to have the complete picture.

The family members of FBLs were also working in agriculture, non-agriculture areas like brick-kiln, digging, roadwork and other works.

There was no Government initiative apparent in the area for securing them a sustainable and secure livelihood. They are in perpetual mode for searching work. There was no awareness regarding minimum wage. Insurance cover, bank credit facilities, or primary agricultural co-operative laws awareness was lacking among them. There was no NGO activity noticed within the FBLs community for organizing them or in raising their awareness on basic income generating and social security issues. NABARD/ similar other institutions, which are associated with Self-Help Groups, were completely missing. ILO, UNICEF, UNFPA, UNIFEM and other international agencies that work with children, women, deprived and old were not working for FBLs in the district. The FBLs were left to fend for themselves. Agriculture and other allied activities was the main domain of their work. The source of livelihood was purely adhoc and daily wage based.

KNOWLEDGE ABOUT THE MINIMUM WAGE

None of the freed bonded labourers knew about the minimum wage, which is prescribed by the Government and enforced by the labour department. They were paid according to the existing wage of the area. The working hours of the freed bonded labourers are normally 7 to 8 hours and they get wage in cash around Rs. 30/- to Rs. 70/- as daily wage.

The labour department has to play an important practical role in implementing minimum wages for them from their employers. The LEOs and Labour Superintendent (agriculture) with ALC in charge agriculture can hold sensitization camps on minimum wages and about punishment for those who do not follow the labour department rules.

Table 4
Government Compensation Package for the FBLs

Sl. No.	*Major things*	*No. of FBLs*	*Per cent*
1.	One buffalo + one Sewing machine	01	1.61
2.	One buffalo + one house	01	1.61
3.	One buffalo + nine petromaxes	03	4.84
4.	One buffalo + one rickshaw	01	1.61
5.	One buffalo + band Baja with 6 drums	01	1.61
6.	One buffalo + one bicycle + cash Rs. 5000/-	02	3.23
7.	One buffalo + one loudspeaker + one bicycle	01	1.61
8.	One buffalo + one dana cutting machine	01	1.61
9.	One buffalo + one horse cart	01	1.61
10.	Two buffaloes	01	1.61
11.	One buffalo + one rickshaw thela	02	3.23
12.	One patta plate making machine	02	3.23
13.	One rickshaw thela	07	11.29
14.	One loudspeaker	03	4.84
15.	One loudspeaker + one rickshaw thela	01	1.61
16.	Cash Rs. 12500/-	02	3.23
17.	One buffalo + one goat + cash Rs. 400/-	17	27.42
18.	One buffalo + cash Rs. 2250/-	05	8.07
19.	One buffalo	09	14.52
20.	Not received any type of assistance	01	1.61
	All	62	100.00

After identification and their release the bonded labourers were provided compensation by the Government agencies. Under this package, the FBLs were given different types of livestock, house cart, machine, petromax, band baja, rickshaw thela, loudspeaker, bicycle and cash money to improve their economic condition and living standard of their family.

- Majority of FBLs (17) received one buffalo, one goat and cash Rs. 400/- for fodder.
- 9 FBLs received one buffalo.
- 7 FBLs received one rickshaw thela.
- 5 FBLs received one buffalo and cash Rs. 2250/-.
- 3 FBLs received one loudspeaker.
- 3 FBLs received one buffalo and nine petromax.
- 2 FBLs received one buffalo, one bicycle and cash Rs. 5000/-.

- 2 FBLs received one buffalo and one rickshaw thela.
- 2 FBLs received one patta platemaking machine.
- 2 FBLs received cash Rs. 12500/-.
- 1 FBL received one buffalo and one sewing machine.
- 1 FBL received one buffalo and one rickshaw.
- 1 FBL received one buffalo and band baja with 6 drums.
- 1 FBL received one loudspeaker and one bicycle.
- 1 FBL received one buffalo and one dana cutting machine.
- 1 FBL received one buffalo and one horse cart.
- 1 FBL received two buffaloes.
- 1 FBL received one loudspeaker and one rickshaw.
- 1 FBL received one loudspeaker and one rickshaw.
- 1 FBL did not receive any type of assistance.

62 freed bonded labourers received working assets to improve economic activities for a sustainable livelihood. The freed bonded labourers reported that the quality of assets were very poor. Almost all have sold their buffalo, horse and goat or they died for want of proper fodder and health care. Cash amount received by the FBLs for business was consumed and they did not start their business. Only two FBLs of village-Khajoori, block Naubatpur, who received cash Rs. 12500/- as rehabilitation amount used it for purchase of 50 decimal land separately.

This was the major rehabilitation carried by the district authorities as per the provisions of the act, but two basic shortcomings were analyzed during the study. The formulation of schemes was not realistic to the ground. The animals were provided to FBLs without basic training regarding its upkeep and how to handle the diseases or whom and where to contact in the time of crisis. There is need to have linkage to department of Animal Husbandry and vetnary for training FBLs on animal maintenance and upkeep before giving animals.

Secondly, it was part of income generating scheme but the implementing agency did not follow up their progress regarding in terms of marketing of goods etc. produced by the given package. In fact, they were forced to sell their animals because they were dying or they were not getting enough return.

As for the district authorities, they never had a blueprint of follow up. The FBLs need constant direction and guidance to come out of the poverty syndrome with concrete schemes, which matches their skills. They have to be empowered first by capacity building to handle or absorb the schemes and its benefits. An arrangement of pre-consultation between the beneficiaries and the donor can be very useful in planning such a humanitarian exercise. The need based assessment with sustainable livelihood approach can bring stability in income with food security. The FBLs are vulnerable and deprived weak link in the socio-economic chain of a village society, hence they require greater care, pain and constant monitoring for their upward mobility.

Table 5
Social Security Pension for FBLs

Sl. No.	Statement	No. of FBLs					
		Yes	%	No	%	Total	%
1.	Do you get social Security Pension ?	57	91.94	05	8.06	62	100.00

The above table reveals that the majority of FBLs (91.94%) avail the social security pension facility of Rs. 100/- per month, which is provided by the Government under the Bonded Labour Rehabilitation Scheme. 5 (8.06%) FBLs don't get this type of facility. There were (three cases) in village Salarpur and (two cases) in the village Malahai of Barh block. Thus, all FBLs of Barh block don't get the social security pension. The matter has been reported to social security office in Patna for corrective action. Otherwise the administration has done satisfactory work on the pension front. The lapse regarding 5 FBLs can be corrected by corrective action. This pension is lifeline for them and it is recommended that the old age family members of the FBLs may be also included as social security measure and safety net for them.

The above table reveals that 44 (70.97%) FBLs received Indira Awas Yojana (IAY) facilities and are using it for their residential purposes. About one-third 18 (29.02%) FBLs reported that they have not got this type of facility and a long period has passed since they were released. They have no clue as to why they were not provided IAY house, but they are still hopeful of getting one from the government. It has been reported to social security office.

Table 6
IAY and IRDP Facilities for FBLs under Poverty Line Scheme

Sl. No.	*Scheme*	*No. of FBLs*					
		Yes	*%*	*No*	*%*	*Total*	*%*
1.	IAY	44	70.97	18	29.03	62	100.00
2.	IRDP	09	14.52	53	85.48	62	100.00

Nine FBLs reported that they received one buffalo, (amounting to Rs. 3000/-) each under IRDP scheme through the nearest bank. But the rest of FBLs got nothing under IRDP assistance.

The Government assistance is evident but it is not in consolidated manner in totality. There is an urgent need to address the issue as to why 18 (20.03%) FBLs were left out from IAY scheme. It can be said that the Government programmes, under the below poverty line and freed bonded labour schemes, are not efficiently provided to the FBLs.

This scheme is about shelter, which is also one of the foremost and important issues in the case of FBLs. As per the direction of the Government of India and the State Government, all DMs have to link the FBLs with IAY schemes as a part of Government's poverty alleviation holistic strategy. Patna district has failed to provide IAY and other development schemes to all rehabilitated FBLs.

Table 7
Lal Card and PDS Facilities among FBLs

Sl. No.	*Statement*	*No. of FBLs*	*Per cent*
1.	Do you have a Red Card ?		
	(i) Yes	47	75.81
	(ii) No	15	24.19
2.	If Yes, then what type of materials received by you at the Govt. rate ?		
	(i) Kerosene oil	40	64.52
	(ii) Kerosene oil and grains	07	11.29
3.	Where are the PDS ?		
	(i) Within the village	49	79.03
	(ii) Outside the village	13	20.97

SJGSY is in practice, since April 1999, as an important scheme for poverty alleviation. The FBLs can be brought under SJGSY, which has multiple inputs for BPL families. It clearly states that within three years with help of all inputs an effort should be made to bring a family above poverty line.

- The Table 7 shows that 75.81% of FBLs have got the facility of Lal Card.
- 24.19% of FBLs didn't receive the Red Card facility which is provided by the Government agencies.
- 64.52% of FBLs are getting benefit of Kerosene oil only from the PDS net work.
- While 11.29% of FBLs (four FBLs of village-Hasanpur, block-Phulwarisharif, two FBLs of village-Babhanpur, block-Phulwarisharif and one FBL of village-Painal, block-Bihta) reported that they are getting benefit of kerosene oil and food grains particularly 15 kg rice and 20 kg wheat in a month.
- They complained that the most beneficial would be the availability of food grains particularly rice/wheat at subsidized rates in PDS fair price shop (Ration shop).
- 79.03% FBLs reported that PDS facility was within the village and 20.97% of FBLs reported that their PDS was outside their village.

Table 8
Property Released and Provided Property through the Government

(a) Distribution of FBLs by Seized Property

Sl. No.	*Statement*	*No.of FBLs*			
		Yes	*%*	*No*	*%*
1.	Did employer seize your property during the Bonded Labour Period?	-	0.00	62	100.00

(b) Distribution of FBLs by providing Basgit paper ?

Sl. No.	*Have you received Basgit paper?*	*No. of FBLs*	*%*
1.	Yes	44	70.97
	If Yes, then:		
	(i) 1-2 decimal	23	37.10
	(ii) 3-4 decimal	18	29.03
	(iii) 5-6 decimal	03	4.84
2.	No	18	29.03
	Total	62	100.00

It is evident from the Table 8 that their previous employer seized no property during the bonded labour period.

Majority of FBLs (44) reported that they have received the basgit papers for their houses, while 18 FBLs reported that they didn't receive the basgit papers.

Table 9
Visit of Vigilance Committee Members in the FBLs-Village/Tola

Sl. No.	*Statement*	*No. of FBLs*			
		Yes	*%*	*No*	*%*
1.	Visit of Vigilance Committee Members	-	0.00	62	100.00

The vigilance committee's members have to visit the FBLs village/tola for the monitoring the development of socia-economic condition of FBLs and their overall progress.

The table reveals that the vigilance committee members never visited any FBLs village/tolas.

This indicates that the organizational performance and monitoring system of vigilance committee in the district is non-functional.

TRAINING FACILITIES

None of the FBLs have received any type of training by any government agency after their release for self-employment. Training is an important component for learning skills for self-employment to generate regular income.

The training for acquiring new skills, developing the existing indigenous skills tradition art and craft can be important mode of income. Vocational training as a mean of securing jobs and creating avenue for self-employment can be included in their rehabilitation package also.

AWARENESS PROGRAMME AMONG THE FBLs

No awareness programme was held among the freed bonded labourers. They were not aware about the Government schemes for them except what they had got at the time of release. It is necessary to make them aware about the other assistance, schemes and programmes being implemented in the district, particularly BPL schemes.

A regular sensitization and capacity building process was not done in the district for the FBLs. The district administration can organize awareness camps for making them aware about their schemes and how they can benefit from them. A district help line with help of PRI representatives can be established. The mukhiya can be involved in reporting, monitoring and sensitization.

They must be sensitized about their right and how to live independently and free from debt bondage. National Human Right Commission resource persons should be invited in such awareness and sensitization camps to establish a direct rapport between FBLs and NHRC network.

Table 10
Availability of Release Letter among the FBLs

Have you received any type of Bonded Labour release letter issued by DM/SDO ?	*No. of FBLs*	*Per cent*
Yes	62	100.00
No	-	0.00
Total	62	100.00

It is evident from the table that all the FBLs had received their release certificate through the District Administration, but their release certificate is missing or not in proper condition.

The District Revenue Office, Patna gave the name and addresses of released FBLs to ANSISS team.

OPINION OF THE FBLS ON WHAT STEPS THE GOVERNMENT SHOULD TAKE TO IMPROVE THEIR CONDITIONS (Table 11)

The expectation of the freed bonded labourers were assessed as to what in their opinion the state should take steps to improve their condition. The suggestions for improving their present situation gave an inside view of their level of expectations :

- The table reveals that most significant suggestions were for improving economic condition of their families (75.81%) in which they demanded loans, business facilities, land for cultivation and animal husbandry–cattle/pig rearing skills.
- 61.29% of FBLs wanted improvement in the infra-structural facilities like electricity, road and public distribution system.

- 38.71% of FBLs felt that the government should provide them more medical and health care facilities.
- Housing drinking water, toilet and drainage facilities (43.55%).
- 30.65% of FBLs suggested that the pension amount should be increased and payment regularly.
- 24.19% of FBLs have demanded educational facilities for their children.
- 33.87% of FBLs have demanded regular work all the year around.
- 12.90% of FBLs wants the increase of their wages for the betterment of their living condition.
- 4.84% of FBLs felt that the development functionaries should pay visit in the villages/tolas of FBLs.
- 56.45% of FBLs wants more facilities through the Government. During the interview of FBLs, it was found that they totally depend on the Government to improve their economic condition.

Table 11
Opinion of FBLs on What Steps the Government should take to Improve their Conditions

	Statement	*No. of FBLs*	*Per cent*
1.	To improve infra-structural facilities –Electricity, Road, PDS	38	61.29
2.	Housing, Drinking water, Toilet and Drainage facilities	27	43.55
3.	Medical and health care facilities	24	38.71
4.	Educational Facilities	15	24.19
5.	For improving economic condition of families loan, vocational training, Business, Land for cultivation, Animal Husbandry–Cattle, Piggary	47	75.81
6.	Pension facilities and increase in Pension amount	19	30.65
7.	Regular work all the around	21	33.87
8.	More facilities by the Government	35	56.45
9.	Development functionaries should pay visit	03	4.84
10.	Enhancement of wage	08	12.90
11.	No response	-	0.00

The Table 11 shows that none of the FBLs of the district knew about the Bonded Labour Act, 1976 under which they were freed, but they were in consensus grateful to the Government agencies for releasing from the clutches of bondage. NHRC and Ministry of Labour, Delhi should direct the district administration to hold camps in FBL panchayats for basic awareness creation about Bonded Labour Act, 1976. This can help in creating a mass awareness to prevent further debt bondage practice.

Table 12
Knowledge of Bonded Labour Act among the FBLs

Do you know about the Bonded Labour Act ?	*No. of FBLs*	%
Yes	-	0.00
No	62	100.00
Total	62	100.00

Table 13
Perception of Change among FBLs

Statement	*No. of FBLs*	%
Freedom of work	47	75.81-
Feeling better than earlier	26	41.94
Enhancement in social prestige	04	6.45
No pressure/binding of work	29	46.77
Improvement in food availability	08	12.90
Enhancement of wages	05	8.06
No change	-	0.00

Not: Figures are non-additive.

This was the major question that whether they felt any perceptible change after being freed. The response was overwhelming. They cherished the freedom of work, which meant liberty to choose their workplace. They valued their mobility without fear and right to live as they wished. It was, a clear departure from bondage to liberty and for availing opportunities, as it had come with great hardship in most of the cases.

The table reveals that the most significant answers were freedom of work (75.81%) followed by no pressure and binding of work (46.77%).

Those who expressed feelings of being better than before were 41.94%.

Some felt improvement in food availability (12.90%).

A very small section felt enhancement in wages 8.06.

Some experienced enhancement in their social prestige (6.45%).

There was no case reported of any pressure or force being applied by former landlords on them to work in their field.

Table 14
Opinion of FBLs on their Uplift after being Released

Activities	*Uplift*			
	Gain		*No Gain*	
	No. of FBLs	*%*	*No. of FBLs*	*%*
Financial condition	58	93.55	04	6.45
Food consumption	58	93.55	04	6.45
Asset acquisition	2	3.22	60	96.78
Social prestige	62	100.00	-	0.00
Voting behavior	62	100.00	-	0.00

There has been an improvement in financial condition, betterment in food consumption, enhancement in social prestige and increase in voting activities after being released. But only two of them have purchased any permanent asset.

The above table demonstrate that the majority of FBLs (63.79%) take better food at present than before. 27.59% of FBLs reported that they have experienced some improvement in food, clothing and housing, while 8.62% FBLs reported that they take food according to their will, which is just enough for subsistence.

Table 15

Sl. No.	*Gain in food consumption*	*No. of FBLs*	*Per cent*
1.	What type of Improvement :		
	(a) Food according to their will	05	8.62
	(b) Take better food	37	63.79
	(c) Improvement in fooding clothing and housing	16	27.59
2.	How many times, do you take food :		
	(a) Twice a day	19	32.76
	(b) Thrice a day	39	67.24

The table further reveals that 67.24% of FBLs take their food thrice a day and 32.76% of FBLs take it twice a day. All the FBLs take rice with potato/salt and chili or rice juice (Maar) and salt/ chatani and achar/chokha etc. They don't consume food rich in protein and Vitamins, particularly non-vegetarian food items, due to their low economic condition. Their consumption in quality food is still low but has improved from past. The thrust is more on the quantitative food compared to qualitative food. Low intake does affect their health and longevity of life. Many FBL children appeared malnourished. They need proper nutrition and guidance on proper food intake. The poor quality in food intake has affected FBL families. There has been slight improvement from the past scenario but much more is required on this issue.

DIFFICULTIES FACED IN THE FIELDWORK

(i) The list of freed bonded labourers was not properly maintained in the Social Security Department. The revenue section of Patna district office provided the FBLs list. No register was maintained. The list of freed bonded labourers was in a file of the revenue section. The social security office was dependent on the revenue section of district office for supply of record data etc. on FBLs. The Assistant Director, Social Security should be the fulcrum of FBL development activities. The documentation needs strengthening.

(ii) The list of freed bonded labourers in the district office was not up-to-date. It was not clear that how many freed bonded labourer were alive or had died or migrated.

(iii) The Assistant Director, Social Security was not updated about the rehabilitated freed bonded labourers status in the district. He was not aware about the social security pension and how many freed bonded labourers received. It was attributed to frequent transfers. The incumbent of the post of Assistant Director, Social Security should be fully aware of all developments on the FBLs.

(iv) Mostly freed bonded labourers were illiterate so the response of many questions was not given properly.

(v) The majority of the FBLs have damaged or have lost their release order certificates.

It can be concluded that the administration sponsored programmes under below the poverty line and freed bonded labourers schemes were not properly implemented to the FBLs. The rehabilitation process needed comprehensive strategy with proper execution.

The district administration has assured that the corrective action would be taken urgently for the benefit of all FBLs in their upliftment.

PART - V

An Evaluation of Bonded Labour Rehabilitation Schemes in WEST CHAMPARAN District

21

INTRODUCTION–WEST CHAMPARAN : A PROFILE

BRIEF HISTORY OF THE DISTRICT

The newly created district of Paschim Champaran was carved out of the old Champaran district in the year 1972 as a result of reorganization of the districts in the state. It was formerly a subdivision of Champaran district known as Bettiah sub division. It consists of 18 community development blocks. The district is bounded on the north by the hilly region of Nepal, on the south by Gopalganj district and part of Purbi Champaran district, on the west by Deoria district of Uttar Pradesh and on the east by Purbi Champaran.

The District Gazetteer mentions Champaran as a corruption of Champa-ananya, i.e., the forest of Champa trees, a designation which is popularly believed to date back to the time when the district was a vast forest uninhabited except by solitary ascetics. The whole district is dotted with places held in religious esteem as the traditional abodes of Hindu rishies, such as Valmiki, in whose hermitage Sidtam, the banished spouse of Rama, is said to have taken shelter. This great sage is reputed to have resided near Sangrampur, and the village is believed to be indebted for its name (which means the city of the battle) to the famous fight between Rama and his two sons, Lava and Kush. There is also a popular belief within this district lay the kingdom of Virat mentioned in the Mahabharata as the tract within which the Pandavas spent the last year of their weary 12 years exist and that its capital, where the five brothers resided a year was situated near a village called Vairati, 9 or 10 kms. west of Ram Nagar.

The district Gazetteer-further mentions that apart from these traditions, it seems probable that Champaran occupied in early period by races of Aryan descent and formed part of the country in which the vedehas settled after their migration from the Punjab, according to the legend preserved in Vedic literature. Again the God of five, accompanied by the vide in their march eastwards from the bank of the Saraswati came to the broad stream of the Gandak. They cleared the forests, cultivated the virgin soil and founded a great and powerful kingdom. This kingdom was ruled over by king Janaka, who is said by local legend to have lived at Chankigarh, known locally Jankigarh, 17 kilometers north of lauriya Nandangarh. Under his rule, according to the Hindu mythology, the kingdom of Mithila was the most civilized kingdom of India. King Janak himself was a scholar and author of Upanishads, and his chief priest; Yajnasvalkya was the renowned codifier of Hindu law. After the decline of the Vedeha empire, the district formed part of the Vrijjan oligarchic republic with its capital at Vaishali. The Lichchhavis were the most prominent, which constituted the Vrijjan confederation. Ajatshatru, the emperor of Magadh succeeded in subduing the Lichchhavi and occupying their capital at Vaishali. He extended his sovereignty over the present district of Paschim Champaran, which continued under the Mauryan rule for the next hundred years. Ashoka's pillars have been found at Lauriya (Nandangarh). After the Maurya, the Sangas and Kanvas ruled over Magadh and its territories. Archaeological evidences. pointing to the influence of the Sanda and Karva culture have been found in the district.

The district thereafter formed part of the Kushan empire ,and later came under the Gupta empire though not much is known about the material culture of the district in that age. Along with Tirhut, Harsha during whose reign Hieun Tsang, the famous Chinese pilgrim, visited India possibly, annexed the district.

The history of the district during the medieval period and the British period is linked with the history of Bettiah Raj.

The district Gazetteer mentions Bettiah Raj as a great estate. It traces its descent from one Ujjain Singh and his son Gaj Singh, who received the title of Raja from the emperor Shahzahan (1628-58). The family came into prominence in the 18th century during the time of the downfall of the Mughal Empire, when one finds frequent references made by Mohammedan historians to the Rajas of Bettiah as independent chiefs. Thus, in the Riyazus-salatin, the Raja is described as a stubborn and turbulent chief, whose territory had never acknowledged the dominion of any of the Subahdars. In order to subdue this, Ali Vardi Khan led an expedition against him in 1729, and brought him and his territory under subjugation. Subsequently, in 1748, the Raja seems to have entered into an alliance with the Afghan rebel chief of Darbhanga and gave shelter to the members of his family. During their revolt against the Bengal victory, when the Afghans were defeated by Ali Vardi Khan, he offered a contribution of 3 lakhs of rupees as support. In 1759 Cailland advanced against the fort of Bettiah and compelled the Raja to submit in 1762. Mir Kasim Ali Khan sent expedition against him and he was again captured. In 1766, a third expedition under Sir Robert Barker became necessary to establish British authority.

At the time when Sarkar Champaran passed under British rule, it was in the possession of Raja Jugal Keshwar Singh, who succeeded Raja Dhurap Singh in 1763. This Raja soon came in conflict with the East India Company. He failed to clear arrears of revenue. After an unsuccessful attempt to resist the British forces, he fled to Buldelkhand for safety. The attempt by company to manage the estate proved, however to be a complete failure. The company finding on that is revenue is getting less and less, persuaded Jugal Keshwar Singh to return. They settled parganas Mahjhawa and Simraon to him and the remainder of the district being given to his cousins, Sri Kishan Singh and Abdhart forming the Sheohar Raj. The same two Parganas of Majhaura and Simra were settled with Sir Keshwar Singh, the son of Jugal Keshwar Singh, at the Decimal Settlement in 1791, which constituted the greater part of the Bettiah Raj estate.

The Bettiah Raj palace occupies a large area in the center of the town. Much of the old palace was removed and the wards made large modern additions. In 1910 at the request of the Maliavavi, the new palace was built after the plan of Grahms place in culture.

The later history of the district is intimately connected with indigo plantation. Britain used to get supplies of indigo from their American colonies but this ceased after the war of independence in 1776 as a result of which the colonies became free. This forced the British to fall back upon India for supplies of indigo in the

Indigo producing areas of Bengal and Bihar. The Bettiah and Ramnagar estate gave leases of land to them for indigo cultivation on rather easy terms.

In the freedom struggle the district played an important role and was among the outstanding districts in the state in regard to national movement.

NATURAL DIVISION

The district consists of a few district tracts. The southern portion of the district is a flat alluvial plain but towards the northwest the surface is more undulating and rises gradually near the Nepal frontier. From the north-western corner a range of low hills extends in a south-easterly direction for a distance of some 32 kms. Between this range and the Sumeshwar range which extends along the whole of the northern portion is composed of old alluvium, and contains much low level admirably suited for rice but unfit for the cultivation of rabi crops. It is a great rice producing area traversed by a number of streams flowing southwards.

The Gandak is the most important river of the district. It rises in the central mountain basin of Nepal known as Sapt Gandaki from the seven streams, which unite to form, this river. After flowing about 50 kms beyond the Indian border, the river descends to the plains at Tribeni, at its confluence with the sonabs and the Panchanand. Being show-fed the Gandak is a torrential stream until leaves the hills, after which it becomes wider and less turbulent. It is navigable up to Tribeni, timber being the chief product transported by river.

The Sikrahna is the second largest river in the district. It originates in the Chautrwa chour, and flows in southeasterly direction through the central portion of the district till it turns south at Lakhausra, north of Motihari. The southern portion of the river is known as Burhi Gandak.

CLIMATE CONDITIONS

The climate of the district of Paschim Champaran is cooler and damper than the adjoining district. The terai area, comprising mainly Ramnagar, Bagha and Narkatiaganj is unhealthy. Except in these tracts, the climate is rather healthy in all other areas. Winter begins in November and lasts till February, followed by the hot summer months when the maximum temperature reaches up to

43 C. Rains set in during the latter part of June. The district reaches some winter rain also.

RAINFALL

The rainfall is heavier than most of the districts and is especially heavy in the sub mountain tract, partly owing to the heavy showers which fall when cyclone storms break up on reaching the hills and partly because the monsoon is stronger towards the west over the parts of the district just under the hills. The normal annual rain fall in the districts is about 56 mm.

FLORA AND FAUNA

The district, which had derived its name from, the thick forests of Champa trees have during the recent past suffered large-scale denudation of forests. Forests are confined to the northern tract and particularly the Sumeshwar and the Dun ranges are covered with forests. Among the trees found in this region are sal, sign etc. Gun the red cotton tree, and khair. In the most lands of terai, clumps of bamboo palm trees, and mango orchards. Riverbanks, which are subject to floods, are covered with growth of needs and bushes.

The land is now becoming too productive to be spared for wild growth. The 1961 census reported mentions that tiger, panther, bear, deer, sambhar, wild boar, leopard and bison are the wild animals found in the forests of the districts.

Among the common birds found in the district are the brown flycatcher, the gray shrike (which is of a French gray color with black stripe above the eye and is usually of the size of a myna), the green willow warbler, and alive green birds, various types of mynas, the pipit, and different types of vultures. Ducks are found in the marshes and on the riverbanks.

MINES AND MINERALS

The Dun and Sumeshwar hills in the extreme north are formed of ill-compacted sand stone. The bare stony beds of watercourses formed by the downstream rush with considerable force in the rains. There are beds of kankar in parts of the district and various mineral is found almost everywhere.

TENANCY

The District Gazetteer describes the land revenue administration of the district, as the one owned mainly by a few big proprietors along with a small number of petty revenue free properties and little subordinate tenure. Three estates held the greater parts of the property viz., the Bettiah Raj, the Madhuban Estate and the Ramnagar Raj. Petty proprietors were fairly numerous in Madhuban Dhakas and Kesharia but everywhere else the Bettiah Raj and a few big zamindars predominated.

There were only three very small Government estates under direct management. Of the three, two estates was originally Government camping grounds being unconditional gift from the Madhuban estate. These camping grounds, which were adjacent, were found to have been cultivated by tenants, who paid no rent. They were consequently brought on the revenue roll and the collectariate staff collected rent. A large numbers of tenant's business was previously the cultivation and manufacture of indigo. In addition since indigo declined, the area directly cultivated by mukarrariadars and thikadars had decreased, as they found it more advantageous to settle as cultivators directly.

LIVESTOCK

This district along with other districts in the state depends absolutely on livestock for cultivation. The plough cattle are breeded locally. In addition there has been for years a large scales of imports from other parts of India especially Bengal.

There are many fine and well conditioned bullocks seen particularly the cart bullocks, but large herds of cow and calves are generally found not in good condition may be due to insufficient round for grazing and few fodder crops grown. Buffaloes are the main source of milk in the district. Goats are numerous everywhere in the district. They are generally of small type but in fairly good condition. There are veterinary hospitals in Bettiah and Bagaha. The veterinary department has popularized vaccination for epidemic disease, which has done a great deal of good. A district branch of the society for prevention of cruelty to animals had recently been formed.

COMMUNICATIONS

The district had no proper road till the year 1800. However, in due course great change were brought about by the enterprising indigo and sugar planters to whom good lines of communications were an absolute necessity. In 1841, the road from Mehasi to

Bettiah (about 80 km) was considered as excellent. The other roads, which were not so good at that time, have improved considerably. The P.W.D. and the District Board as also by the municipalities maintain the roads. The proportion of metalled led roads is small. The most important roads are those which lead from the Nepal border to the banks of the Gandak. Important among the State Highways and District roads are:

(i) Motihari - Madhubani Ghat Road

(ii) Sugauli - Bettiah Road

(iii) Bettiah - Bagaha Road

(iv) Bagaha - Bhaisalotan Road

Passenger buses ply between the following points:

(i) Motihari, Govindpur, Areraj, Ghorasahan, Bettiah and Muzaffarpur

(ii) Bettiah and Pahlezaghat via a Ramnagar, Bagaha and Lauria.

The railway was introduced in 1988 when Bettiah was linked with Muzaffarpur. The line was extended subsequently to Bhikhna Thori on the Indo-Nepal border. A line also runs from Bagaha to Bairagania in Sitamarhi district.

Bettiah also has a landing ground for planes.

TRADE AND COMMERCE

The rich forests of the district have opened the doors of flourishing trade in timber. The district borders Nepal on the North over along street of land. These are some road routes also connecting the district with Nepal. Naturally, therefore, a good bulk of the Indo-Nepal trade is carried on through the district. Nepalese rice, timber are imported into India through the district while textiles, petroleum products etc. are exported to Nepal. The chief trade centers are Bagaha, Bettiah, Chanpatia and Narkatiaganj.

An overall picture and some important facts of Paschim Champaran district are presented in the Table 1. The table demonstrate about the distribution of total population in respect of rural-urban male and female population, areas, density of population, IMR, literacy rate, child population etc.

Further, the table reveals the administrative name of the district is Paschim Champaran. There are 3 sub-divisions, 18 community development blocks, 5 towns, 1487 revenue villages and 319 panchayats. The areas of the district are 5228.0 kms density of population is 582 sq. km and IMR is 83. The total population of the district is 3043044 followed by male 1600853 and female 12998894. Whereas literacy rate is 39.63% followed by female literacy rate is 25.85% and male literacy rate 51.91 respectively.

Table 1
Paschim Champaran: Some Important Facts
(Census 2001)

1.	Administrative name: Paschim Champaran			
2.	No. of Sub-divisions	- 3		
3.	No. of blocks	- 18		
4.	No. of towns	- 5		
5.	No. of revenue villages	- 1487		
6.	No. of Panchayats	- 319		
7.	Area (in kms)	5228.0		
8.	Total Population	*Male*	*Female*	Total
	Rural14336667	1296894	2733561	
	Urban	164186	145297	309430
	Total	1600853	1442191	3043044
9.	Sex ratio	Rural	Urban	Total
	(Per 10000 male)	903	885	901
10.	Density of population	-	582 per sq. kms.	
11.	Infant morality	-	833	
12.	Population growth during 1991–2001			
		Male	*Female*	Total
		3600337	352097	712434
13.	(i) Literacy	662131	293697	955828
	(ii) Literacy rate	51.91	25.85	39.63
14.	Child population in the age-group 0-6:			
		Male child	*Female child*	*Total*
	Rural296590	279494	576084	
	Urban	28613	26715	55328
	Total	325203	306209	631412
15.	C.D. Block having highest sex ratio		Bagaha-II	922
	C.D. Block having lowest sex ratio		Piprasi	681
16.	C.D. Block having highest literacy rateBettiah		67.27	
	C.D. Block having lowest literacy rate		Takrahan	24.37
17.	C.D. Block having highest female literacy rate		Bettiah	56.76
	C.D. Block having lowest female literacy rate		Piprasi	9.10

Table 2
Block-wise Distribution of Population
(Census - 2001)

Sl. No.	*Name of the C.D. Block*	*Population*		
		Male	*Female*	*Total*
1.	Bagaha-II	123268	1136766	236944
2.	Ramnagar	100915	92060	192975
3.	Gaunha	81874	75745	157619
4.	Mainatanr	75806	68578	14438
5.	Narkatiaganj	153689	138125	291814
6.	Lauriya	93941	85443	179384
7.	Bagaha	1677564	148890	316454
8.	Piprasi	1677724	14740	31464
9.	Madhubani	3433392	31162	665554
10.	Bhitaha	27807	24340	52147
11.	Thakrahan	23121	20631	43752
12.	Jogapatti	97925	87235	185160
13.	Chanpatia	118580	106752	225332
14.	Sikta	76655	68794	145449
15.	Majhaulia	134057	120009	254066
16.	Bettiah	97785	87125	184910
17.	Bairiya	84271	75461	159732
18.	Nautan	92479	83425	175904
	Total	1600853	1442191	3043044

Overall the picture of block-wise distribution of male and female population of West Champaran district demonstrates that the highest populated block is Narkatiaganj and the lowest population is in Piparasi block. The Sidhaw block is also known as Bagaha II.

The overall pictures of the workers and non-workers of Paschim Champaran are presented in the above table. The statistic relating to total workers sub-divided into main workers and marginal workers and distribution of main workers into the four broad categories of workers viz. cultivators, agricultural labourers, household industry workers and others workers are presented in the table.

There are 2677643 families below the poverty line in a population of 3043044 in West Champaran district. Bagaha-II (211620), Majhaullia (36297), Narkatiaganj (18488) and Bagaha-I

(20441) are four blocks having a large number of BPL families. It reveals the socio-economic scenario of West Champaran district.

Table 3
Distribution of Workers and Non-workers in the West Champaran District

		1981	*1991*	*2001*
1.	Total population	1972619	2330610	3043044
2.	Total workers	682100	823923	1162855
3.	Main workers	648389	773095	843977
	(i) Cultivators	235592	264371	251320
	(ii) Agricultural labourers	334140	422935	720773
	(iii) Household industry workers	10149	13808	31152
	(iv) Other workers	68508	71981	159610
4.	Marginal workers	37711	50828	318878
5.	Non-workers	1290510	N.A.	1880189

Source: Census of India 2001.

Table 4
BPL Families List of West Champaran Block-wise 2002

1.	Majhaullia	36297
2.	Mainatanr	14710
3.	Chanpattia	18363
4.	Lauriya	16490
5.	Bagaha - I	20441
6.	Siktta	11505
7.	Bagaha - II	211620
8.	Ram Nagar	14691
9.	Narkatiaganj	18488
10.	Bairiya	16805
11.	Thakraha	5783
12.	Madhubani	6885
13.	Bettiah	4882
14.	Nautan	16005
15.	Yogapatti	15466
16.	Gaunaha	15986
17.	Piprasi	4491
18.	Bhitraha	7035
	Total	2677643

Source: DRDA office, West Champaran, Year - 2001-2002.

REFERENCES & ACKNOWLEDGEMENT

1. DRDA office, West Champaran.
2. DM office, West Champaran.
3. Department of Social Security, West Champaran.
4. District Census Handbook: West Champaran, 1981, Series–4, Bihar.
5. Economic Intelligence Service, Profiles of districts, CMIE, Mumbai.
6. Champaran District Gazetteer, P.C. Roy Chaudhry, Gazeteer Revision Section, Revenue Department, Patna, 1960.

22

BONDED LABOUR IN WEST CHAMPARAN DISTRICT

The system of bonded service came into existence when lands were divided and distributed to the individuals for the purpose of cultivation. The system became sterilized when the lands so distributed to the individuals were declared permanent property of the respective individuals. This may be in administrative phraseology called the incidence of land settlement. The vicious nexus started with the society splitting into "haves and have-nots". The bonded labour belongs to the depressed and deprived section of the feudal society based on social and economic inequity.

The present chapter deals with the present and past status of freed bonded labourers of West Champaran district. In this respect, the district administration and the department of social security West Champaran provided the list of 2487 identified and rehabilitated freed bonded labourers, who were spread in the different villages in the different blocks of the district. The West Champaran district contains 18 blocks and 16 out of 18 blocks has more and less freed bonded labourers. The highest number of freed bonded labourers (805) were identified and rehabilitated in Bagha-II block, where as the lowest number of FBLs (02) were identified and rehabilitated in Bettiah block. It is important to point out here that the district administration of West Champaran identified 2502 FBLs up to year 2001 but rehabilitated only 2487 FBLs, because 11 had migrated and 04 had died at the time of rehabilitation process. Thus, in total 2487 FBLs were rehabilitated through the district administration.

In the year 2002-03, the district administration identified more 294 bonded labour and released them. The process of their rehabilitation is still in progress and the amount for their rehabilitation is gradually being sent to different block offices.

The ANSISS research team visited different village of different block of the district and interviewed sampled freed bonded labourers (230) and collected relative data from them. It is important to point out here that the research team did not draw any sample from those 294 FBLs who were identified in the year 2002-03 because their rehabilitation process is in progress. Thus, the sample was drawn only from 2487 rehabilitated freed bonded labourers of the district.

The following table gives details about the freed bonded tabourers of the district.

Table 1
Identified & Rehabilitated FBLs in West Champaran District (upto year 2001)

Sl. No.	*Name of the C.D. Block*	*No. of Freed Bonded labourers*			*Remarks*
		Identi-fied	*Rehabi-litated*	*Not Rehabilitated*	
1.	Bettiah	02	02	-	-
2.	Nautan	37	37	-	-
3.	Bairia	111	109	02	Died
4.	Yogapatti	24	24	-	-
5.	Majhaulia	63	63	-	-
6.	Chanpatia	56	56	-	-
7.	Narkatiaganj	63	63	-	-
8.	Gaunaha	478	467	11	Migrated
9.	Sikta	24	23	01	Died
10.	Mainatarh	130	129	01	Died
11.	Lauriya	74	74	-	-
12.	Madhuwani	35	35	-	-
13.	Ramnagar	399	399	-	-
14.	Bagha-I	195	95	-	-
15.	Bagaha-II	805	805	-	-
16.	Thakrahan	06	06	-	-
	Total	2502	2487	15	-

The above table shows the block wise actual position of freed bonded labourers of the district. The table reveals that about 2502 bonded labourers were identified and released, but 15 freed bonded labourers were not available for rehabilitation, because 11 FBLs had migrated and 04 FBLs were dead.

REHABILITATED FREED BONDED LABOURERS IN WEST CHAMPARAN DISTRICT

The table 2 shows the complete picture of rehabilitated freed bondod labourers in the different blocks of the district. Bagha-II block has the highest number of FBLs (805) rehabilitated by the district administration. Gaunaha block is in the 2nd position with 467 FBLs, whilp Ramnagar block is in the 3rd position with 399 FBLs. Bagaha-I block is in the 4th position with 195 FBLs and in the 5th position is Mainatarh block with 129 FBLs. The ranking of the different blocks in the Table 2 indicates the position of the FBLs in the block.

Table 2
Rehabilitated Freed Bonded Labourers in West Champaran District

Sl. No.	*Name of the C.D Block*	*No. of FBLs*		*Per cent*
1.	Bettiah	02	0.08	16
2.	Nautan	37	1.49	11
3.	Bairiya	109	4.38	6
4.	Yogapatti	24	0.97	13
5.	Majhauli	63	2.53	8
6.	Chanpatia	56	2.25	10
7.	Narkatiaganj	63	2.53	9
8.	Gaunaha	467	18.78	2
9.	Sikata	23	0.92	14
10.	Mainatarh	129	5.19	5
11.	Lauriya	74	2.98	7
12.	Madhubani	35	1.41	12
13.	Ramnagar	399	16.04	3
14.	Bagaha - I	195	7.84	4
15.	Bagaha - II	805	32.37	1
16.	Thakraha	06	0.24	15
	Total	2487	1100.00	

IDENTIFICATION PERIOD OF REHABILITATED FBLs

Since the enforcement of Bonded Labour System (Abolition) Act 1976, a total number of identified and released bonded labour in the district was 5202 and out of this figure 2487, FBLs were rehabilitated through the district administration. The Table 3 shows the identification period of all rehabilitated freed bonded labourers of the district.

124 (4.98%) FBLs were released during the year 1980-81. 80 (3.22%) FBLs were released in the year 1981-82. 286 (11.50%) FBLs were released in the year 1982-83. 338 (13.59%) FBLs were released in the year 1983-84. 504 (20.27%) FBLs were released in the year. 1984-85, 448 (18.01%) FBLs were released in the year 1986-87 271 (10.90%) FBLs were released in the year 1987-88. 293(11.78%) FBLs were released in the years 1990-91 and 143 (5.75%) FBLs were released in the year 1993-94.

The majority of FBLs were released in the year 1984-85 and the next majority of FBLs were released in the year 1986-87.

Table 3
Identification Period of Rehabilitated FBLs

Identification Period	*No. of FBLs*	*Per cent*
1980-81	124	4.98
1981-82	80	3.22
1982-83	286	11.50
1983-84	338	13.59
1984-85	504	20.27
1986-87	448	18.01
1987-88	271	10.90
1990-91	293	11.78
1993-94	143	5.75
Total	2487	100.00

In West Champaran the released FBLs period and their rehabilitation takes two to three years because government machinery problem. The released bonded labourers need immediate support for their livelihood. There is need for copious flow of buffer fund to give immediate relief to bonded labourers. The rehabilitation grant takes time for sanction from State and Central Government.

A permanent corpus should be created to help bonded labourers immediately after release. Hence, the gap of two or three years should minimised as possible as.

Table 4
Block & Village-wise Distribution of Sample FBLs in the West Champaran District

Sl. No.	Block	Village	No. of FBLs			Total
			Inter-viewed	Migrated	Died	
1.	Bettiah	Ganauli	01	-	-	01
		Rupdih	-	-	01	01
2.	Nautan	Pathari	02	-	-	02
		Khadda	01	-	02	03
		Sofiatola	01	-	01	02
		Churiharwa	-	-	01	01
3.	Bairiya	Saraiya	15	01	05	21
4.	Yogapatti	Mahavirpur	-	-	01	01
		Semari	01	-	01	02
		Lakauria	01	03	-	04
5.	Majhaulia	Ramnagar		01	06	11
		Bankat	04			
		Amawa				
		Majhar				
6.	Chanpatia	Jokahan	07	-	05	12
7.	Narkatiaganj	Pakari	03	-	01	04
		Harditerha	04	-	02	06
8.	Gaunahan	Lakshnauta	01	-	01	02
		Pachrukhiya	02	01	04	07
		Ghamaura	01	-	03	04
		Bhatani	01	-	-	
		Kharatia	01	-	01	02
		Banbairia	22	-	09	31
9.	Sikata	Noniyatola	03	02	-	05
10.	Mainatarh	Lipani	03	-	04	07
		Inarwa	01	-	-	01
		Purainiya	01	-	-	01
11.	Lauriya	Mathiya	10	-	01	11
12.	Madhubani	Kerwaniya	04	-	01	05
13.	Ramnagar	Dhanrapa	05	-	03	08
		Dainbharwa	10	01	03	14
		Bhawal	11	01	09	21
14.	Bagaha - I	Bibibankatwa	03	-	01	04
		Bhataura	01	-	01	02
		Kumhiya	01	-	-	01
		Ahirbaliya	09	01	03	13
		Vishunpurwa	05	-	01	06
15.	Bagaha - II	Subhashnagar	15	-	01	16
		Rampur	16	04	03	23
		Kailashnagar	02	-	02	04

Sl. No.	*Block*	*Village*	*No. of FBLs*			*Total*
			Inter-viewed	*Migrated*	*Died*	
		Sherwa	03	-	-	03
		Pipara	01	-	-	01
		Dumbalia	01	-	04	05
		Narainapur	06	-	-	06
		Patkhauli	04	-	01	05
		Malkauli	02	-	01	03
		Narbal Barbal	27	01	06	34
		Total	230	16	97	343

The research team in this evaluation study visited about 343 freed bonded labourers household. Out of 343, 230 were interviewed. It was found that 16 had migrated and 97, a major group of freed bonded labourers, had died. Thus, the evaluation team met and collected the relevant data from 230 FBLs.

This latest information on FBLs has been passed to the district administration and the social security office by the ANSISS team. The evaluation team suggested to the social security department official to collect the latest information about bonded labourers and up date their register also.

DISTRIBUTION OF FBLs BY THEIR CAUSES FOR BONDED LABOUR

One of the most important objectives of the study was to find the causes for becoming bonded labour in the West Champaran district. It can be observed from the Table 5 that the most significant answer was indebtedness (95.65%), followed by the poverty (40.43%). The other major reason was attributed to the low socio-economic status in the society (27.83%) followed by the traditional way (11.74%) and unemployment (9.13%).

The type of most common bondage is debt bondage. Hence, the problem of debt is very important and related to the quantity of loan, previous and subsequent the rate of interest, the source of debt etc. In the same way, a bonded labourer may go on taking subsequent loan from their masters, whenever they are in need of money for daily consumption or marriages purposes or for treatment of own family members. So, debt is the main and dominant reason for bondage.

Table 5
Distribution of FBLs by their Causes for Bonded Labour

Cause	*No. of FBLs*	*Per cent*
Low socio-economic status in the society	64	27.83
Unemployment	21	9.13
Poverty	93	40.43
On the traditional way	27	11.74
Indebtedness	220	95.65
Own choice	-	0.00

Note: The figures are non-additive. It is multiple answer based.

Table 6
Working Place of FBLs before Release

Statement	*No. of FBLs*	*Per cent*
Within the same village	166	72. 17
Outside the village but within the Block	61	26.52
Outside the block but within the District	03	1.31
Outside the district but within the state	-	0.00
Outside the State	-	0.00
Total	230	100.00

Another major objective of the study was to find out where FBLs were working as bonded labour before their release. In response of these findings, the majority of FBLs (72.17%) reported that they worked in the same village during the bonded labour period, where they lived. This affirms the feudal social environment where these FBLs worked. About (26.52%) FBLs reported that they worked outside the village but within the block, while 1.31% FBLs reported that they worked outside the block but within the district.

No sampled FBLs were found working outside the district and the state. It means that majority of freed bonded labourers working place was within the same village or neighboring area of the village. It is important to point out here that all the sample FBLs identified and released were from the agricultural sector.

An overall picture about the working period of FBLs as bonded labour before their release is presented in the Table 7. The table reveals that out of 230 sampled FBLs, 137(59.56%) FBLs worked as bonded labour for 11 years and above, while 32.61% of FBLs reported that they had worked as bonded labour for 6 to 10 years. About 7.83% of FBLs reported that they had worked between 1 to 5 years. It reveals that the majority was in chain of subjugation and bondage for over a decade and had spent their prime years in servitude.

Table 7
Working Period of FBLs as Bonded Labour before Release

Working Period	*No. of FBLs*	*Per cent*
Upto 5 years	18	7.83
6 – 10 years	75	32.61
11 – 15 years	69	30.00
16 – 20 years	40	17.39
21 years and above	28	12.17
Total	230	100.00

Consideration of the duration of bondage is very important, since it indicates the exploitative period of the labourers to bonded service leading to their poor economic conditions, and their natural aspiration to come out of bondage at the earliest and so on.

23

FREED BONDED LABOUR : SOCIAL LIFE

The caste system is deeply embedded in social hierarchy. Some occupations are correlated to forcing them to follow traditional occupation. The rural social situation has revolved around traditional pattern of hierarchical occupation. Hindu social system has a marked influence in the villages. The social fabric is build around the caste status. The majority of the FBLs in West Champaran belonged to scheduled caste category (57.83%), while 16.09% of FBLs belonged to OBC category. About 13.04% of FBLs belonged to scheduled tribe category and muslim category.

The present chapter is concerned about the social characteristics of freed bonded labourers. Under these characteristics of freed bonded labourers, the study focuses on age, sex, family size, marital status, castes, neighbours and availability of infrastructure facilities in the village to understand their social life.

The following table gives details about the social life of freed bonded labourers.

Let us first examine the age pattern of the freed bonded labourers. It is evident from the table that the freed bonded labourers belong to different age groups raging from 31 to 71 and above. They are a composite mix group of young, middle and old age. It is found from the above table that the highest percentage of the FBLs (36.52%) belong to the age group of 51 to 60 years. The second highest percentage of respondents (30.87%) belongs to the age group of 61 to 70 years. The third highest percentage of the respondents (22.61%) belongs to the group 41 to 50 years. The fourth highest percentage of the respondents (5.65%) belongs to age group of 31 to 40 years. This age groups is young and hard working. And the last percentage of respondents (4.35%) belongs to age group of 71 years and above. They are old and not in the position to work hard. They have been long in the vicious circle of bondage till they were freed. It also suggests that a small percentage survived the hardship of bonded period. They have lived long to tell the tales. It emerged during informal discussions that the majority had served their master for a relatively long time and the treatment received from them was cruel unkind and degrading.

Table 1
Age-wise Distribution of Freed Bonded Labourers

Age Group (Yrs.)	*Number*	*Per cent*
31 - 40	13	5.65
41 - 50	52	22.61
51 - 60	84	36.52
61 - 70	71	30.87
71 & above	10	4.35
Total	230	1 00.00

Table 2
Sex-wise Distribution of Freed Bonded Labourers

Sex	*Number*	*Percentage*
Male	225	97.83
Female	05	2.17
Total	230	100.00

The above table shows the distribution of male and female sampled freed bonded labourers in the district. It is evident from the table that there were 225 males and 5 females signifying high prevalence of males in bondage but there were female freed bonded labourers too. The presence of female Freed bonded labourers in the district present a picture where the highest degree of exploitation of the bondage labourers families must have happened where women were compelled to mortgage themselves as debt bondage labourers. These females were mortgaged along with their husbands and were released together. They were working in agriculture sector.

Out of 5 female FBLs, 3 female FBLs (Radhika Devi W/o Bhikhan Ram, Ms. Ram Rajia W/o Shekhar Manjhi and Ms. Jaguia

Devi W/o Pugan Ram) were found in the village Mathiya of Lauriya block; one female FBL (Ms. Panwa Devi) was found in the village Bhawal of Ramnagar block, another one female FBL (Ms. Kushmi Devi W/o Mohan Paswan) was found in the village Narbal-barbal of Bagha-II block. They were identified and released through the district administration from agriculture sector.

Table 3
Family Size-wise Distribution of Freed Bonded Labourers

Family Size	*No. of FBLs*	*Percentage*
Upto 5	86	37.39
6 –10	105	45.65
11–15	31	13.48
16 & above	08	3.48
Total	230	1 00. 00

The above table shows that majority of FBLs (45.65%) had family size of 6-10 members, whereas 37.39% of freed bonded labourers had 5 and less than 5 members in their family. About 13.48% of freed bonded labourers had large family size with 11 to 15 members. Only 3.48% of freed bonded labourers had very large family size with 16 and above members. In view of rural family structure, large family is still prevalent norm and it was true for freed bonded labourer families also, because they are related to the village life.

Table 4
Age & Sex-Wise Distribution of Family Members of Freed Bonded Labourers

Age Group	*Male*		*Female*		*Total*	
	No.	*%*	*No.*	*%*	*No.*	*%*
0-5	109	6.61	107	6.48	216	13.09
6-14	250	15.15	209	12.67	459	27.82
15 - 60	462	28.00	391	23.70	853	51.70
61 & above	76	4.60	46	2.79	122	7.39
Total	897	54.36	753	45.64	1650	100.00

The above table shows that the freed bonded labourers families belong to different age groups. They are in the age group of upto 5 years, 6 to 14 years, 15 to 60 years and 61 and above years. The majority of the freed bonded labourers (51.70%) were found the age group of 15 to 60 years, followed by 28.00% males and 23.70% females. The next age group of FBLs is 6 to 14 years with 27.82% constitute the second large size, with 15.15% males and 12.67% females. Another age group of FBLs below 5 years with 13.09% constitutes the third large size with 6.61% and 6.48% females. The fourth and last age group of FBLs is 61 years and above with 7.39% followed by 4.60% males and 2.79% females.

Table 5
Distribution of Freed Bonded Labourers by Sex & Marital Status

Marital Status	*Male*		*Female*		*Total*	
	No.	*%*	*No.*	*%*	*No.*	*%*
Married	200	86.96	01	0.43	201	87.39
Unmarried	-	0.00	-	0.00	-	0.00
Widow/Widower	25	10.87	04	1.74	29	12.61
Total	225	97.83	05	2.17	230	100.00

Thus, the table indicates that most of the freed bonded labourers families were found in the age group of 15 to 60 years and this age group is more hard working and earning group.

Table 6
Caste Composition of the Freed Bonded Labour

Caste	*Number*	*Percentage*
Scheduled Caste	133	57.83
Scheduled Tribe	30	13.04
Backward	37	16.09
General	–	-
Muslim	30	13.04
Total	230	100.00

An overall picture of marital status of freed bonded labourers are presented in this table. Majority of freed bonded labourers 87.39% (followed by 86.96% males and 0.43% female's respondent) were married and enjoying marital life. No respondent was found unmarried. Only 10.87% males and 1.74% female freed bonded labourers were widow/widower, who live in the village and bear the family responsibilities. The role of the state is to give them secure work, food and health environment to protect their families.

The above table shows the caste composition of sampled freed bonded labourers in West Champaran district. The majority of the freed bonded labourers 57.83 per cent belong to scheduled caste (Chamar, Musahar, Dusadh and Dhobi) community while 13.04 per cent FBLs belongs to scheduled tribes (Tharu & Gorh). Thus, all together 70.87 per cent are scheduled caste and scheduled tribes. 16.09 per cent of the freed bonded labourers are belongs to backward caste (Yadav, Mallah, Koeri, Kurmi, Turaha, Noniya, Kanu, Bin, Paul Barhi and Mali). About 13.04% of freed bonded labourers were found from Muslim community also. None of the FBLs were found in the upper caste category. It is significant and true to the history of debt bondage. It fits the absolute deprivation paradigm, where ritually low status in graded hierarchical society coexists with those below the poverty line status. The social and economic levels are uniformly steeped in the bottom line of an agrarian semi-feudal society.

Table 7
Neighbours of Freed Bonded Labour

Sl. No.	*Statement*	*No. of FBLs*	*%*
1.	Was your neighbour Freed Bonded Labour?		
	(i) Yes	224	97.39
	(ii) No	06	2.61
2.	If yes, how many families?		
	(i) Upto — 5	57	24.78
	(ii) 6 – 10	24	10.43
	(iii) 11 – 15	52	22.61
	(iv) 16 & above	91	39.57

The distribution of figures in above table shows that the majority of freed bonded labourers (97.39%) live in cluster, while 2.61% were not found in cluster. It indicates that the district administration identified and rehabilitated bonded labour in cluster.

Further, the table reveals that 39.57% of FBLs had 16 and above members of FBLs in the neighbourhood, while 22.61% of

FBLs had a neighbours size of 11-15 FBLs members. About 10.43% of FBLs had a neighbor size of 6-10 FBLs member. The rest 24.78% of FBLs had up to 5 members of FBLs in the neighbourhood. The social cohesion was among the FBLs fraternity and felt psychologically more as a unit due to their common background.

Table 8
Availability of Government Infra-structural Facilities in the FBLs Villages/Tolas

Government Facilities	*No. of FBLs*	*Percentage*
1. Post Office	96	41.74
2. PDS	147	63.91
3. Health Centre	20	8.70
4. Electricity	84	36.52
5. Bank	51	22.17
6. Road Facilities		
(i) Kachcha	131	56.96
(ii) Pucca	36	15.65
(iii) Mixed	63	27.39
(iv) No facility	–	0.00

Availability of Governmental infra-structural facilities in the society as basic civic support system for the citizens are an important work for assessing the reach and welfare measures taken to ameliorate the common peoples predicament, particularly in the rural and backward areas. In the present table, the availability of governmental infra-structural facilities for FBLs represents a mixed scenario.

The Table 8 shows that all types of infra-structural facilities are not available in the freed bonded labourers village/tolas of the district, rather it is insufficient for the freed bonded labourers families in several areas. Some are fortunate to enjoy the facilities whereas others are deprived of the basic facilities. There is no uniformity in the availability of these Government conveniences. The table also demonstrates that missed opportunity by the Government agencies in reaching out uniformly to all the FBLs families in their neighbourhood.

The picture emerging is like that 41.74 per cent of freed bonded labourers can utilize the post office facilities, whereas 63.91 per cent of freed bonded labourers can use the public distribution system (PDS) facilities. The heath situation is dismal only 8.70 per cent of freed bonded labourers having access to the health centres. 36.52 per cent of freed bonded labourers can utilize the electricity connection. Only 22.17 per cent of freed bonded labourers can utilize the bank facilities.

The other important issue is transport by road facilities. The katcha road facilities were accessible for 56.96 per cent FBLs families, 15.65 per cent on the pucca road and 27.39 per cent of freed bonded labourers were accessible on the mixed road.

The state facilities used by the freed bonded labourers in extremely backward area, were below standard and needs urgent upgradation. Equity and access are key for their upliftment in development process.

24

FREED BONDED LABOUR : ECONOMIC LIFE

The freed bonded labourers come from socially backward castes and from most of the economically backward sections of the society. They have weak economic status. Their annual income is below poverty line. They are laborious and their economic existence depends upon their physical labour.

The freed bonded labourers are the important segment of the labour and agrarian relations. The freed bonded labourers have no land. They are part of the landless work force. They work as agricultural labourers and non-agricultural labourers. The job market is not stable in agriculture sector. It varies from one season and depends on demand of labour in job market. In the village level development works, under the Swarn Jayanti Rozgar Yojana and other schemes, where number of works like digging the earth, carrying the soils, brick work in the village lane etc. are done by the freed bonded labourers. Further, it was observed that development works were not taken up in their village regularly, hence there was limited scope for work.

The family members of freed bonded labourers also work. They do petty work.

The Table 1 gives the details about the economic life of freed bonded labourers.

It was observed that the freed bonded labourers have no fixed working hours when work is available in the agriculture field. The work is generally available in agriculture sector only for five to six months. Work is not available round the year. There is no employment guarantee and food security. Secondary source of employment and income generating schemes like rearing the animal, dairy, poultry farm etc., are not available in this district.

Table 1
Distribution of FBLs in Terms of Land provided for Cultivation through the District Administration

Statement	*No. of FBLs*	*Per cent*
Land provided for Cultivation		
(i) Yes	40	17.39
(ii) No	190	82.61
If yes, then, how much land ?		
(i) Upto 0.25 acre	03	1.30
(ii) 0.26 - 0.50 acre	04	1.74
(iii) 0.51 - 0.75 acre	01	0.44
(iv) 0.76 - 1.00 acre	17	7.39
(v) 1.00 - 1.25 acre	15	6.52
But the Land and is not in their possession	40	17.39

The distribution of cultivable land among bonded labourers under the rehabilitation scheme was done by the district administration. The district authorities provided ceiling surplus land, bhoodan and gramdan to 40 (17.39%) FBLs, out of 230 freed bonded labourers.

The distributions of surplus land ceiling was done among 40 freed bonded labourers who got the land papers but not in equal size. The above table 1 shows that the 7.39 per cent freed bonded labourers got the land above 75 decimal to 1 acre land 6.52 per cent got the largest size of land between one acre to 1.25 acres. 1.74 per cent got 26 decimal to 50 decimal. 12.30 per cent got less than 25 decimal and only 0.44 per cent have got 51 decimal land for agricultural purposes. But, unfortunately the land is not in their possession. This is due to the landlords, who have filed cases against government for taking their land under the surplus ceiling land. The case is subjudice, hence the government distribution of land to the 40 FBLs remains on paper only. It is only after the legal battle is over, that the clear picture will emerge. Till then, 40 FBLs are also landless.

The majority of freed bonded labourers are agricultural and non-agricultural labourers by occupation. Some of them have little agricultural land, which they purchased, after been released. For cultivation and doing agricultural and non-agricultural works, their most urgent need is the need for farming equipment. So, after their release, they purchased some farming equipment which have become their tool for livelihood and security, which prevents them from wandering into economic obsoleteness. The main tools for cultivation and agricultural and non-agricultural works are plough, shovel, Khurpi, Hasua and other equipments. They are fundamental tools to their fight against hunger and uncertainty.

Table 2
Distribution of FBLs by their Possession of Farming Equipments

Farming Equipments	*No. of FBLs*	*Per cent*
Plough	04	1.74
Shovel	186	80.87
Others Khurpi & Hasua	230	100.00

Table 3
Agriculture Facilities Provided by Government Among FBLs

Statement	*No. of FBLs*	*Per cent*
Farming Equipments provided by the Government	–	0.00
Fertilizer, seeds and pesticides at subsidized rate	–	0.00
Have you agriculture land for cultivation ?	05	2.17
How do you irrigate your land ?		
(i) Well	-	0.00
(ii) Pond	-	0.00
(iii) Canal	-	0.00
(iv) No facility	05	2.17
Not applicable	225	97.83

The above table explains the possession of farming equipments among the freed bonded labourers. Only 4 (1.74%) of freed bonded labourers reported that they had plough, while 186 (80.87%) FBLs reported that they had shovel as the farming equipments. All of them reported that they had Khurpi and Hasua only. Though, the tools are primitive and familiar to least developed feudal agricultural plains of West Champaran, but they have proved to be lifeline for them. It is due to these utilitarian basic tools, they get some work during the non-agricultural season and even during agricultural period like digging excavation etc. work. They are part of their work culture and existence.

Majority of the freed bonded labourers 225 (97.83%) were found landless. Only 5 (2.17%) freed bonded labourers have purchased some cultivable land after been released. But the government till date has not provided any of irrigation facilities to them. They also reported that they haven't received fertilizers, seeds and pesticides at the subsidized rate. For the landless freed bonded labourers, the issue of fertilizers, seeds, pesticides and irrigation facility is baseless. None of them got any type of farming equipment by the district administration.

The following five FBLs have purchased some cultivable land after been released:

- (i) **Lallan Pd. Hazara :** Village Rampur, block Bagaha-II, 12 decimal land.
- (ii) **Bhukhal Ram :** Village Dhanrapa, block Ramnagar, 20 decimal land.
- (iii) **Mahmood Miyan :** Village Semari, block Yagapatti, 20 decimal land.
- (iv) **Sagar Raut :** Village Saraiya, block Bariya, 8 decimal land.
- (v) **Shankar Patwari :** Village Bhatni, block Gaunaha, 25 decimal land.

The rearing of animal is secondary source of income in rural society. Traditionally, livestock possession played an important role in the rural economy. For poor households like landless agricultural labourers etc., the livestock possession plays very important role in their economy and contributes to about two third of the rural poor income. Rural poor population depends on it for their supplementary livelihood. In this connection, landless and agricultural labours mainly depend on goat, cow and buffalo. Though cattle rearing for them are difficult, but they struggle to keep them.

The Table 4 reveals the critical dependence of freed bonded labourers on livestock for their cash incomes. Out of 230 freed bonded labourers, 134 freed bonded labourers had their own livestock and only 7 freed bonded labourers had bataidari livestock, which were given by different types of people to look after their animal on 50 per cent sharing basis.

Table 4
Distribution of FBLs by their Livestock Possession

Sl. No.	*Livestock*	*No. of FBLs having*	
		Own livestock	*Bataidari livestock*
1.	One goat	05	01
2.	Two goats	04	-
3.	Three goats	01	-
4.	Four goats	04	-
5.	Five goats	01	-
6.	Six goats	03	-
7.	One cock	01	-
8.	One cows	21	-
9.	Two cows	08	01
10.	Four cows	01	-
11.	Five cows	01	-
12.	Six cows	01	-
13.	One ox	07	-
14.	Two oxes	08	-
15.	One buffalo	12	01
16.	Two buffaloes	05	02
17.	Three buffaloes	01	-
18.	Two he-buffaloes	07	-
19.	One mare	01	-
20.	One cow + one goat	02	01
21.	One cow + one ox	01	-
22.	One cow + one buffalo	02	-
23.	One cow + two buffaloes	01	-
24.	One cow + five goats	01	-
25.	One buffalo + one goat	02	-
26.	One buffalo + three goats	02	-
27.	One buffalo +	01	-
28.	One buffalo + one ox	01	-
29.	One buffalo + two oxes	02	-
30.	One buffalo + four goats	02	-
31.	One he-buffalo + one goat	-	01
32.	One ox + one goat	01	-
33.	Two buffaloes + three goats	01	-
34.	Two buffaloes + one goat	02	-
35.	Two buffaloes + one He-buffalo	02	-
36.	Three buffaloes + one goat	01	-
37.	Two oxes + one goat	01	-
38.	Two cows + four goats	02	-
39.	Two cows + one ox	01	-
40.	Two cows + two oxes	02	-

Contd...

S. No.	Livestock	No. of FBLs having	
		Own livestock	Bataidari livestock
41.	Three cows + four goats	01	-
42.	One cow + one buffalo + two goats	01	-
43.	One cow + one buffalo + one goat	01	-
44.	One cow + two goats + two pigs	01	-
45.	One cow + one ox + three goats	02	-
46.	One cow + two oxes + two goats	02	-
47.	One buffalo + two cows + two oxes	01	-
48.	One buffalo + one he-buffalo + one goat	01	-
49.	One ox + two cows + one hen	01	-
50.	One buffalo + two oxes + five cows + two goats	01	-
	Total	134	07

The rest of freed bonded labourers had no animals in their possession because they have no means to kept it. This reflects on their poor supplementary source of incomes. They reported that the rearing of livestock was not suitable for them because of the non-availability of cattle shed, grazing lands etc.

Table 5
Distribution of FBLs through their Occupation

Occupation	Male		Female		Total	
	No.	%	No.	%	No.	%
Agricultural labour	183	79.57	05	2.17	188	81.74
Non-Agricultural labour	10	4.35	-	0.00	10	4.35
Service	01	0.43	-	0.00	10	4.35
No work/Old age	31	13.48	-	0.00	31	13.48
Total	225	97.83	05	2.17	230	100.00

The Table 5 demonstrates the contemporary occupation profile of the freed bonded labourers. Majority of freed bonded labourers (81.74%) including the women bonded labourers were found as agricultural labourers. They were engaged in agriculture filed in the vicinity of their households. They don't want to go elsewhere for work due to lack of confidence. It was found that freed bonded labourers were not engaged round the year and the demand was more seasonal, hence during the dull season they work in the non-agricultural areas like digging, house construction, rope making, wood cutting in the village or outside the village, which is their secondary occupation.

About 4.35 per cent of freed bonded labourers were engaged in non-agricultural work round the year. They were engaged in house construction with *Rajmistri,* as tractor driver and as horse cart puller in local areas.

Only one freed bonded labour from Narbal Barbal village of Bagha-II block named Ramprit Kurmi works as a Peon in Gandak canal project after been released. This is rare and it is an exceptional case.

About 13.48 per cent of freed bonded labourers were unable to do any type of work due to their old age and sickness.

Table 6
Wage Structure

Wage Structure	*No. of FBLs*	*Per cent*
In Kinds :		
(i) 3 kg. grains	16	6.96
(ii) 4 kg. grains	28	12.17
(iii) 5 kg. grains	04	1.74
(iv) 6 kg. grains	03	1.30
In Cash :		
Rs. 21 - 30	52	22.61
Rs. 31 - 40	66	28.70
Rs. 41 - 50	24	10.43
Own work	06	2.61
No work	31	13.48

The above table shows overall picture of wage structure of freed bonded labourers in the district. About 22.17% of FBLs reported that they were working in agriculture area and their wages were paid in kinds like rice, paddy, wheat etc. between 3 kg to 6 kg grains per day. The wage of freed bonded labourers varies from place to place in the district. It is seen in the table that 16 (6.96%) freed bonded labourers reported that they get 3 kg. Grains, whereas 28 (12.17%) FBLs reported that they get 4 kg. Grainswhile another 4 (1.74%) FBLs reported that they get 5 kg. Grains. 3 (1.30%) FBLs reported that they get 5 kg. Grains per day. The difference of wage in agriculture sector depends on peak and dull season work.

Out of 230 FBLs, 142 FBLs were working in agricultural and non-agricultural works and they received their wages in cash ranging from Rs. 21/- to Rs. 50/- per day. 6 FBLs reported that they were engaged in their own small business like grocery shop, tea shop, shoe repairing works, rickshaw thela pulling etc. About 13.48% of FBLs reported that they cannot do any type of work for their livelihood due to their old age sickness and they are dependent on their family for their day to day requirement.

Table 7
Knowledge of Minimum wage among FBLs

Do you know about the minimum wage ?	*No. of FBLs*	*Per cent*
Yes	-	0.00
No	230	1.00
Total	230	100.00

The above table shows that none of the freed bonded labourers had the knowledge about the government minimum wage for the agricultural and non-agricultural sector. Due to lack of knowledge and non-availability of work in the village, they work on low wages. They had no support from labour inspectors (LEOs) to enforce minimum wages for them. Till date, they have not met any LEO cadre officers from their respective blocks.

Table 8
Annual Family Income of FBLs

Income categories	*No. of FBLs*	*Per cent*
Upto Rs. 5000/-	07	3.04
Rs. 5001 - 10,000/-	57	24.78
Rs. 10,001 - 15,000/-	60	26.09
Rs. 15,001 - 20,000/-	72	31.31
Rs. 20,001 - 25,000	23	10.00
Above Rs. 25,000/-	11	4.78
Total	230	100.00

The Table 8 indicates about the economic status of freed bonded labourer's family. The poverty syndrome was apparent because 85.22% of FBLs were found below poverty line. It can be inferred from the table that their family income is less than Rs. 20,000/- per annum and which his more less below the poverty line amount i.e. Rs. 24,000/- yearly or Rs. 2000/- per month.

Only 14.78% of FBLs family earned above Rs. 20,000/- in a year, which shows that they were marginally scratching above the poverty line.

Further, the table reveals that the majority of FBLs (31.31%) have income of Rs. 15,001/- to Rs. 20,000/-, while 26.09% of FBLs have income of Rs. 10,001/- to Rs. 15,000/-. Another 24.78% of FBLs have income of Rs. 5,001/- to Rs. 10,000/- and 10.00% of FBLs have income of Rs. 20, 000/- to Rs. 25,000/-. About 4.78% of FBLs have income above Rs. 25,000/- and only 3.04% of FBLs have earned up to Rs. 5,000/-.

The picture in totality grim and dismal and needs major state's economic intervention for uplifting their position.

The family income of freed bonded labourers in West Champaran has not increased in a growth mode as it should have been progressively over the year. The reason is the majority of freed bonded labourers receive their wages in kind (food grains like paddy, wheat and maize etc.) and very few of them receive cash amount against his work. Many of them are not getting even the minimum wages as prescribed by the State Government.

Table 9
Saving Attitude among the FBLs

Have you saving account in the Bank/Post office ?	*No. of FBLs*	*Per cent!*
Yes	20	8.70
No	210	91.30
If yes, then where:		
(i) In the Bank	20	8.70
(ii) In the Post Office	-	0.00

The below table explains about the saving habit of FBLs. The majority of FBLs (91.30%) do not have any type of account in the bank or the post office. Only 8.70% of freed bonded labourers have their account in banks, but they did not operate their account for many years. The saving attitudes of FBLs are not satisfactory. On inquiry the majority of them reported that they earn daily and consume it. There are no spare money from their income for saving. They were always in hand to mouth situation because there is no facility of work round the year. In this connection, the government should provide minimum 100 days of work in a year and food for work programme along with the income-generating schemes among the freed bonded labourers on top priority.

Then another effort may be made for more awareness among them about saving habit for their safe and secure future. No efforts have been made to educate them for operating the savings account in the Post Office or a bank by the Department of Savings, Government of Bihar. The National Saving Departments has not held any awareness programme for inculcating saving habits among them.

Table 10
Debt among Freed Bonded Labourers

Source	*No. of FBLs under loan*	*Per cent*	*Amount of Loan*	*Average Amount of loan*
Formal agency	32	62.75	269400	8418.75
Non-formal agency	19	37.25	151100	7952.63
Total	51	100.00	420500	8245.10

The Table 10 shows that out of 230 FBLs, only 51 FBLs were in debt and had taken loan from formal and non-formal agency which amounted to a total amount of Rs. 4,20,500/-. 32 FBLs took loan from formal agency, which amounted to a total amount of Rs. 2,69,400/- and 19 FBLs had borrowed loans from non-formal agencies (e.g. Landlords, Moneylenders, relatives and friends) which amounted to a total amount of Rs. 1,51,100/-. In case of loans from non-formal agencies, they have to pay a higher rate of interest that is 5 to 10 per cent, which is exploitative in nature. Their dependence on moneylenders, *sahukaars* have to be prevented, because they can be vulnerable to debt bondage trap again.

The distribution of figures in the above table shows that majority of the freed bonded labourers (83.91 per cent) are working anywhere they get an opportunity to work. Only 2.61 per cent of the freed bonded labourers were working with their old landlords, where they worked before their release but today they are working due to their own choice and on better wages and condition. No compulsion to work with old landlord was reported. 13.48 per cent FBLs do not have any work due to their old age and sickness.

Table 11
Present Working Place of FBLs and his Family Members

Statement	*Anywhere*		*Old employer*		*Not applicable*		*Total*	
	No.	%	No.	%	No.	%	No.	%
Where do you Work at present ?	193	83.91	06	2.61	31	13.48	230	100.00
Where does other family members work at present ?	219	95.22	04	1.74	07	3.04	230	100.00

About 95.22% of FBLs family members have been working at different places for earning their livelihood while 1.74% family members were working with their previous landlord, where their father/husband were previously working. 3.04% of FBLs have no family members or their family members are not fit for working due to old age and sickness.

Table 12
Distribution of FBLs by Nature and Types of Dwelling units

No. of Rooms	*Kachcha*	%	*Pucca*	%	*Hut*	%	*Mixed*	%	*All type*	%
1.	-	0.00	44	19.13	12	5.22	-	-	56	24.35
2.	15	6.53	86	37.39	51	22.17	08	3.48	160	69.57
3+	01	0.43	01	0.43	10	4.35	02	0.87	14	6.08
	16	6.96	131	56.95	73	31.74	10	4.35	230	100.00

The above table shows that all freed bonded labourers had their own shelter, which meant a dwelling unit of some kind. The majority of FBLs 142 (56.95%) had pucca houses which has been made by help of the district administration under Indira Awas Yojana Scheme. 73 (31.74%) FBLs had hut, 16 (6.96%) FBLs had kachcha houses, and the rest 10 FBLs had mixed dwelling units. The mixed dwelling units were a combination of Indira Awas Yojana added to their traditional kachcha houses. But, 89 (38.70%) had not received the Indira Awas Yojana. This was a serious matter. It is suggested that the district administration should take necessary steps against this matter and provide the Indira Awas Yojana scheme for the remaining FBLs immediately because shelter is one of the basic needs for the human development.

The dwelling units had different numbers of rooms. The distribution of number of rooms in the Table 12 shows that the majority of freed bonded labourers 160 (69.57%) had two rooms unit, 24.35% of FBLs had one room unit and 6.08% of FBLs had three and more rooms unit. Their condition was far from satisfactory. The district administration must ensure that all FBLs receive Indira Awas Yojana unit urgently, particularly the 89 FBLs in the district who had not received IAY, as found during the study. The state has to be a good social provider for upliftment of FBLs.

25

EDUCATION SCENARIO : FREED BONDED LABOURERS AND THEIR FAMILIES

For human development paradigm, education is one of the major agencies of socialization. Education is most significant instrument for changing the society. Education influences the quality of life. Education is empowerment. It is an instrument to bring qualitative change.

The literacy rate of West Champaran district is 39.63% followed by 51.91 per cent male and 25.85 per cent female. The rate of literacy suggests that the government sponsored literacy programmes have to reach the vulnerable areas of deprived and under privileged. The present literacy and education initiative is not visible, since they remain under the umbra of benightedness. The results of primary data on selected variables pertaining to education have been presented in simple frequency.

Table 1
Classification of Freed Bonded Labourers on the Basis of Education

Education	*Number*	*Per cent*
Illiterate	191	83.04
Literate	28	12.18
Middle	09	3.91
Upto matriculate	02	0.87
Total	230	100.00

An overall picture of education among freed bonded labourers is presented in this table. The educational positions of freed bonded labourers were found low in the district because majority of them

(83.04%) were illiterate and had never received any form of schooling, under any Government educational schemes. Only 12.18% of freed bonded labour were found to be literate or better understood as semi-literate in the sense that they take social security money with signature and another 3.91% of freed bonded labourers were found to have received middle class education. But, it is also important to know that 0.87% of FBLs had education up to Matriculation level. Thus, the freed bonded labourers truly come from the most backward sections of the traditional society, who lives far from the block, district towns in the most interior area (village) of the district. It is too hard to reach these areas because the road facility are extremely deplorable and poor.

Table 2
Educational status of Freed Bonded Labourers Family Members

Category	*Illiterate*		*Literate*		*Upto Middle*		*Matriculate*		*Total*	
	Number	*%*	*Number*	*%*	*Number*	*%*	*Number*	*%*	*Number*	*%*
Adult Male	430	29.98	38	2.65	45	3.14	25	1.75	538	37.52
Adult Female	427	29.78	04	0.28	05	0.35	01	0.06	437	30.47
Male (6-14 yrs.)	119	8.30	-	0.00	131	9.13	-	0.00	250	17.43
Female (6-14 yrs.)	156	10.88	-	0.00	53	3.70	-	0.00	209	14.58
Total	1132	78.94	42	2.93	234	16.32	26	1.81	1434	100.00

As regards literary and educational status of freed bonded labourer's family, the table shows that shadow of darkness has not spared the next generation of freed bonded labourers families. 230 freed bonded labourers had 1,434 family members followed by 538 adult males, 437 adult females, 250 male child and 209 female child. They were predominantly illiterate with highest figure 1132 (78.94%) and only 42 (2.93%) were literate. About 16.32% were educated up to middle standard and 1.8% were found to be matriculate. Further, the table indicates that male and female children between the age group of 6-14 years were not going to school. They were engaged in domestic work in their own houses. Only 9.13% male children and 3.70% female children were going to school for their betterment of future. Thus, the percentage of school going children in FBLs families show that they haven't shown any interest in their wards education. They assume that there is no place of education in their existence because they can survive to by working hard.

There has been no extra efforts made by the state to spread education or raise their education level.

Education is key to mobility in life, but it does not carry any purpose among them.

Table 3
Awareness of FBLs Children Education

Where does your child read?	No. of FBLs	Per cent
Anganwari	02	0.87
If Anganwari, than		
(i) Getting food	02	0.87
Not reading	103	44.78
If not reading, then		
(i) Doing work at home	66	28.70
(ii) Playing here and there	73	31.74
(iii) Due to long distance of school	12	5.22
(iv) Working as a child labour	08	3.48
(v) There is no gain with education	23	10.00
(vi) No needs of education among girls	04	1.74
(vii) Grazing cattle	38	16.52
(viii) Dominant caste people disturb the children inside/outside the school	07	3.04
(ix) Due to low economic condition	14	6.09
School	83	36.09
If School, then		
(i) getting food materials	65	28.26
(ii) getting cash amount	02	0.86
(iii) getting books free	68	29.57
Not Applicable	44	19.13

Note: Figures are non-additive.

Naturally, the question arises why the children of bonded labourer families discontinue their education even at the early levels of primary and middle education. There are some common reasons accounting for this fact, which may be summed upon follows:

Firstly, the very atmosphere of the freed bonded labour families is not favourable. Here, we refer particularly to the domestic atmosphere. In the family of a bonded labourer or labourers, the members are uneducated and they are in unhealthy conditions and some times given to some bad habits and quarrels. In addition to these things, the children do not have convenient place of study. So social and economic conditions of the bonded families are not at all encouraging for the children to continue their studies.

Secondly, when the children of the freed bonded families can not fare well in their studies and show no or very little progress. Naturally, the elderly members of the families discourage the children and withdraw them from the schools and put them to domestic work or earning process.

Thirdly, apart from these two general and common reasons for the discontinuation of education, there are some specific and particular reasons.

The distribution of figures in the table demonstrates about the sampled FBLs children education. Out of 230 FBLs only, two FBLs reported that his children go to the Anganwari centre and are getting mid-day meal (Khichri). 36.09% of FBLs reported that their children go to school, and they reported that they are getting food (28.26%); books free of cost (29.57%) and are getting cash amount as stipend (0.86%). These FBLs were conscious for education and knew about its importance. Further, the table reveals that majority of 103 (44.78%) FBLs children don't go to school.

One more question was asked from the FBLs that where are your children if not in school? In response to this question, majority of them (31.74%) reported that their children were playing here and there, while 28.70% of FBLs reported that their children were doing work at home. 16.52% of FBLs children were engaged in grazing cattle. 10.00% of FBLs did not know the importance and value of education as they reported that there is no gain with education.

5.22% FBLs children did not go to school, due to long distance of school. 3.48% of FBLs children worked as a child labour. 1.74% FBLs were gender biased families, which felt that there was no need of education among the girl child. Some FBLs children were prevented from going to school by the dominant caste men in their areas (3.04%). There were some FBLs families, (6.09%), who wanted to send their children to school but could not do so due to poor and low economic conditions. About 19.13% of FBLs family reported that they have no children or no school going age children.

Majority of FBLs do not send their children to the Anganwari centre due to lack of knowledge and information. There is no approach made by the Anganwari center or concerned ICDS officials to motivate them or extend the Anganwari facilities to them.

Majority of them are illiterates, and few are educated at the lower levels, but they still cherish an ambition to see that their children receive good education. The Government have extended many facilities for their education like literacy programme and Sarva Shiksha Abhiyan for the poor and the oppressed. The Siksha Mitras mass contact programme will help in making education reach at the lowest level. With the improvement of wages, the agricultural labourers and freed bonded labourers also are enabled to spare a little part of their earning for the education of their children. Almost in every village cluster, there is a primary school. There is need to encourage children of the freed bonded labour families to receive primary education.

Table 4
Availability of Educational Facilities in the FBL's Village/tola

Facilities	*No. of FBLs*	*Per cent*
Anganwari	149	64.78
(i) Primary school	117	50.87
(ii) Upto Middle School	91	39.56
(iii) Upto High School	10	4.35
(iv) None of these	12	5.22

The accessibility of the governmental educational facilities as basic need for the betterment of future generation needs improvement. Education brings important change in the life of the people. The present table represents the availability of government educational facilities for the freed bonded labourers children in the village or tola.

The Table 4 indicate that all type of educational facilities are not available in the freed bonded labourers village/tola, rather it is insufficient for the FBLs families children in several areas.

Under the educational facilities, 64.78% of freed bonded labourers can utilize the Anganwari facilities, whereas 94.78% of FBLs can utilize schooling facilities for their children.

Further, the table reveals that the majority of FBLs (50.87%) can use schooling facilities upto primary level, whereas 39.56% of FBLs can utilize these facilities upto middle standard. Only 4.35% of FBLs can utilize these facilities upto High school for their children's education. About 5.22% of FBLs don't have any type of schooling facilities in their village/tola for their children.

In spite of these facilities, the light of education has not spread among the FBLs families. This shows that FBLs families are not taking interest in education. There is no quest for education. The hunger for food over takes the craving for education.

From above discussion and on the basis of field experience, it is recommended that freed bonded labourers need some special literacy package. A focused approach is needed to bring them in education cover totally. The schools presently running in the villages have failed to cover the FBLs children.

26

FREED BONDED LABOUR : HEALTH

The experience and concern in health development and primary health care in India date back to vedic period. In the Indus Valley Civilization as far back as 3000 B.C., one finds evidence of well developed environmental sanitation programmes such as under ground drains, public baths in cities etc. 'Arogya' or 'health' was given high priority in daily life and this concept of health included physical, mental, social and spiritual well-being.

One must take a holistic view of health policy because it is related to human and social development. The WHO has defined health as a state of complete physical, mental, social and spiritual well being and not merely the absence of disease or infirmity. In order to live socially and economically productive life, health is important. It has also been recognized that heath is a function not only of medical care, but a part of over-all integrated development of society, i.e. cultural, economic, educational, social, spiritual and political. It is affected by socio-economic status, family composition, customs, believes, life styles and use of available medical facilities. In fact, health influences man's all activities and shapes his destiny.

'Health for All' has been adopted as the goal with the promotion of primary health care as part of the new international development strategy for the 1980's and beyond. As a signatory to the Alma Alta Declaration adopted by WHO and UNICEF, Government of India has formulated a national policy (1983) to preside Health for All. It sets the goal towards the reduction of death rate in India but it could not achieve the goal 'Health for All' in a holistic manner, because health and medicare facilities is not provided by the Government in the rural areas, particularly in Bihar. The depressed caste people and economically backward family suffers from many types of diseases due to poverty and poor socio-economic conditions.

Health is the most important for freed bonded labourers. They don't understand about malnutrition. They live on poor quality food, which is not nutritious. As they are engaged in strenous work the food they take is not enough to keep them fit for long time and disease makes early entry, which debilitates them and make them grow old in their prime youth. The lack of rural medicare facilities particularly for the freed bonded labourers hits them early and hard. The issue of mortality is predominant.

The availability of safe drinking water is a major problem which is so necessary for good health. Thus, the present table tries to examine the drinking water facilities in the FBLs villages/tolas.

Table 1(a)
Availability of Drinking Water Facilities in the FBLs Villages/tolas

Source	*No. of FBLs*	*Per cent*
Well	15	6.52
Hand Pump	142	61.74
Well + Hand Pump	73	31.74
Total	230	100.00

The positive aspect in the above table is that it represents a mixed picture, which is that some type of drinking water facilities is available in all the FBLs villages/tolas. Majority of FBLs (64.74%) reported that the hand pump facilities is available in their villages/tolas, while 31.74% of FBLs reported that well and hand pump facilities are available in their villages/tolas. Only 6.52% of FBLs reported that they have only well facility for drinking water. Majority were satisfied with the availability of drinking water facilities, but had complains about the repair work of hand pumps and wells. They repair the hand pumps and wells with their own resources.

Freed bonded labourers are not aware about that the water available is safe for drinking. Water is kept in open, due to lack of proper storage system and facilities.

Above table demonstrates about the drinking water facility used by the freed bonded labourers. It is evident from the table that the majority of FBLs (87.39%) use hand pump for drinking water, while 10.87% of FBLs use well and only 1.74% of FBLs used well and hand pump both. Further, the Table 1(b) reveals that 20.87% of FBLs have installed their own hand pump for drinking water, which has not been provided by the district administration. They bored it in their houses on their own cost, but it is not deep tube well. The water appears to be unsafe for drinking purposes. PHED Department can help in installing proper hand pumps.

Table 1(b)
Drinking Water Facility used by the FBLs

Source	*No. of FBLs Used*				*Total*	*Per cent*
	Own Facility	*Per cent*	*Community facility*	*Per cent*		
Well	-	0.0	25	10.87	25	10.87
Hand Pump	48	20.87	153	66.52	201	87.39
Well + Hand Pump	-	-	04	1.74	04	1.74
Total	48	20.87	182	79.13	230	100.00

Drinking water facilities are community assets in many FBL tolas, which has been provided to some extent by the Central and State Government through the help of district administration is still needed for purposes of complete drinking water facility.

Above table shows the availability of toilet facilities in the FBLs houses. Majority of FBLs (98.70%) reported that there are no toilet facilities in their house. They go for open defecation. Even the female satisfies herself from call of nature in open. It is humiliating and hurts dignity.

Table 2
Availability of Toilet Facilities in the House

Response	*No. of FBLs*	*Per cent*
Yes	03	1.30
No	227	98.70
Total	230	100.00

Only 3 (1.30%) of FBLs of the district, who live in the village Saraiya, block-Bairiya, have toilet facility in their houses.

The rural sanitation programme of Government, UNICEF etc., are non-existence in the whole district. The rural sanitation programme is missing in FBLs tolas. It is harmful for their health.

Table 3
Availability of Drainage Facilities in the FBLs Village/tola

Response	*No. of FBLs*	*Per cent*
Kachcha	17	7.39
Pucca	10	4.35
Open flow	203	88.26
All	230	100.00

Table 4
Distance of Primary Health Centre from FBLs Residence

Distance in Km.	*No. of FBLs*	*Per cent*
upto 2	28	12.17
3-4	53	23.04
5-6	116	50.44
7-8	26	11.31
9 & above	07	3.04
Total	230	100.00

Above table demonstrates about the availability of drainage facilities in the FBL's villages/tolas. In this respect, majority of FBLs (88.260/0) reported that the waste water spilled here and there in the village land, due to the absence of any proper drainage system in the village/tola. Some of FBLs (7.39%) reported to have kachcha drains for disposal of wastewater in their villages/tolas. Very few FBLs (4.35%) reported to have pucca drains for disposal of wastewater in their villages/tolas.

It is evident from the above table that the freed bonded labourers face problem to get medical facilities from the government health infrastructure due to long distances from their tolas.

The majority of FBLs (50.4%) have to cover a long distance of 5 to 6 kms to reach the nearest health centre, while 14.35% of FBLs travel such a long distance 7 and above kms to reach the nearest health center.

23.04% of FBLs travel 2-4 kms to reach the nearest health centres, while 12.17% of FBLs travel 1-2 kms to reach the nearest health centre.

There is no outreaching programme for medicare FBLs. Non-availability of transport, makes the health issue for sick and old FBLs complicated. Hence, the freed bonded labourers and their family members face many difficulties about the medical and health care in the district.

Table 5
Medicare Facilities for FBLs

Statement	*No. of FBLs*					
	Yes	*%*	*No*	*%*	*Total*	*%*
Regular check up of Health	-	0.00	230	100.00	230	100.00
Medicare during the illness period	-	0.00	230	100.00	230	100.00

The latest status of government heath care system for the FBLs and their households is presented in this table. There is no doorstep facility for them. There is no concrete FBL's health programme, which gives priority for their regular health check up. There is no provision for medical team visits for check up after their release and rehabilitation. The FBLs complained that they don't get medicine at health centre. They are given prescription to buy medicine on their own cost.

27

EVALUATION OF REHABILITATION SCHEMES AND THEIR IMPACT

The present evaluative study was concerned with the rehabilitation status and their impact on the freed bonded labourers in West Champaran district.

Table 1
Identified & Rehabilitated FBLs in West Champaran District
(Upto Year 2001)

Sl. No.	*Name of the C.D. Block*	*No. of Freed Bonded labourers*			*Remarks*
		Identi-fied	*Rehabi-litated*	*Not Rehabilitated*	
1.	Bettiah	02	02	-	-
2.	Nautan	37	37	-	-
3.	Bairia	111	109	02	Died
4.	Yogapatti	24	24	-	-
5.	Majhaulia	63	63	-	-
6.	Chanpatia	56	56	-	-
7.	Narkatiaganj	63	63	-	-
8.	Gaunaha	478	467	11	Migrated
9.	Sikta	24	23	01	Died
10.	Mainatarh	130	129	01	Died
11.	Lauriya	74	74	-	-
12.	Madhuwani	35	35	-	-
13.	Ramnagar	399	399	-	-
14.	Bagha-I	195	195	-	-
15.	Bagha-II	805	805	-	-
16.	Thakrahan	06	06	-	-
	Total	2502	2487	15	-

The identification of bonded labourers and their release order certificate was given under the District Magistrate leadership.

PRESENT OCCUPATION OF FBLs & THEIR FAMILIES

Freed bonded labourers work as agricultural labourers within the village or outside the village independently. They are free to work with any landlord. Seasonally, they migrated to other place in search of work. Some were found working in non-agricultural work like digging, road work, construction work and other works. A small number of freed bonded labourers were without work due to old age and illness. Some FBLs go for work to nearest towns near their home place.

Table 2
Distribution of FBLs through their Occupation

Occupation	*Male*		*Female*		*Total*	
	No.	*%*	*No.*	*%*	*No.*	*%*
Agricultural Labour	183	79.57	05	2.17	188	81.74
Non-Agricultural Labour	10	4.35	-	0.00	10	4.35
Service	01	0.43	-	0.00	01	0.43
No work/Old age	31	13.48	-	0.00	31	13.48
Total	225	97.83 1	05	2.17	230	100.00

The majority of the family members of FBLs were working in agriculture, non-agriculture areas like brick-klin, digging, road work and other works.

There was no government assistance in their employment sphere. They were self-employed. There was no awareness regarding minimum wage or about insurance cover social protection programmes among them. There was no civil society activity noticed within the FBLs community for organising them or in raising their awareness on fundamental issues. NABARD/ similar other institutions, which are associated with Self-Help Group, were completely missing. ILO and other international agencies that work with children, women, deprived and old were conspicuous by their presence.

KNOWLEDGE ABOUT THE MINIMUM WAGE

None of the freed bonded labourers knew about the minimum wage, which is prescribed by the government and enforced by the labour department. They were paid according to the existing wage of the area. The working hours are normally 7 to 8 hours and get wage not only in cash but in kind also. They get wage of Rs. 20 to 50 in cash and 3 to 6 kg paddy or wheat with breakfast. It varies from village to village and block to block of the district. The FBLs do not receive minimum wage which needs to taken up urgently.

Table 3
Knowledge of Minimum Wage among FBLs

Do you know about the minimum wage ?	*No. of FBLs*	*Per cent*
Yes	-	0.00
No	230	100.00
Total		100.00

The labour department has to play an important role to implement minimum wages for them from their employers.

Table 4
Government Compensation Package for the FBLs

Sl. No.	*Major things*	*No. of FBLs*	*Per cent*
1.	One ox	03	1.31
2.	Two oxes	49	21.31
3.	Three oxes	05	2.18
4.	One buffalo	11	4.79
5.	Two buffaloes	19	8.26
6.	Two cows	01	0.43
7.	Eight goats	01	0.43
8.	Eight tyre carts	01	0.43
9.	One chara-cutting machine	01	0.43
10.	One rope-making machine	04	1.74
11.	One rope-making machine + one he-buffalo	03	1.31
12.	One rope-making machine + one buffalo	03	1.31
13.	One rope-making machine + two he-buffaloes	01	0.43
14.	One rope-making machine + one ox	05	2.18
15.	One chara-cutting machine + two oxes	02	0.87
16.	One buffalo + one ox	14	6.09
17.	One buffalo + one cow	02	0.87

Sl. No.	*Major things*	*No. of FBLs*	*Per cent*
18.	One buffalo + two oxes	24	10.44
19.	One cow + one ox	01	0.431
20.	Three buffaloes + one ox	01	0.43
21.	One buffalo + three oxes	01	0.43
22.	One he-buffalo + two oxes	01	0.431
23.	One buffalo + two oxes + cash Rs.1500/-	01	0.43
24.	One buffalo + two oxes + cash Rs. 300/-	01	043
25.	One cow + one calf + two he-buffaloes	01	0.43
26.	One horse cart + one mare	01	0.43
27.	One tyre cart + two oxes	45	19.57
28.	One tyre cart + two he-buffaloes	22	9.57
29.	One tyre cart + one buffalo + two oxes	04	1.74
30.	One tyre cart + one buffalo	02	0.87
	Total	230	100.001

After identification and their release, the bonded labourers were provided compensation package by the district administration agencies. Under this package, the freed bonded labourers were given different types of livestock, horse cart, tyre cart, chara cutting machine, rope-making machine, and cash to improve their economic condition and living standard of their family.

An overall picture of compensation package for the FBLs, provided through the district administration is presented in this table.

- The majority of FBLs (49) received two oxes.
- Next group of FBLs (45) received two oxes and one tyre cart.
- Another group of FBLs (24) received one buffalo and two oxes.
- The fourth group of FBLs (22) received two he-buffaloes and one tyre cart.
- The fifth group of FBLs (19) received two buffaloes.
- 14 FBLs received one buffalo and one ox.
- 11 FBLs received one buffalo.
- 5 FBLs received one roap-making machine and one ox.
- 5 FBLs received three oxes.
- 4 FBLs received one rope-making machine.

- 4 FBLs received one tyre cart, one buffalo and two oxes.
- 3 FBLs received one ox.
- 3 FBLs received one rope-making machine and one he-buffalo.
- 3 FBLs received one rope-making machine and one buffalo.
- 2 FBLs received one chara-cutting machine and two oxes.
- 2 FBLs received one buffalo and one cow.
- 2 FBLs received one tyre cart and one buffalo.
- 1 FBL received two cows.
- 1 FBL received eight goats.
- 1 FBL received one tyre cart.
- 1 FBL received one chara-cutting machine.
- 1 FBL received one rope-making machine and two he-buffalo.
- 1 FBL received one cow and one ox.
- 1 FBL received one ox and three buffaloes.
- 1 FBL received one bufallo and three oxes.
- 1 FBL received one he-buffalo and two oxes.
- 1 FBL received one buffalo, two oxes and cash Rs. 1500/-.
- 1 FBL received one buffalo, two oxes and cash Rs. 300/-.
- 1 FBL received one cow, one calf and two male buffaloes.
- 1 FBL received one horse cart and one mare.

Table 5
Social Security Pension for FBLs

Sl. No.	*Statement*	*No. of FBLs*					
		Yes	*%*	*No*	*%*	*Total*	*%*
1	Do you get Social Security Pension ?	173	75.22	57	24.78	230	100.00

Above table reveals that the majority of FBLs (75.22%) avail the social security pension facility of Rs. 100/- per month, which is provided by the Government under the Bonded Labour Rehabilitation Scheme, while 57 (24.78%) FBLs reported that they don't get this type of facility.

The break up of FBLs, who don't get the social security pension:

(a) Gaunaha Block:	(i) Banfairiya village	-	19
	(ii) Ekawa village	-	11
	(iii) Supauli village	-	04
	(iv) Lakshnautan village	-	01
	(v) Pachrukhiya village	-	01
	(vi) Bhatani village	-	01
	(vii) Kharatia village	-	01
(b) Mainatarh Block:	(i) Lipani village	-	03
	(ii) Inarawa village	-	01
	(iii) Purainiya village	-	01
(c) Bagaha - II Block:	(i) Rampur village	-	01
	(ii) Sherawa village	-	01
	(iii) Pipara village	-	01
	(iv) Narbal barbal village	-	04
(d) Lauriya Block:	(i) Mathiya village	-	01
(e) Nautan Block:	(i) Safawatola village	-	01
(f) Majhauliya Block:	(i) Ramnagar Bankat village	-	01
(g) Narkatiaganj Block:	(i) Harditerha Village	-	04

Why social security pension was not been given to some of the freed bonded labourers, was inquired from the District Social Security Department Officer. It was reported by officer concerned that he had no knowledge about this and why they have not been paid the social security pension. But, he promised to implement it soon.

The district administration has not done satisfactory work on the pension front because about one-fourth FBLs of the district don't get the social security pension till date.

This pension is lifeline for them and it is recommended that old age family members and widowers of FBLs may be also be included in these social securities scheme immediately.

Table 6
Other Related Programmes for FBLs under Poverty Line Scheme Indira Awas Yojana & IRDP Facilities

Sl. No.	*Scheme*	*No. of FBLs*					
		Yes	*%*	*No*	*%*	*Total*	*%*
1.	IAY	141	61.30	89	38.70	230	100.00
2.	IRDP	32	13.91	198	86.09	230	100.00

- The Table 6 shows that 141(61.30%) FBLs received Indira Awas Yojana (IAY) facilities and were using it for residential purposes.
- 38.70% of FBLs reported that they didn't get this type of facility and a long period has passed since they were released. They had no clue as to why they were not provided IAY house, but they are still hopeful of getting one from the Government.
- 32 (13.91%) FBLs reported that they received loan from the bank to purchase livestock tyre cart, pumping set machine, grinding machine etc. to establish their business. But some of them spent this loan amount on daughter's marriage and in treatment of disease of their family members.
- Majority of then (86.09%) didn't get anything under IRDP assistance.
- The Government assistance is evident but in fragmented manner and not in totality. There is urgent need to address the issue as to why 89 (38.70%) FBLs were left out from the IAY scheme.
- It can be said that the Government programmes under the below poverty line and bonded labour schemes, are not efficiently provided to the FBLs.
- This scheme is about shelter, which is also one of the foremost and important issue in the case of FBLs human development. As per direction of the Government of India and the State Government, all DMs have to link the FBLs with IAY schemes as a part of Government poverty alleviation holistic strategy.
- West Champaran district has failed to meet its mission to provide IAY and other development scheme to all rehabilitated FBLs.
- SJGSY is in practice since April 1999 as an important scheme for poverty alleviation. The FBLs can be brought under SJGSY, which has multiple in put for BPL families. It clearly states that within three years with help of all in puts an effort should be made to bring the family above poverty line.

The Table 7 reveals that the majority of FBLs (76.09%) have received the facility of Lal Card, while 23.91 % of FBLs reported that they didn't receive the Lal Card facility which is provided by the Government agencies. They want reduction of delay tactics at the block offices and petty corruption.

Table 7
Lal Card and PDs Facilities among FBLs

Statement	*No. of FBLs*	*Per cent*
Do you have a red card?		
(i) Yes	175	76.09
(ii) No	55	23.91
If yes, then what type of materials received by you at the Govt. rate ?		
(i) Kerosene oil	124	53.91
(ii) Kerosene oil & grains	05	2.18
(iii) Nothing	46	20.00
Where are the PDS?		
(i) Within the village	147	63.91
(ii) Outside the village	83	36.09

- Further, the table reveals that 124 (53.91 %) of FBLs are getting benefit-of kerosene oil only from the PDS network.
- 2.18% of FBLs-one FBL of village-Jokahan, Block-Chanpatia, one FBL of village-Semario, block-Yodgapatti, one FBL of village Banairiya, block-Gaunaha, one FBL of village -Rampur, block-Bagaha-II and one FBL of village-Sherwa, block-Bagaha-II) reported that they are getting benefit of kerosene oil & food grains particularly 15 kg rice and 20 kg wheat in a month at subsidized rate.
- About 20% of FBLs reported that they don't get anything, either kerosene oil or neither food grains with help of the Lal Card.
- Majority of them complained during the field visit that most beneficial would be availability of food grains particularly rice/ wheat at subsidized rates in the PDS fair price shop (Ration shop).
- 63.91% of FBLs reported that PDS facility is available within the village, while 36.09% of FBLs reported that their PDS is outside their village.

It is evident from Table 8 that their previous employer seized no property during the bonded labour period.

Table 8
Property Released and Provided Property through the Government

(a) Distribution of FBLs by Seized Property

S. No.	Statement	No. of FBLs			
		Yes	%	No.	%
	Did employer seize your property during the Bonded Labour Period ?	-	0.00	230	100.00

(b) Distribution of FBLs by providing Basgit paper

Have you received Basgit Paper?	No. of FBLs	%
Yes	171	74.35
If Yes, then:		
(i) 1-2 decimal	105	45.65
(ii) 3-4 decimal	55	23.92
(iii) 5 decimal	11	4.78
No	59	25.65
Total	230	100.00

- Majority of FBLs (171) reported that they had received basgit papers, while 59 (25.65%) reported that they did not receive the basgit paper for their houses.
- Further, the table reveals that 105 (45.65%) FBLs had received 1-2 decimal of land through the basgit paper, while 55 (23.92%) FBLs reported that they had received 3-4 decimal of land. Only 11 (4.78%) FBLs reported that they had received 5-6 decimal land through the basgit paper.

Table 9
Visit of Vigilance Committee Members in the FBLs Village/tola

S. No.	Statement	No. of FBLs			
		Yes	%	No.	%
1.	Visit of Vigilance Committee Members		0.00	230	100.00

- For the monitoring the development of socio-economic condition of freed bonded labourer, the Vigilance Committee's members have yet to visit the FBLs villages/tolas to monitor the progress.

- The table reveals that the Vigilance Committee members never visited any FBLs village/tolas.
- This indicates that the organizational performance and monitoring system of Vigilance Committee in the district is non-functional.

TRAINING FACILITIES

- None of the FBLs received any training by government agency after their release for self-employment.
- Training, particularly vocational training is an important component for learning skills for self employment.
- The capacity building for acquiring new skills and developing the existing indigenous skills tradition art and craft can become an important mode of income.

AWARENESS PROGRAMME AMONG THE FBLs

- No awareness programme was held among the freed bonded labourers. They were not aware about the government scheme for them except what they had got at the time of release. It is necessary to make them aware about the other assistance, schemes and programmes.
- A regular sensitization and capacity building process was not done in the district for the FBLs. An effort can be made on making them aware about their schemes and how they can benefit from them.
- Exercise can be held to drive home about their right and how to live independently and free from debt bondage.
- It is evident from the Table 10 that all FBLs received their release certificate by the district administration, but at present majority of them have lost the release certificate or were keeping in proper condition. They should be given laminated certificates and periodically it should be checked whether they have it or not, because that will ensure their receiving Government assistance.
- One of the major objectives of the present evaluative study is to find out the opinions or expectations of the freed bonded

labourers. In lieu of this, freed bonded labourers expressed their suggestions for improving their present situation and gave an inside view of their level of expectation.

Table 10
Availability of Releasing letters among the FBLs

Have you received any type of Bonded Labour release letter issued by DM/SDO ?	*No. of FBLs*	*Per cent*
Yes	230	100.00
No	-	0.00
Total	230	100.00

Table 11
Opinion of FBLs on What Steps the Government should take to improve their conditions

	Statement	*No. of FBLs*	*Per cent*
1.	To improve infra-structural facilities–Electricity, Road, PDS	156	67.83
2.	Housing, Drinking water, Toilet & Drainage Facilities	113	49.13
3.	Medical & Health care facilities	87	37.83
4.	Educational Facilities	56	24.35
5.	For improving economic condition of families, loan vocational training, Business, Land for cultivation, Animal Husbandry–Cattle, Piggery	194	84.35
6.	Pension facilities and increase in Pension amount	63	27.39
7.	Regular work all the year around	74	32.17
8.	More facilities by the Government	47	20.43
9.	Development functionaries should pay visit	28	12.17
10.	Enhancement of wage	44	19.13
11.	No response	-	0.00

- The above table reveals that most significant suggestion was for improving economic condition of families (84.35%) in which they demanded food security, work guarantee, loans, income generating facilities, land for cultivation and animal husbandry–cattle/pig rearing.

- 67.83% of FBLs want improvement in the infra-structural facilities like electricity, road and public distribution system.
- 49.13% of FBLs felt that the Government should provide housing, drinking water, toilet and drainage facilities.
- 37.83% of FBLs felt that the government should provide more medical and health care facilities.
- 32.17% of FBLs demanded regular work round the year.
- 27.39% of FBLs suggested that the pension amount should be increased and payment regularly.
- 24.35% of FBLs demanded educational facilities for their children.
- 19.13% of FBLs want to increase their wages for betterment of their living condition.
- 12.17% of FBLs felt that the block development functionaries should pay visit in their village/tolas.
- 20.43% of FBLs want more facilities through the government.
- During the interview of FBLs it was found that they totally depend on the Government to improve their economic condition.

Table 12
Knowledge of Bonded Labour Act among the FBLs

Do you know about the Bonded Labour Act ?	*No. of FBLs*	*%*
Yes		0.00
No	230	100.00
Total	230	100.00

- All freed bonded Labourers of the district don't know about the Bonded Labour Act, 1976 under which they freed.
- They were in consensus grateful to the Government agencies for releasing from the clutches of bondage.
- An overall picture of perception of change among FBLs is presented in this table. But, the most important question was that whether they felt any perceptible change after being freed. The response was overwhelming.

Table 13
Perception of Change among FBLs

Statement	*No. of FBLs*	*Per cent*
Freedom of work	203	88.26
Feeling better than earlier	148	64.35
Enhancement in social prestige	26	11.30
Improvement in food availability	24	10.43
Enhancement of wages	15	6.52
No pressure/binding of work	172	74.78
No change	07	3.04

Note: Figures are non-additive.

- They cherished the freedom of work, which meant liberty to choose their workplace.
- They adored mobility and right to live as they wished. It was clear departure from bondage to liberty and to availing opportunities, as its came through with great hardship in many cases.
- The above table shows that the most significant answers were freedom of work (88.26%), followed by no pressure and binding of work (74.78%).
- 64.35% of FBLs expressed their feelings of being better than before.
- Some experienced enhancement in their social prestige (11.30%).
- A very small section of FBLs felt improvement in food availability (10.43%).
- And enhancement in wages (6.52%).
- The revelation of this study was that few FBLs, who were freed, continued to work in their old master's field. They had no complaint against them because the old masters were giving them batter wages now than before, and liberty and mobility and choice to work or not with them.
- There has been a slight improvement in financial condition, betterment in food consumption, enhancement in social prestige and increase in voting activities after their release.
- But majority of them (9%) haven't purchased any permanent or durable assets for their income and livelihood.

Table 14
Opinion of FBLs on their uplift after being Released

Activities	*Uplift*			
	Gain		*No Gain*	
	No. of FBLs	*%*	*No. of FBLs*	*%*
Financial condition	203	88.26	27	11.74
Food consumption	216	93.91	14	6.09
Asset acquisition	09	3.91	221	96.09
Social prestige	224	97.39	06	2.61
Voting behaviour	230	100.00	-	0.00
No response				

- There is marginal change in their better food consumption, living pattern as in past and in use of clothes.
- They like to eat rice and bread with vegetable regularly and also the consumption of pulse frednently. It was marked progress from the previous bondage life. They were trying to have neat and clean clothes.
- Some had better accommodation facilities due to houses provided under the Indira Awas Yojana through the district administration.

Table 15(a)
Classification of FBLs with Gain in Food Consumption

Statement	*No. of FBLs*	*Per cent*
(a) If Gain in food consumption, then what type of improvement ?		
(i) Food according to their will	27	11.74
(ii) Take better food:	134	58.26
(iii) Improvement in fooding clothing and housing	65	28.26
(b) No Gain:	04	1.74
How many times, do you take food ?		
(a) Twice a day	53	23.04
(b) Thrice a day	177	76.96

- The above table reveals that the majority of FBLs (58.26%) take better food at present.
- 28.26% of FBLs reported that they have experienced improvement in fooding, clothing and housing.

- While 11.74% of FBLs reported that they take food according to their will, which is just enough for subsistence.
- Further, the table reveals that 76.96% of FBLs take their food thrice a day and 23.04% of FBLs take it twice a day.
- All the FBLs take rice and bread with potato/salt & chili or rice juice (Maar) and salt/chattani and achar/chakha etc.
- They don't consume food rich in protein and vitamins, particularly non-vegetarian food items, due to their low economic condition. Their consumption in qualitative food is still low but improved from, past. The thrust of intake is more on the quantitative food compared to qualitative food.
- Low intake does affect their health standard and longevity of life.

Table 15 (b)
Classification of FBLs with Gain in Asset Acquisition

Statement	*No. of FBLs*	*Per cent*
If Gain in asset acquisition, then what type of asset ?		
(i) Purchasing of land	06	2.61
(ii) Purchasing of livestock	03	1.30
No Gain	221	96.09
Total	230	100.00

- The above table demonstrates that majority of FBLs (96.09%) haven't purchased any permanent or durable assets for their income and livelihood.
- While 2.61 % of FBLs reported that they purchased some land for agriculture or housing purpose after the release.
- Only 1.30% of FBLs reported that they purchased two buffaloes each in village-Jokahan, block-Chanpatia.
- The break up of FBLs, who have purchased land after the release :
- (a) Bairiya block: (i) Saraiya village - 02
- (b) Yogapatti block: (i) Semari village - 01
- (c) Gaunaha block: (i) Bhatani village - 01
- (d) Ramnagar block: (i) Dhanrapa village - 01
- (e) Bagha - II block: (i) Rampur village - 01

DIFFICULTIES FACED IN THE FIELD WORK & FEEDBACK

(i) The list of freed bonded labourers was properly maintained in the social security department, but the addresses of the FBLs was very vague and proved to be a daunting task to find FBLs in the field since West Champaran terrain is ardous and tough and there is poor road connectivity and public transportation facility. It was painful and distressing at times because the addresses provided were incorrect. No register was maintained. The list of freed bonded labourers was typed and kept neatly in a file, but the data was not proper in most cases.

(ii) The list of freed bonded labourers was not up-to-date. It was not clear that how many freed bonded labourers were alive or how many had died or migrated.

(iii) It was surprising the Assistant Director, Social Security was not fully updated about the freed bonded labourers rehabilitation status particularly about the latest released FBLs. He informed that the rehabilitation process was on but had no clue when will it be completed. There was no time schedule fixed either at district level or at block level.

(iv) He was not aware about the total picture of the social security pension scenario and how many FBLs were actually receiving the pension.

(v) Mostly freed bonded labourers were illiterate so the response of many questions was not given properly.

(vi) Many were not keeping the release order certificate to verify their identity. The certificate should have their photograph and be laminated for their long life.

(vii) It can be said that the government sponsored programme under the below the poverty line and freed bonded labourers schemes were not efficiently implemented.

(viii) The field administration had not pursued any follow up programme and monitoring to assess the progress of the freed and rehabilitated bonded labourers.

(ix) The programmes were devoid of human touch. Some had benefited while others were left out. There was lack of holistic approach.

(x) There was no mechanism to review progress of the freed bonded labourers by the block, sub-division and district administration officials. The Vigilance Committee can play a key role, provided it is functional.

(xi) The FBLs complained that rehabilitation was just one time affair, and no constant nurturing or monitoring was done to see whether they have benefited or not. There is scope for greater involvement by field agencies, since FBLs are the most important segment of anti-poverty strategy in the district. The holistic effort should be to prevent them for falling back to debt bondage. The sustainability of their livelihood and regular income, with support of district administration, is basic to their rehabilitation.

(xii) The district administration has assured that immediate corrective measures would be taken for benefit of all FBLs in the district in their upliftment, development and progress in the district.

PART - VI

An Evaluation of Bonded Labour Rehabilitation Schemes in MUNGER District

28

INTRODUCTION – MUNGER : A PROFILE

BRIEF HISTORY OF THE DISTRICT

The district of Munger lies in the central part of the state. It was carved out of the other district of Bhagalpur around 1812. It is named after Munger, which is the most important town and the administrative headquarters of the district.

Comprised within Bhagalpur division, Munger is bounded on the north by Begusarai and Saharsa district, on the south by the Santhal Parganas and Hazaribagh district of Jharkhand state and on the west by Gaya and Patna. As the result of the reorganization of the districts in the state, Begusarai, which was a sub-division of the old Munger attained the status of an independent district with effect from 2nd October, 1972. The trimmed Munger district now contains two sub-divisions and nine community development blocks.

'Munger' was the spelling adopted by the early Britishers, which continued to be used till the 1971 census. However, in the recent part it was decided to adopt the Hindi name, which could be better spelt as Munger. There are various hypotheses about the origin of the name of the district. The Mahabharat mentions the place as Muda-Giri or Mods-Giri. It was also known as Maudagalaysgiri after Mandagalys, a famous Buddhist monk. However, a widely prevalent tradition ascribe the name of the sages Mudgals Rishi, the grandfather of the epical Ahilyas, who was turned into stone on account of her husband's curse but was redeemed later in Trets-yug by lord Shri Ramchandra. Mudgalgiri, so named after Mudgals Rishi, was in course of time corrupted to Munger.

EARLY HISTORY

The district of Munger comprised the eastern portion of Madhyadesh or the midland of the original Aryan settlers. Later, Munger formed part of the kingdom old Angs with its capital at Champa, near Bhagalpur, on the western part of the district and it constituted part of the Magadh empire. Anga was overtaken by the Magadh Emperor Bimbisar in the sixth century B.C., when Brahmadatta, the last independent ruller of Anga was overthrown. Hereafter, the history of Munger was virtually that of the Magadh empire.

It is believed that the town of Munger is also associated with Buddha's disciple Maudhadgalya. There is enough historical and archaeological evidence to show that Buddha himself had visited different places in the district, and there are ruins and remains of stapes and viharas built by royal converts of Buddhism all over the district. Recently, scholars have also tried to prove conclusively that Mahavir Tirthankar was born at a place called Lachchaur lying in the southern part of the district. Thousands of jain pilgrims visit this small hamlet, high up in the hills, to celebrate the birth anniversary of Lord Mahavira.

The earliest written account of the district is available in the travel memories of Hiuen Tsang, who traveled through some parts of the district towards the middle of the seventh century A.D. He had passed through the south portion of the district, now corresponding to Sheikhpura, Kharagpur and Kajra.

There is a gap in the history of the district for a several centuries after Hieun Tsang's visit. Dhannpal, one of the Pala kings, resided in Munger in about 770 A.D., while Deva Pal carried out further conquest. A copper plate showing the grant of a village by Deva Pal in modern Patna was executed in Mudagiri or the present Munger. Another place shows the grant of land by Narayan Pal, fifth in the line of Pals Kings, who is described as the Lord of Anga, i.e., Bhagalpur and Munger.

MUSLIM PERIOD

Towards the close of the twelfth century A.D., when Bakhtiar Khilji involved and conquered Bihar, Munger passed into the hands of muslims without offering, much resistance. In 1225 A.D., Sultan Iltutmish probably met the forces of Sultan Gyasuddin Khilji of Bengal at Munger, which ultimately led to signing of a treaty. During the time of early muslims, Munger was the secured town in south Bihar. It continued to be a part of Bengal till 1332, when it was annexed to Delhi by Md. Tughlak. From 1397, Munger become a part of the kingdom of Jaunpur and continued as such for about one hundred years until the time of Bahlol Lodi, whose son Sikandar Lodi over ran Bihar as far as the frontier of Bengal in 1489. Earlier, from, 1459 to 1474, Munger was brought under the control of Rukmuddin Barkurk. After a temporary control by Afghan chiefs, Daniyal, son of Sultan Hussain Shah of Bengal, met Sultan Sikandar Lodi of Delhi near Barh in the year 1499, and the province was acknowledged as a part of Bengal.

Munger was for sometimes the station from where Akbar's forces led by Todar Mal directed their operations against the insurgents of the military revolt in Bengal in 1580. Todar Mal succeeded in winning over the rebel chiefs without much fighting, Raja Sangrampur and Raja Puran Mal of Gidhaur because they thought it was better to submit to Akbar Khan than wage an useless war.

In 1745, Mustafa Khan, a rebel general of Ali Vardi Khan advanced upon Munger and captured the fort. Two years earlier, the army of Balaji Rao, the Peswa of Poona had marched through Munger and caused heavy suffering to its people.

BRITISH PERIOD

As the empire of Moghuls weakened and disintegrated by the middle of the 18th century, Bihar came under the control of the Subhash of Bengal, which had become practically independent of Delhi.

Once again Munger came into prominence, when in 1762 Kasim Ali Khan or Mirkashim shifted his capital from Murshidabad in Bengal to Munger. Mirkashim Ali, soon came in for trouble with the English when a company of sepoys was sent by the English manager of the factory at Patna to search the Munger Fort on the suspicion that some deserters were harboured there, subsequently, in the events that followed a British from under Major Adam defeated Mir Kasim's troops at Suti. Ultimately, the Fort of Munger was taken over by the British in 1763.

With the extension of their domination by the British, the town of Munger ceased to be an important military station. In the subsequent period, it owed its prominence more as a health resort than an administrative center.

Unlike other parts of the state, the National Movement of 1857 did not affect Munger district to any appreciable extent. The timely dispatch of troops to the town of Munger nipped the trouble in the bud.

Geomorphological setting—Munger district has a diverse landscape made up of the hills, the plateau, the erosion plain, and the terraced alluvial plain. The terrain on either side of the eastwardly articulate Kharagpur hill tract descends in steps from the Chakai plateau (340 m above MSL) in the south to the channel of Ganga (32 m above MSL) in the north. Weighable the hills and the plateau including undulating recessional plain (pedi plain) are restricted within 60 to 300 m and above (above MSL), high level (alluvial plain) Jamui Terrace occurs between 40 m above MSL). The major part of Ganga plain including parts of Diara plain has elevation from, 37 m to 40 m above MSL, while that of the lowest, relief representing the core area of back swamp depressions is between 34 m and 37 m above MSL.

Flood and water logging—The belt of the Ganga including their tributaries like Harohar and Kiul are prone to flood and or water logging to a raring extent. The Ganga-Kiul plain and Diara plain are the most affected areas. Again, even in a low-flood year, water logging by drainage congestion and back flow sometime takes place in Tal area of Ganga belt. The Tal areas has in general a minimum depth of inundation of 2 m and above from the end of July to the end of October, whereas in the peripheral part water logging takes place for about two months during August and September. Parts of Jamui terrace areas adjoining Kiul, Badua and Barnar river channels are also occasionally affected by flash flood.

Soil Erosion and drought—The rocky upland, the plateau and the pediplain is also a part of Jamui terrace and are the areas prone for hill erosion. The surface runs off down slope gravitational fall and removal of protective green cover are some of the factors which are responsible for soil erosion and formation of barren hill slopes. It is in this southern part of the district recurrence of the drought is felt almost every year. The drought not only affects cultivation but also causes chronic shortage of drinking water problem. In addition, there is annual variation in the rainfall to the extent of 250 mm to 300 mm from, the average of 1234 mm at the district. The other factor, which contribute the drought conditions are the delay on the onset of monsoon, its early withdrawal and abnormal distribution of rainfall like major downpour in July-August and very meager incidence of rainfall in September and October etc.

Climate—The climate of Munger can be described as a transition between the dry and moderately extreme climate of the Northern India and the warm, humid climate of Bengal basin viz.

(i) Winter : The winter actually begins from the end of November and extends up to ethic end off February. In December and January the weather is delightful being dry and bracing during the day while the nights are distinctly cold when there is a gradual fall in temperature from north to south.

(ii) Summer : Summer begins from the mid of March and extends up to the end of May. These are the driest months of the year when hot winds start bellowing causing severe heat during the day.

(iii) Monsoon : Normally the monsoon starts from mid June and continues till the end of September. During this period about 80% of the annual precipitation is received.

(iv) Autumn : This season commences with retreat of the monsoon from early mid October and lasts till upto the end of November thus the climate is salubrious in the entire district during the autumn and winter, whereas summer is uncomfortable.

Rainfall—The average rainfall in the district is 1234 mm. The areas around Chakai, Sono, Jhajha and Lakhisarai gets rainfall below the district average, while towards the south as well as east rainfall increases. August is the month of highest rainfall.

Soil—Important soil in district are sandy soil, red and yellow soil, and younger alluvial. Younger alluvial soil is restricted in the northern, flood prone areas of the district along the river Ganga. The soil is generally alkaline and characterized by deficiency in nitrogen, phosphoric acid and humus. It is most fertile soil and suitable for extensive cultivation of rice, pulses and sugar cane. Rest of the areas is occupied by red sandy soil and red yellow soil. Red sandy soil is acidic pH ranging between 5.0 to 6.5 and is deficient in nitrogen, phosphates and organic matters. Red and yellow soils acidic to alkaline in reaction (pH value ranging between 5.5 to 8.5) and is poor in calcium phosphate, nitrogen and humus.

Land use—The land use is the dynamic pattern of the human uses of land resources of areas which evolve through the combined influence of terrain characteristics, natural resources, hazards, socio-cultural and tech-economic factors.

Markets—The important markets of the district are situated at Munger, Jamalpur and Lakhisarai. In addition to these there are markets at Barbighas, Jamui, Barahys, Jhajha and Kharagpur. All these markets have good roads links. The agriculture products market committee based at Munger have five sale points/sub-yards in the district nearly at Jamalpur, Sangrampur, Tarapur and Asarganj having principal market at Safia Sarai (Munger). As regards the marketing of industrial products at present 183.51 units are gathering order every month from I.T.E. Few units are getting order from the other Government Department like PHED, Hospitals etc. Three cattle markets are held at Barbighas, Tarapur and Sikandra in the district. There are 15 regulated markets and 35 non-regulated markets in the district.

Banking—The principal banking in the Munger district comprises of commercial banks, Munger Regional Rural Banks, Munger-Jamui central co-operative banks and land development banks. In addition the institutional finance in the district is also provided by Bihar state Financial Corporation and Life Insurance Corporation of India.

Demographic characteristics—Population growth-The total population of Munger district is according to 2001 census is 1135499. The distribution of male and female population as per 2001 census is 604662 and 530837 respectively. The cultivators and agricultural laborers are the two most important categories of the working forces. The total working population is engaged in agricultural and allied activists. The people engaged in household industry manufacturing and processing and other services were marginal workers were the total working forces.

Agriculture—Munger district comprises of various types of land form, with undiluted type of topography. The land form of the district can be broadly divided in the following major crops:

1. Gangatic plain
2. Diara Plain
3. Tal land
4. Hilly and forest hilly area

Agriculture condition is quite different in the north and south of the district. Some of the good fertile lands in the district are found under Diara of Ganga which are alluvial and diluvial. Some Diara lands are most fertile producing good Bhadai kharif crops before flood and good rabi crops after flood in winter.

Cropping pattern—In this district there are two distinguished seasons i.e. kharif and rabi. The summer crops are a supplementary one.

Irrigation—Utilization of surface water for irrigation purposes although not is not adequate, but it is being carried through the following surface water irrigation schemes:

- Lower Kiul Valley Irrigation Project (right)
- Lower Kiul Valley Irrigation Project (left)
- Beha Irrigation Project
- Vajan Irrigation Project
- Lift Irrigation Kaurihari River
- Kund Ghat Irrigation Project
- Tali Irrigation Project
- Phirangi Bigha Irrigation Project
- Amriti Reservoir Project
- Shrikhandi Reservoir Project
- Morve Reservoir Project
- Kamihari Irrigation Project
- Kailash Ghati Reservior Project

Industry—There are two large scale industries in the district namely :

- Railway workshop at Jamalpur
- Cigarette factory at Munger.

At present, the largest industrial concern in the district is the workshop of the Eastern Railway at Jamalpur. These workshops are among the largest in India and have been established for the construction and repair of rolling stock. The plant connected with the railway and all the constituent parts of a locomotive engine can be manufactured.

The next important industries establishment in the district is the cigarette factory at Munger. The factory is owned by the Indian tobacco company, makers of certain famous brand of cigarettes. One of oldest industry of Munger is iron and steel work, in particular, for the manufacture of Guns.

Education—There are number of education institutions in different blocks of Munger district. Besides this there is one industrial training institution in the district.

Fisheries—Munger district offers immense potential for fresh water fisheries is large system of rivers, canals and inland water bodies. The Ganga's tributaries and sub-tributaries constitute the drainage network in munger district. The tributaries to the Ganga are usually perennial with varying amount of surface flow round the year.

Besides the district is also blessed with a number of ponds and seasonal streams. In addition to these, there are a large number of Reservoirs, jheels and irrigation channels, which from a large network of water bodies. The large water bodies are utilized for multiplying and growing fishes on a commercial scale, the small water bodies is utilized for production of fish seeds.

Livestock—The terms 'livestock' includes cattle (cows, bulls and bullocks) buffaloes, sheep, goat and pigs. The cattle are generally of small size and poor quality. Except, the north Gangetic plains, whose grass lands are available, the grazing lands are generally deficient on the district. The usual fodder of the cattle consists of the scanty grass, which grows along the road side, and the weeds which spring up among the stubble after the crops have been harvested. Efforts are being made by the Animal Husbandry Dept. to improve the breed of the cattle by various upgrading programmes.

Forest—The forest area of Munger district is speared over to 4 out of 9 blocks of the district. The total forest area of the district is 344148 hectares.

Rail—Communication facilities are still lacking in the districts. The headquarters of Munger district is itself on the loop line crosses through northern part of the district from east to west.

The main railway line passes from north to south of the district touching Lakhisarai, Jamui, Jhajha and Simultalla.

Road network: There are several types of roads in the district. There has been no National High way passing through the district.

Munger is essentially an under developed over populated district having terrain condition and varied but limited endowments of nature. The district is unique in its exposure to frequent natural hazards–flood waterlogging, river erosion in the northern part and drought and soil erosion or the southern sector. Any national plan for the district therefore must recognize the various environmental elements, which cause such natural vagary and identify the priority sector, where rapid development can be effected to improve socio-economic conditions of large population.

Keeping this perspective in view, it has been attempted to analyse the present status of development of Munger district.

Table 1
Munger : Some Important facts (Census 2001)

1.	Administrative name		Munger		
2.	No. of Sub-divisions	:	2		
3.	No. of Blocks	:	9		
4.	No. of Towns	:	4		
5.	No. of Revenue village	:	866		
6.	No. of Panchayats	:	101		
7.	Area (in kms.)	:	1419.0		
8.	Total population	:	*Male*	*Female*	Total
		Rural	818913	435774	1254687
					135474
		Total	604662	604662	1135499
9.	Sex ratio (per 1000 male)		Rural	Urban	Total
10.	Density of population		800		
11.	Population growth during 1991 - 2001				
			Male	*Female*	Total
12.	Infant mortality				
13.			*Male*	*Female*	*Total*
	(i) Literacy		35461	209432	564043
	(ii) Literacy rate		70.68	47.97	60.11
13.	Child population in the age group 0-6				
			Male child	Female child	Total
			Rural	78809	71347
			Urban	24119	22869

Source: Census of India 2001, Series 11, Bihar.

Physical features—Munger district lying between north latitudes 24°23′ and 25°30′ east longitude 85°35′ and 86°44′ covers and area of 5228.0 sq.m. It is bounded on the North by the river Ganga, on the south of Giridih and Deoghar district (Jharkhand state), on the East by Bhagalpur district and on the west by Nawada, Nalanda and Patna districts.

General Administrative Divisions—Munger district consists of two subdivisions and 9 revenue circles. For development administration, the district is divided into 9 development blocks. There are 866 revenue villages and 101 panchayats.

An overall picture of some important facts of Munger district is presented in the Table 1. The table reveals the distribution of total population in respective of rural-urban, males/females, population, areas, density of population, population growth rate, infant mortality rate, literacy rate, child population. Further, the tables demonstrate the administrative name of the district in Munger There is 2 sub-divisions, 9 C.D. blocks, 4 towns, 866 revenue villages and 101 panchayats.

C.D. BLOCK BY RURAL-URBAN

An overall picture of block-wise distribution of rural-urban population is presented in this table. The table reveals the highest rural population is in Munger sadar block followed by Kharagpur and in third position is Dhanahara block. The total rural population in the district is 8,18,913 and total urban population is 3,16,586 and total rural-urban population is 11,35,499.

Table 2
C.D. Block of Munger Districts of Rural-Urban Population

	Rural	*Urban*	*Total*
Munger	109639	187311	296950
Bariarpur	92431	-	92431
Jamalpur	84912	96659	181571
Dharahara	103919	-	103919
Kharagpur	1540988	26910	181008
Asarganj	53856	5706	59562
Tarapur	84341	-	84341
Tetia Bomber	57622	-	57622
Sangrampur	78095	-	57622
Total	818913	316586	11,35499

	Male	*Female*	*Total*
Munger	159243	13 7707	296950
Bariarpur	49632	42799	92431
Jamalpur	96522	85049	181571
Dharahara	55197	48722	103919
Kharagpur	95183	84825	181008
Asarganj	31620	27942	59562
Tarapur	44060	40281	84341
Tetia Bomber	30869	26753	57622
Sangrampur	41336	36759	78095

Source: Census of India, 2001.

An overall picture of block-wise distribution of males and females population is presented in this table. The table reveals, the highest population is in the Munger sadar block, followed by 1,59,243 males and 137707 females and the lowest population is in the Titia Bombar block, followed by 30,869 males and 26,753 females.

Table 3
Block-wise Literates

	Total	*Male*	*Female*
Munger	168940	101494	67446
Bararpur	40604	26816	13788
Jamalpur	114768	68267	46501
Dharahara	42986	28509	14477
Kharagpur	77249	51253	25996
Asarganj	25108	16175	8933
Tarapur	36289	23470	12819
Tetia Bomber	23882	16395	7487
Sangrampur	34217	22232	11985

Source: Census of India, 2001.

An overall picture represents the literacy scenario of the Munger district. Total literate male people 3,54,611 and female 2,09,432. Munger sadar block is first position for literate persons, followed by Jamalpur and Kharagpur blocks. The very low number of literates people belongs to Titia Bomber block.

Table 4 reveals that there are 83.965 families below the poverty line in a population of 11,35,499 in Munger district. Jamalpur (22,171), Harnaut (11,001), Tarapur (15,745) are three blocks having a large number of BLP families. It also reveals the socio-economic scenario of Munger district.

Table 4
Block-wise List of BPL Families

Block	*No.* of families
Jamalpur	22171
Dharhara	10344
Tarapur	15745
Sangrampur	8688
Kharagpur	1614
Titia Bombar	7181
Bariarpur	7221
Munger	11 00 1
Total	83,965

Source: DRDA office, Munger year 1997-98.

REFERENCES & ACKNOWLEDGEMENT

1. Census 2001.
2. District Census Handbook: Munger district, 1981, Series–4, Bihar.
3. Economic Intelligence Services, Profile of Districts, CMIE, Mumbai.
4. DRDA, Munger.
5. Department of Social Security, Munger.
6. Dr. Almas Ali and Dr. B.P. Thiagarajan, District Profile-Bihar, PFI, New Delhi.
7. Munger District Gazetteer, P.C. Roy Chaudhry, Gazetteer Revision Section, Revenue Department, Patna 1960.

29

BONDED LABOUR IN MUNGER DISTRICT

The system of bonded service came into existence when lands were divided and distributed to the individuals for the purpose of cultivation. The system became sterilized when the lands so distributed to the individuals were declared permanent property of the respective individuals. This may be in administrative phraseology called the incidence of land settlement. The vicious nexus started with the society splitting into 'haves and have-not'. The bonded labour belongs to the depressed and deprived section of the feudal society based on social and economic inequity.

The present chapter deals with the present and past status of freed bonded labourers of Munger district. In this respect, the district administration and the department of social security Munger provided a list of 790 identified FBLS, but only 745 FBLs were rehabilitated, who were spread in the different villages in: the different blocks of the district. The Munger district contains 9 blocks, and 6 out of 9 blocks has more and less freed bonded labourers. The highest number of freed bonded labourers (257) were identified and rehabilitated in Jamalpur block, where as the lowest number of FBLs (46) were identified and rehabilitated in Sangrampur block. It is important to point out here that the district administration of Munger identified 790 FBLs upto year 1987, but rehabilitated only 745 FBLs. Thus, in total 745 FBLs were rehabilitated through the district administration.

The ANSISS research team visited different village of different blocks of the district and interviewed sampled freed bonded labourers (151) and collected relative data from them. Thus, the sample was drawn only from 151 rehabilitated freed bonded labourers of the district.

The following table gives details about the freed bonded labourers of the district.

Table 1
Identified and Rehabilitated FBLs in Munger District

Sl. No.	*Name of the C.D. Block*	*No. of Freed Bonded labourers*			*Remarks*
		Identi-fied	*Rehabi-litated*	*Not Rehabi-litated*	
1.	Jamalpur	257	257	-	-
2.	Dharahara	66	62	04	-
3.	Tarapur	61	60	01	-
4.	Sagrampur	47	46	01	-
5.	Munger	86	86	-	-
6.	Kharagpur	273	234	39	-
	Total	790	745	45	-

The above table shows the block-wise actual position of freed bonded labourers of the district. The table reveals that about 790 bonded labourers were identified and released, but 45 freed bonded labourers were not rehabilitated.

REHABILITATED FREED BONDED LABOURERS IN MUNGER DISTRICT

The Table 2 shows the complete picture of rehabilitated freed bonded labourers in the different blocks of the district. Jamalpur block has the highest number of FBLs (257) rehabilitated by the district administration. Kharagpur block is in the 2nd position with 234 FBLs, while Munger block is in the 3rd position with 86 FBLs. Dharahara block is in the 4th position with 62 FBLs and in the 5th position is Tarapur block with 60 FBLs. On the 6th position is Sangrampur block with 46 FBLs. The ranking of the different blocks in the table indicates the position of the FBLs in the block.

IDENTIFICATION PERIOD OF REHABILITATED FBLs

Since the enforcement of Bonded Labour System (Abolition) Act 1976, a total number of identified and released bonded labour in the district was 790 and out of this figure, 745 FBLs were rehabilitated through the district administration. The table 3 shows the identification period of all rehabilitated freed bonded labourers of the district.

Table 2
Block-wise Distribution of Identified FBLs in Munger District

Sl. No.	*Name of the C.D. Block*	*No. of FBLs*	*Per cent*	*Rank*
1.	Jamalpur	257	32.53	1
2.	Dharhara	66	8.35	4
3.	Tarapur	61	7.72	5
4.	Sangrampur	47	5.95	6
5.	Munger	86	10.89	3
6.	Kharagpur	273	34.56	2
	Total	790	100.00	

108 (14.50%) FBLs were released during the year 1980-81. 365 (48.99%) FBLs were released in the year 1982-83. 130 (17.45%) FBLs were released in the year 1984-85 and the rest 142(19.06%) FBLs were released in the year 1986-87.

The majority of FBLs were released in the year 1982-83 and the next majority of FBLs were released in the year 1986-87.

Table 3
Identification Period of FBLs in Munger

Identification Period	*No. of FBLs*	*Per cent*
1980-81	108	14.50
1982-83	365	48.99
1984-85	130	17.45
1986-87	142	19.06
Total	745	100.00

In Munger, the released FBLs period and their rehabilitation takes two to three years, because of the government machinery problem. The released bonded labourers need immediate support for their livelihood. There is fundamental need for creation of buffer fund to give immediate relief to bonded labourers. The rehabilitation grant takes time for sanction from State and Central Government.

A permanent corpus should be created at DM level to help bonded labourers immediately after release. Hence, the gap of two or three years should minimised as much as possible.

The research team in this evaluation study visited about 332 freed bonded labourers household. Out of 332 FBLs, 151 FBLs were interviewed. It was found that 13 FBLs had migrated and 168 FBLs, a major group of freed bonded labourers, had died. Thus, the evaluation team met and collected the relevant data from 151 FBLs.

Table 4
Block & Village-wise Distribution of Sample FBLs in the Munger District

Sl. No.	*Block*	*Village*	*No. of FBLs*			*Total*
			Inter-viewed	*Mig-rated*	*Died*	
1.	Jamalpur	Ahra Mushari	13	1	24	38
		Ratanpur	15	1	7	23
		Chamargarh	16	2	17	35
		Fulkia	8	-	7	15
2.	Dharhara	Dasrathi	4	-	10	14
		Barmsia	4	-	2	6
		Bilokhar	3	1	5	9
		Sarobag	1	-	4	5
		Bhalari	1	-	1	2
3.	Tarapur	Launa	10	1	8	19
		Devgaon	2	1	2	5
4.	Sangrampur	Rampur	3	-	3	6
		Maggai	1	-	2	3
		Narayanpur	6	-	5	11
5.	Munger	Maniarchak	13	2	9	24
		Nawagarhi	2	-	2	4
		Tothi	1	-	1	2
		Chandan Nagar	1	-	2	3
6.	Kharagpur	Madanpur	17	1	20	38
		Laxmipur	7	-	9	16
		Mohanpur	7	-	8	15
		Shampur	-	-	04	04
		Saraiyan	6	1	5	12
		Kausalpur	1	-	1	02
		Kathulitya	9	2	10	21
		Total	151	13	168	332

This latest information on FBLs has been passed to the district administration and the social security office by the ANSISS team. The evaluation team suggested to the social security department official to collect the latest information about bonded labourers regularly and update their register also.

DISTRIBUTION OF FBLs BY THEIR CAUSES FOR BONDED LABOUR

Bonded service is generally traced out to be the inevitable consequence of the degenerated social and economic conditions of the labourers in villages. But at what particular period of life and circumstance the labourers become vulnerable to require a large sum of money is an important aspect of study. It is during that particular period only that they are initiated to bonded service.

Table 5
Distribution of FBLs by their Causes for Bonded Labour

Cause	*No. of FBLs*	*Per cent*
Low socio-economic status in the society	43	28.48
Unemployment	18	11.92
Poverty	76	50.33
On the traditional way	29	19.21
Indebtedness	111	73.51
Own choice	4	2.65
Total	151	100.00

Note: The figures are non-additive. It is multiple answer based.

One of the most important objectives of the study was to find the causes for becoming bonded labour in the Munger district. It can be observed from the above table that the most significant answer was indebtedness (73.51%), followed by the poverty (50.33%). The other major reason was attributed to the low socio-economic status in the society (28.48%), followed by the traditional way (19.21%) and unemployment (11.92%).

In respect of causes of bonded labour, there was multiple answers given by the FBLs but the problem of indebtedness, poverty, low socio-economic status in the society and unemployment was most dominant causes for falling into vicious bonded labour trap. It is classic example of absolute deprivation praxis in the social and economic structure. The feudal environment and graded caste hierarchy also played an important role in bringing the landless and the helpless in the exploitative practices of the bonded labour system where the dominant landlords lured them into bondage.

Another major objective of the study was to find out where FBLs were working as bonded labour before their release. In response of these findings, the majority of FBLs (59.61%) reported that they worked in the same village during the bonded labour period, where they lived. This affirms the feudal social environment where these FBLs worked. About 39.07% FBLs reported that they worked outside the village but within the block, while 1.32% FBLs reported that they worked outside the block but within the district.

Table 6
Working Place of FBLs before Release

Statement	*No. of FBLs*	*Per cent*
Within the same village	90	59.61
Outside the village but within the block	59	39.07
Outside the block but within the district	02	1.32
Outside the district but within the state	-	0.00
Outside the State	-	0.00
Total	151	100.00

Table 7
Working Period of FBLs as Bonded Labour before Release

Working Period	*No. of FBLs*	*Per cent*
Upto 5 years	4	2.65
6 - 10 years	40	26.49
11 - 15 years	43	28.48
16 - 20 years	35	23.18
21 years and above	29	19.20
Total	151	100.00

A complete picture about the working period of FBLs as bonded labour before their release is presented in the Table 7. The table reveals that out of 151 sampled FBLs, 107 FBLs (70.86%) FBLs worked as bonded labour for 11 years and above, while 26.49% of FBLs reported that they had worked as bonded labour for 6 to 10 years. About 2.65% of FBLs reported that they had worked between 1 to 5 years. It reveals that the majority was in chain of subjugation and bondage for over a decade and had spent their prime years in servitude.

30

FREED BONDED LABOUR : SOCIAL LIFE

The present chapter deals about the social characteristics of freed bonded labourers. Under these characteristics of the FBLs, the study focuses on the age, sex, family size, caste, marital status, family members, neighbours and availability of infrastructure facilities in the village to understand their social life. The majority of the FBLs in Munger belonged to Scheduled Caste category (79.47%), while 15.89% of FBLs belonged to OBC category. About 4.64% of FBLs belonged to Scheduled Tribe category.

Before analyzing the sample data, it would be essential to note that these freed bonded labourers are from ritually deprived strata in degraded social hierarchy of peasant village society. The social disadvantaged position combines with economic deprivation. Their backwardness not only showed their ascribed position, but also their achieved position. The FBLs quality of life was found at the low end. It was also found that this community (FBLs), still suffers from social and economic infirmity. They were not in the local mainstream of the village society. The freedom from bondage appeared meaning less since liberty was limited. The social mixing was not evident and the scar of bondage was apparent socially. The ladder of social mobility was still elusive.

The Table 1 gives details about the social life of freed bonded labourers.

Let us first examine the age pattern of the freed bonded labourers. It is evident from the table that the freed bonded labourers belong to different age groups ranging from 41 to 71 and above. They are a composite mix group of young, middle and old age. It is found from this table that the highest percentage of the FBLs (48.34%) belong to the age group of 61 to 70 years, which suggest that they are old and have been long in the iniquitous cycle of bondage till they were freed. They have lived long to relate their harrowing experiences. It also emerged that the majority had served their masters for a long time.

Table 1
Age-wise Distribution of Freed Bonded Labourers

Age Group (Yrs.)	*Number*	*Per cent*
41 - 50	21	13.91
51 - 60	46	30.46
61 - 70	73	48.34
71 and above	11	7.29
Total	151	100.00

The second highest percentage of respondents (30.46%) belonged to the age group of 51 to 60 years, which implies that they were in the master's domain also for a reasonable period of time. The third highest percentage of the respondents (13.91%) belongs to the group 41 to 50 years. This group was small but provided in depth view of bonded scenario. It also suggests that a small percentage survived the bonded period. The fourth highest percentage of the respondents (7.29%) belongs to age group of 71 and above. This age group is dominated by the old survivors. They are old and not in the position to work hard. They have been long in the vicious circle of bondage till they were freed. It also suggests that they survived the hardship of bonded period and are wealth of information on bonded period. They have lived long to tell their stories of hardship. It emerged during informal discussions that the majority had served their master for a relatively long time and the treatment received from them was not proper and were treated in inhuman manner.

The Table 2 shows the distribution of male and female sampled freed bonded labourers in the district. It is evident from the table that there were 149 males and 2 females signifying high prevalence of males in bondage but there were two female freed bonded labourers too. The females FBLs were found in the Ratanpur village of Jamalpur block only. The location of these female bonded labourers village was about 12 kms from CD block office. They were released in the year 1982-83.

Table 2
Sex-wise Distribution of Freed Bonded Labourers

Sex	*Number*	*Percentage*
Male	149	98.68
Female	02	01.32
Total	151	100.00

The presence of female Freed bonded labourers in the district depicts a scenario where the highest degree of exploitation of the bonded labourers families happened, where women were compelled to mortgage themselves as debt bondage labourers. These females were mortgaged along with their husbands and were released together. They were working in agriculture sector.

Table 3
Family Size-wise Distribution of Freed Bonded Labourers

Family Size	*No. of FBLs*	*Percentage*
Upto 5	46	30.46
6-10	82	54.30
11-15	20	13.25
16 and above	3	1.99
Total	151	100.00

The above table shows that majority of FBLs (54.30%) had family size of 6-10 members, whereas 30.46% of freed bonded labourers had up to family size of 5 members. About 13.25% of freed bonded labourers had large family size with 11 to 15 members. Only 1.99% of freed bonded labourers had very large family size with 16 and above members.

In view of rural family structure, large family is still prevalent in-norm, and it was true for freed bonded labourer families in Munger also, because they are related to the rural life. Thus, the family size of FBLs was found large in the district because they were related to village life, where large and joint family is the main characteristics. The families of all rehabilitated FBLs belong to traditional family system with two or three generation living together and sharing common kitchen. It is very interesting to point out that the no concept of family planning among the FBLs was evident.

Table 4
Age & Sex-wise distribution of Family Members of Freed Bonded Labourers

Age Group	*Male*		*Female*		*Total*	
	No.	*%*	*No.*	*%*	*No.*	*%*
0 - 5	19	1.77	25	2.33	44	4.10
6 - 14	179	16.68	141	13.14	320	29.82
15 - 60	304	28.34	258	24.04	562	52.38
61 and above	82	7.64	165	6.06	147	13.70
Total	584	54.43	489	45.57	1073	100.00

The above table shows that the freed bonded labourers' families belong to different age groups. They are in the age group of up to 5 years, 6 to 14 years, 15 to 60 years and 61 and above years. The majority of the freed bonded labourers (52.38%) were found the age group of 15 to 60 years, having 28.34% males and 24.04% females.

The next age group of FBLs is 6 to 14 years with 29.82% constitute the second large size, with 16.68% males and 13.14% females. Another age group of FBLs 61 and above years with 13.70% constitutes the third large size, with 7.64% and 6.06% females. The fourth and last age group of FBLs is less than 5 years with 4.10% followed by 1.77% males and 2.33% females.

Table 5
Distribution of Freed Bonded Labourers by Sex and Marital Status

Marital Status	*Male*		*Female*		*Total*	
	No.	*%*	*No.*	*%*	*No.*	*%*
Married/Unmarried	125	82.78	-	-	125	82.78
Widow/Widower	24	15.89	2	1.32	26	17.22
Total	149	98.67	2	1.32	151	100.00

Thus, the table indicates that most of the freed bonded labourers families were found in the age group of 15 to 60 years and this age group is diligent and very hard working group.

An overall picture of marital status of freed bonded labourers are presented in this table. The majority of freed bonded labourers 82.78% are married. Only 15.89% male and 1.32% female freed bonded labourers were widow/widower, who live in village and bear the family responsibilities. The district administration has to give them work, food and secure environment to protect their families.

The two female FBLs belonged to Ratanpur village of Jamalpur block. They were released in 1983 and have settled in their own village. The female FBLs need special intervention from administration.

Table 6
Caste Composition of the Freed Bonded Labourers

Caste	*Number*	*Percentage*
Scheduled Caste	120	79.47
Scheduled Tribe	7	4.64
Backward	24	15.89
General	-	-
Total	151	100.00

The above table shows the caste composition of sampled freed bonded labourers in Munger district. The majority of the freed bonded labourers 79.47 per cent belong to Scheduled Caste (Chamar, Musahar, Dusadh and Nonia) community, while 4.64 per cent FBLs belongs to scheduled tribes. 15.89 per cent of the freed bonded labourers belong to backward caste (Tatwa, Yadav, Koeri). None of the FBLs were found in the upper caste category. It is true to the picture of the history of debt bondage. It fits the absolute deprivation paradigm, where ritually low status in graded hierarchical society coexists with those below the poverty line status. The social and economic levels are uniformly steeped in the bottom line of an agrarian semi-feudal society.

The distribution of figures in above table shows that the majority of freed bonded labourers live in cluster. It indicates that the district administration identified and rehabilitated bonded labour in a cluster.

Further, the table reveals that 58.28% of FBLs had 16 and above members of FBLs in their neighbourhood, while 11.92% of FBLs had a neighbour's size of 11-15 FBLs members. About 21.85% of FBLs had a neighbour size of 6-10 FBLs member. The rest 7.95% of FBLs had up to 5 members of FBLs in the neighbourhood. The social cohesiveness as a unit was apparent among the FBLs fraternity. They felt psychologically more as an extended family due to their common heritage and past.

Table 7
Neighbours of Freed Bonded Labourers

Sl. No.	*Statement*	*No. of FBLs*	*%*
1.	Was your neighbour Freed Bonded Labour?		
	(i) Yes	151	100.00
	(ii) No	–	–
2.	If Yes, how many families?		
	(i) Upto 5	12	7.95
	(ii) 6 –10	33	21.85
	(iii) 11 – 15	18	11.92
	(iv) 16 and above	88	58.28
	Total	151	100.00

The availability of government infra-structural facilities in the rural society as basic civic, support system for the citizens are an important measurement for evaluating the expanse of welfare steps taken to uplift the common citizen in rural Bihar. In the present table, the availability of governmental infra-structural facilities for FBLs represents a mixed scenario.

Table 8
Availability of Government Infra-Structural Facilities in the Villages/Tolas of FBLs

Government Facilities		*No. of FBLs*	*Percentage*
1.	Post Office	70	46.36
2.	PDS	151	100.00
3.	Health Centre	2	1.32
4.	Electricity	72	47.68
5.	Bank	2	1.32
6.	Road Facilities :	–	–
	(i) Kachcha	144	95.37
	(ii) Pucca	5	3.11
	(iii) Mixed	2	1.32
	(iv) No other facility	–	–

The table 8 shows that all type of infra-structural facilities are not available in the freed bonded labourers village/tolas of the district, rather it is insufficient for the freed bonded labourers families in several areas. Some are fortunate to enjoy the facilities where as others are deprived of the basic facilities. There is no uniformity in the availability of these government conveniences except in PDS facility in Munger. The table also demonstrates about missed opportunity by the Government agencies in reaching out to all the FBLs families.

The picture emerging is like that, 46.36 per cent of freed bonded labourers can utilize the post office facilities, where as 100 per cent of freed bonded labourers can use the Public Distribution System (PDS) facilities, which is excellent in Munger. The health situation is dismal with only 1.32 per cent of freed bonded labourers having access to the health centres. 47.68 per cent of freed bonded labourer can utilize the electricity connection. Only 1.32 per cent of freed bonded labourers can utilize the bank facilities, which is very poor.

Another most important issue is road facilities. The kachcha road facilities were accessible for 95.37 per cent FBLs families, 3.11 per cent on the pucca road and 1.32 per cent of freed bonded labourers were accessible on the mixed road.

The facilities used by the freed bonded labourer shows mixed availability in a backward area of Bihar, where there is lopsided provision of infrastructure and basic amenities.

31

FREED BONDED LABOUR : ECONOMIC LIFE

The freed bonded labourers are from socially backward castes and the economically deprived sections. They have low economic status. They are below the poverty line. Their economic survival depends upon their labour. They have no secondary source for income generation.

The freed bonded labourers are the important segment of the local agriculture labour. The freed bonded labourers are part of the landless labourers. The limited job market is unstable. The FBLs with their families work either in agriculture field or in the non-agriculture works like brick-kiln, building construction, railway work, cart pulling, digging soil etc. The older people do minor work.

It varies from one season to another. They are dependent on demand of labour in rural market. In the village development works, under the Swaran Jayanti Rozgar Yojana and other schemes, where number of minor works like digging the earth, carrying the soils, brick work in the village lane etc., are done by the freed bonded labourers. Due to few development works in their villages, there was limited scope for work.

The family members of freed bonded labourers also work in order to support their families. They do petty work Children work as child labour.

The table 1 gives the details about the economic life of freed bonded labourers.

It was observed that the freed bonded labourers have no fixed working hours when work is available in the agriculture field. The work is generally available in agriculture sector only for five to six months. There is no employment guarantee and food security. Secondary source of employment and income generating schemes like rearing the animal, dairy, poultry farm etc., are limited.

Table 1
Distribution of FBLs in Terms of Land provided for Cultivation through the District Administration

Statement	*No. of FBLs*	*Per cent*
Land provided for Cultivation		
(i) Yes	5	3.31
(ii) No	146	96.69
If Yes, then how much land		
(i) Upto 18 decimal	1	-
(ii) 50 decimal	2	-
(iii) 90 decimal	1	-
(iv) 1 acre	1	-

The distribution of cultivable land among bonded labourers under the rehabilitation scheme was done by the district administration for 5 FBLs. The district authorities provided land, which was acquired under ceiling. The quality of land is poor and barren. So, the FBLs who had received the land could not cultivate it.

The distributions of surplus land ceiling was done among five freed bonded labourers, who got the land papers, but not in equal size. The above Table 1 shows that one freed bonded labourer got 18 decimal land. Two FBLs got 50 decimals of land, whereas one FBL got the largest size of land-one acre. One FBL got 90 decimal of land. All were meant for agricultural purposes. But, unfortunately the land is not in good quality. 146 FBLs got no land and are fully dependent on working in others field.

The majority of freed bonded labourers are agricultural and non-agricultural labourers by occupation. For cultivation and doing agricultural and non-agricultural works, their most urgent need is the need for farming equipment. So, after their release, they purchased some farming equipment which has become their tool for livelihood and security, which prevents them from wandering into economic non-entity. The main tools for cultivation and agricultural and non-agricultural works are plough, shovel, khurpi, hasua and other equipments. They are fundamental tools to their fight against hunger and economic uncertainty.

Table 2
Distribution of FBLs by their Possession of Farming Equipments

Farming Equipments	*No. of FBLs*	*Per cent*
Plough	16	10.59
Shovel	135	89.41
Others Khurpi & Hasua	151	100.00

Table 3
Agriculture Facilities provided by Government among FBLs

Statement	*No. of FBLs*	*Per cent*
Farming Equipments provided by the Government	–	–
Fertilizer, seeds and pesticides at subsidized rate	–	–
How do you irrigate your land ?		
(i) Well	–	–
(ii) Pond	–	–
(iii) Canal	–	–
(iv) No facility	03	1.99
Not applicable	148	98.01

The above table explains the possession of farming equipments among the freed bonded labourers. Only 16 (10.59%) of freed bonded labourers reported that they had plough, while 135 (89.41%) FBLs reported that they had shovel as the farming equipments. All FBLs reported that they had khurpi and hasua only. Though, the tools are primitive and familiar to least developed feudal agricultural -plains of Munger, but they have proved to be lifeline for them. It is due to these utilitarian basic tools, they get some work during the agricultural season and even during non-agricultural period like digging excavation etc. work. They are part of their work culture and economic existence.

Majority of the freed bonded labourers 148 (98.01%) were found to be landless. For the rest of 5 FBLs, the government till date has not provided any irrigation facility to them. They also reported that they haven't received fertilizers, seeds and pesticides at the subsidized rate. For the landless freed bonded labourers, the issue of fertilizer, seeds, pesticides and irrigation facility is baseless. None of them got any type of farming equipment by the district administration.

Table 4
Distribution of FBLs by their Livestock Possession

Sl. No.	*Name of Livestock*	*No. of FBLs having*	
		Own livestock	*Bataidari livestock*
1.	One buffalo	02	-
2.	Two buffaloes	01	02
3.	One cow	23	04
4.	Two cows	04	-
5.	One goat	07	-
6.	Two goata	06	-
7.	Three goata	03	-
8.	Two oxes	04	-
	Total	50	06

The rearing of animal is secondary source of income in rural society. Traditionally, livestock possession played an important role in the rural economy. For poor households like landless agricultural labourers etc., the livestock possession plays an important role in their economy and contributes to about two third of the rural poor income. Rural poor population depends on it for their supplementary livelihood. In this connection, landless and agricultural labourers mainly depend on goat, cow and buffalo. Though cattle rearing for them are difficult, but they make lot of effort to keep them.

The Table 4 reveals the critical dependence of freed bonded labourers on livestock for their cash incomes. Out of 151 freed bonded labourers, 50 freed bonded labourers had their own livestock and only 6 freed bonded labourers had bataidari livestock, which were given by different types of people to look after their animal on 50 per cent sharing basis.

The rest of freed bonded labourers had no animals in their possession because they have no means to keep it. This reflects on their poor supplementary source of income.

The Table 5 demonstrates the contemporary occupation profile of the freed bonded labourers. Majority of freed bonded labourers (72.19%) including the women bonded labourers were found as agricultural labourers. They were engaged in agriculture filed in the vicinity of their households. They don't want to go elsewhere for work due to lack of confidence. It was found that freed bonded labourers were not engaged round the year and the demand was more seasonal, hence during the dull season they work in the non-agricultural areas like digging, house construction, rope making, wood cutting in the village or outside the village, which is their secondary occupation.

Table 5
Distribution of FBLs through their Occupation

Occupation	*Male*		*Female*		*Total*	
	No.	*%*	*No.*	*%*	*No.*	*%*
Agricultural labour	108	71.52	01	0.66	109	72.19
Non-Agricultural labour	26	17.22	1	0.66	27	17.88
No work/Old age	15	9.94	-	-	15	9.93
Total	149	98.68	2	1.32	151	100.00

About 17.88 per cent of freed bonded labourers were engaged in non-agricultural work round the year. They were engaged in house construction as mason (rajmistri) and as horse cart-puller.

About 9.93 per cent of freed bonded labourers were unable to do any type of work due to their old age and sickness.

The below table shows overall picture of wage structure of freed bonded labourers in the district.

Table 6
Wage Structure of FBLs

Wage Structure	*No. of FBLs*	Per cent
Cash		
Upto Rs. 40	18	11.92
Rs. 40 - 50	73	48.34
Rs. 51 - 60	45	29.80
No work	15	9.94
Not taking wage	-	-
Total	151	100.00

Out of 151 FBLs, 136 FBLs were working in agricultural and non-agricultural works, and they received their wages in cash ranging from Rs. 40/- to Rs. 60/- per day. About 9.94% of FBLs reported that they cannot do any type of work for their livelihood due to their old age sickness. They are dependent on their family for their day-to-day requirement.

Table 7
Knowledge of Minimum Wage among FBLs

Do you know about the minimum wage ?	*No. of FBLs*	*Per cent*
Yes	-	-
No	151	100.00
Total	151	100.00

The table shows that none of the freed bonded labourers had the knowledge about the government minimum wage for the agricultural and non-agricultural sector. Due to lack of knowledge and non-availability of work in the village, they work on low wages. They had no support from Labour Inspectors (LEOs) to enforce minimum wages for them. Till date, they have not any met LEO cadre officers from their respective blocks. The Government should organize sensitization awareness camps at their tolas.

The Table 8 indicates about the economic status of freed bonded labourer's family. The poverty syndrome was apparent because 92.04% (139) FBLs were found below poverty line. It can be inferred from the table that their family income is less than Rs. 20,000/- per annum, which is more or less below the poverty line amount i.e. Rs. 24,000/- yearly or Rs. 2000/- per month.

Table 8
Annual Family Income of FBLs

Income categories	*No. of FBLs*	*Per cent*
Upto Rs. 5000/-	07	4.64
Rs. 5001 - 10000/-	51	33.77
Rs. 10001 - 15000/-	42	27.81
Rs. 15001 - 20000/-	39	25.83
Rs. 20001 - 25000/-	8	5.30
Above Rs. 25000/-	4	2.65
Total	151	100.00

Only 7.95% (12) FBLs family earned above Rs. 20,000/- in a year, which shows that they were marginally scratching above the poverty line.

Further, the table reveals that the majority of FBLs (25.83%) have income of Rs. 15,001/- to Rs. 20,000/-, while 27.81% of FBLs have income of Rs. 10,001/- to Rs. 15,000/-. Another 33.77% of FBLs have income of Rs. 5001/- to Rs. 10,000/- and 5.30% of FBLs have income of Rs. 20,000/- to Rs. 25,000/-. About 2.65% of FBLs have income above Rs. 25, 000/-. Only 4.64% of FBLs have earned upto Rs. 5,000/-.

The picture in totality bleak and miserable and needs major state's economic intervention for elevating their position.

The family income of freed bonded labourers in Munger has not increased as it should have been progressively over the year. Many of them are not getting even the minimum wages as prescribed by the State Government.

Table 9
Saving Attitude among the FBLs

Have you saving account in the Bank/Post office ?	*No. of FBLs*	*Per cent*
Yes	16	10.60
No	135	89.40
If yes, then where:		
(i). In the Bank	16	10.60
(ii) In the Post Office	-	-

The above table explains about the saving habit of FBLs. The majority of FBLs (89.40%) do not have any type of account in the bank or the post office. Only 10.60% of freed bonded labourers have their account in banks, but they did not operate their account for many years. The saving attitudes of FBLs are not satisfactory. On inquiry, the majority of them reported that they earn daily and consume what they earn. There is no spare money from their income for saving. They were always in hand-to-mouth situation because there is no facility of work round the year. In this connection, the Government should provide minimum 100 days of work in a year and food for work programme along with the income-generating schemes among the freed bonded labourers on top priority.

Then, another effort may be made for generating more awareness among them about saving habit for their safe and secure future. No effort has been made to educate them for operating the savings account in the Post Office or a bank by the Department of Savings, Government of Bihar. The National Savings

Department has not held any awareness programme for inculcating saving habits among them.

Table 10
Debt among Freed Bonded Labourers

Source	*No. of FBLs under loan*	*Per cent*	*Amount of loan*	*Average Amount of loan*
Formal agency	15	10.00	68000.00	4533.33
Non-formal agency	-	-	-	-
Total	15	100.00	68000.00	4533.33

The Table 10 shows that out of 151 FBLs, only 15 FBLs were in debt and had taken loan from formal, which amounted to a total amount of Rs. 68,000/-. No FBLs had borrowed loans from, non-formal agencies (eg. landlord, moneylender, relatives and friends).

The distribution of figures in the above table shows that majority of the freed bonded labourers (88.74%) are working anywhere they get an opportunity to work. Only 1.32% of the freed bonded labourers were working with their old landlords, where they worked before their release but today they are working due to their own choice and on better wages and condition. No compulsion to work with old landlord was reported. 5.30% FBLs do not have any work due to their old age and sickness.

Table 11
Present Working Place of FBLs and their Family Members

Statement	*Anywhere*		*Old Employer*		*Not Applicable*		*Total*	
	No.	*%*	*No.*	*%*	*No*	*%*	*No*	*%*
Where do you work at present ?	134	88.74	02	1.32	15	9.94	151	100.00
Where does other family members work at present ?	143	94.70	08	5.30	-	-	151	100.00

The above table shows that all freed bonded labourers had their own shelter, which meant a dwelling unit of some kind. The majority of FBLs 76 (50.33%) had pucca houses which has been made by help of the district administration under Indira Awas

Yojana Scheme. 40 (26.49%) FBLs had kachcha houses, and the rest 35 FBLs had mixed dwelling units. The mixed dwelling units were a combination of Indira Awas Yojana added to their traditional kachcha houses. But, 40 (26.49%) had not received the Indira Awas Yojana. This was a serious matter. It is suggested that the district administration should take necessary steps against this matter and provide the Indira Awas Yojana Scheme for the remaining FBLs immediately because shelter is one of the basic needs for the human development.

Table 12
Distribution of FBLs by Nature and Types of Dwelling Units

No. of Rooms	*Kachcha*	*%*	*Pucca*	*%*	*Mixed*	*%*	*All Type*	*%*
1.	12	7.95	27	17.88	14	9.27	53	35.10
2.	24	15.89	48	31.79	18	11.92	90	59.60
3.	04	2.65	1	0.66	03	1.99	08	5.30
Total	40	26.49	76	50.33	35	23.18	151	100.00

The dwelling units had different numbers of rooms. The distribution of number of rooms in the above table shows that the majority of freed bonded labourers 90 (59.60%) had two rooms unit, 53 (35.10%) FBLs had one room unit and 5.30% of FBLs had three and more rooms unit. Their condition was far from satisfactory. The district administration must ensure that 40 FBLs receive Indira Awas Yojana unit urgently in the district, who had not received IAY, as found during the study. The state has to act as facilitate to provide basic economic security and minimum standard of life in order to prevent their slipping into deep ocean of poverty.

32

EDUCATION SCENARIO : FREED BONDED LABOURERS AND THEIR FAMILIES

In human development model, education is one of the major agencies of mobility. Education is important agency for changing the poor and underdeveloped society. Education is linked with the quality of life. Education is empowerment. It is a mean to bring basic and fundamental change.

The literacy rate of Munger district is 60.11% followed by 70.68% male and 47.97% female. The present literacy and education initiative has not gone to the freed bonded labourers, since they remain under the umbrella of darkness.

Table 1
Classification of Sampled Freed Bonded Labourers on the basis of Education

Education	*Number*	*Per cent*
Illiterate	142	94.05
Literate	6	3.97
Middle	2	1.32
Upto Matriculate	1	0.66
Total	151	100.00

An overall picture of education among freed bonded labourers are presented in this table. The educational position of freed bonded labourers were found to be miserable in the district because majority of them (94.05%) were illiterate and had never received any form of schooling. Only 3.97% of freed bonded labour was found to be literate or better understood as semi-literate in the sense that they take social security payment with signature and another 1.32% of freed bonded labourers were found to have received middle class education. But, it is also important to know that 0.66% of FBLs had education upto Matriculation level. It can be said that the freed bonded labourers are from the most deprived section of the rural society, who are far residing in the most in accessible villages of the district. The road linkages are not well maintained and are in bad shape.

Table 2
Educational Status of Freed Bonded Labourers' Family Members

Category	*Illiterate*		*Literate*		*Upto Middle*		*Matriculate*		*Total*	
	Number	*%*	*Number*	*%*	*Number*	*%*	*Number*	*%*	*Number*	*%*
Adult Male	367	35.67	6	0.58	5	0.49	8	0.78	386	37.51
Adult female	314	30.52	2	0.19	7	0.68	-	-	323	31.39
Male (6-14 yrs.)	85	8.26	4	0.39	9	8.75	-	-	179	17.40
Female (6-14 yrs.)	76	739	3	0.29	62	6.03	-	-	141	13.70
Total	842	81.83	15	1.46	164	15.94	8	0.78	1029	100.00

As regards literary and educational status of freed bonded labourers family, the table shows that the next generation of freed bonded labourers families are also in educationally disadvantaged position. The 151 freed bonded labourers had total 1029 family members followed by 386 adult males, 323 adult females, 179 male children and 141 female children. They were predominantly illiterate with highest figure 842 (81.83%) and only 15 (1.46%) were literate.

About 15.94% were educated upto middle standard and only 8 (0.78%) were found to be Matriculate. Further, the table indicates that male and female children between the age group of 6-14 years were not going to school. They were engaged in domestic work. Only 8.75% male children and 6.03% female children were going to school. Thus, the low percentage of school-going children in FBLs families showed that they haven't existed any interest in their children's education. They do not understand the need of education. They believe that hard work will bring them food security. Earning two square meals is their main priority.

Table 3
Awareness of FBLs Children Education

Where does your child read?	*No. of FBLs*	*Per cent*
Anganwari	12	7.95
If Anganwari, then :		
(i) Getting food		
Not reading	49	32.45
If not reading, then :		
(i) Doing work at home	37	24.50
(ii) Playing here and there	27	17.88
(iii) Due to long distance of school	05	3.31
(iv) Working as a child labour	03	1.98
(v) There is no gain with education	04	2.65
(vi) No needs of education among girls	12	7.94
(vii) Grazing cattle	08	5.30
(viii) Dominant caste people disturb the children inside/outside the school	02	1.32
(ix) Due to low economic condition	34	15.23
School	60	39.74
If School, then :		
(i) getting food materials	58	38.41
(ii) getting cash amount	00	0.00
(iii) getting books free	58	38.41
Not Applicable	42	27.81

Note: Figures are non-additive.

The distribution of figures in the table demonstrates about the sampled FBLs children education. Out of 151 FBLs only, 12 FBLs reported that his children go to the Anganwari centre and are getting mid-day meal (Khichri). 7.95% of FBLs reported that their children go to school and they reported that they are getting food (38.41%), books free of cost (38.41%). These FBLs were conscious for education and knew about its importance. 02 (1.32%) reported that they were not getting anything. Further, the table reveals that majority of 49 (32.45%) FBLs children don't go to school.

One more question was asked from the FBLs that where are your children if not in school? In response to this question, majority of them (17.88%) reported that their children were playing here and there, while 24.50% of FBLs reported that their children were doing work at home. 5.30% of FBLs children were engaged in grazing cattle. 2.65% of FBLs did not know the importance and value of education as they reported that there is no gain with education.

3.31% FBLs children did not go to school, due to long distance of school. 1.98% of FBLs children worked as a child labour. 7.94% FBLs were gender biased families, which felt that there was no need of education among the girl child. Some FBLs children were prevented from going to school by the dominant caste men in their areas (1.32%). There were some FBLs families, (15.23%), who wanted to send their children to school but could not do so due to poor and low economic conditions. About 27.85% FBLs family reported that they have no children or no school-going age children.

Majority of FBLs do not send their children to the Anganwari centre due to lack of knowledge and information. There is no approach made by the Anganwari centre or concerned ICDS officials to reach them or extend the Anganwari facilities.

Table 4
Availability of Educational Facilities in the Village/tolas of FBLs

Facilities	*No. of FBLs*	*Per cent*
Anganwari	51	33.77
(i) Primary school	137	90.73
(ii) Upto Middle School	8	5.30
(iii) Upto High School	2	1.32
(iv) None of these	4	2.65

The convenience of the governmental educational facilities as basic need for the development of future generation requires upgrading. The present table represents the availability of government educational facilities for the freed bonded labourers children in the village or tola.

The table indicates that all types of educational facilities are not available in the freed bonded labourers village/tola, rather it is inadequate for the FBLs families children in several areas. Under the educational facilities, 33.77% of freed bonded labourer can utilize the Anganwari facilities, whereas 90.73% of FBLs can use schooling facilities for their children.

Further the table reveals that the majority of FBLs (90.73%) can use schooling facilities up to primary level, whereas 5.30% of FBLs can utilize these facilities up to middle standard. Only 1.32% of FBLs can utilize these facilities upto High School for their children's education. About 2.65% of FBLs don't have any type of schooling facilities in their village/tola for their children.

In spite of these facilities, education has not gone down to them. FBLs families are not sensitized for children's education. There is no pursuit for education. The livelihood race over takes the passion for education. Food insecurity syndrome has to be replaced with zeal for education.

The economically and socially oppressed and deprived need special pedagogical intervention for their educational empowerment and climbing the ladder of socio-economic mobility. No society has developed without education hence, education should be the foundation stone of all major government initiative to bring around a basic change in freed bonded labourers' status.

33

FREED BONDED LABOUR : HEALTH

The value of positive and good health is oblivious among the freed bonded labourers, due to their poor economic condition. They survive through hard physical labour. They have limited resources to take their health care. They consider themselves healthy and fit as long as they can earn by hard toil. The concept of holistic health care is missing among them.

Minor ailments are not taken care by them. They pay attention to major ailments, but at times it is too late to do anything to improve the health situation. There is no organised medical check up programme for them.

One of the prime necessities for the better upkeep of man is the provision of safe drinking water. Most of the diseases can be attributed to contaminated water. Water facilities available to the weaker and lower section of people are by no means adequate.

Table 1(a)
Availability of Drinking Water Facilities in the villages/tolas of FBLs

Source	*No. of FBLs*	*Per cent*
Well	20	13.25
Hand Pump	93	61.59
Well + Hand Pump	38	25.16
Total	151	100.00

The availability of safe drinking water is a huge problem for the freed bonded labourers, which is the key for good health. Thus, the present table tries to examine the drinking water facilities in the FBLs villages/tolas.

The positive aspect in the Table 1(a) is that it represents a mixed picture, which is that some type of drinking water facilities is available in all the FBLs villages/tolas. Majority of FBLs (61.59%) reported that the hand pump facilities is available in their villages/tolas, while 25.16% of FBLs reported that well and hand pump facilities are available in their villages/tolas. Only 13.25% of FBLs reported that they have only well facility for drinking water. Majority were satisfied with the availability of drinking water facilities but had complains about the repair work of hand pumps and wells. They repair the hand pumps and wells with their little resources, but wants the local government assistance for maintenance.

Freed bonded labourers don't know whether the water available is safe for drinking. They simply know that food and water is important for survival. Water is kept in open, due to lack of awareness and lack of proper storage system and required utensils.

Table 1(b) demonstrates about the drinking water facility used by the freed bonded labourers. It is evident from the table that the majority of FBLs (76.16%) use hand pump for drinking water, while 14.57% of FBLs use well and only 9.27% of FBLs used well and hand pump both. The water appears to be unsafe for drinking purposes. PHED department can help in installing proper hand pumps.

Table 1(b)
Drinking Water Facility used by the FBLs

Source	*No. of FBLs Used*	
	No	*Percentage*
Well	22	14.57
Hand Pump	115	76.16
Well + Hand Pump	14	9.27
Total	151	100.00

Table 2
Availability of Toilet Facilities in the Homes of FBLs

Response	*No. of FBLs*	*Per cent*
Yes	-	-
No	151	100.00
Total	151	100.00

Drinking water facilities are community assets in FBLs tolas, which have been provided by the Central and State Government through the help of district administration for purposes of safe drinking water. Safe drinking water is the essential need of weaker section people as well as the freed bonded labourers. It guarantees good health and ensures less proneness to diseases.

Table 2 shows the availability of toilet facilities in the FBLs houses. All FBLs (100%) reported that there are no toilet facilities in their house of any type. They use open defecation in places outside the village for this purpose. There is no provision of toilets and bathrooms. They do it in open. Even the female satisfies herself from call of nature in open. They feel bad about it, but are helpless.

The rural sanitation programme of government, UNICEF etc. are non-existence in the whole district. The rural sanitation programme is not available to this segment of FBLs.

Table 3
Availability of Drainage Facilities in the Villages/tolas of FBLs

Response	*No. of FBLs*	*Per cent*
Kachcha	16	10.60
Pucca	-	-
Open flow	135	89.40
All	151	100.00

Above table demonstrates about the availability of drainage facilities in the FBL's villages/tolas. In this respect, majority of FBLs (89.40%) reported that the waste water spilled here and there in the village land, due to the absence of any proper drainage system in the village/tola. Some of FBLs (10.60%) reported to have kachcha drains for disposal of wastewater in their villages/tolas.

Table 4
Distance of Primary Health Centre from FBLs Residence

Distance in Km.	*No. of FBLs*	*Per cent*
1-2	4	2.65
3-4	76	50.33
5-6	19	12.58
7-8	52	34.44
Total	151	100.00

It is evident from the Table 4 that the freed bonded labourers face great difficulties to get adequate medical and health care facilities from the government health infrastructure due to long distances.

The majority of FBLs (50.33%) have to cover a long distance of 3-4 kms to reach the nearest health centre, while 34.44% of FBLs travel such a long distance 7 and above kms to reach the nearest government health center.

2.65% of FBLs travel 1-2 kms to reach the nearest health centre, while 12.58% of FBLs travel 5-6 kms to reach the nearest government health centre.

There is no PHC or APHC contact programme for medicare of FBLs. Due to poor transport, it makes life more difficult for sick and old FBLs. They face severe difficulties about the medical and health care and exposed to health insecurity syndrome.

Table 5
Medicare Facilities for FBLs

Statement	*No. of FBLs*					
	Yes	*%*	*No*	*%*	*Total*	*%*
Regular check of health	-	-	151	100.00	151	100.00
Medicare during the illness period	-	-	151	100.00	151	100.00

Although, health centres are available at the block level, but it is not accessible for freed bonded labourers due to distance and absenteeism among the PHC staff. The government doctors are not visiting them. In many PHCs, no female doctors are posted. ANMs are also posted, but are of no use. They confide more in the local quacks and their touts who visits them regularly. The vicious nexus of touts and FBLs have to be broken to enrich their longevity and quality of life by providing good medicare.

34

EVALUATION OF REHABILITATION SCHEMES AND THEIR IMPACT

The present evaluative study was concerned with the rehabilitation status and their impact on the freed bonded labourers in Munger district.

Table 1
Identified & Rehabilitated FBLs in Munger District

Sl. No.	*Name of the C.D. Block*	*No. of Freed Bonded labourers*		
		Identified	*Rehabilitated*	*Not Rehabilitated*
1.	Jamalpur	257	257	-
2.	Dharhara	66	62	04
3.	Tarapur	61	60	01
4.	Sangrampur	47	46	01
5.	Munger	86	86	-
6.	Kharagpur	273	234	39
	Total	790	745	45

The identification of bonded labourers and their release order certificate was given under District Magistrate's leadership. In 1980-81 release order was given to 108 bonded labourers. In 1982-83 release order was given to 365 bonded labourers. In 1984-85 release order was given to 130 bonded labourers. In 1986-87 release order was given to 142 bonded labourers. The total number of FBLs released was 745. No bonded labour were identified after 1988.

PRESENT OCCUPATION OF FBLs & THEIR FAMILIES

71.52% Freed bonded labourers work as agricultural labourers within the village or outside the village independently. They are free to work with any landlord. Seasonally, they migrated to other place in search of work.

Table 2
Distribution of FBLs through their Occupation

Occupation	*Male*		*Female*		*Total*	
	No.	*%*	*No.*	*%*	*No.*	*%*
Agricultural labour	108	71.52	1	0.66	109	72.18
Non-Agricultural labour	26	17.22	1	0.66	27	17.88
No work/Old age	15	9.94	-	-	15	9.94
Total	149	98.68	2	1.32	151	1 00.00

17.22% were found working in non-agricultural work like digging, road work, construction work and other works.

A small number of freed bonded labourers (9.94%) were without work due to old age and illness.

Some FBLs go for work to nearest towns near their home place.

The majority of the family members of FBLs were engaged in agriculture and non-agriculture activities like brick-klin, digging, road work and other works.

There was no government help seen in their self-employed sphere. There was lack of information regarding minimum wage. There was absence NGO activity within the FBLs community for organising them or in raising their awareness on core issues. NABARD/similar other institutions, which are associated with Self-Help Group, were not working in this area; ILO and other international agencies that work with children, women, deprived and old were not working among FBLs for their upliftment.

Table 3
Knowledge of Minimum wage among FBLs

Do you know about the minimum wage ?	*No. of FBLs*	*Per cent*
Yes	–	–
No	151	100.00
Total	151	100.00

KNOWLEDGE ABOUT THE MINIMUM WAGE

None of the freed bonded labourers knew about the minimum wage, which is prescribed by the Government and enforced by the labour department. They were paid according to the existing wage of the area. The working hours are normally 7 to 8 hours and get wage not only in cash but in kind also. They get wage of Rs. 40 to 60 in cash. It varies from village to village and block to block of the district. The FBLs do not receive minimum wage which needs to taken up urgently.

The labour department has to play a key role to implement minimum wages for them from their employers.

Table 4
Government Compensation Package for the FBLs

Sl. No.	*Major things*	*No. of FBLs*	*Per cent*
1.	One cow	20	13.25
2.	Two cows	49	32.45
3.	Three cows	01	0.66
4.	One buffalo	05	3.31
5.	Two buffaloes	04	2.64
6.	Two oxes	30	19.86
7.	Four oxes	01	0.66
8.	Four goats	01	0.06
9.	Two he-buffaloes	02	1.32
10.	Horse cart	08	5.29
11.	Bullock cart	04	2.64
12.	Two rickshaws	06	3.97
13.	Loudspeaker	02	1.32
14.	Leather & Shoe repair shop	02	1.32
15.	Kirana shop	02	1.32
16.	Cash Rs. 4000/-	02	1.32
17.	One ox + one cow	02	1.32
18.	Two oxes + one cow	02	1.32
19.	Two oxes + one he-buffalo	03	1.98
20.	One cow + Cash Rs. 2500/-	01	0.66
21.	One cow + one rickshaw	02	1.32
22.	Two cows + one rickshaw	01	0.66
23.	Two cows + five goats	01	0.66
	Total	151	100.00

After identification and their release, the bonded labourers were provided compensation package by the district administration agencies. Under this package, the freed bonded labourers were given different types of livestock, horse cart, tyre cart, loudspeaker, rickshaw, kirana shop, leather and shoe repairing shop, etc. and cash to improve their economic condition and living standard of their family.

An overall picture of compensation package for the FBLs, provided through the district administration is presented in this table.

- The majority 49 FBLs (32.45%) received two cows.
- Next group of 30 FBLs (19.86%) received two oxes.
- Another group of 20 FBLs (13.25%) received one cow.
- The fourth group of 8 FBLs (5.29%) received one horse cart.
- The fifth group of 6 FBLs (3.97%) received two rickshaws.
- 5 FBLs (3.31%) received one buffalo.
- 4 FBLs (2.64%) received two buffaloes.
- 3 FBLs (1.98%) received two oxes and one male buffalo.
- 2 FBLs (1.32%) received two male buffaloes.
- 2 FBLs (1.32%) received one loudspeaker.
- 2 FBLs (1.32%) received leather and shoe repair shop.
- 2 FBLs (1.32%) received kirana shop.
- 2 FBLs (1.32%) received cash Rs. 4000/-.
- 2 FBLs (1.32%) received one ox and one cow.
- 2 FBLs (1.32%) received two oxes and one cow.
- 2 FBLs (1.32%) received one cow and one rickshaw.
- 1 FBL (0.66%) received three cows.
- 1 FBL (0.66%) received four oxes.
- 1 FBL (0.66%) received four goats.
- 1 FBL (0.66%) received one cow.
- 1 FBL (0.66%) received one cow and cash Rs. 2500/- only.
- 1 FBL (0.66%) received two cows and one rickshaw.
- 1 FBL (0.66%) received two cows and five goats.

The above table reveals that the majority of 120 FBLs (79.47%) avail the social security pension facility of Rs. 100/- per month, which is provided by the Government under the Bonded Labour

Rehabilitation Scheme, while 31 (20.53%) FBLs reported that they don't get this type of facility. The district administration should urgently provide this facility to them.

Table 5
Social Security Pension for FBLs

Sl. No.	*Statement*	*No. of FBLs*					
		Yes	*%*	*No*	*%*	*Total*	*%*
1.	Do you get social Security Pension ?	120	79.47	31	20.53	151	100.00

The break up of FBLs don't get the social security pension:

(a) Jamalpur Block :	(i)	Chamangarh	05
	(ii)	Ahra Musahari	05
(b) Sangrampur Block :	(i)	Rampur	01
(c) Munger Block :	(i)	Maniharchak	02
	(ii)	Nawagarhi	02
(d) Dharahara Block :	(i)	Sarobag-	01
(e) Kharagpur Block :	(i)	Madanpur	07
	(ii)	Laxamipur	07
	(iii)	Mohanpur	01

This was not been given to some of the freed bonded labourers, was inquired from the District Social Security Department Officer. He reported that he has no knowledge about this that why they have not been paid the social security pension.

Table 6
Other Related Programmes for FBLs under Poverty Line Scheme : Indira Awas Yojana and IRDP Facilities

Sl. No.	*Scheme*	*No. of FBLs*					
		Yes	*%*	*No*	*%*	*Total*	*%*
1.	IAY	75	49.67	76	50.13	151	100.00
2.	IRDP	10	6.62	141	93.38	151	100.00
3.	Schedule caste Development Finance Corporation	5	3.31	146	96.69	151	100.00

The district administration has not done satisfactory work on the pension front because about one-fourth FBLs of the district don't get the social security pension till date.

This pension is lifeline for them and it is recommended that old age family members and widowers of FBLs may be also be included in these social securities scheme immediately.

- The Table 6 shows that 75 (49.6%) FBLs received Indira Awas Yojana (IAY) facilities and were using it for residential purposes.
- 76 (50.13%) of FBLs reported that they didn't get this type of facility and a long period has passed since they were released. They had no clue as to why they were not provided IAY house, but they are still hopeful of getting one from the government.
- 5 (13.31%) FBLs reported that they received loan from the scheduled caste finance and development corporation to leather and shoe repair shop.
- 10 (6.62%) FBLs get under IRDP assistance.
- The Government assistance is evident but in fragmented manner and not in totality. There is urgent need to address the issue as to why 76 (50.13%) FBLs were left out from the IAY scheme.
- It can be said that the Government programmes under the below poverty line and bonded labour schemes, are not efficiently provided to the FBLs.
- This scheme is about shelter, which is also one of the foremost and important issue in the case of FBLs human development. As per direction of the Government of India and the State Government, all DMs have to link the FBLs with IAY schemes as a part of Government poverty alleviation holistic strategy.
- Munger district has failed to meet its mission to provide IAY and other development scheme to all rehabilitated FBLs.
- SJGSY is in practice since April 1999 as an important scheme for poverty alleviation. The FBLs can be brought under SJGSY, which has multiple input for BPL families. It clearly states that within three years with help of all in puts an effort should be made to bring the family above poverty line.

The Table 7 reveals that the majority of FBLs 127(84.11%) have received the facility of Lal Card, while 24 (15.89%) of FBLs reported that they didn't receive the Lal Card facility which is provided by the Government agencies. They want reduction of delay tactics at the block offices and petty corruption.

Table 7
Lal Card and PDs Facilities among FBLs

Statement	*No. of FBLs*	*Per cent*
Do you have a red card?		
(i) Yes	127	84.11
(ii) No	24	15.89
If yes, then what types of materials received by you at the Govt. rate		
(i) Kerosene oil	125	82.78
(ii) Kerosene oil & grains	-	-
(iii) Nothing	2	1.32
Where are the PDS?		
(i) Within the village	139	92.05
(ii) Outside the village	12	7.95

- Further, the table reveals that 125 (82.78%) of FBLs are getting benefit of kerosene oil only from the PDS network.
- 2.18% of FBLs–one FBL of village.
- About 1.32% of FBLs reported that they don't get anything, either kerosene oil or food grains with help of the Lal Card.
- Majority of them complained during the field visit that most beneficial would be availability of food grains particularly rice/ wheat at subsidized rates in the PDS fair price shop (Ration shop).

Table 8
Property Released and Provided Property through the Government

(a) Distribution of FBLs by Seized Property

Sl. No.	*Statement*	*No. of FBLs*			
		Yes	*%*	*No*	*%*
	Did employer seize your property during the Bonded Labour Period?	-	-	151 100.00	

- 139 FBLs (92.05%) reported that PDS facility is available within the village, while 7.95% of FBLs reported that their PDS is outside their village.

It is evident from the Table 8 that their previous employer seized no property during the bonded labour period. -

(b) Distribution of FBLs by Providing Basgit Paper

Have you received Basgit Paper?	*No. of FBLs*	*%*
Yes	133	80.08
If Yes, then:		
(i) 2 decimal	39	25.83
(ii) 3.5 decimal	26	17.22
(iii) 10.5 decimal	68	45.03
No	18	11.92
Total	151	100.00

- Majority of FBLs (133) reported that they had received basgit paper, while 18 (11.92%) reported that they did not receive the basgit paper for constructing their house.
- Further, the table reveals that 39 (25.83%) FBLs had received 2 decimal of land through the basgit paper, while 26 (17.22%) FBLs reported that they had received 3.5 decimal of land. Only 68 (45.03%) FBLs reported that they had received 10.5 decimal land through the basgit paper.

Table 9
Visit of Vigilance Committee Members in the FBLs Village/tola

Sl. No.	*Statement*	*No. of FBLs*			
		Yes	*%*	*No*	*%*
1.	Visit of Vigilance Committee Members	-	-	151	100.00

- For the monitoring the development of socio-economic condition of freed bonded labourer, the vigilance committee's members have yet to visit the FBLs villages/tolas to monitor the progress.
- The table reveals that the vigilance committee members never visited any FBLs village/tolas.
- This indicates that the organizational performance and monitoring system of vigilance committee in the district is non-functional.

TRAINING FACILITIES

- None of the FBLs received any training by Government agency after their release for self-employment.
- The capacity building for acquiring new skills and developing the existing indigenous skills tradition art & craft can become an important mode of regular income for the released FBLs.

AWARENESS PROGRAMME AMONG THE FBLs

- No awareness programme was held among the freed bonded labourers. They were not aware about the Government scheme for them except what they had got at the time of release. It is necessary to make them aware about the other assistance schemes and programmes.
- A regular sensitization and capacity building process was not done in the district for the FBLs. An effort can be made on making them aware about their schemes and how they can benefit from them.
- Exercise can be held to drive home about their right and how to live independently and free from debt bondage.

Table 10
Availability of Releasing Letters among the FBLs

Have you received any type of Bonded Labour release letter issued by DM/SDO ?	*No. of FBLs*	*Per cent*
Yes	151	100.00
No	-	-
Total	151	100.00

- It is evident from the table that all FBLs received their release certificate by the district administration, but at present majority of them have lost the release certificate or were keeping in proper condition. They should be given laminated certificates and periodically it should be checked whether they have it or not, because that will ensure their receiving government assistance.
- One of the major objectives of the present evaluative study is to find out the opinions or expectations of the freed bonded labourers. In lieu of this, freed bonded labourers expressed

their suggestions for improving their present situation and gave an inside view of their level of expectation.

Table 11
Opinion of FBLs on What Steps the Government should take to Improve their Conditions

	Statement	*No of FBLs*	*Per cent*
1.	To improve infra-structural facilities—Electricity, Road, PDS	18	11.92
2.	Housing, Drinking water, Toilet and Drainage facilities	37	24.50
3.	Medical and health care facilities	24	15.89
4.	Educational facilities	-	-
5.	For Improving economic condition of families–loan, Vocational training, Business, Land for cultivation, Animal Husbandry–Cattle, Piggery	41	27.15
6.	Pension facilities and increase in Pension amount	07	4.63
7.	Regular work all the year around	37	24.50
8.	More facilities by the Government	04	2.65
9.	Development functionaries should pay visit	27	17.88
10.	Enhancement of wage, food security, work guarantee, loans, income generating facilities, land for cultivation and animal husbandry–cattle/pig rearing	71	47.02
11.	No response	02	1.32

- The table reveals that most significant suggestion was for improving economic condition of families (47.02%) in which they demanded enhancement of wage, food security, work guarantee, loans, income generating facilities, land for cultivation and animal husbandry, cattle/pig rearing.
- 11.92% of FBLs want improvement in the infra-structural facilities like electricity, road and public distribution system.
- 24.50% of FBLs felt that the government should provide housing, drinking water, toilet and drainage facilities.
- 15.89% of FBLs felt that the government should provide more medical and health care facilities.
- 24.50% of FBLs demanded regular work round the year.

- 4.63% of FBLs suggested that the pension amount should be increased and payment regularly.
- 47.02% of FBLs want to increase their wages for betterment of their living condition.
- 17.88% of FBLs felt that the block development functionaries should pay visit in their village/tolas.
- 2.65% of FBLs want more facilities through the Government.
- During the interview of FBLs it was found that they totally depend on the Government to improve their economic condition.

Table 12
Knowledge of Bonded Labour Act among the FBLs

Do you know about the Bonded Labour Act ?	*No. of FBLs*	*Per cent*
Yes	-	-
No	151	100.00
Total	151	100.00

- All freed bonded labourers of the district don't know about the Bonded labour Act, 1976 under which they freed.
- They were in consensus grateful to the Government agencies for releasing from the clutches of bondage.
- An over all picture of perception of change among FBLs is presented in this table. It was mother of all questions that whether they felt any perceptible change after being freed. The response was overwhelming.
- They cherished the freedom of work, which meant liberty to choose their workplace.
- They adored mobility and right to live as they wished. It was clear departure from bondage to liberty and to availing opportunities, as it came through with great hardship in many cases.
- The above table shows that the most significant answers were
- Enhancement in their social prestige (98.01 %).
- No pressure and binding of·work (95.36%).
- Followed by freedom of work (92.05%).

- 41.06% of FBLs expressed their feelings of being better than before.

Table 13
Perception of Change among FBLs

Statement	*No. of FBLs*	*Per cent*
Freedom of work	139	92.05
Feeling better than earlier	62	41.06
Enhancement in social prestige	148	98.01
Improvement in food availability	67	44.37
Enhancement of wages	23	15.23
No pressure/binding of work	144	95.36
No change	03	1.98

Note: Figures are non-additive.

- A section of FBLs felt improvement in food availability (44.37%).
- And enhancement in wages (15.23%).
- Few expressed that they did not want any change: No change (1.98%).
- The revelation of this study was that few FBLs, who were freed, continued to work in their old master's field. They had no complaint against them because the old masters were giving them better wages now than before, and liberty and mobility and choice to work or not with them.
- There has been a slight improvement in financial condition (99.34%).
- Betterment in food consumption (100%).
- Enhancement in social prestige (98.01%).
- And increase in voting activities (100%)after their release.
- But majority of them (98.68%) haven't purchased any permanent or durable assets for their income and livelihood.
- There is significant change in their food consumption, living pattern as in past and in use of clothes.
- They like to eat rice and bread with vegetable regularly and also the consumption of pulse frequently. It was marked progress from the previous bondage life. They were trying to have neat and clean clothes.

- Some had better accommodation facilities due to houses provided under the Indira Awas Yojana through the district administration.

Table 14
Opinion of FBLs on their uplift after being Released

Activities	*Uplift*			
	Gain		*No Gain*	
	No. of FBls	*%*	*No. of FBLs*	*%*
Financial condition	150	99.34	01	0.66
Food consumption	151	100.00	0	0.00
Asset acquisition	02	1.32	149	98.68
Social prestige	148	98.01	3	1.99
Voting behaviour	151	100.00	-	-
No response		-	-	-

Table 15(a)
Classification of FBLs with Gain in Food Consumption

Statement	*No. of FBLs*	*Per cent*
(A) If Gain in Food Consumption, then what type of improvement :		
(i) Food according to their will	23	15.23
(ii) Take better feed	109	72.19
Improvement in feeding, clothing and Housing	19	12.58
How many times, do you take food :		
(a) Twice a day	84	55.63
(b) Thrice a day	67	44.37

- The above table reveals that the majority of FBLs (72.19%) take better food at present.
- 12.58% of FBLs reported that they have experienced improvement in fooding, clothing and housing.
- While 15.23% of FBLs reported that they take food according to their will, which is just enough for subsistence.
- Further, the table reveals that 44.37% of FBLs take their food thrice a day and 55.63% of FBLs take it twice a day.

- All FBLs take rice and bread with potato/salt and chili or rice juice (Maar) and salt/chattani and achar/chakha etc.
- They don't consume food rich in protein and vitamins, particularly non-vegetarian food items, due to their low economic condition. Their consumption in qualitative food is still low but improved from past. The thrust of intake is more on the quantitative food compared to qualitative food.
- Low intake does affect their health standard and longevity of life.

Table 15(b)
Classification of FBLs with Gain in Asset Acquisition

Statement	*No. of FBLs*	*Per cent*
If Gain in asset acquisition, then what type of asset :		
(i) Purchasing of land	02	1.32
(ii) Purchasing of livestock	02	1.32
No Gain	149	97.36
Total	151	100.00

- The above table demonstrates that majority of FBLs (97.36%) haven't purchased any permanent or durable assets for their income and livelihood.
- While 2.64% of FBLs reported that they purchased some land for agriculture or housing purpose after the release.

DIFFICULTIES FACED IN THE FIELD WORK & FEEDBACK

(i) The team faced difficulty for completing the sample size due to high rate of FBLs mortality.

(ii) The list of freed bonded labourers was properly maintained in the social security department but the addresses of the FBLs was very vague and proved to be a daunting task to find FBLs in the field. There is poor road connectivity and public transportation facility. It was painful and distressing at times because the addresses provided were not exact. But, the register was maintained. The list of freed bonded labourers was typed and kept neatly in a file, but the data was not proper in most cases.

(iii) The list of freed bonded labourers was not up-to-date. It was not clear that how many freed bonded labourers were alive or how many had died or migrated.

(iv) It was surprising the Assistant Director, Social Security could not be contacted. The team was informed that he is on long medical leave.

(v) The office staff was not aware about the total picture of the social security pension scenario and how many FBLs were actually receiving the pension.

(vi) Mostly freed bonded labourers were illiterate so the response of many questions was not given properly.

(vii) Many were not keeping the release order certificate to verify their identity. The certificate should have their photograph laminated on them for their official assistance programme.

(viii) Regarding the government sponsored programme under the below the poverty line and freed bonded labourers schemes, they were not efficiently executed. There is scope for improvement.

(ix) No official agency had pursued follow up programme and monitoring to constantly measure the progress of the freed and rehabilitated bonded labourers.

(x) The programmes were executed without human touch. Some had benefited while others were left out. There was lack of holistic approach. The effort should be to bring all within the settlement and upliftment process.

(xi) There was no communication between the freed bonded labourers and the block, sub-division and district administration officials, due to non-functional role of the vigilance committee.

(xii) The FBLs complained that rehabilitation was just one time administrative affair. There is need for constant nurturing and monitoring to see whether they have gained or not from government rehabilitation package.

(xiii) Munger district has vigilance committee on paper, but it has not held any meeting to review the progress of FBLs.

(xiv) The study indicates that as an anti-poverty programme, bonded labour rehabilitation process is not adequately envisaged by the planners. The problem is deep-rooted, complex and has wider socio-economic dimension, which needs deeper understanding of the bonded labour rehabilitation phenomenon. They need economic intervention but more than that they need human touch. The agency should have positive commitment. It requires comprehensive planning and determined implementation efforts.

(xv) The district administration has expressed intention to use corrective measures urgently to deliver benefit to all freed bonded labour in the district.

PART - VII

Conclusion

35

CONCLUSION

1. A systematic discussion of the study's findings will serve as the basis for drawing conclusion and recommendations in this concluding chapter. The chapter also helps in understanding the persistence of certain conditions and situations in the families of bonded labourers even after liberation and extent of change in their conditions and situations from their pre-liberation period. In this way, various aspects of physical, social economic and psychological of this target group have been analyzed in the light of the data obtained from the respondents who were freed from the bondage.
2. During the study, it was observed that the system of landlord and bonded labour was established almost several decades ago. In old times, the wages were meager and paid in form of share of the produce. Labourers were not free to choose their master and lacked mobility. Debt bondage became a form of bonded labour system in which they were stuck for a long period of time. On analysing into the reason for their first entry in bondage, it was found that poverty is the major cause. Every case is based upon it. The first entry in to bonded service is due to economic stringency, but a part of poverty is also due to particular events. For example, sickness, death, or a marriage ceremony in the family always acted as an immediate cause. Another event, which becomes responsible to attachment in bondage is the burden of loan, under which they were heavily pressed. So, they entered into debt bondage. The finding fundamentally points to the need to eradicate poverty and ensure durable income in all the seasons, without allowing them to fall into the iniquitous debt trap again.

3. The data concerning economic life of the liberated (freed bonded) labour and their families analyzed suggest that they are poorly paid people, because the wages are highly dissatisfactory. But, the crux of the problem lies in the fact that the prices of essential commodities increase so rapidly that their daily wages cannot cope with the inflated cost of living. Hence, even some marginal increase in their income has not improved their economic conditions, rather due to price rise at a higher rate; the economic problems have become more complicated.
4. The respondents have themselves accepted that they are not satisfied with their daily wages. Hence, it may be concluded that even after liberation, the economic condition of this class of freed bonded has not improved and they still constitute the most economically backward segment of the rural society.
5. All the freed bonded labourers are illiterate or semi-literate, and had not received education in their childhood. No effort has been made by the Government agencies as special case to make them fully literate, after their liberation from yoke of bondage. In general, the condition of literacy and education among the FBLs are pathetic and miserable.
6. The data collected from the field suggests that these freed bonded labourers aspire for educating their children. Hence it may be resolved that in spite of being educationally and economically backward status, they have developed an awareness and consciousness in favour of education. They realize the importance and significance of education in the present times, and feel that they had missed the real bus to decent learning and living mode in their life, but would not like their children suffer on this account. They have great expectations from Government agencies to look into this area seriously. The mothers were very vociferous in their desire to educate their children.
7. Hence, it can be opined that there has been a considerable change in their attitude and outlook. The challenge is to the government agencies to address this issue and give special attention to the freed bonded labourer's children for education in decent environment without fear of discrimination due to their parenthood or caste. A motivation and hunger for

education can keep the school-going children of the freed bonded labourers away from being engaged in domestic work or as a child labour. They are conscious of the fact that education enhances status and helps in improving economic condition.

8. It may be resolved that their attitude have remarkably changed and there is awareness in respect of rights, privileges and social respect, in spite of suffering from poor economic condition and educational backwardness.
9. The freed bonded labourers housing facilities, toilet facilities, and drinking water facilities also needs urgent attention. Top priority has to be given to make their habitat congenial and a role model of good living by Government intervention. The housing is mix of kachha and pucca including the Indira Awas houses. Drinking water facilities are not satisfactory. Some are fortunate to have Government hand pumps in their clusters. Most of the freed bonded labourers, female members and children were using toilet facilities outside the home. No toilet facility is available in the home. Drainage facilities are also not very satisfactory.
10. The Government agencies should consider and try to provide these facilities on a priority basis. The Indira Awas House for each freed bonded labourer, installation of hand pumps in every FBLs cluster, provision of low cost sanitation facility such as Sulabh shauchalaya toilets, will improve their living conditions and enhance their quality of living.
11. It was discovered that there was a strong co-relation of consumption with the large family size. The economic conditions of the freed bonded labourer families were utterly hopeless, and if the family was of a large size, then the problem became more serious. The information collected from the freed bonded labourers about their family size showed that family planning and population control methods have to be educated in order to make their children life convenient and meaningful including their own lives. The FBLs were victim of age-old myth that more hands meant more earning hands, hence prosperity rather it was gospel of doom for them. Massive and intensive village based family welfare and Government should hold health camps regularly and NGO agencies including

WHO, UNICEF and PFI to sensitize them about reproductive and child health care benefits.

12. The FBLs were found to be spending more on consumption, social rites and rituals such as marriages, birth functions and death ceremonies (Shraddh), alcohol drinking and other local custom ceremonies. They were spending but without saving or from saved money. They were borrowing heavily from local vicious money suppliers and other like institutions.
13. There was little knowledge about savings schemes, and related programmes of financial institutions at the rural level among the FBLs. The level of awareness showed that a positive savings attitude was missing. Moneylenders or such unholy institutions still play a significant role in their lives. Their borrowings for consumption, sickness bouts, marriages, death rite functions are the areas of vulnerability in these FBLs. It is a deep-rooted malaise, which can be fought with massive savings campaign by Department of Savings, NABARD, commercial banks, cooperative banks, gramin banks etc. There is need for developing micro-credit societies, Self-Help Groups and small income generating groups among them to motivate towards strengthening earning and savings attitude.
14. The study found that the knowledge about Minimum Wages Act and knowledge of Bonded Labour (Abolition) Act 1976, which were fundamental to their lives, was not known to them at all. They understood that the Government has freed them from bondage but nothing beyond that. There has been no attempt made by neither the civil society bodies nor the Government agencies to hold such training camps in order to make them aware about their rights so that they are not exploited under the shadow of ignorance.
15. **Psychological rehabilitation:** Freed bonded labour feels psychological freedom from bondage after government released them. This is of great relevance for the bonded labour and their family.
16. **Physical and Economic Rehabilitation:** (First major rehabilitation component) The district administration provided compensation to them in kind as per the Act provisions prevalent then after their release along with their release certificates. The district administration provided

Animal husbandry and rickshaw (Cow, Buffalo, Goat, Rickshaw etc.) in lieu of cash, that is, in kind. All freed bonded labourers received this rehabilitation component. But at the time of evaluation study most of them were found without the animal and rickshaw given to them. They complained that due to lack of knowledge and skill in upkeep of animal husbandry, their animals died without being of any use to them. Their rickshaws were also destroyed due to poor maintenance and negligence. Their choice was not taken or they were not consulted as to what will be best for them in kind if they were not given cash for the compensation amount. All agreed that kind in place of cash was good planning because they would have spent the cash on drinking or some trivial issue. But they were not happy with what they had got, so it can be expressed that the role of district authorities was not satisfactory. There was no follow up programme done by district administration to observe the progress they were making with the cows, goats, pigs or rickshaw. There was no monitoring done at all.

17. The second major rehabilitation component provided by the district administration was allotment of house-site and agricultural land. The district authorities provided ceiling's surplus land, Bhoodan and Gramdan land to them. It is apparent from the study that the land provided by the district administration was not useful. It was far away from their residences, and the land was in low lying area, where there was water logging round the year. There are cases where the freed bonded labourer did not have the lands in their possession. The insensitivity of rehabilitation approach is evident. There is need to put all programmes with proper sensitivity and with a sense of belonging to the work being done.

18. The third major rehabilitation component, provided by the district administration, was social security pension @ Rs. 100/- per month for life. But, it is not satisfactory. It needs more care and proper check-up for this programme. Due to lack of district administration ignorance and indifference, some freed bonded labourers were not receiving this security pension. It is the foremost duty of district administration or

department of social security to cover all the freed bonded labour under the social security pension scheme. ANSISS team was quick to point it out and have been promised immediate corrective action to bring the left outs in the social security net.

19. Another rehabilitation provided by the district component administration was the low cost dwelling units (Indira Awas Yojana). But, all freed bonded labourers were not getting this component. The district administration should allot it to all freed bonded labourers. The positive and good thing in this exercise was that some dwelling units were provided in their same caste/community. They had no complaints and were comfortable to be in a friendlier environment.
20. The district administration under IRDP (Integrated Rural Development Programme) had taken few FBL, cases to develop their economic life but it is not satisfactory. It needs more care and follow-up.
21. There is protection of civil rights of FBLs in the district. There was no case of harassment reported by the FBLs about the landlords or about the previous masters forcibly engaging them. So it is full civil freedom for FBLs in the districts.
22. It was observed that district administration are not providing adequals help under components like:
    (i) Agriculture credit.
    (ii) Horticulture-training, loan etc.
    (iii) Training for acquiring new skills, developing skills and TRYSEM programmes.
    (iv) Traditional arts and crafts conservation and training.
    (v) Education to children of bonded labourers.
23. The Government should take care of the above-mentioned components for the betterment of the freed bonded labour.
24. There should be freedom of choice in selection of occupation by FBLs.
25. Bonded labour represents the extremes of poverty and backwardness among the category of landless agricultural labourers. They need special care, therefore it is suggested that all the development programmes for the freed bonded labours

should be implemented in the district to improve the over all socio-economic conditions. The district authorities should organize follow-up programme.

26. The role of the vigilance committee in the districts are negligible. The frequency of meeting and the follow up of the rehabilitation programme by them are missing. Not a single member of vigilance committee visits the freed bonded labourers. It is negligence on the part of the vigilance committee. Vigilance committee must be active and sincere in their responsibilities.
27. The district level vigilance committee is responsible for the whole district and the sub-divisional level vigilance committee looks at the areas under them, but at sub-divisional level the vigilance committee has not been constituted in some districts. There is no effective role of the vigilance committee at the village and block level.
28. In the light of above facts and discussion of the findings, it may be concluded that the process of liberation has not brought significant qualitative change as envisaged in the socio-economic condition of the freed bonded labourers community. The programme was not taken so seriously by the implementing agencies, hence there is full scope for improvement.

I. FUTURE ASPIRATION OF FREED BONDED LABOURERS OF NAWADA

During the study, an attempt was made to find their needs. It is as follows:

(i) 91-bonded labourers wanted loan for improving economic condition of their families.

(ii) Beside the pension, 59 bonded labourers expressed for more income generating facilities by the government to enhance their economic condition.

(iii) 48 bonded labourers showed concern for medical and health care facilities. 45 bonded laborers demanded better housing, drinking water, toilet and drainage facilities.

(iv) 42 bonded labourers wanted improvement in infra structural facilities like electricity, Road and Public Distribution System (PDS).

(v) 24 bonded labourers demanded regular work round the year;

(vi) 23 thought that they should get more pensions.

(vii) 22 bonded laborers didn't say any thing about their future plan.

(vii) Few were keen to have vocational training for self-employment.

II. FUTURE ASPIRATION OF FREED BONDED LABOURERS FOR NALANDA

During the study attempt was made to know their future needs. It is as follows:

(i) 27 freed bonded labourers wanted loan for improving economic condition of their families.

(ii) 15 bonded labourers showed concern for medical and health care facilities.

(iii) 18 bonded labourers demanded better housing, drinking water, toilet and drainage facilities.

(iv) 21 free bonded labourers wanted improvement in infra-structural facilities like electricity, road, school and public distribution system.

(v) 14 freed bonded labourers demanded regular work round the year.

(vi) 4 freed bonded labourers wants to increase in pension amount.

(vii) 11 freed bonded labourers wants to increase in daily wage and that is in cash.

(viii) 2 freed bonded labourers did not say anything about their future plan.

III. FUTURE ASPIRATION OF FREED BONDED LABOURERS FOR PATNA

During the study an attempt was made to know their future needs. It is as follows:

(i) 47 freed bonded labourers wanted loan for improving economic condition of their families.

(ii) 24 bonded labourers showed concern for medical and health care facilities.

(iii) 27 bonded labourers demanded better housing, drinking water, toilet and drainage facilities.

(iv) 38 freed bonded labourers wanted improvement in infra--structural facilities like electricity, road, school and public distribution system.

(v) 21 freed bonded labourers demanded regular work round the year.

(vi) 15 freed boded labourers demanded educational facilities for their children.

(vii) 19 freed bonded labourers wants to increase in pension amount.

(viii) 8 freed bonded labourers wants to increase in daily wage.

(ix) 3 freed bonded labourers felt that the development functionaries should pay visit in their villages/tolas.

IV. FUTURE ASPIRATION OF FREED BONDED LABOURERS FOR WEST CHAMPARAN

During the study attempt was made to know their future needs. It is as follows:

(i) 84.35% of freed bonded labourers wanted loan for improving economic condition of their families.

(ii) 37.83% of freed bonded labourers showed concern for medical and health care facilities.

(iii) 49.13% of bonded labourers demanded better housing, drinking water, toilet and drainage facilities.

(iv) 67.83% of free bonded labourers wanted improvement in infra-structural facilities like electricity, road, school and public distribution system.

(v) 32.17% freed bonded labourers demanded regular work round the year.

(vi) 27.39% of freed bonded labourers wanted increase in pension amount.

(vii) 24.35% of freed bonded demanded labourers educational facilities for their children.

(viii) 20.43% of freed bonded labourers wants more civic amenities and other basic facilities through the Government.

(ix) 19.13% of freed bonded labourers wants increase in daily wages and that to in cash.

(x) 12.17% of freed bonded labourers wanted regular visit of the concerned development functionaries.

V. FUTURE ASPIRATION OF FREED BONDED LABOURERS FOR MUNGER

During the study attempt was made to know their future needs. It is as follows:

(i) 27.15% of bonded labourers wanted loan for improving economic condition of their families.

(ii) 15.89% of freed bonded labourers showed concern for medical and health care facilities.

(iii) 24.50% of bonded labourers demanded better housing, drinking water, toilet and drainage facilities.

(iv) 11.92% of free bonded labourers wanted improvement in infra-structural facilities like electricity, road, school and public distribution system.

(v) 24.50% freed bonded labourers demanded regular work round the year.

(vi) 4.63% of freed bonded labourers wanted increase in pension amount.

(vii) None freed bonded labourers demanded educational facilities for their children.

(viii) 47.02% of freed bonded labourers wants increase in daily wages and that to in cash.

(ix) 17.88 % of freed bonded labourers wanted regular visit of the concerned development functionaries.

RECOMMENDATIONS

1. The system of bonded service should be rejected on social, political and moral basis. The task is to put an effective end to the evil system.
2. In order to achieve this, they should be freed from the existing load of debts. They should be given loans by the Government until the rehabilitation of a family is attained.

3. It must be seen that he should have job opportunities and change of occupation. In short, the bonded labourers should be freed from debts and their general economic conditions should be improved.
4. An Act was made in 1976, which is an important landmark in the social and political history of India. Side by side with the social Act, many other measures of rehabilitation are needed to crush the evil system of bonded service.
5. Even after two and half decade from the passing of the Act of 1976 no case has been filed in the district. The prosecution arm of the government needs to get its act together to deliver justice.
6. The concerned authorities do not strictly implement the measures of rehabilitation.
7. There should be honesty and sincerity in the efforts. Mere passing of an Act will not help them.
8. The Government should, without any delay, constitute vigilance committee in each district and sub-division in compliance with requirements of Section 13 of the Bonded Labour System (Abolition) Act, 1976.
9. The District Magistrate should also seek assistance of non-political social groups and voluntary agencies to ensure implementation of the provisions of the Bonded Labour System (Abolition) Act, 1976.
10. The district administration should take all necessary measures to ensure that minimum wages are paid.
11. The district administration should provide housing and toilet facilities to the Freed Bonded Labourer.
12. The district administration should provide pure drinking water facilities and drainages facilities in the FBLs tolas.
13. The district administration should immediately take steps to ensure proper and adequate medical facilities for the FBLs and to the members of their families free of cost.
14. The District Magistrate should take up steps for creating awareness among local population about the programmes and the activities for the FBLs. It should seek assistance of the local media and organize camps and exhibition frequently.

15. The local NGOs, VOs, School teachers and students of local colleges should be encouraged for creating awareness among local population about the programmes and activities for FBLs.
16. The schemes and programmes of vocational training should be based on the basic needs of the areas.
17. The District Magistrate should hold the meeting of vigilance committee at least twice a month at the district level as well as at the sub-division level. In absence of such meeting, many crucial issues are kept in abeyance as a result several programmes and schemes cannot be implemented.
18. During training, the FBLs and their respective families should be motivated and encouraged to form Self-Help Groups (SHGs). The trainers should provide information among the FBLs, so that they can form SHGs.
19. The State Government should set up a special cell at Department of Social Security under Director for extending assistance to FBLs. The proposed cell can be helpful in completing formalities for seeking loan from financial institutions and banks. The cell can also extend help to those who would like to form SHG.
20. The State Government should organize post-training activities for the FBLs by organizing workshops etc.
21. The workshop can be helpful to the FBLs in preparing schemes for self-employment and acquainting them with the procedures to be followed for securing financial assistance from bank.
22. The State Government should also carry out post-training survey in the form of follow-up exercise to examine the setting up of vocations or enter gainful economic activities by the FBLs.
23. It may be noted that the District Magistrate have vital role under the Act, and Government of Bihar can, therefore, instruct the District Magistrates to take up the work of identification of bonded labour on priority basis and to pin point areas in the bonded labour where they may be found. They are suspected to be found in stone quarries, brick-kilns etc. The DM should assign task forces for identification and release of bonded labour. The Labour Department can hold

labour camps in these areas, particularly to enforce minimum wages and to detect debt bondage.

24. Most of the FBLs and their family members were found to be illiterate in the district. Most of their children were not attending any school. Concrete effort should be made to connect the youth with the literacy campaign and enroll the children in the schools under Sarva Siksha Abhiyan.
25. Some FBLs were getting the benefit of Indira Awas Yojana (IAY) and very few of them were associated with the IRDP. Therefore, it is suggested that FBLs be consulted in all the development programmes in the district in order to improve their overall socio-economic conditions, standard of living and ouality of life. They should be associated with Swarn Jayanti Gram Swarojgar Yojana (SJGSY).
26. The performances of Anganwari Centre in the FBLs Villages/ Tolas were found to be poor. The FBLs were hesitant in sending their children in the Anganwari Centre. District Magistrate, should ensure that the CDPOs of all the blocks in the district, take the necessary steps to improve functioning of Anganwari Centre in their respective areas and they should be instructed to take special care of women and children or FBLs families. The Sevikas/workers of anganwadi can be recruited from the FBL families in consultation with the ICDS directorate. This will be a reassuring gesture for the beneficiaries.
27. The list of Free Bonded Labourers maintained by the Social Security Department at the district level need to be updated through fresh assessment in the districts. It will be helpful in knowing the current status of the FBLs and accordingly developmental programmes can be provided to them.
28. The district level Social Security Department should maintain a register dealing with court cases related to FBLs. It will help in knowing about the total number of cases, cases in the court hearing stage, pending cases and the number of cases where conviction has been done.
29. The FBLs should be resettled and rehabilitated far away from the old landlords, where they can have alternative sources of employment. Self-employment with a view to avoid the chances of becoming bonded labour again.

30. The district administration should organize seminars and camps on freed bonded labourers issue for creating awareness among the local population for the benefit of the FBLs.
31. These are some of the real challenges for district administration even after years of the Bonded Labour System (Abolition) Act, 1976.
32. There is need for macro and micro planning to further improve the implementing schemes of rehabilitation for the bonded labour, immediately after their release.
33. The rehabilitation assistance should include allotment of agricultural land, house-sites, provision of income generating units like milch animals i.e., cows/buffaloes, other animal husbandry units like sheep, goats, mules, poultry, etc., provision of agricultural implements and inputs, assistance for promotion of crafts/skills like carpentry, black smith, weaving, tailoring, knitting, etc. The rehabilitation amount is meagre. It should be increased with rise in costs of goods.
34. An awareness campaign should be held regularly in the villages and blocks for the purpose of enlightening them about the BL Act (1976), its provisions as well as the various schemes required to be translated into success story. The awareness literature should be simple with picture charts and in the local language so as to make them intelligible to the target groups.
35. Audio-visual shows of the various development schemes would be the most effective way of communication to them. A success story in visual documentary form can be made and shown to the FBLs and their families.
36. The district information and public relations department will have a very useful role to play in this direction. DPRO should make it a monthly exercise, in every block, to hold sensitization and information sharing camp. The various statutes such as the Land Reforms Act, Minimum Wages Act, Protection of Civil Rights Act and Bonded Labour System (Abolition) Act can be taught in such information and awareness camps.
37. Section 7(1) of the Bonded Labour System (Abolition) Act, 1976, no doubt, specifically provides that immediately after the bonded labourer had been identified and released, his

property, which might have been under any mortgage, charge, lien, etc., should be freed from such mortgage and restored to this possession. This needs to be taken seriously in order to generate confidence and faith on his new status of freedom.

38. The provision of low-cost dwelling units is another essential component of rehabilitation. The programme of construction of low-cost dwelling units should be based on local designs, local material and local skills.

39. In allotting a house-site or a plot of agricultural land, segregation and isolation approach should be avoided. The focus is that all freed bonded labourers are rehabilitated at a place in such a way that help them in getting mainstreamed to village community.

40. It should also be ensured that common facilities and back-up services like drinking water; electricity, drainage and convenient access to the main road, to dispensaries and educational institutions are provided. This is to ensure that he has a sense of belonging and a feeling for the community in which he lives.

41. The programme for distribution/handing over possession of agricultural land should be backed by provision of a complete package of various services and facilities such as a provision of plough, bullocks and agricultural implements to the freed bonded labour. Training and support programme should be provided so that they can utilize their land provided by government.

42. The district administration should ensure that all the land holdings of freed bonded labourers are covered with irrigation wells.

43. They should get regular medical check up and doctors of primary health centers should arrange such checks. The PHC staff should hold regular camps in the FBL villages.

44. The Government (PHED department) should ensure to provide a drinking water well/handpump in every tola/ village where freed bonded labourers have been rehabilitated.

45. The district block authorities should open Fair Price Shops in the tolas/villages, where freed bonded labourers have been

rehabilitated for supply of essential commodities like rice, wheat, sugar, kerosene, etc. at controlled prices. Lal card should be provided to all FBLs.

46. Balwadis is essential where freed bonded labourers have been rehabilitated for primary education of their children. This can be taken up in consultation with respective department.

47. The district administration should promote adult literacy among the senior and adult FBL illiterates.

48. The local police station can keep watch against the possibility of atrocities being committed on them by the powerful former masters, who once held them in bondage.

49. The SUDHA BIHAR movement can play a lead role in income generating activities of FBLs by linking them to their milk procurement programme. The Department of Animal Husbandry can facilitate their animal procurement through credit in liaison with NABARD, Cooperative Bank, Grameen Bank or the Commercial Banks. The department can support the animal check up and maintenance through its mobile animal clinics and veterinary doctors. A preliminary training can be provided by SUDHA dairy and the animal husbandry department to the FBLs on dairy intricacies. SUDHA is a huge success story in dairy and it is pride of Bihar, hence they can become instrumental in improving the economic capacity of the FBLs.

50. This is the type of linkages and convergence strategy, which has to be adopted to eradicate poverty among the FBLs and change their conditions permanently for better. All FBLs have to linked to the district's Below Poverty Line programme to bring basic change in their present situation.

51. There is need to develop a sustainable livelihood approach for FBL to freed from the poverty syndrome.

52. The district administration, under DM, should make district level special action plan in light of contemporary developments and should make dedicated effort to bring holistic development of the FBLs.

53. A Monitoring Information System (MIS) should be set up in DM's office with the Assistant Director, Social Security, being fully responsible for updating their progress report received

from the block and panchayat, after every quarter. The data can be sent to NHRC, New Delhi and Ministry of Labour. A surveillance by field administration should be kept to prevent the FBLs slipping again into the field of landlords.

54. A dedicated website can bring transparency and control over administered development initiatives for FBLs. The leading human rights watch groups and NGO's can give some feedback in the district from their perspective. Their feedback can further help in consolidating FBLs development, growth and socio-economic mainstreaming.
55. The DM should hold special drive for recruitment of FBLs and their family members in government jobs like the post of driver, peon, village dafadar, VLWs, chaukidar etc. It would increase their self confidence and prestige. It would go a long way in establishing role model of success among the FBLs and their community. The FBLs need such special intervention.
56. FBLs need to be treated in holistic rehabilitation mode in totality, and not in ad hoc administrative rehabilitation manner. It should display human touch.
57. The corrective measures, as assured by the concerned agencies, must be completed within a time period to fill the gaps in the rehabilitation process.

INDEX

J

K

L

M